FRENCH AEROPLANES BEFORE THE GREAT WAR

FRENCH AEROPLANES BEFORE THE GREAT WAR

Including Many Rare Photos from the Musée de l'Air et de l'Espace

Octave Gilbert testing his 1909 glider as an unmanned kite. Note the hammock slung between the wings from which he planned to control his machine. (Courtesy of the Musée de l'Air et de l'Espace/Le Bourget-France)

Leonard E. Opdycke

Schiffer Military History
Atglen, PA

Acknowledgments

I dreamed of this project more than 15 years ago, and Michel Bénichou, the editor of the French aviation magazine then titled *Le Fanatique de l'Aviation,* also became excited about it. Together we began surveying books, magazines, catalogs, patents; we checked out the libraries of aviation museums in Europe and North America. After some time, Michel felt pressed by time and other responsibilities, and for the past 10 years or so I continued the work on my own. The current text and photographs represents some of his work along with the contributions of many others, as noted under Credits, below, interleaved with mine. Further special mention should be made of the assistance of Stéphane Nicolaou and the staff and friends at the Musée de l'Air et de l'Espace at Le Bourget, and of the enthusiastic support for lo, these many years by the membership of World War I Aeroplanes, Inc, who have expressed their eagerness to hear about this project, to assist with it where possible, and finally – we hope! – to purchase the completed product. And I hope you the readers get as much joy from studying this outpouring of aeronautical invention as I did.

Credits, primarily for assistance with the photographs, but also for further information, and encouragement of all kinds.

So many people have contributed to this work that it is difficult or impossible to do each one proper justice. Some have worked to answer questions; some have donated advice; some have donated photographs or drawings or original or xeroxed material; some have donated time in scanning materials or proof-reading mine. The number of hours which my friends have contributed to this book is inconceivable. Thank you, one and all.

Ray Atkinson	James Davilla	William Lewis	Wesley Smith
Paul Badré	Gilbert Deloisis	Nigel Mills	D'Alt Swift
Michel Bénichou	Nicholas Forder	Stéphane Nicolau	John WR Taylor
Rolly Bliss	George Fuller	Robert Owens	Bruce J Vander Mark
Peter Bowers	Frederick Freeman	Guy Roberty	Henry S Villard
JM Bruce	Bill Hannan	Jean-Louis Rosman	Beverly Williams
Hugo Byttebier	Phil Jarrett	William Sayer	Harry Woodman

Dedication

To my dear wife Sandy, who made our visits to Paris a joy after my day's work at the Musée de l'Air; and whose steady enthusiasm and support and advice – and delight! – and proofing – made this book possible.

Book Design by Robert Biondi.

Copyright © 1999 by Leonard E. Opdycke.
Library of Congress Catalog Number: 98-87946.

Printed in China.
ISBN: 0-7643-0752-5

We are interested in hearing from authors with book ideas on military topics.

Published by Schiffer Publishing Ltd.
4880 Lower Valley Road
Atglen, PA 19310
Phone: (610) 593-1777
FAX: (610) 593-2002
E-mail: Schifferbk@aol.com.
Visit our web site at: www.schifferbooks.com
Please write for a free catalog.
This book may be purchased from the publisher.
Please include $3.95 postage.
Try your bookstore first.

Foreword

by JM Bruce

From early times there was something about aerial flight that captured the imagination of the French nation with a unique fervency. Practical ballooning had begun in France with the work of the Montgolfier brothers, but the idea of flight in a heavier-than-air machine was ever-present. Although the pioneering work of Sir George Cayley at the beginning of the 19th century in England seems to have been unknown in France, early thoughts on heavier-than-air flying machines in the latter half of that century were pursued in that country by a fair number of French pioneers.

A focus for this thinking and aspiration was provided in 1863 by the talented and versatile novelist, essayist, caricaturist and photographer Gaspard Felix Tournachon (1820-1910), better known by his professional name Nadar. In that year he founded La Société d'Encouragement pour la Navigation Aérienne with the specific objective of promoting heavier-than-air flying machines. One who took up this cause enthusiastically was Victor Hugo, the celebrated poet and author, who had already foreseen a great future for aerial navigation, primarily as a cultural and commercial bond between nations. On 9 March 1869 he wrote a strongly supportive exhortation to the contemporary aeronaut Gaston Tissandier, urging the development of flight.

Among those 19th century French pioneers who pursued various aeronautical activities and experiments were such men such as Félix du Temple, Alphonse Pénaud, Jean-Marie Le Bris, Ferdinand Ferber, Clément Ader, Joseph Pline, Louis-Pierre Mouillard, Victor Tatin. Some of their designs and ideas showed remarkably advanced thinking, several anticipating, at least in appearance, the configuration of aeroplanes of decades later.

All such ideas were frustrated by lack of supporting technologies, most notably in appropriate power units and fuels.

European aviation in general received a powerful fillip when the Wright brothers demonstrated their aeroplane in 1908, and showed the world what properly controlled mechanical flight could be. The effect on France's pioneers was the more dramatic because these demonstration flights were made in France.

It was as if French national pride had been dealt a severe blow: to many French citizens of the time the conquest of the air and the development of mechanical flight was, or should be, a French prerogative. A welcome restorative to the nation's pride came in July 1909, when Louis Blériot made the first crossing of the English Channel in an aeroplane.

In the five years preceding the outbreak of World War I in August 1914, an ever-growing army of determined French pioneers worked tirelessly on the building of many score types of aeroplane. Their name was Legion, their creations wondrously varied, their achievements – some of them, at least – heroic. Development was quick, on the whole constructive, and forward-looking. Although some designs could only be described as bizarre, the aircraft created by such design teams as those of Blériot, Breguet, Morane-Saulnier and Nieuport pointed aviation's way ahead with exemplary clarity. The best of them outstripped the Wrights' biplane that had inspired the strong growth of French aviation, but France had little time to enjoy the restoration of its eminence in the field, for war came to apply far sterner pressures on the country's aviation industry.

With such a vast range of designs and designers, of ideas and achievements, the task of the historian bold enough to attempt to chronicle them must be one of the most daunting and demanding that could be imagined. Now, the debt owed by students of aviation history to Leo Opdycke is correspondingly huge, for this is what he has done; the pages that follow record his many discoveries, and perpetuate many names that deserve to be remembered in the history of aviation. This book has been many years in the making: its size and scope are and will be an enduring testimonial to the author's endurance, determination, percipience and competence quite as much as it is a worthy monument to so many who toiled with such dedication in the pre-1914 period to establish the foundations of aviation in Europe.

Contents

Foreword, *by JM Bruce* 5

Introduction 8

One   The Pioneers 10

Two   The Aeroplanes 15

Appendix I: More Aeroplanes, Perhaps 278

Appendix II: More Aeroplanes, But Which? 279

Appendix III: The Names 282

Bibliography 287

Introduction

These marvelous aeroplanes have never shared a hangar before, and it has been a delight for me to become acquainted with them and to bring them together here. The period before World War I was an exciting one for aviation pioneers: anything seemed possible, and while in some cases the understanding of aerodynamics and structural engineering was minimal and its absence filled in with enthusiasm, in others it was surprisingly full. Today when so many aircraft designs are similar to the point of real confusion, it is wonderful to look back to a time when even the numbers of wings and tails varied, not to speak of their placement – to a time so unlike our own when many of these early machines failed to fly at all. The energy in France, especially, was remarkable, and this book offers the work of more than 700 builders. For some there was but one aircraft designed, and perhaps not even finished; for a few others there were many designed, and hundreds built.

My interest was primarily in getting these early machines, especially the lesser-known ones, out into the light of day. I chose to include gliders, ornithopters, helicopters, as well as more standard powered machines; I chose to omit the aviettes, the little bicycle-based flying things, partly because they seemed less like aircraft and partly because there were so many, undocumented: they might make an interesting study of their own some day.

Some aircraft which showed themselves in several interesting variants appear in several separate photographs or drawings; others, perhaps more familiar at least by name, have to be satisfied with fewer pictures. Especially interesting, at least to me, are the photographs of the interiors of workshops, or of exhibitions, where the subject of the photo may appear in front; but in the rear, perhaps in pieces against the wall, or half-assembled at one side, appears the fuselage or wing of a very rare and perhaps unidentified structure. Some of the rarer machines seem to exist now only in relatively fuzzy book or magazine photos, and appear in this book in relatively unsatisfactory photo-copy form. Nevertheless, the selection printed here represents the best choices I could make.

The first chapter is titled "The Pioneers", and catalogs in chronological order 16 of the earliest French efforts to get off the ground – or leap off the tower. The list starts in 1678 and ends in 1888; doubtless there were others, but these fearless fliers are perhaps the better known.

The second chapter is titled "The Aeroplanes", and describes in alphabetical order the aeroplanes of nearly 700 different builders.

Appendix I is titled "More Aeroplanes, Perhaps", and lists over 100 names for which I have so far been unable to find any information at all – no picture, no details. Some of these may in fact be variant spellings or misunderstandings of the names in the main list.

Appendix II is titled "More Aeroplanes, But Which?", a display of some of the aeroplanes for which I have so far found no names nor any information at all.

Appendix III is titled "The Names" and offers the 700-odd builders/designers detailed in the text. In addition, it includes some 450 designations or spellings alternative to the ones chosen to be standard in the main list. This includes names of people involved who may have been described in the contemporary press as designers or builders. Granted, this choice was sometimes pretty arbitrary.

But this book is not to be considered the definitive work; in fact, after spending over 10 years on it, I find it hard to imagine what a definitive work might look like. The documentation has been hard to come by, often erratic, often inconsistent and self-contradictory. Over time, designations and information have frequently been copied directly from earlier sources which are themselves suspect; authors attempting to put at least some of these aircraft in order have been plagued with errors and omissions; contemporary photographs and contemporary magazines were often mislabeled from the very beginning. Numbering and lettering systems have been very difficult to decipher. The brief lists of specifications following some of the types represent the best of what I could find – for some machines there was a good deal that seemed reliable; for others, little or nothing.

It is interesting to note how few Wright copies there were: certainly the Wrights' influence was great, but less in terms of specific design features. And unlike in the United States, the Curtiss pusher did not serve the French as a model, except in a couple of instances. The serious models for French builders were the Blériot XI, the Antoinette, the Hanriot, the Demoiselle, the Farman, the Nieuport, and the Morane-Saulnier: this book is full of their look-alikes. Some of the larger builders, like Blériot, sold parts and complete assemblies, so the similarities between many of these early fabricators are not accidental. And it is interesting to see how designers might start with a configuration that seemed far from the beaten track; but by the time they had worked out 2 or 3 more, their conceptions tended to be more like what were becoming norms.

I offer this catalog in this form as a beginning, rather than an ending, to the study, to which should be added further information as it is unearthed. Please feel free to contribute further names, photos, and other data as you may come across them.

ONE

The Pioneers

Early French aviation did not begin in 1900, or 1800, either. So this section titled The Pioneers features the works of 16 early aviators whose earliest efforts go back almost into mythology and whose later efforts begin to foretell the machines of 1900-1914:

1678	Besnier
1742	De Bacqueville
1772	Desforges
1781	Blanchard
1784	Renaux
1784	Gérard
1784	Thibault de St André
1788	Resnier
1852	Letur
1856	Mouillard
1856	Le Bris
1870	Pénaud
1874	Du Temple
1879	Biot-Massia
1883	Goupil
1888	Hérard

1678 Besnier

Le Journal des Sciences of 12 December 1678 reported the work of a iron-worker (or locksmith?) named Besnier on his flying machine, at Sablé, in the Maine. The picture has been often reprinted: a man with a long beam across each shoulder, and a small creased panel at each end; the rear of each beam was attached to the man's feet with cords. The description notes that the diagonal twisting motion of the flapping wings provided the lift. The machine could not take off, but given a height to start from, could apparently glide some distance. Two men named J-J Bourcart et de Gruebweiler managed some lift-offs and tiny flights (?) with Besnier's device, restored, in 1868.

1742 de Bacqueville

Around 1742 the Marquis de Bacqueville is reported to have thrown himself from the roof of his house and managed to fly "with artificial wings" across the Seine, at which point he fell heavily into a boat and broke his thigh. He was more than 60 years old, "slightly crazy but with a lot of spirit." There seems no record of how the wings worked.

1772 Desforges

A monk at d'Etampes, the abbot Desforges, reportedly built in 1772 a machine of wicker with rapidly flapping wings, all under a big parachute for landing: part aeroplane, part ornithopter. On one occasion he leaped from the tower at Guinette, but sustained only bruises – no doubt because he was fortified with a helmet and goggles!

1781 Blanchard

Jean-Pierre Blanchard was to become famous as a pioneer of ballooning, but a few years earlier, in 1781 in Paris, he was building his flying ship – a hull with a mast and an assortment of flapping wings – when news arrived of the Montgolfier ballooning experiments. He gave up his balloonless device and went on to the balloons that made him famous, always trying to retain something of his interest in a guided vessel.

1784 Renaux

In 1784 AJ Renaux built an ornithopter with a variety of wing shapes, basically an aerial kayak-paddle with the 2 blades themselves of different shapes.

1784 Gérard

Also in 1784, a M Gérard offered another ornithopter machine with flapping wings.

1784 Thibault

1784 was a good year for these experiments: Thibault de St André offered a sort of balloon-cum-flexible surfaces attached at the ends of the pilot's arms, whereby he might guide his disabled (and quite small) balloon to the ground in safety.

1788 Resnier de Goué

General de Goué had had a brilliant career in the army; in 1788 under the pseudonym Reinser II he published a book in which he described a flying machine consisting of a sort of corset with bat-wings attached. He retired from the army in 1801, and in his home town, Angoulême, built a version of his design with feathers for wings. At age 62 he threw himself from the 30-meter high tower at Petit-Beaulieu and fell into the river, without apparent damage. He tried again and broke his leg, and lived on to the age 82.

1852 Letur

François Letur designed and built a parachute-cum-paddles machine in 1852; he exhibited it at the Hippodrome in Paris at the end of May 1853. He went to England and tested his device on 27 June 1854 under a balloon operated by a WH Adam. Unfortunately he was not able to disengage in time, and was dragged by the balloon over the ground, suffering contusions from which he died.

1856 Mouillard

Louis-Pierre Mouillard was born in Lyon in 1835, and early became interested in flight, especially bird-flight: he began weighing and measuring birds. His actual experiments and patents in the course of his life amounted to very little, but his big book L'*Empire de l'Air*, published in 1881 and republished

Mouillard's glider in Cairo, his fourth. (Author's collection)

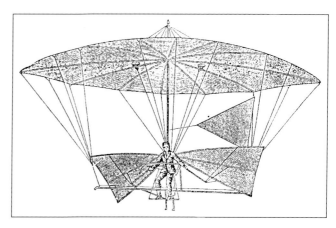

A drawing of Letur in his machine, controlling his wings through a system of treadles and pedals. (Author's collection)

in their Annual Report by the Smithsonian Institution in 1893 as *The Empire of the Air*, was widely read, and served to focus attention on the need to understand gliding and soaring before undertaking powered flight.

He built his first glider in 1856 in Lyon, but it was too weak, and he abandoned it. Moving later to Algeria, he built 2 more; the last one weighed 72.6 kg, and consisted of monoplane wings made of thin wood stiffened by aloe ribs, with the pilot standing in an opening cut between them. The wings were hinged upwards, and at the conclusion of his first hop (unexpected), which covered some 45 meters, he fell, breaking the glider. Rebuilt, it flew once more, but in a gust the wings folded up on him, and he sprained his shoulder. He moved to Cairo in 1865, where in 1878 he began his 4th glider, a monoplane with a fan-shaped tail, adjustable sweep-back and what looked like ailerons but were in fact differential air-brakes to slow down one wing or the other for turn control.

In 1891 Octave Chanute got in touch with Mouillard, and offered to help him finance the new glider. In the course of his work Mouillard suggested to Chanute the use of rockets for propulsion and aluminum for structure, but was dissuaded in both cases. The machine was finished in 1895 and tested unsuccessfully in 1896. His US patent was awarded in 1897.

1856 Le Bris

In his book *Progress in Flying Machines*, Octave Chanute wrote about Captain Joseph Marie Le Bris, taking his material from a brief historical account written in 1884 by de la Landelle, and a semi-historical novel by the same man.

Le Bris was a ship captain who had become interested in flight through observing albatrosses in action; he killed one, and felt he had discovered the secret. In 1857 he designed and built the first of his 2 albatross-like gliders; each had a boat-shaped hull, swallow tail, and bird-shaped wings. 2 levers controlled the leading edges, which rotated and allowed a variable angle of attack. The pilot stood upright and worked the rudder with foot-pedals. He tested his bird on a road near Trefeuntec, near Duarnenez, placing it on a moving cart. Le Bris tried to release the tow-rope as the glider began to lift from the vehicle, but the rope caught on a nail, ripping loose part of the cart. The glider then rose in the air; but since the rope had also wound around the driver, he was lifted up as well. His weight acted like the tail of a kite, stabilizing the glider, and all together they rose some 300 m into the air under perfect control. Seeing the driver hanging below him, Le Bris brought his glider down so the man could get off. But now, unbalanced, it would not fly again. His second try was from a tower built over a quarry, but this time the glider, adjusted for weight, sailed out, hit a gust of wind, crashed, and was destroyed. The pilot was only slightly injured.

(Span: 15.2 m; length of hull: 4.1 m; wing area: 20 sqm; empty weight: 202 kg)

Now nearly penniless, Le Bris waited 13 years until a public subscription brought him enough money to build a second albatross, similar to the first, but lighter. It featured a movable counter-weight for automatically maintaining longitudinal balance. On the urging of his friends he tried the glider with ballast only; sometimes it rose, but not far, and was frequently damaged. On one occasion, flown as a kite, it lifted and then advanced against the wind; the rope slackened, and the bird glided on its own some 200 m. A final attempt ended in wreckage: Le Bris had never piloted his last machine.

He seems not to have planned any kind of power for his projects, though he had wanted to tow his glider behind a ship, since the hull itself was waterproof. Le Bris served in the war in 1870, and was murdered 2 years later while serving as a policeman.

1870 Pénaud

Born on 18 May 1850, Alphonse Pénaud meant to be a naval officer, but was soon crippled by a hip disease, and used crutches all his life. He determined to research the work done on aerial navigation and aviation itself, and in 1870 developed a model helicopter with shaped flexible blades using a rubber band for power – the first rubber-powered model aeroplane ever. The following year he built his Planophore, a little pusher stick model, rubber-powered, with wing and stabilizer – no rudder. And on 17 February 1876 Pénaud took out a patent for a full-scale powered machine. Unfortunately it was never built; he

One of the Le Bris gliders in flight. (Author's collection)

Another Le Bris glider, perhaps the unlucky one on the cart. (Author's collection)

and his mechanic Paolo Gauchot had conceived a twin tractor propeller monoplane with retractable undercarriage. The 4-bladed all-metal propellers turned in opposite directions, and allowed for ground-adjustable pitch changes. The hull was to be able to float and the machine to be amphibious. The elliptical wingtips curved upward for lateral stability. Pénaud realized that at the moment there was no suitable engine, but he expressed faith that science would produce one sooner or later. He gave Henri Giffard, the dirigible pioneer, all his research work, not having been successful in finding a substantial backer; and deeply depressed and ill, he shot himself in 1880, aged 30.

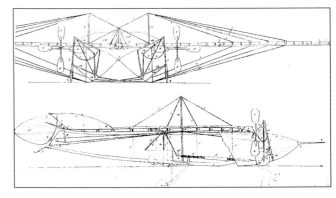

A drawing of the remarkable Pénaud amphibian with retractable undercarriage and twin propellers. (Author's collection)

In 1899 Wilbur Wright wrote the Smithsonian Institution: "I have been interested in the problem of mechanical and human flight ever since as a boy I constructed a number of bats of various sizes after the styles of Cayley's and Pénaud's machines. My observations since then have only convinced me more firmly that human flight is possible and practicable."

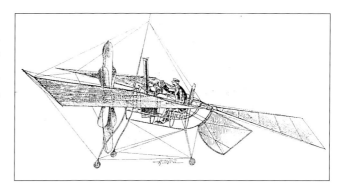

The du Temple brothers' steam-powered machine of 1874. (Author's collection)

1874 Du Temple

After studying the flight of birds, Félix and his brother Louis du Temple, naval officers, built first a small model flying machine that actually hopped, powered by watch-springs; then he and his brother undertook a huge 17-meter span steam-powered machine set high on 3 small wheels. The pilot sat behind the 6 hp steam engine in a neat basket-like frame, with a single long triangular tail behind him and a small rudder underneath, both arranged to move for control. 2 long angular wings built on 2 intersecting curved spars swept forward from the pilot's position, and the 8-bladed tractor propeller spun between them. It weighed about a ton. By 1874 they were ready to test it: a sailor piloted it as it ran down a ramp, hopped off the end and landed.

1879 Biot-Massia

Interested in kites as early as 1861, Gaston Biot built a conical tailless kite, and in 1880 a version stabilized by a free-wheeling propeller. In 1881 the Société Française de Navigation Aérienne reviewed a project submitted by Biot and Dandrieux. Earlier, in 1879, financed and probably assisted by Massia, Biot had built a birdlike glider based on the work of Mouillard, and flew it several times at Clamart. The pilot was placed between 2 perpendicularly-arranged metal rectangles, to which were attached V-struts on either side, at the ends of which were fitted 7 long feather-like surfaces which could be swung back and forth to serve as rudders. The tail consisted of 7 more such feathers arranged to lie flat in a flexible frame which could be twisted for vertical control. It was donated to the Musée de l'Air in 1925 and restored in 1960: it is the world's oldest surviving heavier-than-air machine.

(Span: 8.6 m; length: 4.2 m; wing area: 6.48 sqm; empty weight: 37 kg)

On 7 July 1882, the Count ED Massia wrote Louis Mouillard describing a glider for which, Mouillard wrote Octave Chanute in 1991, Mouillard had given Massia the technical information. The glider proved too heavy, and Massia gave it to Biot, who rebuilt it lighter. In its final version it was of monoplane form, the pilot positioned just forward of the wing

The 1879 Biot-Massia glider exhibited at the Musée de l'Air et de l'Espace. (Author's collection)

The more developed Massia-Biot glider of 1882. (Library of Congress)

and immediately behind a forward control surface; a swallow-tail surface extended aft from the trailing edge of the wing. Biot seems to have made this a twisting surface, like his first one. (It is this machine to which Chanute referred, erroneously, as Biot's 1879 design.)

1883 Goupil

In 1883 Alexandre Goupil built a birdlike monoplane glider, which seemed stable under a restraining rope. He intended to power it with his new steam engine which weighed about 1000 lbs and produced 15 horsepower. The aircraft featured a streamlined bird-shaped hull, tractor propeller, and rudder and hori-

Glenn Curtiss' reproduction of the Goupil Duck, on floats at Hammondsport. On wheels, it flew in 1917. (Peter M Bowers collection)

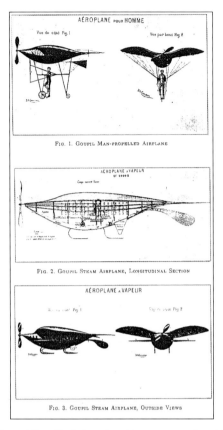

Three drawings of Goupil's designs: first, his man-powered machine, and second, his steam-powered aeroplane. (Albert F Zahm, Aeronautical Papers)

zontal tail aft; it rested on skids. 2 stubby horizontal surfaces forward were controlled by the pilot's moving around on a pivoted seat: they could work together as elevators or in opposite directions as ailerons, though their purpose was rather to restore lateral balance than to facilitate banking and turning. He called his machine an "aeroplane," apparently one of the first to use the name.

(Span: 6 m; length: 8 m; wing area: 27 sqm; weight: 50 kg)

In a 1916 attempt to avoid the Wright patent on wing-warping and its equivalents, Glenn Curtiss had his Buffalo, NY, factory built the Duck from Goupil's original patent drawings and a description in *La Locomotion Aérienne*. Curtiss put it first on wheels instead of skids like the original, and then on the original Langley floats, and then again on wheels. Powered by a Curtiss OXX-6, it flew on 19 January 1917, succeeding first in a straight and level flight, and then in a circle. As with his rebuilt Langley Aerodrome, Curtiss made some significant changes in the original design – control linkages, engine – and longer wings than what Goupil seems to have intended. But Curtiss never made use of his "evidence" that the Wrights were not the first to invent lateral control: the famous Curtiss-Wright patent fight was settled by arbitration as World War I approached.

1888 Hérard

Around 1888 a man named Hérard built a large rotating-wing machine set on 4 wheels. A sort of mill-wheel with 5 rotating Venetian-blind wing panels spun above the chassis on a horizontal axis. He seems to have had oars in mind as a model for his propulsion arrangement.

Hérard's paddle-wheel flyer of 1888 – which probably did not fly. (Author's collection)

TWO

The Aeroplanes

The aeroplanes in this section are listed alphabetically by their most reasonable names – sometimes designer – builder – pilot – and sometimes financier. It was often hard to sort them out, and some of the resulting choices were fairly arbitrary. The author tried to choose the most useful, locating the aeroplane where it might be the easiest to find, where the place made sense in the light of the firm's history. Aircraft were often known by the more famous customer's name, and often built to order, sometimes to the customer's own design; some designers and builders might go off to another firm and built their own designs there under the new name. The problem of designation then becomes a matter of philosophy rather than history.

A list of all the designers and builders and others under whose names the particular aircraft might be known is given in Appendix III, The Names.

A

Abric-Calas

In 1909 this short-lived association of 2 amateurs from southern France built several models, a biplane glider and a powered biplane; both full-sized machines were modeled on the Wright. The powered aircraft was built by Montel, a car-body builder in Marseille. It had a Voisin airfoil, a forward biplane elevator, a single rudder perhaps mounted just aft of it as on one of their earlier models, and a fixed but adjustable tailplane.

Since it was thought at the time that wing-warping was more efficient but ailerons safer, Abric and Calas thought that double ailerons in tandem pairs between the wings would have the advantage of both. They also designed the twin pusher propellers of thin wood sheets and fabric, of 2.9 meters in diameter, 1.6-1.8 meters in pitch, turning at only 500 rpm.

(Span: 11 m; wing area: 44 sqm; gross weight: 540 kg; 18 hp 4-cylinder water-cooled Turcat-Méry weighing 170 kg with radiator and water – a Grégoire-Gyp engine is also reported)

Acier

A metal monoplane flown by Olivier?

Ader

Clément Ader was born in Muret, near Toulouse, on 2 April 1841, and by 1855 he was already experimenting with gliding, using a big overcoat for his wings. In 1867 he patented a bicycle with rubber tires, and in 1873 he was back to gliding, this time with a big bird-shaped machine with an articulated 10-meter wing covered with goose-feathers. He tethered it to the ground at its center of gravity, got inside it, and controlled its ascents and descents in a moderate wind. From then until about 1910 he was busy with electric devices, especially in connection with the telephone. But in 1882 he began to work again on the problem of flight, and undertook the construction of his first powered machine.

Avion 1, Eole: The pilot was seated inside the enclosed hull behind the boiler of a 20 hp steam engine of Ader's own design driving a 4-bladed propeller whose blades were shaped like feathers. There was no elevator, probably no rudder, and no flight controls other than a device for swinging each bat-shaped wing differentially to shift the center of pressure, another for varying wing area on each side, a third to vary the camber, and a fourth to raise and lower each wing. In addition to the engine controls, the pilot was faced with 6 separate wheel controls and a pair of foot pedals. The Eole was to run on caterpillar tracks whose design was borrowed from Ader's earlier "Rail-without-End" trailer-truck invention, but it was in fact built with 3 wheels.

On 9 October 1890 it was tested at Armanvilliers, making the first powered take-off in history, starting on level ground and covering about 165 m at a height of about 20 cm: in 1906 Ader was to refer in his book *La Première Etape de l'Aviation Militaire* to this occurrence as "ce petit évènement," and made no claims for it as a significant flight. In 1891 the boiler was rebuilt, and Ader later claimed to have made a real flight of 800 m at Satory – though later he was unable to recall the exact date, nor was the test referred to in any contemporary correspondence between

15

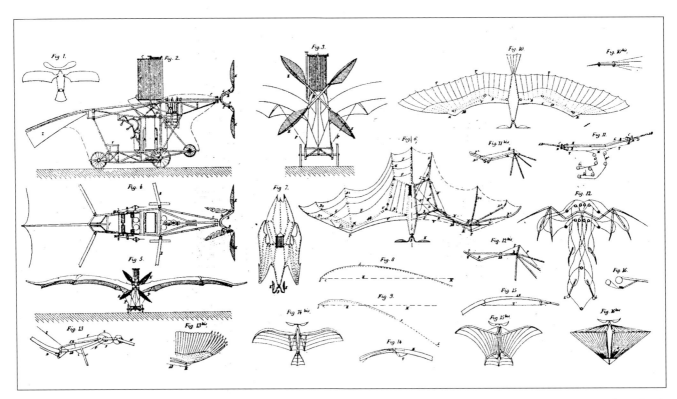

Clément Ader's Eole; the complex controls and bird-like structure show clearly in this single-propeller machine. (From drawings in Octave Chanute's epic Progress in Flying Machines)

Ader and the military – nor indeed in Ader's own account of the Eole, written in 1893.

(Span: 13.7 m; length: 4.6 m; wing area: 29.2 sqm; empty weight: 167 kg; gross weight: 298 kg)

<u>Avion II</u>: The French Ministry of War commissioned Ader to build a second machine, and he began building both the structure and the steam engine for Avion II in June 1893. He then calculated the torque of the 3-meter diameter 4-bladed propeller and frightened himself; he abandoned Avion II on the spot and undertook a new design.

<u>Avion III</u>: It featured 2 slightly smaller steam engines driving 2 slightly smaller counter-rotating propellers, one of which was mounted slightly ahead of the other. The airframe was built, laboriously and beautifully, of small lengths of wood and bamboo joined together with glue and wrapped with fabric; the result was very light. The propellers were made of light strips of bamboo assembled exactly like bird feathers. The wings were intricately articulated: a main spar hinged, with smaller spars towards the ends branching off; the sections of spar and the joints themselves were referred to as elbow, hand, thumb, and fingers. Fabric was applied to the wing with thousands of tiny buttons, none taking much stress. The multiple wing adjustments of Eole had been reduced to one: both wings could be swung forwards and backwards to move the center of pressure, controlled by a single wheel requiring 20-30 turns for full travel. A small fabric rudder

was attached to the steerable rear wheel for control of yaw, and the 2 propellers could be adjusted to turn at different speeds for further effect.

On 12 October 1897 he made the first test on a circular track of his own design at Satory: it was a driving test only, and showed the machine could travel under its own power. It did not leave the ground, nor was that the purpose of this test.

The second trial occurred on 15 October, and Avion III circled the track until the wind came from behind; the machine tipped forward enough to lift the rear steering wheel off the

The Avion III as exhibited at the Paris Exposition Internationale de Locomotion Aérienne of 1908. (Author's collection)

ground, and careened off the track into the field, slewed around in a sort of groundloop, and came to a halt, badly damaged. General Mensier's report on this trial, describing it exactly in this way, was not released to the public until November 1910, long after Ader had been exhibiting Avion III and had made claims for this final trial as a real flight, completely at variance with the official military report.

Avion III was recently under study at Chalais-Meudon, one of the original wings being restored, complete with curved hollow wooden spars, hinges, and cover, with the aim of proving the design's aerodynamic qualities.

(Span: 15.3 m; length: 5.45 m; wing area: 37.95 sqm; empty weight: 246 kg; gross weight with pilot: 455 kg)

Avion IV: While Ader was repairing Avion III, he began work on Avion IV, similar to III but with the twin propellers further apart, and with fully castering wheels. But in February 1898 the Army canceled Ader's contracts and gave up research into flying machines; Avion III was preserved for posterity, now at the Musée des Arts et Métiers and fully restored and recovered in pink fabric; and Avion IV was never finished.

Aimé-Salmson

Emmanuel Aimé was a mathematics teacher who began working early in the century with Santos-Dumont; later in the 1909 Paris Salon he and Salmson showed their Autoplane, a curious direct-lift biplane consisting of a long slightly up-curved rectangular panel tangent at its center to the top of the arch formed by a similar long panel bowed down at each end. A centrally-mounted engine sat on a skid-equipped frame of steel tubing and drove 2 pusher propellers; and at right angles to them on each side another propeller drove air against the underside of the curved lower wing for lift.

Albert

In 1910 a Jean Albert built a monoplane.

Albessard

Albessard worked first with Louis Clément (no relation to the Clément of Clément-Bayard), and in the spring of 1912 completed his first and

The fuselage and cabin of Avion III as it was being restored at the Musée de l'Air in 1982. (Author's collection)

Two views of the Albessard Autostable. Note flattened top, and the keel aft of the passenger compartment. (From The Scientific American)

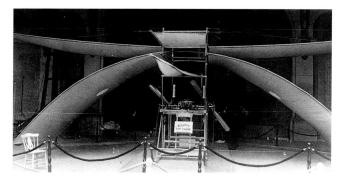

The Aimé-Salmson Autoplane; the exact position of the third and fourth propellers – and their function – is not clear here. (Courtesy of the Musée de l'Air et de l'Espace/Le Bourget-France)

only machine, which he named Autostable. It was a large tandem high-wing monoplane, in which the pilot and unknown number of passengers sat in a 2.5-meter wide cabin behind big rectangular Emaillite windows. The top of the fuselage was flat for extra lift, and was extended into fins along the side for still more. All 4 wing panels were the same, with greater angle of attack for the front pair, and warped for lateral control, through an automatic pendulum device – hence the name Autostable. The aeroplane was tricky to fly, apparently partly because it was heavy for the 85 hp 10-cylinder Anzani, and partly because it was excessively stable. Tests were completed by June 1912 at La Vidamée (Chantilly), north of Paris.

(Spans: 2.5 m; length c 14 m; wing area: 44 sqm; speed reported as 75 kmh)

Alexandre

The firm built the Garaix/ACR 2-seater monoplane at Chartres in 1912, fitted with a 10-cylinder 80 hp Anzani. The triangular section aft fuselage was uncovered, and the 2 cockpits were set into a long curved coaming. An odd small kidney-shaped rudder brought up the rear.

Alkan

Oscar Alkan built Le Enfin in 1910.

Alvarez et de Condé

De Condé worked with a Lieutenant Saunier (not Saulnier), a military expert attached to the laboratory at Chalais-Meudon. Traces of 3 designs remain:

1. Seaplane or flyingboat, model only.

2. An odd high-wing flyingboat with streamlined hull and pointed nose, fabricated from 2 layers of cedrat, a kind of lemon-wood, with fabric in between; the pilot was enclosed along with the engine which drove 2 pusher propellers set on the trailing edge. 4 windows provided him with a view, and small winglets provided stability on the water. The low-aspect-ratio wing was in 3 panels with large ailerons, and was supported on the struts based on special floats; it was entirely of metal construction without welding. The machine was tested around August 1913 at Bellevue on the Seine; the results are not known.

(Span: 12 m; chord: 2.2 m; wing area: 26.5 sqm, Eiffel No 8 airfoil; length: 8.4 m; winglet span: 5.7 m; 60 hp water-cooled engine)

3. Existed in proposal only: an all-steel 3-seater armored amphibian combat aircraft for the Navy. It featured an auxiliary 8 hp motor to power the radio, and to start the main engine.

Amiot

An aircraft begun and not finished.

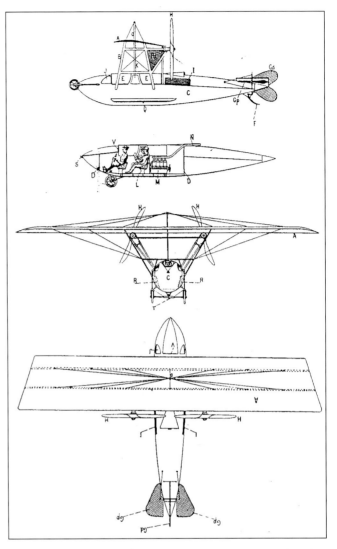

A contemporary drawing of the Alvarez et de Condé No 2. The tiny fins along the sides would probably not help much in the water. (Author's collection)

D'André

D'André built a hang-glider, the Aérovoile, in 1908: a large flat rectangular wing trailed a long triangular tailplane behind it. The pilot hung from 2 parallel bars underneath.

Antoinette

In May 1906 Léon Levavasseur and Captain Ferdinand Ferber founded the Société Anonyme Antoinette to build fast motorboats; it was named for the daughter of Jules Gastambide, just as the Mercedes firm in Germany was named after the daughter of the Spanish ambassador stationed in Germany. Among the shareholders were Jules Gastambide, Chairman; Louis Blériot, Deputy Chairman; Burgeat; Mengin; Demanest; and several others.

Antoinette I: In December 1906 the Board allowed Levavasseur to build one aeroplane for Captain Ferber; they did not believe in aviation, but thought the project would help promote their engines. The construction of the monoplane was undertaken in February 1907 after much research and testing of models. The structure foreshadowed the later more famous Antoinette designs: a long slender wooden fuselage of triangular section with wooden diagonal bracing; pylon-braced multi-spar wings (in this case, 5 main spars) with innumerable light built-up ribs; false ribs and false spars; centrally-mounted undercarriage with skid; propeller built of oval aluminum blades riveted to a steel shaft; Antoinette motor; triangular fin and tailplane.

But No I was very different from its successors: a forward stabilizer was to have been mounted directly above the engine, with Blériot-style tip elevators; the wings were elliptical and cupped like spoons. These wings were exhibited at the 1908 Paris Salon; the machine itself was later completed or nearly completed, but never tested; Levavasseur was persuaded by his shareholders to work on other designs.

(Span: 10 m; length: 15.5 m; wing area: 30 sqm; gross weight: 500 kg; propeller diameter/pitch: 1.2/1.2 m)

It showed the way for the Gastambide-Mengin, later to be known as Antoinette II. It should be noted here that these numbers are not type numbers, but construction numbers, and that Levavasseur's earlier series of motor-boats were known as Antoinette I, II, etc.

Gastambide-Mengin: There may have been just one aeroplane with this name, and it appeared in 5 different forms. All were tractor monoplanes resembling more or less the familiar later Antoinette shape.

The first version had a tricycle undercarriage, all 3 wheels castering, the aft pair mounted on an outrigger on each side of the fuselage. The rudder was rectangular, set below the tail; a pair of masts in tandem carried the upper wing bracing. As in later Antoinettes, the airfoil section was symmetrical fore and aft. It was uncompleted in October or November 1907; when

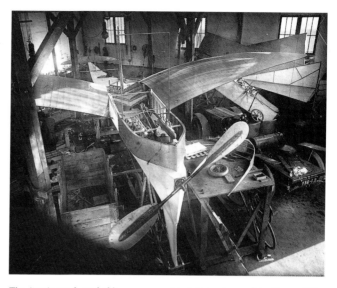

The Antoinette 1, probably never completed. Note pieces of the Gastambide-Mengin in various forms at the back of the shop. (Courtesy of Musée de l'Air et de l'Espace/Le Bourget-France)

Another view of the Antoinette I wing. (Courtesy of the Musée de l'Air et de l'Espace/Le Bourget-France)

The wing of the Antoinette 1 under construction, resembling that of the later models. This structure has often appeared identified as the wing of a Blériot or other early aeroplane. (Author's collection)

The first version of the Gastambide-Mengin, with castering tricycle landing gear. (Courtesy of the Musée de l'Air et de l'Espace/Le Bourget-France)

finished, the mechanic Boyer flew it in February 1908 at Bagatelle, taking off in 30 m, rising to 4 or 5 m. Boyer cut the engine, and the undercarriage was broken in the ensuing hard landing.

In its second configuration the front wheel was replaced by a pair slightly closer together than the aft pair; the new gear was broken again on 12 February. The third form had close-set twin wheels in front. Boyer managed 2 flights of 100 and 150 m, and another of 80 m, and then one wingtip touched the ground while taxiing; the machine flipped onto its back, badly damaged.

In August the Gastambide-Mengin appeared again, much modified, now with 2 wheels, a fully-covered fuselage, a single mast above and below for wing bracing, an odd small moveable elevator on each side of the fuselage amidships, a large triangular fin and tailplane, and an uncharacteristic semicircular rudder bringing up the rear. The pilot, Welferinger, complained of the controls, and it was modified again for the fifth and last time.

Now it had a 4-wheeled undercarriage like a baby-carriage, trailing the familiar triangular ailerons hung from the wingtips, and the tail had the sail-like fins and rudders of the Antoinettes to come. But even in this configuration the machine was reported too flexible, and testing continued on Tournedos Island, in Normandy, in space rented from Hervé Raoul-Duval.

(Span: 10 m; length: 7-9 m; wing area: 24 sqm; weight: 350 kg)

Antoinette III: This was the modified eighth Ferber design, also known as Ferber IX; it was built by Antoinette in 1908, and described under Ferber.

Antoinette IV: The next design, resembling somewhat the Gastambide-Mengin, rolled out at Issy in November 1908. This single machine was radically modified over a short period of time: changes could have been made even within a few hours, making photographic sequencing nearly impossible.

All versions shared the long triangular-sectioned fuselage of the later Antoinettes, similar wide trapezoidal wings, centrally-mounted undercarriage and triangular sail-like tail surfaces; No IV was the only model with ailerons, the rest having warping wings.

Probably the fifth and last version of the Gastambide-Mengin, with 4 wheels equally spaced. (Author's collection)

One of many variants of the first Antoinette IV. (Peter M Bowers collection)

The following brief sketch of the design progression of the first No IV is an estimation; some of the features described here overlapped across several changes. The first undercarriage consisted of 2 wheels on what looked like enlarged bicycle forks, in tandem; triangular ailerons hung loosely, with loose fabric for the trailing edges. The rudder was a rectangular panel between the forward triangular fin and a trailing triangular fin, and the elevator corresponded to it, without the trailing surface. Then the undercarriage was reversed with a single trailing wheel set into the rear of a long skid girder which had a small wheel set out in front of the tip. The rectangular elevator was fixed, and a triangular surface was hinged behind it. The name Antoinette was painted on the sides of the radiators. Further changes included a roller set into the front of the skid, the rectangular rudder taken out and the familiar pair of triangular rudders substituted, the familiar spoked control wheels appeared on the sides of the cockpit, the nose was covered, and small wheels were fixed to the wingtip skids.

Then the bracing mast was set right above the undercarriage strut; the familiar long diagonal skid replaced the horizontal girder; and a close-set pair of wheels were fitted on a cross-axle. Then the fuselage, at least, must have been re-covered, since diagonal tapes showed between the diagonal fuselage bracing, giving a series of diamond patterns; a small wheel was set the tip of the skid. A curved wooden fairing was added to the bow and another fastened to the forward undercarriage brace. Latham attempted the Channel crossing in it when the fuselage veneer extended to the rear of the side radiators, the diagonal nose-wheel strut had been re-set, and the trailing wing skids had been taken off. The machine was destroyed when it crashed in the water.

At Reims in August 1909 another Antoinette, very similar to Latham's No IV, was entered with the number 13 painted on the sides. It differed from Latham's in having a second horizontal brace in the undercarriage, and lacked the little nosewheel on the skid. In the Champagne meet later the same year, this machine appeared again, with a second diagonal brace crossing the skid, now fitted once more with the nosewheel.

Ferber had designed the controls, consisting first of a left-side-mounted wheel for ailerons and rudder, a right-side-mounted wheel for elevator, 2 small wheels in front of the pilot for engine controls, and a foot-pedal with the ignition switch. Revised, the controls were similar, except that the foot-pedal now controlled the rudder. Levavasseur was said to have been asked why he retained such a complicated system, and he replied that flying was not simple, either. But his machines proved very stable and easy to fly, in spite of his control system.

The wing plan was of the type known as 6:3:2 (each panel had a 6-meter span, a 3-meter chord at the root, and 2-meter chord at the tip). The dimensions of the machine remained generally unchanged during its lifetime; in August 1909 they were described as follows:

(Span: 12.8 m; airfoil symmetrical front and back, as on the Antoinette I; angle of attack: 4°; length: 12 m; wing area: 34 sqm; empty weight: 460 kg; 50 hp Antoinette V8, with a propeller similar to that on Antoinette I)

After Antoinette IV was completed and before it was sent to the Channel, at least 4 other Antoinettes had been built, Nos V, VI, VII, and VIII, the latter flying in August 1909. Little is known about Nos

Another variation. Both still have the long wing skids. (Author's collection)

Demanest's Antoinette V, still with wing-skids. Note wing cut-outs. (Peter M Bowers collection)

V, VI, and VIII. Since Nos IV and VII were progressively retrofitted with the latest improvements, it is reasonable to suppose the same occurred with the other 3, unless they were abandoned too early for this process. Nos V and VI were similar to the first versions of No IV.

Antoinette V: It was built for Demanest with more aluminum parts, especially in the wing, than were used in No IV. It had trapezoidal ailerons, closely-paired wheels at the rear of the heavy girder skid with a front-mounted roller, no forward under-fin, and a curved cut-out at each wing-root.

(Span: 12.5 m; length: 10.8 m)

Antoinette VI: This one was built for Captain Burgeat, at first with ailerons. These were later removed and replaced by a wing-warping system which proved more effective and which was used in No VII. With Levavasseur's system, the front spar was fixed and the rear one could pivot up and down. There was a control wheel on the right side as on all Antoinettes, but a second one was mounted like a steering wheel in front of the pilot, with a cushion between him and it.

Antoinette VII: This was the second of Latham's Antoinettes, used on his second unsuccessful Channel attempt; it was much photographed in its variant forms. It first appeared with a vertical front support for the diagonal landing-gear skid with a roller at the tip and a horizontal brace to the center of the main axle. The familiar separate pair of triangular rudders was replaced by a single triangle with its base well below the bottom line of the fuselage, and the single big triangular elevator was no longer a pair of oddly curved surfaces. 2 small kingposts appeared toward the ends of each wing. After Latham's second crash in this machine, on 25 July 1909, he ordered another No VII, but this time with the familiar raked front support and rudders formed in

2 small triangles. The skid roller disappeared in favor of an up-turned skid. On 29 September 1909 Latham flew it to a world's altitude record of 155 m. It appeared at Reims with the race number 13, and was the first of several production Antoinette VII monoplanes.

The first Antoinette VII, like the IV also to be frequently modified. (Author's collection)

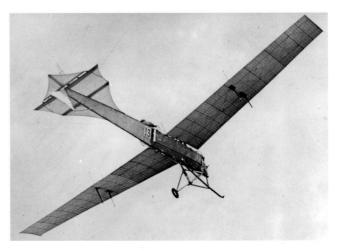

Latham's second Antoinette VII, at Reims with the number 13. (Courtesy of the Musée de l'Air et de l'Espace/Le Bourget-France)

22

Antoinette VIII: Little is known about this one, other than that it was flown by Ruchonnet in 1909 at Bordeaux; it probably had a greater span (14 m), a single wheel and a wooden propeller.

It is almost impossible to distinguish the individual Antoinettes after No VIII. There were several cases of the same fuselage being equipped with different sets of wings; No XII was probably under construction towards the end of 1909.

But an overhaul of the firm in October 1909 allowed the development of new engines and aircraft. Levavasseur and Gastambide were forced out of the company when new share-holders led by Pierre Chalmard, the former manager of the Louis Blériot lamp company, and Maurice Blériot, Louis' cousin, bought the bulk of the assets. Maurice became Executive Manager, and Hubert Latham, Chairman. Before the return of Gastambide in March 1910, the firm introduced the ENV V8 and the 50 hp Gnôme as powerplants for their products. Hubert Latham ordered a new 2-seater, endeavoring to produce a school aircraft with larger wings of 15-meter span. It was probably the same machine shown in French reviews at the end of 1909, with ailerons which were later removed. The wing-roots were cut out in a curve to provide a better view of the ground. The student sat between the pilot's knees, and both seats were further forward for balance.

The firm also built a ground trainer, a sort of rolling barrel in which the pilot sat and controlled its movement with Antoinette controls. The school machine and all subsequent designs were equipped with wooden propellers: Chauvière Intégrales or Ratmanoff Normales, or similar makes. Other significant developments during this period were modifications of the airfoil with flattened under-surfaces. A new 100 hp 16-cylinder engine was introduced for Latham's attempt on the Gordon-Bennett Cup Race in October 1910, with the pilot's upper body emerging from a protective cylindrical coaming, a specially modified machine with 3 tanks mounted between the wings for Thomas to use in the long-distance Coupe Michelin in December 1910.

The most remarkable designs of 1910 were the streamlined machines: one of these was named for Wachter after his fatal crash at Reims in 1910; the fuselage was decked over with wood frames and tight canvas from the cockpit forward, with only the cylinder-heads exposed. The second racer was fitted with only a 50 hp motor completely cowled; the wheels were covered over and the landing gear legs were faired. The wings were shortened.

In 1911 the company's position was still bad, and the performance of the Antoinette engines was a distinct drawback: they were generally underpowered for the firm's aircraft, which tended to be heavy. The landing gear was not strong enough for prolonged taxiing, and there were too many unexplained wing failures – the problem of most contemporary monoplanes.

Antoinette Monobloc (or Latham Type): This large new 3-seater, also known as the Military 3-Seater, was nearly finished by the end of 1910; it was Levavasseur's and Gastambide's entry for the Concours Militaire in October 1911. (At this time there was only one Antoinette military 2-seater, of 16-meter span.) The big wooden wing was built around 4 spars, one fixed and the other 3 (1 fore, 2 aft) pivoting for the wing-warping. The controls them-

The big Antoinette Monobloc or Military Scout, 1910, under construction. The sharp leading edge and flat airfoil bottom shows clearly. (Courtesy of the Musée de l'Air et de l'Espace/Le Bourget-France)

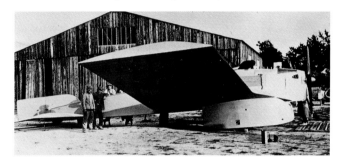

The completed and unflyable Monobloc. A later fin was larger. (Courtesy Harry Woodman)

selves were in the form of a distortable rectangular fame which could be pushed fore-and-aft or rocked from side to side for warping. Highly streamlined, the aeroplane stood on 2 large covered legs, each housing 2 wheels on a single short axle towards the rear, and a single smaller wheel at the front, in case of nose-overs. The crew sat in a single opening in the smooth turtle-deck of the top, and copper-tube radiators for the inadequate 60 hp Antoinette ran back along each side. The airfoil section was very thick, to allow for internal heavy bracing "similar to a biplane" – 70 cm at the root. The tail appears in 2 configurations: a long low fin and rectangular rudder both with and without an oddly curved high extension over the fin.

It arrived at Chalons for the competition with a small 16-liter tank and was unable to fly because of excessive weight, although it may have managed a short hop of several meters.

(Span 15.9 m; length 12.25 m; wing area (probably including horizontal tail): 56 sqm; wing chord from 4 to 3 m; empty weight (official): 935 kg; gross weight (never achieved): 1300 kg)

In 1912 the company tried to sell another Antoinette monoplane to the Army: it was a classic design similar to the Wachter machine, called the Triplette – perhaps because it was to be a 3-seater. It retained the classic Antoinette undercarriage with a small front outrigger wheel added. On 17 October Blanc demonstrated it in front of an Army commission, and in the climb a wing tore off. This machine is often called the last pre-War Antoinette design.

Levavasseur died in 1921, after having completed 2 other monoplanes with Jules Gastambide as a partner, these with experimental variable surfaces. The only surviving wing of this type, painted blue, white, and red, was destroyed in the fire at Le Bourget in 1990.

How many aircraft did the company build before WWI? *Jane's* reported 50 in 1909 and 30 in 1910, but there is no proof for such high numbers for a rather ill-fated design. An inventory of the factory is mentioned by Wachter in May 1910 at Chalons, describing the highest serial number stocked there as 32. Henri Levavasseur, the last son of Léon, claimed that he did not think that more than 50 were built altogether.

Herbert Latham demonstrated his No VII at Johannisthal on 23 September 1909, and Dr Hirth ordered one for himself upon seeing the demonstration; he and Otto Wiener founded the Albatros Flugzeugwerke shortly after, on 29 December, hiring Michael Gabriel as Chief Engineer. One French-built Antoinette VII was delivered in 1909, and Gabriel worked out drawings; a second one was delivered in 1910, fitted with a 50 or 70 hp Gnôme. The design proved too heavy for the German army. One was exported from France to Argentina; Harry S Harkness lent 3 of his own machines to the US Navy, and they appeared at the Curtiss training station on North Island, off San Diego. The price of an Antoinette with either an Antoinette or an ENV engine was 25,000F, average for the aircraft of the period, though these aeroplanes were probably the most carefully built and handsomest aircraft of the pre-1914 years.

There are 3 surviving Antoinettes: the aircraft at the Science Museum in London, No 50, is probably the most original; this No VII was used by Latham and flown also by Robert Blackburn. The 2-seater fuselage and 50 hp Antoinette motor are the only original parts of the newly restored machine in Paris. The Antoinette in Krakow will be restored, but information as to its history and serial number is so far missing.

Anzani

Alexandre Anzani was a famous engine designer and builder, and he encouraged aeroplane construction by sponsoring some builders and modestly awarding prizes to special performers. One aeroplane carried his own name, introduced late in 1909. The pilot sat aft of the high wing behind a 40 hp 3-cylinder Anzani driving the tractor propeller through belts. A 4-leg undercarriage bore 2 wheels and long skids. Alternately, the same engine appeared mounted just forward of the leading edge of the wing.

This aircraft was sometimes referred to as the de Mas: since Anzani was not wealthy in 1909, he may have asked de Mas to finance the monoplane.

Archdeacon

The wealthy lawyer Ernest Archdeacon, long an enthusiast of mechanical speed, and one of the most eager and efficient proselytes for aeronautics, became interested in it in 1902; in 1903, with Renard,

The sole Anzani aeroplane, of 1909. Note the all-flying tail surfaces and castering tailwheel. (Peter M Bowers collection)

Hervé, Drzwiecki, Tatin, Besançon, Balsan, Soreau, and Ferber, he founded the Aviation Committee of the Aéro Club de France, and thus gave worldwide aviation a significant boost. It is less well known that he worked out the designs for 3 gliders, whose primary significance was that they helped launch the aviation career of Gabriel Voisin.

In 1904 Archdeacon commissioned Dargent, a model-builder at Chalais-Meudon, to build a glider patterned on the Hargrave kites and the 1902 Wright. Both Gabriel Voisin, then a young art student from Lyon, and Captain Ferdinand Ferber, on leave from the French artillery, flew it in April 1904 at Merlimont on the Channel coast near the town of Berck-sur-mer: Voisin recalled making 34 "flights" in it. Covered with silk, it had no elevator and a single tail fin, but later underwent many modifications with a front elevator, tail fins, and skids.

Voisin built Archdeacon's first glider in 1904; this photograph was taken at St Cloud. (Courtesy of the Musée de l'Air et de l'Espace/Le Bourget-France)

Voisin built Archdeacon's third glider as well; Voisin was nearly drowned in it. (Author's collection)

(Span: 7.5 m; wing area: 21.6 sqm; weight: 34 kg)

By October 1904 Archdeacon had formed the Syndicat de l'Aéronautique with Girardot, Maas, Turgan, de Vogüe and Loisel, and he commissioned Voisin to build a second glider, similar to the first, with tailplane and fins added for stability; the design resembled a stabilized Wright. Archdeacon thought the elevator would do better at the rear, and put it there.

Voisin built the glider for the Syndicate at Levallois, northwest of Paris, in Turgan's workshop; it was tested there with twin propellers driven by an unsuccessful flat-twin 16 hp Turgan engine. The work was then transferred to the Etablissements Surcouf, later to become the Astra Company. Voisin wisely tested the glider unmanned, with a sandbag and no engine; on 26 March 1905 it was towed down a slipway by automobile at Issy-les-Moulineaux, the tail broke off, and the glider was demolished.

(Span: 9.6 m; length: 4.5 m; wing area: 27 sqm)

In 1905 the Voisins built a balloon for Bertelli, and that same year Archdeacon commissioned Voisin to build him yet another glider at Surcouf, similar to No 2 but more substantial. It showed what were to become Voisin characteristics, 4 side-curtains and a biplane cell tail unit. The glider was mounted on 4 floats of inflated varnished fabric. On 8 June 1905, towed on the Seine by Alphonse Tellier's motorboat La Rapière, it managed flights of 600 and 100 m. A wind-speed indicator and a dynamometer were attached to the towline, where Archdeacon computed that 28 hp were necessary for take-off. Voisin was at the controls on the last attempt, when it pitched down and flipped over onto its port side. Voisin's wrist was badly injured, and he gave up flying on the spot.

(Span: 10 m; wing area: 37.4 sqm; tailplane area: c 20 sqm; length: 10 m; weight: 360 kg)

Archdeacon took the same glider, now fitted with heavier floats, to Evian-les-Bains on Lake Geneva to continue his experiments on a larger area of water, where towing straight into the wind was possible. Voisin reported one such experiment with the glider at anchor, when a high wind came up; the pilot was able to control the machine perfectly, taking off and alighting without incident. It was later sold to an Englishman, Bellamy, who took off the floats and installed a 50 hp motor driving 4 propellers. He took it to England in 1906 and tested it suspended from a balloon as Santos-Dumont had done earlier the same year.

At the end of 1905 Gabriel Voisin went off on his own. For a while Archdeacon took up further experiments with Delagrange, founding the Aéro Club de France: in 1906 the group did research and built several gliders on Chanute's model near Palaisseau. Archdeacon himself had planned a new glider for 1907, but it was probably never built. He then went on to offer his name and his money for a series of prizes to develop the powered machines of other designers. His last participation in aeroplane construction was with Clerget and Marquézy at Juvisy in 1911, on the CAM monoplane.

Archdeacon was also the author of a drama, *La Conquête de l'Air*, the story of a poor inventor who fails to fly and then kills himself. The play was performed, also unsuccessfully, in Paris, in January 1905.

Arnaud

A biplane of this name was tested at Montélimard starting in April 1911, powered by a 25 hp Anzani.

Arnoux

Before World War I René Arnoux was known as a designer and builder of recording gasometer equipment for automobiles, some of them, like his fuel-flow meter for gas engines, extremely advanced. He was at the same time vice-president of the Technical Committee of the French Automobile Club and member of the Technical Committee of the Ligue Nationale Aérienne, when he designed the first of his tailless aeroplanes in 1909: none was successful. In about 1912 he coined the names Stabloplane and Stablavion for his designs which were to be automatically stable.

No 1: This tailless biplane with a 4-bladed pusher propeller driven by a chain was built by Astra and was to be tested by Gaudard in

The first Arnoux with the engine not yet installed. (Courtesy of the Musée de l'Air et de l'Espace/Le Bourget-France)

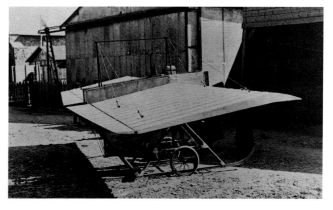

The second Arnoux aeroplane; note the full-span controllers. (Courtesy of the Musée de l'Air et de l'Espace/Le Bourget-France)

1910. The frame looked heavy; it was supported on 2 wheels with up-curved skids forward and aft.

<u>No 2</u>: Garsonin likely test-flew this monoplane at Issy in 1912 only once, after which it was damaged. A tractor engine was fitted at the front of a short rectangular box fuselage which sat in the middle of a broad plank-like wing with full-span controllers with stops to prevent excess downward movement, preventing the reflex airfoil from becoming in effect a simple-cambered section with unstable center of pressure. A simple 2-wheel undercarriage with a pair of skids upturned at each end provided stability on the ground. Other controls are not known, but Arnoux retained the floor accelerator of the automobile.

(Span: 10.05 m; weight: 400 kg)

<u>No 3</u>: Also a monoplane, this one was probably also built by Astra shortly after No 2 and shown at the 1912 Salon before its unsuccessful tests in 1913. The squared-off box fuselage of No 2 was now streamlined, and the low wing was wire-braced to the fuselage with no pylon support. The undercarriage was built with 2 pairs of wheels and short skids forward; the rear rested on a single braced extension. A 55 hp water-cooled Chenu drove a 2-bladed Régy propeller behind a high square radiator. Arnoux had expected to control the machine with throttle and foot-pedal only: it was to fly level with a constant angle of attack controlled through the coupling of the throttle and elevator.

But what Arnoux did not understand was that with the elevator up, the angle of attack decreased. He had throttle problems as well, since because of his poor carburetor he could not accurately manage the rpm: the engine turned at full rpm or stopped entirely. At the end of 1912 he suggested using "a modified automotive carburetor."

The fourth Arnoux. Note the hinged forward skid. (Author's collection)

<u>No 4</u>: A much heavier tractor design appeared in December 1912 or January 1913, with an upright 4-cylinder water-cooled motor, a Blériot-style double pylon, end-plates on the wingtips, and a 2-wheel undercarriage mounted on semicircular supports; a cleaver-shaped rudder was fitted under the rear fuselage. It is not clear which was No 3 and which was No 4, since they may have been built at nearly the same time.

<u>No 5</u>: The last Stablavion, a 2-seat pusher monoplane with an 80 hp Gnôme, resembled No 3 but with a quadrilateral 4-wheel undercarriage, the Blériot double pylon, and high vertical fins at each wingtip. It was tested at Issy in June 1914.

Observers as late as 1913 reported that Arnoux had succeeded only with his gliders. After the War he worked with Félix Madon, the WWI ace with 41 confirmed victories, to develop a series of tailless racing planes under the name Arnoux-Simplex.

Arondel

Paul Arondel was appearing in the aeronautical records by mid-1912, though he had already been flying for at least a year. At the end of

The fifth Arnoux of 1914. Compare the airfoil sections of the wings of Nos 1, 2, 4, and 5. (Courtesy of the Musée de l'Air et de l'Espace/Le Bourget-France)

1911 he was associated with Argoult, and began a flying school at Issy-les-Moulineaux; his chief pilot was Hanouille, a Morane-Saulnier pilot. The school aircraft was a Blériot XI. An undated postcard shows a so-called Monoplan Arondel, with a caption describing it as powered by an Anzani: it is clearly a 1911 Morane. Unless the publisher of the card was in error – quite likely – the chances are that Paul Arondel was flying a Morane, later modified with spares from other aircraft as necessary, probably the school Blériot. Other postcards show Arondel's monoplane in late 1912 with 2 different engines, first a 3-cylinder Anzani; and later, by September 1912, a 6-cylinder Anzani. The machine clearly had the fuselage and tail unit from a 1911 Morane, coupled to the wings of a Blériot XI: the Arondel pylon was a single inverted V, unlike that of the Morane. It is likely that the Arondel machine was a much-modified Morane-Borel fitted with various engines.

(Span (Blériot style): 8.65m; (Morane-style): 8.9 m; length varied from 7.6 to 7.65 m; gross weight with the 3-cylinder Anzani: 225 kg)

In 1911 Arondel and Argoult ran a flying school at Issy, using Blériots. In December 1912 Arondel was killed in a crash at Juvisy; he was not yet 25.

D'Artois (Chantiers de l'Artois)

By mid-1912 Louis Schreck was forced to abandon the Anciens Chantiers Tellier he had created at St Omer after he had purchased Alphonse Tellier's monoplane patents. He then formed the Chantiers de l'Artois (workshops of Artois), generally referred to as d'Artois, after the name of the region in northwestern France in which it was located. This short-lived firm produced 3 types of biplanes designed by Louis Gaudard, famous in French aviation since 1909. The first 2 machines were shown at the 1912 Paris Exposition, one a landplane, the other a flyingboat. To save drag, each aeroplane had a 50 hp Gnôme mounted inside the plywood-covered fuselage; each was painted white.

Aérotorpille: This was the landplane. The Gnôme drove a pusher propeller behind the tail, and the rectangular-section fuselage was left uncovered around the engine. The upper wings were of longer span than the lower; both sets pivoted around a single spar, similar to the Breguet design, with a single interplane strut on each side. A simple 2-wheel undercarriage was fitted under the engine, and a long skid kept the propeller off the ground. It was exhibited at the 1912 Paris Salon and probably flew in 1913.

(Span: 10 m, 6 m; length: 7 m wing area: 26 sqm; top speed estimated: 135 kmh; empty weight: 250 kg; 50 hp Gnôme, or a 50/75 hp Chenu)

Flyingboat: The second d'Artois design used what appeared to be the same wings as on the Aérotorpille. The bulky hull resembled earlier Denhaut or Donnet-Levêque designs, of rectangular section forward and triangular behind the wings. The enclosed Gnôme drove a pusher 4-blade propeller through chains

and a short drive-shaft under the juncture of the top wings. The single pointed-topped rudder was hinged on the stern below the tailplane.

(Span: 11 m; length: 7 m; wing area: 26 sqm; weight empty: 350 kg; speed: 90 kmh; 50 hp Gnôme, and also a 50/75 hp Chenu)

The third d'Artois may have been the flyingboat modified or an entirely new machine. It was built in January 1913, and showed a hull similar to that of No 2 but darker in appearance, probably of varnished mahogany plywood. A pair of trapezoidal rudders were fitted above and below the tailplane and its single elevator. The upper and lower wings were of narrower chord and greater span, with only 2 intermediate interplane struts instead of 4; large ailerons were built into the top wing. Some photographs show the machine with 2 radiators and a single streamlined tank, but it was likely fitted early on with a 100 hp Gnôme mounted low in the hull, and 2 tanks. At the 1913 Monaco meet Gaudard damaged the hull and could not enter the qualification trials; on 15 April at the same meet he tried again, with the race number 7. He took off and found he had a problem with the

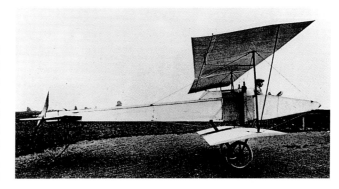

The d'Artois Aérotorpille of 1912. The wings pivot on the front spars – note absence of diagonal bracing aft of the spars. (Courtesy of the Musée de l'Air et de l'Espace/Le Bourget-France)

The third d'Artois at the meet at Monaco in 1913. (Courtesy of the Musée de l'Air et de l'Espace/Le Bourget-France)

machine. In trying to land, he pulled up hard to avoid some boats, fell back against the seat-back and broke it, and then fell hard against the starting crank. Injured, he stood up, and the machine, out of control, crashed into the sea.

(Span (top): 15 m; (lower): 10 m; length: 8 m; empty weight: 450 kg; loaded weight: 740 kg; 100 hp Gnôme)

The Chantiers d'Artois disappeared when Louis Schreck founded the FBA, shortly after Gaudard's death.

Asquier-Régence

Little is known of this monoplane, usually called Asquier. Powered by a 3-cylinder 40 hp Anzani, it crashed on a test flight early in 1910 at the field at Mandelieu-la-Napoule. The specially-appointed pilot, Thomas, was a former motorbike racer; Asquier was the general secretary of the Automobile Club of Toulon; Régence was the name of a company owned by a M Leriche in Marseilles.

Association Générale Aéronautique

A monoplane of this name may have been built in 1913 by students for the Army. But perhaps this firm only bought aircraft and did not build them.

Astra

Edouard Surcouf, the successor to Maurice Mallet, began his aviation career by repairing and building balloons. His firm, Etablissements Surcouf, went on to build dirigibles – the Lebaudy was his first – and became extremely successful: income for 1908 was 3 million francs. In 1908 Surcouf built its first heavier-than-air machine, a tandem monoplane probably inspired by the Langley Aerodrome by way of Blériot's tandem Libellule; it was designed by Louis Paulhan and was tested, unsuccessfully, the same year. Gabriel Voisin built his float-equipped glider for Ernest Archdeacon in the buildings of the Surcouf firm. Early in 1909 Henri Deutsch de la Meurthe took over the firm and renamed it Ateliers de Construction Aéronautiques Astra, with Surcouf as manager. In May the aeroplane part of the firm was established in another part of the factory with some 60 workers to build Wright aeroplanes; the firm had acquired the "monopoly of the construction of the Wrights."

The Compagnie Générale de Navigation Aérienne (CGNA) had been founded on 14 December 1908 by the banker Lazare Weiller, with partners Henry Kapferer, Hart O Berg, and the bank Dernheim et Compagnie. The latter supported the Ateliers et Chantiers de France at Dunkirk, small shipyards in serious financial difficulties. It was first announced that the yards would build a dozen Wright Flyers in 1909, but early that year the company and its supporting bank went bankrupt, and there remained only the more stable Astra company. CGNA was formed to own and make use of the Wright patents in France.

Astra started work without drawings, copying an original machine under the supervision of Wilbur himself; and by February 1909 14 machines had been ordered; by May a total of 50 were said to be on order. From Astra, Surcouf and Kapferer founded yet another firm,

the Compagnie Générale Transaérienne (CGT) for aerial tourism, beginning with ballooning (this CGT had a Belgian subsidiary called AVIA, not to be confused with the French company). This firm was revived for a short period after WWI and can be considered as the earliest air transport company in the world.

Astra-built Wright Type A: These were later modified with an undercarriage and full tail units.

(Span: 12.32 m; length: 8.5 m; empty weight: 420 kg; 35 hp Barriquand et Marre)

From this design, Astra developed 2 families of biplanes, Astra-Wright and Astra, all retaining more or less modified Wright wings.

Astra-Wright Type 1910: The factory designation for this single example shown at the Paris Exposition of 1910 is unknown. It had the typical Wright wings, a nacelle for 2 pilots in tandem seated in front of a 55 hp Chenu motor driving a single pusher propeller. There were no forward surfaces, and the rudder consisted of 2 small triangles placed above and below a single rear elevator mounted at the ends of the 4 tailbooms.

(Span: 12.5 m; length: 12 m; wing area: 248 sqm; empty weight: 450 kg)

Astra-Wright BB: At least one Wright Baby was imported to France and then marked Astra-Wright Type BB (in French BB sounds like the word for baby, bébé). It is now exhibited at the Musée de l'Air in Paris.

Astra-Wright Type L: This designation appeared in Astra advertisements in 1911 for a new school machine used at the Wright Flying School Pau-Pont, south of Bordeaux. It was a 2-seater with dual control without front elevators and with a full tail unit – this machine was very likely a Dayton-built Wright Type B.

Astra-Wright Type E: This designation rarely appeared in print; the aeroplane was developed from the Type 1910, but was larger and more like the original Wright design: no front surfaces, and

The Astra-Wright Type E. The nacelle holds 2, and the Renault is cowled with a large circular ring. (Author's collection)

classical tail configuration. The wheels were paired. The 2-seated nacelle was faired with windows, and a 50 hp Renault cowled in a distinctive big ring was mounted on the lower wing to starboard of the nacelle. In 1912 the nacelle was widened and the windows were made larger and square; the bombardier lay on the floor to the right of the pilot, working a Scott bomb-release device; a machine so equipped won the 1912 Coupe Aéro Cible Michelin. The design was still in use in 1913 with a slightly different nacelle fairing.

(Span: 16 m; length: 10.64 m; wing area: 60 sqm; empty weight: 624 kg; 50 hp Renault V-8)

<u>Astra Type C</u>: The first typically Astra design first appeared in 1910 and flew in August 1911. It was built in small numbers through 1913, a 2-seater first of wood and later of steel and wood. It had the long triangular-section fuselage and cross-axle-and-post undercarriage of the Antoinettes.

(Span: 12.5 m; length: 10.4 m; wing area: c 48 sqm; empty weight: 500 kg; gross weight: 800 kg; speed 81 kmh; 60 hp Chenu)

Below: An Astra Hydro was shown at the 1912 Paris Salon with the long triangular fuselage uncovered. (Courtesy of the Musée de l'Air et de l'Espace/Le Bourget-France)

The Greek-owned Type C named Nautilos. (Author's collection)

The Astra CM with 3 seats; it rather resembles a biplane Antoinette. (Author's collection)

A seaplane variant was developed directly from the Type C; perhaps the original aircraft was also mounted on Tellier floats. Another, with a 160 hp Gnôme, was entered at Deauville in August, but failed to appear.

(Span: 16 m; length: 12 m; wing area: 54.2 sqm)

The Greek government bought one, named it Nautilos, and fitted it with a bomb-release mechanism. The British Navy ordered one, to be numbered 25, but the order was canceled.

Astra Type CM: Type C was developed as the military CM, with 3 seats, rounder wingtips and wider wings; more metal was used in the frame.

(Span: 12.32 m; length: 10.95 m; empty weight: 673 kg; gross weight: 1000 kg; speed: 85 kmh; 80 hp Chenu, or an 85 hp air-cooled Renault)

Astra Hydro: In 1912 the CM was fitted with 3 Tellier floats; at least 2 were built powered by 100 hp V12 Renaults. The first was flown by Labouret to win the St Malô race on 14-26 August 1912. 2 seem to have been ordered by the British Navy, to be numbered 106 and 107, but they never materialized.

(Span: 12.3 m; length: 11 m; wing area: 50 sqm; empty weight: 800 kg; 2 main floats 4.5 x 1.15 m, and one small tail float)

The second, with unequal-span wings and powered by a 110 hp flat radial liquid-cooled Salmson Système Canton-Unné engine, flew and crashed at Monaco. At St Malô the rules favored competing aircraft with the most seats, so Labouret's machine was introduced with 5 seats.

In 1912 a C or CM was tested with exhaust pipes on a 75 hp Renault, and at the 1912 Salon an identical aircraft was shown all made of steel tubing, the fuselage uncovered. The CGT flew this one between Nice and Monaco in regular charter service for several weeks.

Astra Triplane: Sponsored by Henri de la Meurthe, this marvelous large machine was built by Gabriel Voisin; it is described under Voisin.

In 1912, Astra took over Train, and former Train designs were then called Astra-Train. In 1913, Henri Deutsch de la Meurthe merged the heavier-than-air division of Astra with the Nieuport firm he had just bought; the merger was completed after the War, and gave rise to the later Nieuport-Astra designs. In 1915-1916 the firm designed a big twin-boom biplane with a span of 25.5 m; propellers were mounted at the nose of each boom, driven either by a single central engine or one in each boom. The machine was either not begun or not completed.

The flat-mounted Canton-Unné installed in the Astra Hydro at Monaco. (Author's collection)

Astruc

In the 9 March 1933 issue of *Les Ailes*, Edmond Astruc described the experiments he had made with heavier-than-air machines since 1908:

In 1908 I built my first aircraft, a tailless biplane with heavily-staggered wings. 2 7 hp engines moved the craft. A twin-engine? Yes, indeed, the very first... The propellers which I cut out myself were contra-rotating, and were geared down with the ratio of 1 to 3. I succeeded in taking off at Miramas.

I worked at a blacksmith's in Septèmes, named Brémond. We followed up with other tests on a field at Septèmes. In 1909 I achieved short flights, straight forward, at Miramas, with a semi-cantilever monoplane with a canvas-covered fuselage, built by the Blanc brothers. Unfortunately, once I wished to turn... what a disaster! The aircraft was not prepared for turns... no matter, anyway.

I built another aircraft then, with only one motor. It was tested at St Victoret, near Marseilles. At that time I was commissioned as an instructor by the director of the Lyon-Bron airfield to take over the instruction of military pilots. I was appointed chief pilot on Henry Farmans equipped with 50 hp Gnômes. Shortly after, I was transferred to Reims to test the first Hanriot military monoplanes.

1911, first drill, I came a cropper for the first time and quite seriously at Reims. The undercarriage gave me the slip at the start, and the crash was rough: months at the hospital, open fracture, one year with crutches. Note that despite my job and rank, I still had no brevet (Astruc was still a civilian – Ed).

This brings us to 1913. I joined Fabre to test the company's hydro-gliders; I won the first prize at the Monaco meeting, and the prize for the race up the Rhone River, from Marseilles to Aix-les-Bains. Thereafter I was entrusted with the transformation of landplanes into floatplanes. I modified Caudron G-2s, G-4s, and Sopwiths. We were also involved with the design of the Schmitt seaplane with the 300 hp Renault.

Edmond Astruc worked with Henri Potez after WWI, and ceased his aeronautical activities in 1925. (In an interview with Jean Liron in *Aviation* magazine in the mid-1960s, Etienne Romano claimed to have designed and built an unsuccessful biplane in 1908, powered with 2-27 hp Anzanis, which crashed almost on its first flight. Romano had been 19 in 1908, and had worked with Astruc on the first Astruc aeroplane: but the machine was totally Astruc's. Romano went on to become a minor designer in the 1930s.)

Ateliers Aéronautiques de l'Est

One of the several Lecomtes appearing in French aviation history, Alfred bought assets from the defunct Avia firm and founded the AAE, later transferring it to Luneville. The firm built at least one rather awkward-looking and crudely-built aircraft, a monoplane with a long box fuselage covered at the forward end only, and an odd triangular rudder hinged at its point. The tricycle undercarriage was tall and set forward, and a Blériot-style looped cane skid protected the rear. The wings had distinctive elliptical tips, in which the 3 tip ribs fanned out from a point on the leading edge.

(Span: 12.6 m; length: 8.6 m; wing area: 22 sqm; 30 hp 3-cylinder Viale)

Ateliers et Chantiers de Dunkerque

In 1908-1909 the directors of the shipyards Ateliers et Chantiers de Dunkerque attempted to convert the ailing firm to aircraft construction. Lazare Weiller, owner of the Wright patents in France, was among these directors. 12 Flyers were ordered, 2 of which were to be delivered to the Army, and were sent to Chalais-Meudon in February 1910. The construction was judged untidy and the machines unsatisfactory: it is likely the company went bankrupt before the entire order of 12 was completed. Other Wrights were built by Astra.

The 1910 Audineau. One hopes the aft fuselage was very lightly built! (Author's collection)

Aubry

Before the war Météor was the name of a large cab company which owned some 200 cars in 1910; the name was also given to a monoplane designed by Aubry, chief pilot and designer at the Desprat flying school at the Camp de Chalôns. Similar to the Hanriots but with triangular tail surfaces like the Antoinettes, it was finished in May 1911, but not flown. The wings had gracefully curved and scalloped trailing edges. In August a lightened version appeared and flew, after "careful fitting."

(Span: 8.6 m; length: 7.5 m; wing area: 14 sqm; empty weight: 200 kg; 50 hp Anzani)

Audineau

This firm was best known for building horse-drawn vehicles and later car bodies. At the 1910 Paris Exposition, they showed a monoplane with a long streamlined tubular fuselage made of cylinders assembled on wooden spars. The wing ribs were built from a web of cork with ash flanges; the wings were tapered, with curved tips. The tailplane was of long chord with split elevators. The undercarriage resembled that of the Blériot XI with forward skids, but with a different springing arrangement. It was flown or at least tested at Juvisy in 1910 by a pilot named Merle. Audineau also built the 1911 Pivot-Koechlin.

The first Auffm-Ordt; note the inner wing panels. The machine seems a little loose on its landing gear. (Courtesy of the Musée de l'Air et de l'Espace/Le Bourget-France)

Auffm-Ordt

Clement Auffm-Ordt, associated with a M Heeren, designed his first aeroplane in 1908, a light monoplane similar to the Demoiselle. The tail at the end of the single curved fuselage boom was a Hargrave box cell with the elevator in the middle and the rudder at the rear. The inner sections in each wing panel were adjustable apparently differentially for balance from dihedral to cathedral, and the wingtips curved up elliptically. The machine was built by Voisin and tested at Buc.

(Span: 8 m; wing area: 20 sqm; moving surfaces: span 2.4 m; 30 hp REP engine, with a 2-bladed REP prop of c 2.5 m in diameter)

The second machine was built in 1909, perhaps a radical modification of the first. This one had an aluminum frame, skids instead of wheels, a biplane tail with twin rudders, and control panels in the wings similar to those of the first design, though the wingtips did not curve upwards. It seems likely that the wings could be swept backwards independently. Powered by the same REP engine, it was tested for 2 months at St Moritz in Switzerland before managing at least one flight at an altitude of 2 m. One photograph shows what seems to be the end of a ramp; perhaps the flight that ended in a crash was attempted down this artificial slope.

Auzely

An aeroplane of this name is reported to have been photographed in southwestern France.

Auto-fiacre

The name is apparently a trademark, meaning "automobile taxi." Perhaps it was a builder's or operator's name, though more likely it was the name of a cab company. A machine of this name was reported to be flown early in 1912 at Villacoublay piloted by a M Coupart, and later flown at Chartres by a M Goulard, powered then by a 90 hp engine.

Aventino, Mingozi, et Paletta

A 1910 monoplane at Nice?

Avia

Charles Roux and Emil Bonnet-Labranche founded Avia in April 1909 at St Die, at the foot of the Vosges mountains in eastern France. The Dutheil et Chalmers motor company were share-holders; they expected to put together a capital of 1,000,000F, but never achieved this. At about the same time Roux, who had the reputation of an imaginative inventor with little sense of business, together with a M Kempf, founded the Aéro Club des Vosges, to be based on future Avia designs – most of which never succeeded in flying.

Their first powered aeroplane, built in mid-1909, was the big Scott biplane of 12-meter span designed by Bueno and Demaurex and tested in Switzerland. In May 1909 appeared the first of the series of Avia gliders, this one towed behind a car on 23 May. Their catalogue lists 7 types of gliders, all built to resemble small Voisins: biplane wings and tail, and a front elevator; it is likely they were later known as Bonnet-Labranche gliders.

The second Auffm-Ordt being tested at St Moritz in 1909. Note apparent sweepback of the wings. (Bill Lewis collection)

1. Uncambered wings covered on one side, no undercarriage. Probably a hang-type glider of 6-meter span.
2. Similar, but with cambered surfaces.
3. Similar, with surfaces covered on both sides.
4. Similar, with landing skids.
5. Similar, with 7-meter span.
6. The first monoplane, with 7-meter span.

4 types of big powered biplanes were also built. The various postcards showing them in flight are suspect: 3 were referred to, optimistically, as "vedettes aériennes" (aerial scouts).

1. The first design was inspired by the Voisin, but looked rather like the smaller Henry Farman. At least 2 were built, one for Terentchenko, the other for Bonnet-Labranche, and sold for 9500F – very cheap. (Cf Bonnet-Labranche.)

2. The second was similar and larger, and featured small extra wing panels which extended outward from the center pair of wing struts; a nose wheel was fitted. One was sold to Bonnet-Labranche for 10,500F.

(Span: 8.5 m; 30 hp water-cooled engine)

3. The third was inspired by the Sommer biplane; it was a 2-seater designed for the military, and sold for 17,000F. Probably it was built by Bonnet-Labranche as the ABL No 5; cf Bonnet-Labranche.

(Span: 10 m; 40 hp engine)

4. The fourth was single-seat tractor, built for the Morlat school at Pont Leroy. It resembled the first Goupy biplane, with a Blériot rudder and biplane tail surfaces, and an uncovered fuselage similar to the Blériot XI's. The undercarriage resembled that of the Avia monoplanes, but with small steel-plate skids. The Avia motto was painted on the rudder.

Avia designed and built at least 4 types of monoplanes as well.

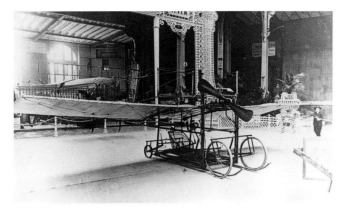

The first Avia monoplane, at the 1909 Paris Salon. Note the remarkable Gangler monoplane in the room in back at the left. (Courtesy of the Musée de l'Air et de l'Espace/Le Bourget-France)

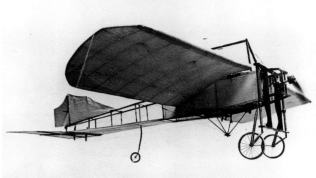

The second Avia monoplane. This photograph may be of a model; it appeared in many of the Avia catalogs. The propeller turns, but the stationary Anzani doesn't show here. One other very poor photo shows a full-sized machine in the Avia stand. (Courtesy of the Musée de l'Air et de l'Espace/Le Bourget-France)

1. The first was readied for the 1909 Exposition in September, but it never flew. It was a single-seater with an awkward 4-wheel undercarriage, a long fuselage and a small rectangular rudder mounted above the rear end.

(Span: 7 m; length: 7.75 m; 20 hp Dutheil et Chalmers)

2. The second was a 2-seater of 8-meter span which may never have flown. A monoplane appeared in the Avia stand in the Exposition of 1910, fitted with a 5-cylinder 40 hp Anzani; contemporary ads list it for 12,000F. It was similar to the current Blériot, but with a big deckled-edged rudder set on the top of the rear fuselage, and a long fan-shaped tailplane set underneath. A single tailwheel on a long stalk supported the aft end of the machine.

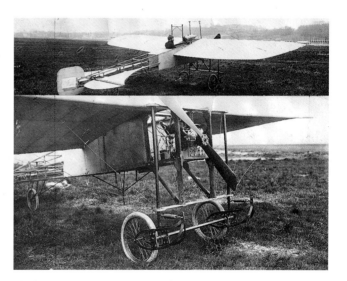

The third Avia monoplane: note the elaborate landing-gear springing method. (Peter M Bowers collection)

3. The third was a single-seater copy of the Blériot XI; at least 4 were built. The trailing main wheels were attached through a complex metal cage; 4 vertical struts comprised the main pylon. The rudder was like the Blériot, but the tailplane was of swallowtail shape with semicircular elevators.

4. There was also a small training plane for Avia students, a high-wing monoplane resembling the Demoiselle.

(Span: 9 m; 30 hp Dutheil et Chalmers)

Besides building these machines of their own design, Avia offered to build the 1909-type Henry Farman and the type américain, Wright copies with larger front elevators and tailplanes – but no rudder. These were shown in 3 variations with extended wings as on their own earlier biplanes. The first, with one seat and 30 hp, sold for 16,000F (7,000F for airframe alone), spanned 8 m. The second, a 2-seater of 30 hp, sold for 17,000F and spanned 13 m. The third spanned 14 m without the wing extension, and sold for 22,000F with a 40 hp engine.

Avia's monoplane trainer. A curious feature is what appears to be an inverted airfoil section. Perhaps the training method did not include flying! (Courtesy of the Musée de l'Air et de l'Espace/Le Bourget-France)

Avia also offered Dutheil et Chalmers engines as Avia Type A1, and Eole engines as Avia Type B. It may have been because of their connection with Dutheil et Chalmers that the photograph of a Santos-Dumont Demoiselle appeared briefly in their catalog; it was fitted with a Dutheil et Chalmers engine, and they had planned to build the machine in quantity. None was so produced, and the aeroplane in the picture was eventually preserved in the Musée de l'Air.

In 1910 Avia began building spares, accessories, propellers, and hangars. But before the 1910 Salon opened, they were forced to give up their business and sell out to Lecomte for only 5,900F; Roux went on to found ACR (Aéroplanes Charles Roux) with Garaix; Emile Bonnet joined his brothers at ABL (Aéroplanes Bonnet-Labranche). In the 1930s another firm took over the name and for 3 years built gliders.

The Avia name was also used by other firms; several cabinet-makers who claimed to build aircraft to the purchasers' designs used it as well.

Aviator

During the summer of 1910, a Blériot-like monoplane designed by the Aviator firm in Belgium was completed at the Laon Foundries in Northern France. The uncovered fuselage was triangular in section, and the undercarriage was of a completely different design with 3 struts on each side. It was test-flown at Quévy in Belgium.

(Span: 10 m; length: 10.8 m; wing area: 24 sqm; gross weight: 250 kg; 45 hp Labor)

B

Bachelard

This was an awkwardly rectangular monoplane of 1910, with a long rectangular covered fuselage, 4 vertical struts to support the undercarriage – the rear pair rose above the fuselage as a pylon. A complicated arrangement of spanwise struts below the wings served to support them.

Bachelier-Dupont-Baudrin

This large flyingboat was designed for military use and completed during the spring of 1913. The hull, in the shape of a half nutshell, had a steel-tube frame covered with wood strips and 2 coats of waterproofed fabric; it formed an unsinkable boat. The pilots sat side by side directly on the deck at the front; the tail was carried high on a single steel-tube outrigger. The engine was set below the upper wing and drove a 4-bladed pusher propeller through a one-meter driveshaft. The aeroplane may not have actually flown, though it is said to have remained for a whole month in the water with no problem.

(Span (upper): 11.2 m; (lower): 9 m; length: 8 m; wing area: 22 sqm; empty weight 380 kg; 50 hp 6-cylinder Anzani)

The Bachelier-Dupont-Baudrin flyingboat. Note the spoon-shaped forward hull. (Author's collection)

Badaire

In August 1913 Maurice Badaire tested an "automatically stable monoplane with elastic wings linked together by a common axis." It had a covered fuselage with a tiny front elevator mounted on struts on each side of the propeller. The machine was registered for the 1914 Concours de Sécurité, but may not have been actually entered.

Baillod

This seaplane was registered for the 1912 contest at Monaco; it may not have been completed.

Bailly

A helicopter of this name was built in 1902.

Balassian de Manawas

At the Concours de Sécurité of 1914, the monoplane designed by Balassian de Manawas was one of the curiosities. Thinking to improve the stability of his machine, especially in the case of engine failure, he arranged the wings of his "avion planeur" to be attached to the fuselage with springs so as to vary the position of the center of lift: the wings could move fore and aft automatically or under pilot control – as he claimed it occurred with gliding birds. The fuselage

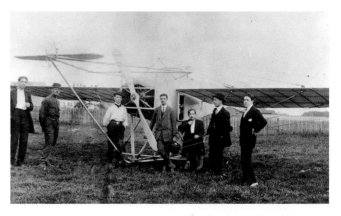

The Badaire safety aeroplane for the Concours de Sécurité of 1914. (Courtesy of the Musée de l'Air et de l'Espace/Le Bourget-France)

consisted only of 2 spars with a fabric seat slung between them; the large tank mounted on the same spars behind the motor provided little protection against the wind, but completely blocked forward vision. The springing of the undercarriage was unique: each wheel was set into a horizontal frame pivoting on the steel tube axle, the wheels forward and below the axle, with a long horn extending backward from each frame, the end hung from 2 heavy shock cords attached to the underside of the fuselage. Damaged during the qualification tests, it did not participate in the contest.

(Span: 11 m; length: 6 m; empty weight: 225 kg; 50 hp Gnôme with Chauvière Intégrale propeller)

Balaye

Balaye's aeroplane was named Robur, after the master engineer in one of Jules Verne's novels. It may have been an original design by Balaye, or merely a production aeroplane with that name; it was seen in 1912 at Malô des Bains.

Balsan

A wealthy businessman and Deputy Chairman of the Aéro Club de France, Jacques Balsan had been one of the first members of the Aviation Committee, an experienced pilot in both lighter – and heavier-than-air machines. In 1911 Lioré et Olivier had completed the graceful Balsan monoplane, and Balsan was flying it at Mourmelon in the summer of 1911 and most of 1912, fitted with a 60-70 hp semi-radial REP motor; it was exhibited at the 1911 Salon de la Locomotion Aérienne with a 50 hp Gnôme, mounted between steel and copper plates. Balsan donated it to the French army in September 1912 – a common practice with single prototypes. It is not clear who designed this neat monoplane, Balsan himself or engineers at Lioré et Olivier.

Below: Jacques Balsan's neat monoplane of 1911. (Courtesy of the Musée de l'Air et de l'Espace/Le Bourget-France)

Balassian de Manawas' entry for the Concours de Sécurité of 1914. As described in the text, the wings moved in various directions. Note the ingenious springing of the undercarriage wheels. A handsome photograph of the 50 hp Gnôme and the Intégrale propeller. (Courtesy of the Musée de l'Air et de l'Espace/Le Bourget-France)

The rectangular wings had elliptical tips and built-in ailerons; the front of the fuselage was rectangular in section and covered with 2 mm ply; the rear was triangular, with the spine at the top. The machine was all wood, fabric-covered, and remarkably clean, the finish being comparable to that of the 1912 Deperdussins. The cross-shaped tail was made of fabric-covered steel tubing; the 4-wheel undercarriage was of Zens design.

(Span: 11.4 m; length: 9 m; wing area: 18 sqm; gross weight: 438 kg)

Barillon

Pierre Barillon designed and built several monoplanes. He was only 18 in 1908-1909 when he built his first one with his brother. Powered with a 12 hp engine, it was said to have flown for short distances.

He got his brevet in October 1909 flying his second machine, a shoulder-wing monoplane with long tapered wings like the Antoinette's, mounted at shoulder level on an uncovered rectangular box fuselage. The undercarriage was similar to that of the Blériot XI, but with a central rocking skid under the propeller and distinctive perforated beams pivoting to hold the wheels. Controls were through large side-mounted wheels as on the Antoinette; the wings had a large dihedral angle – perhaps they warped.

(Span: 9.4 m; length: 8 m; wing area: 19 sqm; gross weight: 325 kg; 25 hp 2-cylinder incline Prini-Berthaud)

Another big monoplane appeared at Juvisy, this one with a longer uncovered rectangular box fuselage, Antoinette-shaped wings but with wingtip ailerons, a tailplane with tip elevators, and a high-set rectan-

The second Barillon, at Juvisy. Note the control wheel. (Courtesy of the Musée de l'Air et de l'Espace/Le Bourget-France)

Barillon's third design. Note the small round windows in the side. (Courtesy of the Musée de l'Air et de l'Espace/Le Bourget-France)

gular rudder. The big steering/control wheel was very apparent. The radiator was mounted above and behind the motor, tipped slightly forward.

Barillon registered his third design for the Paris-Madrid race and later for the Circuit Européan. Even more like the Antoinette, it had a long triangular fuselage completely covered – the front part with linoleum. The passenger sat in front of the pilot and could view the undercarriage through 2 small windows. Small trailing-edge ailerons were fitted.

Pierre Barillon's 1909 monoplane, his second machine. Note the rocking arms for the undercarriage springing. (Courtesy of the Musée de l'Air et de l'Espace/ Le Bourget-France)

(Span: 8 m; length: 9 m; chord: 9 m; gross weight: 450 kg; 2-blade Woirin propeller, said to be of variable pitch; top speed reported more than 130 kmh; 50 hp Gnôme)

Sometimes described as a racer, his fourth design was so similar to the Nieuport that Edouard Nieuport threatened a suit. But Barillon was flying Nieuports at Pau by the spring of 1912 and was appointed by Nieuport as Chief Pilot by June. Shorter than the Nieuport, No 4 carried 2 side – by-side and a third, if required, behind them. The wings had curved cut-outs at the roots to "improve downward visibility and the dropping of bombs"; the wings warped and could be folded for storage. The metal parts of the frame were of nickel-chrome vanadium steel.

(Span: 7.3 m; length: 5.95 m; wing area: 8.8 sqm; empty weight: 215 kg; 40/50 hp 7-cylinder Rossel-Peugeot; Normale propeller; top speed expected to be 65 kmh)

At the time of Barillon's death from typhoid in August 1912, he was working on a 50 hp single-seater and an automatically-stabilized 6-seat machine.

Barker

Barker (or Barkers et Lefevre?) built a Voisin copy at Dijon in 1909 with a 50 hp Anzani and 2 pusher propellers; he was planning to fly it to Spain.

Barlazzi

A glider was reported with this name.

Baron

The Aéro Ramo-Planeur designed in 1911 and perhaps built by A Baron seems to have been based on an uncovered Blériot-style fuselage, with a more or less standard set of wings and tailplane. In addition, a pair of long narrow fore-and-aft panels were fitted behind of the trailing edge of the wings, and odd leaf-shaped surfaces fitted forward of the wings. All these surfaces were arranged to pivot, and some of them perhaps to flap. A small rudder at the tail seemed conventional in shape and function.

Bastier

In 1911 Bastier was studying aviation at Juvisy with de Brageas and Sotinel; the following year he designed a biplane similar to the Goupy. It was finished in April 1912 and flown by Francpourmoi at Juvisy. The design featured deeply-curved staggered wings at a time when flat sections were generally in fashion, and a lifting-Blériot-style tailplane with inset elevators. The wooden fuselage, as on the Blériots, was covered only in the forward section.

(Spans: 10 m and 7 m; length: 9.5 m; total weight: 490 kg; 60 hp BJ 4-cylinder incline water-cooled motor)

Right: The Bastier biplane of 1911. (Courtesy of the Musée de l'Air et de l'Espace/Le Bourget-France)

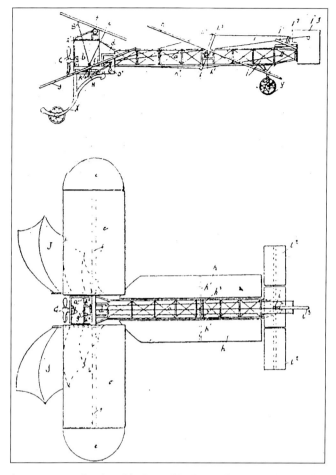

A contemporary drawing of the Baron Aéro Ramo-Planeur. (Author's collection)

Baylac

In 1909 Jean Baylac in Bordeaux was building a large helicopter to be fitted with an engine of no more than 100 hp. It was designed like an aeroplane, with wings and propellers; one wing was horizontal, the other vertical, each with 2 flaps for control in the appropriate directions. Though it was designed for a regular propeller, it was in fact equipped with 4 new "airscrews" for horizontal and 2 for vertical motion.

Bazin

One of the numerous and mostly forgotten heavier-than-air enthusiasts of the early part of the century, Alfred Bazin worked in Marseille from 1904-1907. He built a series of gliders with the wings in the shapes of birds; and hanging underneath, he tested them from local hills and in the Camargue. Some of his gliders were built with wing panels that could be swept backward or forward separately or together, to restore equilibrium in gusts. Since he believed that the aeroplane of the future would fly only in the most direct way, that is to say in a straight line, he did not include rudders. After all, he said, did we expect that aeroplanes would circulate in our streets, along the roads, around race-tracks, pull the stopper off the Eiffel Tower? In 1905 he built a more ambitious machine with streamlined fuselage, warping wings and warping swallowtail; it was reported sold to Ferdinand Ferber.

(Span: 11 m; chord: 1.5 m; length: 5 m; weight: 30 kg)

Towards the end of 1907 he designed and built an ornithopter based on his experience with his gliders. It had the general shape of a bird, with a streamlined fuselage; an unidentified 3-cylinder 12 hp engine drove the wingtips up and down over a 40° range, at .8 – 1.6 beats per second. Both wing and tail were bird-shaped in plan, made of bamboo, wire, and silk; there was no rudder, since the machine "was built to fly straight forward, the shortest distance between one point and another being the straight line." A special control allowed the pilot to loosen or tighten the wing fabric. He installed a small motor of 3 cylinders and 12 hp.

(Span: 14 m; length: 8 m; wing area: 22 sqm; gross weight: 178 kg)

Beaufeist

Little is known about this machine, except that the designer in 1909 was reported to have been Beaufeist, a private soldier of the third Regiment at Verdun.

Beaurin

In 1909 at the Compiègne Corbeaulieu airfield where Legagneux and Martinet had started their aeronautical career, a M Beaurin tested "a tandem biplane with automatic stability, a propeller of 2-meter diameter turning in the middle." No further information is available; Beaurin was either the owner, designer, or builder. The machine was described in an aviation magazine of 1909 by an amateur reporter who may have mis-identified a Farman or Voisin or other standard pusher aircraft.

Bebin

An aircraft of this name was registered at the 1911 Concours Militaire.

Bédelia

The firm Bédelia (B + D + lia) founded by Bourbeau and Devaux was known for its small 2-seater automobiles known as voiturettes. Al-

One of the Bazin gliders of 1904. There was no rudder, since as the designer explained, aeroplanes of the future were to travel only in straight lines. (Courtesy of the Musée de l'Air et de l'Espace/Le Bourget-France)

The Bédelia flyingboat. (Courtesy of the Musée de l'Air et de l'Espace/Le Bourget-France)

though reported to have been working on flyingboats since 1908, their first and only design appeared first at the 1912 Salon de la Locomotion Aérienne. It was ambitious and unsuccessful, a small-span all-steel biplane with a short wide teardrop-shaped hull of rectangular section, on top of which was mounted the biplane cellule. The 2 wings were supported on 4 vertical struts, almost side-curtains, with interplane ailerons, Curtiss-style, mounted behind the outermost struts. The large tailplane was mounted on 2 similar struts, with the rudder between them. A 4-cylinder uncowled 50 hp Clerget sat next to the pilot in the hull, driving an overhead shaft which ran between the upper wing and the tailplane, with the pusher propeller just forward of the tailplane leading edge. On occasion the Bédelia appeared fitted with wheels and 2 long skids reaching far ahead of the hull.

Bourbeau and Devaux founded a hydroplane center on the coast of Picardy, without much success; at the time, they modified the Bédelia with a tractor propeller, smaller struts without the side-curtains, twin tail-booms and twin rudders.

De Beer

The third and fourth designs by the Belgian designer de Beer were built in France by Ratmanoff, a design firm in its own right and builder of the Normale propellers. The de Beer monoplanes were among the most complicated of the pre-War period. He wanted to vary the incidence of the mainplanes to control the speed, but he realized that the stability of his machine varied more or less with the angle of attack of the wings, and so he built different sets of wings with different airfoils, searching for the unique section which would have its lift in the center regardless of angle of attack.

Type 3: In his effort to provide a fully stable aeroplane, de Beer settled on a rather conventional-appearing monoplane, with rectangular wings and rectangular fabric-covered fuselage, small rudder and triangular tailplane with rectangular elevator set forward of the rudder on the sides of the fuselage. Through a complex control system the pilot could vary the angle of attack from +3° to +18°; by pushing the stick sideways he could vary the incidence differentially to serve instead of ailerons; the same stick controlled the elevators. The wings were not locked and could turn freely on their axes in gusts of wind

Type 4: This 2-seater was similar to Type 3 with simpler undercarriage, slightly enlarged tail surfaces, and better finish. Current reports mentioned a weakness of the airframe.

(Span: 9.8 m; length: 7.35 m; low speed: 40 kmh; high speed: 115 kmh; optimum speed: 70 kmh; 80 hp Anzani)

At the same time that Type 4 was built, Ratmanoff produced a 2-seat trainer, quite similar, which may also have been a de Beer design.

Bellamy

This 1906 design was similar to the Voisin-Archdeacon and Voisin-Blériot seaplanes, with a biplane tail cell with 3 vertical surfaces, a forward elevator, twin floats, and 4 side-curtains between the flat-surfaced biplane wings. 2 tractor propellers chain-driven similar to the Wright were set between the outer bays; it also appeared with 4 tractor propellers, photographed on the Lac du Bourget.

Bénégent

One of the pioneers of steel welding in France, Bénégent built a monoplane later called Sirius in mid-1910 at La Courneuve, north of Paris, next to what is today Le Bourget airport. He was assisted by a mechanic, Piat, who became the foreman at Voisin in 1913. The frame was of welded steel tubing; only the wings and tail were covered, in fabric. The fuselage was of triangular section, spine down; the pilot sat on top, high between the rectangular wings, which although of short span, were supported by 24 piano wires.

The Bellamy hydro. The purpose of the single (or double?) sail between the wings and the tail is unclear. (Author's collection)

Three views of the third de Beer monoplane, showing 3 wing incidence positions for (T) landing and take-off; (C) normal flight; (B) position for braking after landing. (Author's collection)

The fourth de Beer. (Courtesy of the Musée de l'Air et de l'Espace/Le Bourget-France)

The undercarriage consisted of 2 wheels and a long central skid. His engine, also called Sirius, was likely to have attracted more attention than his airframe: 2 opposed water-cooled cylinders 140 mm x 130 mm produced 30 hp at 1200 rpm; the shield-shaped radiator was mounted below and behind the engine at the front of the fuselage.

(Span: 8 m; length: 7 m; weight empty: 130 kg; loaded weight: 230 kg; speed: 90 kmh; 30 hp Bénégent)

A few months later Bénégent founded a school at Issy and built at least one monoplane under the trademark Sirius, and claimed to have pioneered in oxyacetylene welding, which was at this time considered a skill for experts; he founded a company, also called Sirius, which specialized in this form of welding.

This new aircraft was smaller – or perhaps just lower – than the old one. The rectangular wings now had rounded tips; the fuselage, still triangular in section, was now fabric-covered; there was now a large tailplane on top of the fuselage. The same 5-tube pylon on top supported the wing-warping controls.

Berger-Gardey
Between 1904-1907 there was a lot of gliding experimentation throughout France; among the oddest of the machines was a glider built at Lyon by Berger, and tested by 19-year-old Gardey, who proceeded to break a leg after taking off down a steep 45° ramp while slung underneath his glider. The glider is said to have flown for 20 m. It was in the form of a flat rectangle c 2 m long and 3 m wide, with 4 little paddle-shaped flaps at each tip. A photograph under the same name – perhaps the same designer? – shows a model of what might be a powered version of this same glider; it stood on 4 small wheels, with a curious arched shape set between the flat forward and rearward surfaces.

Another much more modern monoplane appears under the name Berger in September 1913, at Vidamée: it is clearly a copy of the Nieuport IV, with the same wings and tail, but with a more graceful fuselage and simpler undercarriage.

Berliaux et Salètes
These 2 officers of the French Army, assigned to Fontainebleau in 1909, built and tested at least 2 machines, probably gliders. On 14 August 1909 they tested the Pourquoi Pas? II, which was reported to have remained 32 seconds in the air. It was described as rather crude.

(Span: 6.5 m; length: 7 m; weight: 61 kg)

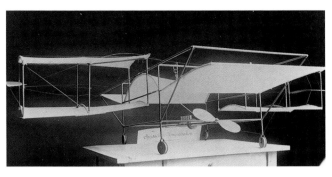

The model of perhaps a powered version of the Berger-Gardey glider. The outer wing panels seem to be warpable. (Courtesy of the Musée de l'Air et de l'Espace/Le Bourget-France)

Berthaud
The name of the designer Berthaud is better-known in connection with the automobile firm of Prini-Berthaud in Lyon. But in collaboration with Prini, Moreau, and Wroblesky-Salvez, he achieved some aeronautic success as well, particularly in metal construction. With Prini, he designed a 2-cylinder inline 2-cycle engine in 1910-1911, a year after they had built the Prini-Berthaud biplane.

Prini-Berthaud: This 1908 design was clearly a Wright copy and probably an unsuccessful one, judging by its nearly flat and inverted airfoil and its heavy all-steel frame. There was no forward outrigger: instead, a low elevator was fitted below the rudder at the rear of the long fuselage formed by elliptical skids. Ailerons were mounted between the outer wing panels. Pusher propellers, Wright-style, were driven by an odd semi-radial 3-cylinder water-cooled Anzani. The pilot sat in front of a large radiator at the left of the motor.

(Span: 10.8 m; length: 9.49 m; chord: 2.2 m; wing area: c

The 1913 Berger monoplane of 1913. (Author's collection)

The Prini-Berthaud: note similarities to and differences from the contemporary Wrights. (Peter M Bowers collection)

50 sqm; gross weight 550 kg; 3-cylinder water-cooled Anzani)

For other machines it is likely that Berthaud was the builder and financial partner – cf Mélin.

<u>Moreau-Berthaud</u>: Associated with a Moreau (not the famous Albert Moreau), Berthaud built this monoplane similar to the early Sommer design: an uncovered fuselage, possibly made of steel tubing; Blériot-style inverted-V cabane struts which ran down to the skids which in turn supported the wheels. It was powered by a 50 hp 2-stroke double-acting 4-cylinder radial Berthaud.

<u>Berthaud Monoplane W</u>: Designed and built in 1911-12, this successful machine was referred to as a Berthaud, in fact designed by Pierre Wroblewsky – who with his brother Gabriel were known as the Salvez brothers! Like a former Salvez design of 1909, the W was based on the Antoinette model, but of metal construction, with 2 seats in tandem; the engine was mounted at the front of the triangular-sectioned fuselage whose aft end was diamond-shaped; a small steel ladder was attached to the port mid-fuselage longeron for easy access to the cockpit. In 1913 the Monoplane W was mentioned in flight reports at Amberieu, and on 1 Mar 1914 Gabriel Wroblewsky was reported "killed in the crash of a monoplane designed by his brother Pierre, who was injured," after a wing broke off. The boy Antoine de Saint Exupéry took his first flight in one of these machines.

(Span: 13.5 m; length: 10.5 m; wing area: 32 sqm; empty weight: 420 kg; 70 hp water-cooled Aviatik)

Another view of the Prini-Berthaud. (Author's collection)

A very poor copy of a copy of the original postcard showing the Berthaud Monoplane W in which Antoine de St Exupéry took his first flight. The postcard is signed by St Ex; the author got the copy from a private collection in the Hôtel du Grand Balcon, in Toulouse, in which the crews of the airline Aéro-Postale stayed between flights, and in which St Exupéry wrote Le Petit Prince. (Author's collection)

From 1912 to the start of the War, Berthaud worked with Moreau at building automobiles in Vincennes under the trade-mark Moreau-Berthaud or Moreau-Luxior.

Bertin

By 1899 Léonce Bertin, known earlier as a long-distance bicycle road-racer and trainer, had designed and built an air-cooled motor for his bicycles (probably a V2), and became the first motor-bicyclist to reach a speed of 100 kmh. He also built a small air-cooled flat twin, later developed into a flat 8, as well as an 8-cylinder in X-form and another 8 in twin-X; at the same time he was working on a heavier-than-air flying machine, a helicopter.

It was built in 1907 at Puteaux with the help of a mechanic named Bouline; the 150 hp flat 8 drove with direct drive a 1.7-meter tractor propeller at 2500 rpm, and at the same time, through a reduction gear, a horizontal 2-blade 2.4-meter rotor at 1200 rpm. This unsuccessful machine weighed c 300 kg. His second design, also unsuccessful, was called a helicoplan; the same engine higher in a smaller airframe

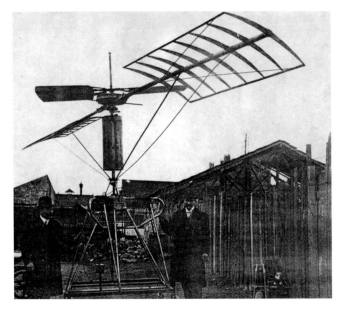

Below: The first Bertin monoplane, semi-Blériot and semi-Antoinette. (Courtesy of the Musée de l'Air et de l'Espace/Le Bourget-France)

Bottom: The fifth Bertin, in which Bertin was killed. (Courtesy of the Musée de l'Air et de l'Espace/Le Bourget-France)

The third Bertin helicopter. (Author's collection)

drove 2 propellers, but in this version the tractor was 2.2 m in diameter and the rotor was 2.5 m. Both propellers were Voisin-style, with aluminum plates and a steel-tube axis. The airframe was mounted on 4 wheels and fitted with a pair of folding biplane wings behind the tractor propeller; and a large swallowtailed tailplane with a large rudder and 2 elevators was underneath. Only the horizontal surfaces were covered, and the lower wing may have had variable incidence for use as elevators. After much testing the machine was converted to a monoplane through the removal of the horizontal rotor.

His third helicopter was a simpler design done with Lieber for exhibition on cycle-racing tracks where Bertin was already famous as a champion. The Bertin-Lieber consisted of a tetrahedral frame on 4 wheels with a 55 hp 4-cylinder Bertin radial at the top, driving 2 horizontal rotors, the smaller one 1.3 m in diameter driven directly at 1000 rpm, and the larger, fabric-covered, clutch-driven at 120 rpm. The drive-shaft ran vertically through the center of the high cylindrical fuel tank. The rig stood c 3.5 m high.

After the failure of his third helicopter, Bertin built a small monoplane also at Puteaux, more or less derived from the early Antoinettes and Deperdussins, with a slender rectangular-sectioned covered rear fuselage. Powered with the new 60 hp flat 6-cylinder 68 kg Bertin, it was brought to the Terrain des Courlis (Curlews Field) at Houeilles in southern France, where Bertin's son René flew it for the first time on 25 March 1910. In September Léonce Bertin won a 5000F prize with it at the same field. A year later, in November 1911, it crashed at Chateaufort (now Toussus Le Noble, southwest of Paris). It was fitted with a 2.3-meter diameter Roland propeller.

His 5th design, a 2-seat racing monoplane, was announced in January 1912, but appeared only later in the year in time for the 1912 Paris Salon. The long fuselage was of pentagonal section with the deck flat; the wings were rigged without dihedral, and to warp. It flew successfully until 14 July 1913 when one of the wings collapsed; Bertin as passenger and his son René as pilot were both killed.

(Span: 10.4m; length: 8.8 m; wing area: 21 sqm; empty weight: 350 kg; top speed 115 kmh; 100 hp twin X 8-cylinder motor)

Bertrand

The name Bertrand appears in several different connections. In 1909 a curious machine (also known as Unic-Bertrand) was completed at the Avionnerie, the workshop of the Société Anonyme de Construction d'Appareils Aériennes (SACAA) managed by de Marthe, Ader's son-in-law; and Espinosa, formerly Ader's mechanic. Designed by René Bertrand, it consisted of a 2-meter diameter tunnel covered with fabric; a heavy automobile engine was mounted towards the front end, driving counter-rotating propellers at 400 rpm, one at each end of the tunnel. Large oval monoplane wings sprouted from each side; a high-mounted forward horizontal surface with tip elevators reached out in front, and 2 trailing elevators brought up the rear. It rode on fore and aft pairs of Blériot-style undercarriage wheels. In May 1910 it was returned to the Avionnerie for unknown modifications.

(Span: 13.4 m; chord: 2.4 m; wing area: 40 sqm; gross weight: 461 kg; 25-30 hp Unic)

A handsome photograph of the strange Bertrand of 1909 under construction. The S-curve airfoil shows clearly and the pivoted joint for the forward outrigger. (Courtesy of the Musée de l'Air et de l'Espace/Le Bourget-France)

The completed Bertrand. The elevators seem to have needed uncommonly heavy bracing. (Peter M Bowers collection)

A classic monoplane, this second machine with the name Bertrand had a fuselage of rounded triangular section, warping wings, no rudder pedals but a single control stick with a wheel mounted at the top.

(Span: 8.6 m; length: 7.3 m; gross weight: 190 kg; 25-30 hp 2-cylinder Velox-Suère)

Another, probably the third, Bertrand, was a Blériot XI copy with a 2-cylinder opposed engine; its Blériot-style undercarriage was dam-

A more conventional aeroplane, the third Bertrand. (Courtesy of the Musée de l'Air et de l'Espace/Le Bourget-France)

aged in December 1910. The Roman numeral III was painted on the rudder. Since René Bertrand had family connections in southern France, this design which appeared in Montpellier (southern France) was probably his.

(Span: 13.3 m; length: 11.8 m; gross weight: 540 kg; 40 hp Labor-Picker)

Besson
Inspired by Voisin's canard, the designs of Marcel Besson raised expectations for performance which they did not always meet. They were built by Louis Clément, one of the few 1910 enthusiasts of all-metal construction. (Louis Clément is unrelated to Maurice Clément or Adolphe Clément-Bayard – he was also the French representative for the Aviatik aero engines.)

Besson's first canard design was nearly completed in August 1911 and was presented at the 1911 Salon de la Locomotion Aérienne. The all-steel fuselage alone weighed only 32 kg; the wings, of metal and wood, weighed only 62 kg; and the undercarriage 22 kg. The wings were rigid, without ailerons, but the tips could be warped up and down; a rudder was fixed on the nose. The pilot sat in the rear of the fully-covered fuselage, just forward of the buried engine which drove through a chain a pusher propeller mounted on the trailing edge of the wing. At the 1911 Salon, a second fuselage was shown beside the completed aircraft. It was tested in October 1911 at La Vidamée, near Chantilly, north of Paris, but it proved unstable.

(Span: 11.6 m; length: 7.5 m; wing area: 26 sqm; empty weight: 350 kg; propeller diameter: 2.5 m, pitch: 2.45 m; engines: Rossel-Aviatik 70 hp, 50 hp Clément-Bayard, 70 hp Labor)

Reports of the second Besson canard appeared in the press as early as March 1912; the completed machine was shown at the 1912 Exposition and was tested at Reims by the Army. It was a landplane, and a model of a seaplane version was shown beside it. The faired fuselage seating 3 ended in a long forward triangular outrigger with the tailplane mounted on top with elevators on the trailing edge, and a rudder mounted below. The wingtips no longer flexed, and were fitted with ailerons; the wheels castered.

(Span: (main) 13.5 m; (tailplane) 4 m; length: 6.6 m; wing area: 30 sqm; top speed: c 110 kmh; 80 hp Gnôme)

A similar aircraft appeared as a floatplane, with 2 all-steel floats mounted so they splayed outwards as seen from the front, with a small float under the nose; the rudder was raised from the landplane version. In December 1912 it was being tested.

The fourth Besson design, probably never built, was for a flyingboat.

In July 1911, however, a "Besson and Pajo" biplane Type Spéciale is mentioned in a brief press report as being tested with a 40 hp Labor motor at La Vidamée near Chantilly.

Besson's first canard; the Voisin influence is clear. (Courtesy of the Musée de l'Air et de l'Espace/Le Bourget-France)

Billard
A machine of this name was registered at the 1911 Concours Militaire.

Blanc, Henri
Henri Blanc was a lawyer; Emile Barlatier was a balloonist and chairman of the Automobile Club de France in Marseille. Early in the century they built and studied kites, and then constructed 2 large powered model kites, one with a 1.25 hp Herdtle-Bruneau engine, the other with a 2.25 hp Buchet, each kite with 2 tractor propellers. In 1906 they began work on a full-scale single-seater monoplane with batlike wings and a large forward elevator surface; it was not successful. Like the kites, it had a centrally-mounted engine driving 2 tractor propellers.

(Span: 14 m; wing area: 60 sqm; 3-cylinder 14 hp Buchet)

Barlatier went off to Canada to become famous as a balloonist, and Henri Blanc worked on with his brother. In 1910 the Blancs developed a new aviation site, the Aérodrome de la Crau, at Miramas, now the location of the test base of the Armée de l'Air at Istres, and they tested a new light monoplane. In 1913 Henri Blanc invented an automatic stabilizer and then disappeared from the aviation chronicles.

Barlatier et Blanc: Their first monoplane was tested at the end of March 1908 at the military camp of Le Rouet, near Marseille, fitted with a 30 hp 7-cylinder REP. The fuselage consisted of 2 parallel wooden box spars with the pilot between them, and a large tailplane at the rear, supporting 4 triangular fins and rudder. Automatic stability was to come through the action of a moving tailplane set ahead of the rearmost one. The REP motor drove a 2-bladed tractor aluminum propeller coupled to a cooling fan, which might also have served as flywheel.

(Span: 14 m; length: 9.5 m; wing area: 45 sqm; empty weight: 240 kg)

Blanc monoplane: It had a fully-covered fuselage with a flat bottom and curved top; 2 oblong upper and lower fins, the upper with a rudder; a large rear elevator; a Blériot-style undercarriage; spoon-shaped wings. It was powered by an Anzani engine and weighed altogether only 120 kg. Its construction was sponsored

The Barlatier et Blanc monoplane. The fuselage seems built of heavy timber. (Courtesy of the Musée de l'Air et de l'Espace/Le Bourget-France)

by a M Mopuro de Livoll, whose name does not appear again. This may well have been the monoplane described by Astruc, built by the Blancs and crashed by Astruc.

Blanc, Maurice: A monoplane of this name appeared in 1914.

Blanc (?): There was also a Blanc Morane-style mid-wing monoplane – perhaps the same? – with a long covered tapered fuselage and odd comma-shaped rudder set above the end on its point. Curved ailerons were set into the wings.

(Span: 10 m; length: 8 m; weight: 350 kg; Anzani)

The spoon-winged Blanc monoplane under construction. Note other parts being built nearby. (Courtesy of the Musée de l'Air et de l'Espace/Le Bourget-France)

A different Blanc monoplane – perhaps a different Blanc? Note simplicity of construction, and Blériot-style upright/longeron joints. (Courtesy of the Musée de l'Air et de l'Espace/Le Bourget-France)

The completed Blanc in flight. (Courtesy of the Musée de l'Air et de l'Espace/ Le Bourget-France)

Left: Another Blanc monoplane, perhaps by a different designer entirely. (Courtesy of the Musée de l'Air et de l'Espace/Le Bourget-France)

Blanchard et Viriot

In 1909 Ferdinand Blanchard and Jack Viriot had a monoplane built in Nantes; a second one is said to have followed it, built by a car-body builder. This machine was tested on the beach at La Baule and crashed. Later Blanchard went to Paris and bought a Blériot, in which he was killed on 26 0ctober 1910.

Blard

Lt Blard's pretty all-metal canard was designed secretly for military use: the plan was to combine the generally better performance of the monoplane with the generally better downward visibility of the bi-plane. It is reported to have been present, though "under adjustment," when President Fallières reviewed the "groupe central de l'escadrille volante" at Villacoublay in April 1912; it was tested over a long period with no favorable outcomes. Resembling the Blériot 33 canard monoplane, it consisted of a simple horizontal tripod, with the pilot and tailplane with tip elevators the engine mounted at the rear, and a forward-mounted tailplane with tip elevators at the extended tip with a curved skid below. The aeroplane sat on 2 wheels and a small rear-mounted skid. Inadequately-sized triangular tip fins and rudders were fitted below the wingtips; these were later enlarged and the machine could then make large-radius turns.

(Span: 10 m; length: 7 m; wing area: 19 sqm; empty weight: 280 kg; 50 hp Gnôme)

Blériot

Louis Blériot made his fortune in carbonic-gas lamps for automobiles, but he soon became fascinated with the problems of flight. Captain Ferdinand Ferber, of Chalais-Meudon, persuaded Gabriel Voisin to visit Blériot in his workshop where he was experimenting with his first ornithopter, and the 2 began a brief and provocative collaboration. Blériot's first efforts were imitations of the work of others, notably the Wrights and Langley, but only when he began working with his own designs and those of Raymond Saulnier did his work take wing.

I: In 1900 Blériot built a 1.5-meter span model of his ornithopter design, powered by a carbonic acid motor, and started the full-scale machine the following year. The design called for a single pair of flapping wings each braced with a single long kingpost, centered on what looked like a tall tank for the gas below and the engine mounted above. He built 3 motors in succession and each one exploded. He gave up the project, though the model had seemed promising.

II: Blériot had watched Gabriel Voisin at work, and commissioned him to build a glider at the Surcouf works. Blériot towed the machine, piloted by Voisin, from a motorboat named Antoinette II, on the Seine at Billancourt; on 18 July 1905 the unstable glider caught its left wing in the water and crashed, almost drowning Voisin. It was built with 2 large Hargrave cells, one for the tail and one for the wings, with a single elevator forward. 2 sets of side-curtains were set between the wings on

Above and below: two close-ups of the unsuccessful Blard canard. Note landing-gear strut springing up at the pylon. (Author's collection)

each side, the outer set at an angle. 2 long floats supported the aeroplane.

(Span (forward wing): 7 m; wing area (forward wing): 29 sqm; weight: less than 200 kg)

III: Undaunted, Blériot had Voisin build a second machine, this one powered, with 2 large equal-size elliptical cells for wing and tail, the whole rig floating on 3 pairs of small pontoons. An Antoinette engine was installed sideways, driving 2 tractor propellers through flexible shafts. It was tested, unsuccessfully, in

A drawing of the model Blériot I ornithopter. (Author's collection)

The Blériot Type II in the water, and the motorboat Antoinette II, 18 July 1905. (Courtesy of the Musée de l'Air et de l'Espace/Le Bourget-France)

May 1906 at Lake Enghien, and Blériot planned to replace the single Antoinette engine with 2.

> (Wing area: 60 sqm; empty weight (with 2 engines): 430 kg; 24 hp Antoinette)

<u>IV</u>: This new machine, also built by Voisin, retained the elliptical tail cell, but the new wing cell was rectangular again and there was a biplane forward elevator cell. This time there were 2-24 hp Antoinette engines driving 2 pusher propellers. The seaplane was tested on 2 long floats on 18 October 1905, but it did not achieve more than 30 kmh, and could not take off. It was then fitted with wheels and retested at Bagatelle on 12 November, but was wrecked when crossing a gutter. Blériot planned to rebuild it with a single 50 hp Antoinette. This was the last Blériot type to be built by Voisin.

> (Span (forward wing): 10.5 m; wing area (forward wing): 47 sqm; total wing area: 78.5 sqm; weight: 430 kg; 2-24 hp Antoinettes)

<u>V</u>: Built and developed from January through March 1907, this little canard was powered with a 24 hp Antoinette and covered in varnished paper. The nose carried a small elevator surface, and a tall forward fin was set under the nose and acted as front skid; the rear of the machine supported on 2 close-set wheels. The wings had upturned tips like a bird's. Damaged at Bagatelle during tests, it was quickly modified. In April it appeared again, this time with a big semicircular rudder behind the aft propeller, the forward vertical surface now equally above and below the nose, and the wings upturned with long trailing areas at the tips.

Blériot's third try. The forward elevator cell is set between the wings, with the 2 propellers in front of it. (Author's collection)

In this version Blériot managed a first small jump on 5 April. A final modification removed the forward vertical surfaces and added a rectangular keel amidships. The forward fuselage covering was taken off. A brief 4-5-meter flight followed, after which the canard was wrecked at Bagatelle on 8 April. This was the only one of Louis Blériot's machines known to have been designed by Louis himself.

> (Span: 7.8 m; length: 8.5 m; weight: 260 kg; 24 hp Antoinette)

<u>VI</u>: Patterned on the Langley Aerodrome, Blériot built this new tandem, named Libellule (dragonfly) at the suggestion of Louis Peyret; Blériot installed the 24 hp Antoinette and hoped for better stability. The 2 sets of wings were approximately the same size and shape, the forward pair having oyster-shell tip ailerons. 2 close-set wheels in front and one large tailwheel carried the

Above and two at right: These 3 photographs make a good study in early aeroplane experimentation. The Blériot IV is shown on 2 different kinds of floats, evidently in an effort to assist take-off. This third variation shows a different main wing cell, shorter, with more dihedral, and inter-wing ailerons. (Courtesy of the Musée de l'Air et de l'Espace/Le Bourget-France)

again modified with a larger forward wing and rear end of its fuselage and rudder lengthened, it managed brief flights from 25-143 m in length.

Other changes, from the 24 hp Antoinette to one of 50 hp, and a much longer vertical tail, allowed flights of over 100 m in September; this version was sometimes known as Type VIbis. A final change reduced the aft wing to the size and function of a stabilizer, the long fin and rudder moved to the top of the fuselage, and it crashed on a 184-meter flight on 7 September.

(Span (each wing): 5.85 m; wing area: 18 sqm; weight: 280

The Blériot V under construction, showing the big forward lower fin. (Courtesy of the Musée de l'Air et de l'Espace/Le Bourget-France)

The same machine as reconstructed in April 1905. The narrow tread and short wheel-base must have made it hard to taxi – at least 2 men needed here! (Courtesy of the Musée de l'Air et de l'Espace/Le Bourget-France)

stabilizer, the long fin and rudder moved to the top of the fuse-lage, and it crashed on a 184-meter flight on 7 September.

(Span (each wing): 5.85 m; wing area: 18 sqm; weight: 280 kg; 24 hp Antoinette)

<u>VII</u>: This was a handsome modern-looking low-wing monoplane, fully covered, with broad rectangular surfaces and what would become the typical Blériot rudder. A 50 hp Antoinette drove a 4-bladed propeller. Tests in October and November 1907 showed the landing gear to be weak, and it was replaced in November and December by what would become the typical Blériot arrange-ment with castering wheels and bedstead supporting beams. On 16 November it flew some 500 m, and flew often and well after that; and then it was damaged in its hangar.

In December it appeared again, this time with wings set high on the sides of the fuselage, with a new trapezoidal cabane structure now required to brace the higher wing. Landing after a long flight on 18 December, a wheel broke and the machine was damaged.

(Span: 11 m; length: 9 m; wing area: 25 sqm; weight: 425 kg; 50 hp Antoinette)

<u>VIII</u>: Blériot had avoided serious injury in the crash of Type VII due to the presence of the new cabane, and he used it regularly on his monoplanes for years after. Built and tested between Feb-ruary and May 1908, Type VIII was a big high rectangular-wing monoplane, all covered with varnished paper, powered by the 50 hp Antoinette; the distinctive big flat radiator was set under the nose between the landing gear legs. The VIIIbis was tested in June with a new broad wing of increased incidence, camber, and curved tips; the rear end of the fuselage was uncovered. It made flights of 400-700 m at Issy. Refitted again with drooping aile-rons and the first of Blériot's famous cloche controls, it made some good flights and impressive turns, and then crashed badly on 23 July.

Reconstructed again, this time as the VIIIter, its fuselage was shorter and the ailerons were replaced by the old oyster-

The first version of the Type VI. The pilot looks like Louis himself. (Courtesy of the Musée de l'Air et de l'Espace/Le Bourget-France)

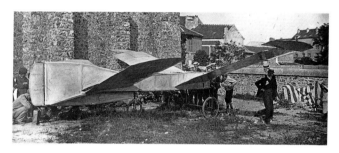
The VIbis, the penultimate version, with wider-track undercarriage and longer fin. (Courtesy of the Musée de l'Air et de l'Espace/Le Bourget-France)

The Type VII under construction, showing the first version of its undercar-riage, low-set wing, and uncompromising sprung tailwheel strut. (Courtesy of the Musée de l'Air et de l'Espace/Le Bourget-France)

The last version of the Type VII, with the more familiar landing gear and the higher wing. (Author's collection)

The Type VIII in flight. Note tip elevators, single tailplane. (Courtesy of the Musée de l'Air et de l'Espace/Le Bourget-France)

The Type VIIIter, with staggered tailplanes and a shorter fuselage. (Peter M Bowers collection)

shell tip surfaces; there were 2 staggered horizontal tail surfaces, one above and one below the aft fuselage, which was still uncovered. It flew from August till 4 November, when it was destroyed in a crash, Blériot himself undamaged.

(Span: 11.2 m (later 8.5 m); wing area: 22 sqm; weight: 480 kg; 50 hp Antoinette)

IX: In process from February to March 1908, at the same time as the VIII, the Type IX had the most powerful engine Blériot had used so far, a 60 hp Antoinette. The 2 radiators stood like ladders on each side of the nose; the aft fuselage was triangular in section; the wings were broad, shaped like the later Blériots, and warped. Although the IX never flew, it is the only one of the pre-Channel types to survive – in the Musée de l'Air in Paris.

(Span: 9 m; length: 12 m; wing area: 26 sqm; weight: 558.7 kg; 60 hp Antoinette)

X: This big tail-first biplane was shown at the Paris Salon of 1908; it had been under construction since September, and the original 50 hp Antoinette had been replaced with one of 90 hp.

The pilot and passenger sat in bentwood chairs on the lower wing, flanked on each side by full-gap radiators made of linked loops like doughnuts; the plan was to carry 3 passengers. The engine sat at their right, driving the big pusher propeller through chains. A single elevator and 3 rectangular rudders were set forward on outriggers, and tall triangular fins were fitted to the rearmost of the outboard struts. Interplane elevators which also served as ailerons were set behind the wingtips on outriggers and controlled by the single cloche; there were no rear tail surfaces. It ran on a pair of large doughnut wheels.

(Span: 13 m; length: 8.2 m; wing area: 68 sqm; weight: 620 kg; 50/90 hp Antoinette)

From its first appearance at the 1908 Paris Exposition, the next new design, the Type XI monoplane, was a success: it was built in various forms and sizes and for various purposes well into WWI, and the designations of these various models have frequently puzzled historians. We will list the variations one after the other, even though some were built while much later type numbers were being designed and flown.

The Type IX, which never flew. Note transparent streamlined windshield, which did not appear again. (Courtesy of the Musée de l'Air et de l'Espace/Le Bourget-France)

<u>XI Type REP</u>: Beside the big Type X at the 1908 Exposition stood the tiny new Type XI, commissioned by Blériot and designed by several people including his chief designer, Raymond Saulnier, in some combination of skills. It was fitted with a large tailwheel, which made landings difficult. The soon-to-be-famous bedstead frame for the undercarriage was sprung with shock cord. The rudder was very small, with almost square corners at the rear; and an odd teardrop-shaped fin was at first attached to the top bar of the support pylon. It first flew at Issy on 18 January 1909 with its heavy 30 hp REP engine attached to a 4-bladed metal propeller.

<u>XI Type Anzani</u>: The wing area was quickly increased from 12 to 14 sqm, the rudder enlarged as well, the engine from the 30 hp REP to a lighter 25 hp Anzani with a Chauvière propeller, and the field at Issy to a longer one at Buc. In June and July the cabane fin was removed and the side-covering extended further back. Blériot flew his new machine in various meets, until he heard of the *Daily Mail* prize for the first flight across the Channel – and then he heard that Latham had crashed in his Antoinette Type IV in the water on 19 July. He brought his XI, now equipped with an inflatable bag in the aft fuselage, to Calais, and prepared to make the attempt. When the weather finally broke, he took off and flew to a crash-landing at Dover Castle. Latham tried again in his new Antoinette VII after Blériot had landed, but failed

The cross-Channel Anzani Blériot XI safely back in France. Note the bladder inside the fuselage, against sinking, and the tall rudder. (Author's collection)

The Type X canard biplane of 1908 never flew. Note the aileron surfaces attached to the outboard interplane struts, and the side-curtains made of circular radiator sections. (Courtesy of the Musée de l'Air et de l'Espace/Le Bourget-France)

A fine close-up of the operating center of the Blériot X. Note the offset propeller blades; the enormous cloche on the control column; the battery and the rudder bar on the step; the big doughnut wheels. (Courtesy of the Musée de l'Air et de l'Espace/Le Bourget-France)

Left: The experimental springing system devised by a man named Sacotte for the XI, with frontal bumpers and under-seat springs. Another photo shows it wrecked. (Peter M Bowers collection)

once more, again being pulled from his wrecked aeroplane in the Channel.

> (Span: 7.8 m; wing area: 14 sqm; gross weight: 300 kg; speed: 36 kmh; 30 hp Anzani)

The XI was built well into 1914, with many other engine combinations, such as the 50 and 100 hp Gnômes, the 50 hp Anzani, the 2-cylinder Coudert, the 2-cylinder Dutheil et Chalmers, the 4-cylinder Humber, the 2-cylinder Clément-Bayard, and the 4-cylinder Labor-Picker. A common development was the substitution of the 1911-style one – or 2-piece elevators, often with a reverse-curve airfoil, for the initial tip surfaces. The big tailwheel was retained in many of the later aeroplanes, as was the trapezoidal cabane structure. A M Sacotte experimented with a complex system of shock absorbers and springs designed to cushion the pilot no matter how the aeroplane hit the ground; a small third wheel was set under the pilot's seat.

The famous stunt-flier Pégoud used at least 3 different XIs. His most famous achievement, the first loop, was in 1913 in a half-Blériot, half-Borel machine with a 2-piece elevator and a single inverted-V pylon. His experiment with a parachute attached to the top of the fuselage in 1913 was in another XI with a V-leg undercarriage and the tip elevators of a much earlier period. A third one appeared with the high tailskid set shortly behind the cockpit.

Sometimes aircraft were reported under different names: a Blériot XI belonging to a man named de Villeneuve was described as L'Epervier, which seemed a whole new type.

<u>XI Type Ecole</u>: This April 1912 design was distinguished by considerable dihedral, tip elevators, looped-cane tailskid, and a sharply back-sloping diagonal edge to the forward fuselage covering. It was fitted with a 25/30 or a 30/35 hp Anzani.

<u>XI Type Taxi-Pinguin</u>: Short wings allowed this version of January 1912 barely to "grass-cut," and a remarkably wide tread and 2 long forward skids kept the novice from turning over. The tail was kept up by the high skid aft of the cockpit. It was built in both military and school versions.

> (Span: 8.9 m; length: 7.8 m (school: 7.65 m); empty weight: 265 kg (school: 220 kg); gross weight: 415 kg (school: 350 kg); speed: 95 kmh (school: 65 kmh); 50 hp Gnôme (school: 30 hp Anzani)

<u>XI Type Artillerie</u>: There were at least 2 versions in March 1912 of this 50 hp Gnôme-powered single-seater spotter, one with a rectangular one-piece elevator, the other with a small elevator surface with an oddly-curved trailing edge. The fuselage folded upward onto its own back, for easy transport; the high skid supported the end of the front section.

One of Pégoud's Type XIs, this one fitted with the parachute with which he made at least one successful jump in 1913; note the inverted rudder to make room for the opening parachute. His machines featured a taller cabane pylon, needed in his looping experiments. (Author's collection)

At least one of Pégoud's XIs had a one-piece elevator, the 2 halves connected with the elevator spar. Note their reverse curve, and the added extensions at the ends. (Author's collection)

Right: A frequently-printed photograph of a 50 hp Gnôme mounted in front of the propeller of a Type XI. This mounting was common in the big Farman pusher biplanes, where the engine was therefore aft of the propeller; this photograph, however, shows the engine mounted in Delagrange's first Blériot XI.

Delagrange's Type XI in flight; the engine has been moved back to its normal position. (Author's collection)

<u>XI Type 1912</u>: Another single-seater with 2-piece elevators and high fuselage skid appeared in March, this one also featured a single inverted-V cabane and a cut-out in the right-hand wing-root.

    (Span: 8.9 m; length: 7.8 m; wing area: 15 sqm; gross weight: 300 kg; speed: 90 kmh; 50 hp Gnôme)

<u>XI Type 1913</u>: A German Rozendaal drawing shows what seems to be a straight Channel model, but with the top fuselage long-erons arched up over the wing and then down to the motor-mounts.

Above and below: Two views of a Type XI Pinguin ground-trainer. Note the heavy protective forward skids and the abbreviated wingspan. (Author's collection)

<u>XI Type Parasol</u>: Lieutenant Gouin is known as the designer of a Blériot parasol monoplane, though he had also contributed to at least one aeroplane built with Henri Chazal. In 1913 he modi-fied and patented a Blériot with the wings set on 4 struts above the fuselage, slightly higher than the pilot's eyes. First shown at the 1914 Concours de Sécurité, it was Blériot's effort to compete with the Morane parasol and improve the visibility over the stan-dard midwing monoplane. Since the military specifications also called for short landing runs, Gouin introduced on the first – and only the first – of his parasols his "crocodile rudder," the 2 halves of which were hinged at the leading edge and could be opened wide as air-brakes after landing. The so-called Blériot-Gouin was also produced for the British RFC, which ordered 15. A 2-seater version was also developed. Production machines were known as Blériot Parasols.

    (Span: 8.95 m; length: 7.8 m; wing area: 7.8 sqm; 80 hp Gnôme)

Right: The prototype Blériot Type Parasol, this one fitted with the split "croco-dile" rudder. (Author's collection)

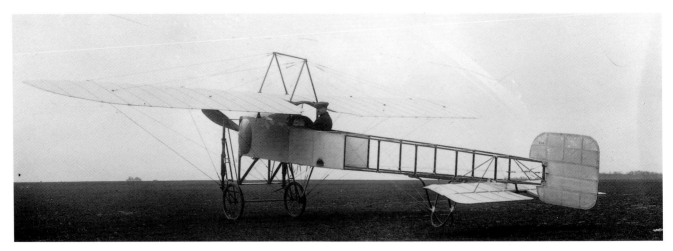

Another Type Parasol; note the differences from the first one. (Courtesy of the Musée de l'Air et de l'Espace/Le Bourget-France)

XIbis: This variant of January 1910 was short in appearance, with a pigeon-tail and elliptical elevators, combined with a standard XI-type rudder. The Gnôme was half-cowled; the big tailwheel was fitted again. It is sometimes erroneously labeled Type XIII.

(Span: 9 m; length: 8 m; wing area: 16 sqm; weight: 250 kg; Gnôme)

XI-2bis: In February 1910 an enlarged XI appeared, with side-by-side seating, to supplement the single-place machines already in use in training schools. Powered with a 50 hp Gnôme, it featured a pigeon tail with elliptical elevators, and a handsome elliptical rudder surface. The first one was rebuilt with the engine out ahead of the bedstead, and was sold in large numbers as the XIbis Militaire.

(Span: 11 m; length: 8.3 m; wing area: 19 sqm; gross weight: 350 kg; 80 hp Gnôme)

XI-2 Tandem: In February 1911 the XI-2 itself came in several versions. One had a lengthened nose and odd curved tailskid, another was a 3-float hydro with a tall rudder. Some had oyster-shell elevators, others had the 2-piece design. Some had half-covered fuselages like the XI, others were fully covered. Perreyon's 160 hp model had a single seat and V-leg undercarriage. But most of them were longer than the XI, with a raised cowling ahead of the first cockpit, and the tall mid-fuselage skid.

(1912: Span: 9.7 m; length: 8.3 m; wing area: 20 sqm; empty/gross weight: 300/550 kg; 70 hp Gnôme)
(1913: Span: 10.35 m; length: 8.4 m; wing area: 19 sqm; empty/gross weight: 335/585 kg; top speed: 115/120 kmh; 80 hp Gnôme)

XI-2 Type Génie (engineer): Similar to the XI-2, the April 1912 70 hp Gnôme Génie had an odd horizontal tail unit set on struts below the aft fuselage, with a one-piece elevator with an S-curved trailing edge. The rudder did not hang below the tailpost, and the bottom rear corner was clipped to allow for the elevator below it. The 2 cockpits were separated; the cabane was now a 4-strut pyramid, and the tailskid was the single high design aft of the rear cockpit. The fuselage of the machine used for the Circuit d'Anjou race was fully covered.

(Span: 9.7 m; length: 8.3 m; wing area: 18 sqm; empty eight: 320 kg; loaded weight: 550 kg; speed: 110-115 kmh; 70 hp Gnôme)

The XI-2bis in flight. (Courtesy of the Musée de l'Air et de l'Espace/Le Bourget-France)

A Type XI-2 Tandem hydro, this one with a short rudder. (Author's collection)

XI-2 Vision Totale: The standard XI-2 design was modified in July 1914 with a parasol wing on 4 vertical cabane struts, and a Blériot XI-2-style rudder. The pilot sat aft of the wing, and the observer in front with his head up between the wing spars. The fuselage was covered only up to aft of the cockpit, and a streamlined fabric pyramid was fitted inside the longerons to cap off the covered section. It was powered with the 80 hp Le Rhône or the 100 hp Gnôme.

(Span: 10.36 m; length: 8.427 m; wing area: 19.5 sqm; empty weight: 600 kg; speed: 100 kmh; 80 hp Gnôme)

XI-2 Type Hauteur: Powered with the 80 hp Gnôme, this one was used by Roland Garros in his altitude flights in August 1912 and March 1913. With a 4-strut pyramidal cabane, it stood on a V-leg undercarriage. The machine used in the later attempts had a fully covered fuselage; in June a similar machine with 2 seats beat Garros' records.

XI-3 Type Concours Militaire: A big 3-seater, it carried 300 kg load for 300 km. 2 were built, one with a Gnôme of 100 hp, the other of 140 hp. The engine was mounted out in front in a heavy box frame, and the heavy landing gear featured a pair of triple wheels mounted together on the same axle.

(Span: 11.35 m; length: 8.2 m; wing area: 25 sqm; gross weight: 519 kg; 140 hp Gnôme)

XII: In April 1909 the Blériot firm designed and built a new monoplane in which the pilot sat under the high wing, behind the 35 hp ENV which drove the tractor propeller with chains. The fuselage was completely uncovered, the top curving downward to the tailpost; a Blériot XI-style rudder was flanked by 2 smaller rectangular rudders, with 2 tailplanes set just ahead of them. Small winglets serving as ailerons protruded from each side behind the pilot. The typical Blériot landing-gear and cabane structures appeared here. After its flights in May, the rudders were all removed and replaced by an awkward-looking rectangular surface mounted high on a post. Blériot experimented with covering the forward sides of the fuselage. In June he added a long curved fin to the top of the fuselage, and in July a whole new curved fin and rudder assembly.

In August he built the first so-called Type XII for Reims, this one fitted with a 60 hp ENV and a 4-bladed propeller, and a new down-curved rear fuselage, still with the 2 tailplanes. The winglets were gone, and the wing area was reduced for speed by uncovering the trailing edge section from tip to tip. No 22 raced in the Gordon-Bennett meet, but crashed and burned. Grahame-White bought the third aircraft off the line and named it the White Eagle. Replacing the ENV with a 50 hp Gnôme saved weight, and one was used as a 2-seat trainer at Pau.

(Span: 10 m; length: 9.5 m; wing area: 22 sqm; empty weight: 600 kg; speed: 100 kmh; 35-50 hp ENV)

The XI-2 Vision Totale of July 1914: the XI-2 Tandem was modified as a parasol to take an observer. (Author's collection)

The first of the Type XIIs. (Peter M Bowers collection)

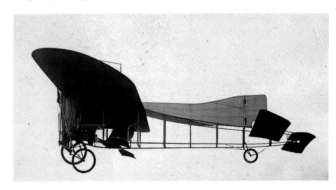

A later modification of the Type XII. This photo shows Blériot himself on board flying before the members of the Senate. (Peter M Bowers collection)

XIII: This big 4-passenger monoplane was conceived in 1909 and built in 1910. Powered with only a 100 hp Gnôme set on the trailing edge with its pusher propeller, it carried not only 4 but on occasion 10 people. The big rectangular wing had drooping ailerons, a long uncovered box-girder fuselage, and single large rectangular tail surfaces all set slightly above the fuselage. 2 big wheels supported the front, and a shallow skid the rear. A forward elevator was set on outriggers. One photograph shows one passenger sitting precariously just ahead of the stabilizer.

(Span: 13 m; length: 12 m; wing area: 40 sqm; gross weight: 600 kg; 100 hp Gnôme)

XIV: This handsome side-by-side aeroplane introduced in November 1910 the new fishtail design, in which the rear fuselage tapered quickly down into the leading edge of the stabilizer, with a curved one-piece elevator at the end, and 2 small oval rudder surfaces, one above and the other below. The wings were braced above and below from inverted-V pylons. Access to the seats was through a trap in the bottom of the fuselage. A version with a single angular rudder flew at Hendon. All had the 50 hp Gnôme; but it is possible one was fitted with a more powerful engine.

XV: Type XV may not have been built: an August 1910 drawing shows a slender single-seater with a graceful covered fuselage of circular section, a pigeon-tail with 2 oval rudders above and below. Most remarkable: the wing was strut-braced from the landing-gear structure.

XVI – XIX: ?

XX: Another fishtail design, also with the 50 hp Gnôme, this single-seater was known initially as Le Poisson (fish), because of the small angular fins above and below the fishtail stabilizer. The lower fin was later removed. The design featured a new rectangular wing with flattened camber and special construction to make it more flexible and easier to disassemble. The trailing edges of the wing ribs could be uncovered for less surface and more speed.

XXI: This handsome side-by-side fishtail design of February 1911 came from both the XI-2bis and the XIV, and was bought by several different air services. It could be easily disassembled, and the crew sat aft of the inverted-V pylon instead of in front, making access easier than with the XIV. It had a single angular rudder surface set over the stabilizer. It also appeared on floats.

(Span: 11 m; length: 8.24 m; wing area: 25 sqm; empty weight: 350 kg; top speed: 90/95 kmh; 70 hp Gnôme)

XXII: ?

XXIII: 100 hp Gnômes powered these racing aircraft of March 1911, with extremely narrow rectangular wings with curved tips, the fish-tail, and a single angular rudder on top. Alfred Leblanc and Gustav Hamel each flew one in the Gordon-Bennett race, with Leblanc winning a second and Hamel wrecking his machine.

(Spans: 7.16 m, 6.71 m; length: 7.62 m; wing area: 9 sqm, 6.75 sqm; speed: 128 kmh; 100 hp Gnôme)

XXIV: The big Limousine was built in November 1911 for Henri Deutsch de la Meurthe, based on the earlier XIII but with an elaborate closed cabin structure for 4 passengers; the pilot sat like a coachman on an exposed seat under the speaking tube and the front windows of the cabin. A small celluloid cone was placed out ahead to provide him with a windbreak. Long curved outriggers supported a forward elevator, and their aft extensions supported a large rectangular tailplane and oddly curved single

Right: A drawing from the patent for the Blériot XV. (Author's collection)

The big Type XIII of 1910. With 100 hp it carried 10 people. (Author's collection)

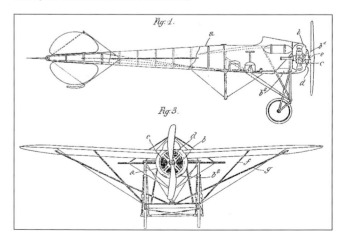

The Type XIV. The photograph is a copy of a copy, but it shows clearly the lines of this machine. (Author's collection)

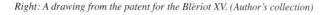

The Type XX. Note revised airfoil section, swallow-tailed stabilizer faired into the fuselage sides. (Courtesy of the Musée de l'Air et de l'Espace/Le Bourget-France)

The swallow-tailed Blériot XXI sat 2 side by side. (Courtesy of the Musée de l'Air et de l'Espace/Le Bourget-France)

rudder on top. The original 100 hp Gnôme was replaced with one of 140 hp, and then the project was given up.

(Span: 13 m; length: 14 m; wing area: 40 sqm; empty weight: 700 kg; 100 and 140 hp Gnôme)

XXV: Planned as a 2-seat naval machine with the observer seated forward, it was designed to float on the water in an emergency. But it was built in August 1911 as a single-seater, similar to the 1907 canard, and presumably, not much more successful. The wings carried drooping ailerons and small rudder surfaces mounted above the tips; a single elevator was set into the nose, and the wheels were fixed to a single U-shaped spring leg, similar to the early Nieuports.

(Span: 8.9 m; length: 5.5 m; wing area: 12 sqm; weight: 400 kg; 50 hp Gnôme mounted aft of the pusher propeller)

XXVI: Another canard, the XXVI was built in September 1911 but apparently not flown. It was a triplane, with short rectangular wings; several short skids under the lower wing supported the rear, and a single wheel forward carried the front: this wheel was designed to retract back up into the fuselage in front of the pilot. The engine was again mounted aft of the pusher propeller.

The Type XXI Hydro. (Courtesy of the Musée de l'Air et de l'Espace/Le Bourget-France)

The Type XXIII racer. (Author's collection)

XXVII: This single-seat racing monoplane with a 50 hp Gnôme was built in July 1911; it stood high on its bedstead-undercarriage. Resembling the XXI but slenderer and with a half-overhanging cowling, it had a short inverted-V cabane made of streamlined tubing.

(Span: 8.9 m; length: 7.5 m; wing area: 12 sqm; gross weight: 430 kg; speed: 125 kg; 70 hp Gnôme)

XXVIII Populaire: The top cylinder of the Anzani Y was hidden in the tiny overhanging cowl; otherwise this was a sporting version of the standard XI; the nose section of the fuselage was thinner, and a long heavy diagonal brace supported each side of the landing gear. The looped-cane tailskid was set amidships instead of under the tail. This design appeared in December 1911, and may also have been built in a 2-seat version.

The pilot at the controls of the Type XXIV, in front of the 4-passenger cabin. Note conical windshield mounted forward. (Courtesy of the Musée de l'Air et de l'Espace/Le Bourget-France)

(Span: 8.9 m; length: 7.2 m; empty weight: 210 kg; 30/35 hp Anzani)

XXIX: Designed for military observation, this 2-seat side-by-side pusher monoplane was never built. The crew was forward in the nacelle, with the 70 hp Gnôme at the rear, with outrigger structures on each side coming to a point and supporting a monoplane tail and an odd oval rudder set below it. A pair of large wheels was set under the leading edge, with a smaller pair on the skids forward. But similar designs would be built later. Among drawings dated 1912 are some of the same aeroplane but with the tail outriggers enlarged and brought together with the propeller turning inside and between them; these are marked XXIXbis.

XXX-XXXI: ?

XXXII: An odd little monoplane design that was never built, the XXXII had an uncovered fuselage shaped like an inverted airfoil, a narrow-tread undercarriage whose axle ran through the bottom of the fuselage. The wings were short and rectangular, the engine was a little 2-cylinder designed by the engineering director of the Blériot firm. The controls were "natural," meaning 2 control wheels moved sideways for turning and rotated for

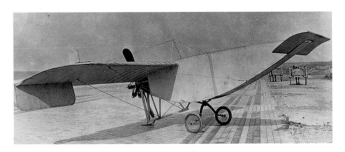

The canard Type XXV. No apparent rudder or fin surfaces. (Courtesy of the Musée de l'Air et de l'Espace/Le Bourget-France)

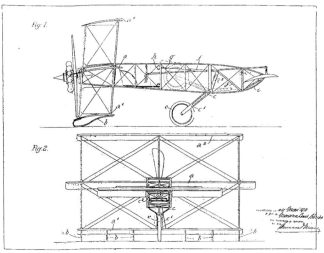

Patent drawing of the Type XXVI of 1911. Note the planned retractable front wheel. (Author's collection)

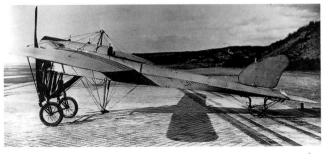

The Type XXVII, similar to the XXI. (Courtesy of the Musée de l'Air et de l'Espace/Le Bourget-France)

The Y Anzani in the Type XXVIII Populaire. (Courtesy of the Musée de l'Air et de l'Espace/Le Bourget-France)

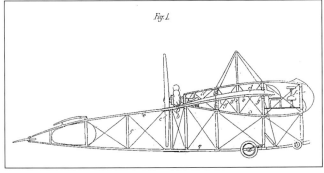

The patent drawing for the Type XXIX project. (Author's collection)

elevation; they were to be moved by the hands or by the knees.

<u>XXXIII Canard Bleu</u>: The 70 hp Gnôme for this big 2-seater canard was meant to be mounted amidships, driving the pusher propeller with a shaft; the whole machine rested on 4 wheels. But when the June 1912 tests proved unsuccessful, it was rebuilt with an 80 hp Gnôme at the tail, and what looked like a standard Blériot bedstead undercarriage, with a tall skid mounted forward. The nacelle was uncovered forward, with a long tapered boom carrying the forward elevator. A big triangular rudder was fitted aft of the propeller with another surface forward of the propeller: the 2 were braced together at the top. A third rectangular surface was mounted below the nacelle.

(Span: 10.5 m; length: 8 m; wing area: 24 sqm; weight: 330 kg; speed: 115 kmh; 70 hp Gnôme)

<u>XXXIV-XXXV</u>: ?

<u>XXXVI Torpille</u>: In October 1912 this neatly streamlined military side-by-side monoplane was shown at the Paris Exposition. The 80 hp Gnôme was accessible and easily removed from its bullet-shaped cowling, and the rigging was quickly demountable from the 3-legged pylon; the occupants were protected from rifle fire by a sheet of armor plate. The landing gear was formed

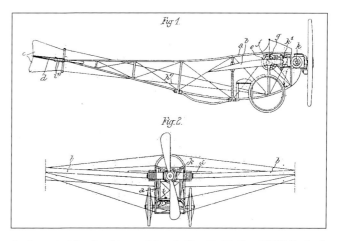

Another patent drawing, this one of the unbuilt pretty little Type XXXII. (Author's collection)

The "Blue Canard" Type XXXIII, second version. (Courtesy of the Musée de l'Air et de l'Espace/Le Bourget-France)

Below: The armored Type XXXVI Torpille at the 1912 Salon. Note simplified all-steel undercarriage. (Courtesy of the Musée de l'Air et de l'Espace/Le Bourget-France)

of simple steel struts and a long forward skid. The curved rudder was in 2 pieces top and bottom. A single photograph shows what seems like a modification of the XXXVI, with a standard Blériot rudder and undercarriage; it may have been the 160 hp Gnôme referred to in contemporary Blériot correspondence concerning a projected XXXVIbis.

(Span: 12.25 m; wing area: 25 sqm; weight: 375 kg; speed: 75 kmh; 80 hp Gnôme)

<u>XXXVII</u>: This seems to have been a further development of the Type XXIX and XXIXbis, designed in January 1913. This time the pusher propeller turned on the top aft longeron outrigger; this, with the 2 lower longerons, supported a standard tail unit. The 2 crew sat forward, the nose of the nacelle hinging downward to allow them access. The centrally-mounted 80 hp Gnôme was replaced with one of 100 hp, and after some 10 months of tests, the pilot Perreyon killed himself in it. (Although a photograph was probably shown at the Olympia show in London in February 1913, no single photograph seems to have survived.)

<u>XXXVIII</u>: ?

<u>XXXIX</u>: A single-seater armored monocoque monoplane, this handsome machine intended for reconnaissance appeared in October 1913. The triangular stabilizer was soon replaced with a smaller rectangular lifting tail, and the rudder replaced with a rudder like the Type XI-2.

<u>XL</u>: This was a tandem-seated nacelle pusher biplane, similar to some of the early Farman designs: the top wing overhung the lower by a great deal, and the single oval rudder was suspended below a big rectangular tail surface. The wheels were mounted on long hinged arms, unlike other Blériots. It was first presented at the May 1913 Salon de Turin, and was probably influenced by the work of the Italian firm of Società Italiana Transaerea (SIT), a licensed Blériot subsidiary. It was shown to the services at Buc, and then at the December Exposition in Paris.

<u>XLI</u>: ?

<u>XLII</u>: This was another canard pusher, built in March 1913, meant for observation, apparently an improvement over the Type XXXVII, though it seems unlikely the changes were helpful. The nacelle was short, with a forward window for the observers to look downward, and a long hooked uncovered outrigger structure out in front with the forward elevator. The wings carried ailerons, along with 3 little rudder surfaces on each panel. A big boomerang-shaped rudder was hung behind the propeller, and the whole thing rested on a traditional Blériot bedstead gear and an awkward rear skid under the 80 hp Gnôme and the pusher propeller. The machine was later modified with a tailwheel and only 2 fins on each wing panel.

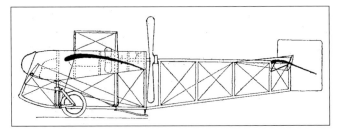

A contemporary drawing of the unlucky Type XXXVII; the crew sat side by side in front. (Author's collection)

The Type XXXIX armored single-seater of 1913. (Courtesy of the Musée de l'Air et de l'Espace/Le Bourget-France)

The tandem Type XL. Note landing gear suspension, semi-spherical nacelle nose. (Courtesy of the Musée de l'Air et de l'Espace/Le Bourget-France)

The canard Type XLII. (Author's collection)

The leggy tandem armored XLIII. (Peter M Bowers collection)

The XLIV Type Artillerie, with aft-sitting pilot. Note the 2 different size struts in the pylon. (Courtesy of the Musée de l'Air et de l'Espace/Le Bourget-France)

(Span: 8.9 m; length: 7.3 m; wing area: 18 sqm; 80 hp Gnôme)

<u>XLIII</u>: This tandem 2-seat armored monocoque monoplane was built in November 1913. The engine was set ahead of the landing gear and covered with a horseshoe-shaped cowl. The 2 occupants sat in separated cockpits, communicating through a horn. The landing gear was very tall, with the diagonal braces shown on the Populaire. The horizontal tail was of more conventional shape than most of the Blériots, the rudder was hinged so part was above and part below the fuselage, and the cabane was a tall 4-strut pyramid.

The Type XLV resembles most of the earlier Blériot monoplanes – until you notice the Anzani set behind the pilot, evidently to allow him to sit far forward for better visibility. (Courtesy of the Musée de l'Air et de l'Espace/Le Bourget-France)

(Span: 10.1 m; length: 6.02 m; empty weight: 350 kg; gross weight: 625 kg; speed: 120 kmh; 80 hp Gnôme)

<u>XLIV Type Artillerie</u>: Built in February 1913, this was similar to the XI, with the pilot seated far back for better visibility, a tall 4-strut pylon, and deep curved cut-outs at the wing-roots. It was powered with an 80 hp Gnôme.

<u>XLV</u>: Another observation single-seater, this one had a 60 hp Anzani mounted amidships inside the fuselage driving the tractor propeller through a shaft. The pilot was seated far forward, ahead of the leading edge, and straddling the drive-shaft. This even exchange of major weights in the fuselage allowed the use of the same tail surfaces as on the XLIV.

In 1913 several other aeroplanes were designed – some were even built – whose designations have been lost. One of them was probably the big side-by-side 3-float seaplane flown by Perreyon; it resembled a float version of the XXI, and was photographed in November 1913. Another was a very modern-looking midwing monoplane designed to shoot down dirigibles: it had a 37 mm cannon firing through the center of the propeller hub.

In July 1914 still another Blériot armored monocoque monoplane appeared. There may have been only the one; its factory designation is unknown. It had the words La Vache (the cow) painted on the side. A small rudder hung at the aft point of the fuselage, preceded by a tail surface with horn-balanced elevators. It was powered by a 160 hp Gnôme.

The Type XI in its various forms, and some of the later models as well, served until 1915 when the monoplane design fell into disfa-

The type number of the armored monoplane La Vache seems not to have been listed. The aircraft looks heavy – note the 3 men's efforts and the large tires. (Courtesy of the Musée de l'Air et de l'Espace/Le Bourget-France)

vor. Blériot joined the Spad firm (la Société Provisoire des Aéroplanes Deperdussin), and became its president. When Armand Déperdussin was disgraced for his financial misdealings, Blériot absorbed the firm, becoming president and changing its name to la Société pour l'Aviation et ses Dérivés, with Béchereau as chief engineer. After the war, Deperdussin committed suicide.

Blériot now concentrated on building Spads, and with the designer Herbemont, racing aircraft; he also built a 26-passenger 4-engined transport in 1919. The firm diversified as well, into motorbicycles, boats, and knock-down furniture. Back into aircraft, he produced pursuit and heavy transport designs. Blériot died on 1 August 1936, and on 20 March 1937 his factories were nationalized.

Bobenreith

A single photo reprinted in *La Voix du Nord* may be of the Bobenreith. It is a Wright copy, with biplane forward elevator and biplane rear surfaces – perhaps also elevators – with a rudder between them. Unlike the Wright designs, it had mid-wing ailerons, 2 close-set wheels and curved wing skids. It was built in Turcoing, in the vicinity of Lille (where *La Voix du Nord* was published).

De Bolotoff

Serge de Bolotoff, son of the wealthy Russian Princess Wiasemsky, was not much more than 20 in 1908 when he ordered his triplane from Gabriel Voisin. Although it shared some features with other Voisins, other features were unique – in particular the heavy vertical wooden beams to support the landing gear. It first appeared in the press of 1908 as "the 100 hp de Bolotoff," a big machine with a 100 hp Panhard-Levassor driving a tractor propeller, with a covered fuselage and biplane tail cellule. It continued to attract notice as late as March 1910 at Mourmelon, where it ran here and there around the field. One journalist observed that "the enormous apparatus" designed to cross the Channel had never flown, and "some think it would be better if it never did so." It crashed at Brooklands in 1914. So it did cross the Channel – in a boat.

(Span: 11 m; length: 12 m; gross weight: 1200 kg; 100 hp Panhard-Levassor)

Bonamy

The single Bonamy aeroplane was entered in the Concours de Sécurité of 1914, promising perfect stability even with the engine not running. It was built from a Ponnier (Hanriot Type D) fuselage, and had 2 pairs of wings in tandem, with greater dihedral on the forward wing, and sweepback on the rear wing. Each wing had 2 spars, the front fixed and the rear pivoted at a rib at mid-span: with the engine on, the forced draft raised the rear spar at the inner ends so that the tips were lowered and incidence at the wingtips increased. The difference at the tips was from 4° to 10°. The machine flew with a rotary engine, type unknown.

It is likely that Bonamy's design was based on a misinterpretation of Ferber's theory of the three Vs on aircraft stability: the 1st V was positive dihedral; the 2d V was sweepback on the mainplanes; the third V was positive incidence on the mainplane, negative incidence on the tailplane.

Bonnet-Labranche

In Bordeaux in 1869 the father of Albert and Emile Bonnet-Labranche had designed and built a large and unsuccessful 4-passenger "helicoplane," with propeller, turbine, and warpable wings; the following year he built a gas balloon. His sons came by their interest in flying naturally – though their designs were not always much more successful.

No 1: Their first machine, more or less a copy of a big Voisin, was built by Espinosa in his Avionnerie. To the basic Voisin design the brothers had added a long extension from the trailing upper edge of the upper wing back to the tail. The pilot and passenger sat inside a partly-covered Voisin-style nacelle; the engine drove a pusher propeller directly, and a tractor propeller in the nose through a long drive-shaft. A forward elevator was in-

Right and top of opposite page: Two views of the first Bonnet-Labranche. The wingtip ailerons are fitted here, so the aircraft is probably the Ibis. Note the long forward drive-shaft for the second propeller. (Courtesy of the Musée de l'Air et de l'Espace/Le Bourget-France)

Any further information on the Bobenreith – if indeed this is the Bobenreith – would be welcome. (Author's collection)

A close-up of the big de Bolotoff triplane. The massive wooden uprights in the landing gear show more clearly in photos of the machine being built at the Voisin factory. (Courtesy of the Musée de l'Air et de l'Espace/Le Bourget-France)

The Bonamy was entered in the Concours de Sécurité of 1914. At least we know it flew. (Courtesy of the Musée de l'Air et de l'Espace/Le Bourget-France)

terconnected with the rear elevator – the first time this had been attempted. The machine proved unflyable after tests at Palaiseau (south of Paris), even after the upper wing had been lightened and tip ailerons pivoting on the upper wing leading edge had been added (No 1bis). This aeroplane was reproduced, flying, on the 3-lira stamp of the Republic of San Marino.

(Span: 12.5 m upper span; 10 m at the leading edge, 4 m at the trailing edge at the rear of the machine; height: 3 m; wing area: 80 sqm; 80 hp Antoinette)

No 2: Their second machine was probably the first with still more modifications, since the 2 were very similar. It looked lighter than No 1 and retained the large upper wing, which was to pro-

vide lift and also, in an emergency, to serve as a parachute. The earlier covered nacelle was replaced by 4 outriggers attached to the leading edges of both wings, and bearing a Voisin-like forward elevator in 2 panels, flat, unlike those of No 1. A second pair, slightly smaller, were mounted between the outer pair of forward struts as ailerons. The biplane tail unit was now without the earlier side-curtains; the forward propeller and the fin in front of the central rudder were gone. Power was provided by a 30 hp G Filtz-Arion, driving at 1100 rpm a 2-blade all-metal pusher propeller.

(Same specifications as for No 1, except the upper span is sometimes given as 11.5 m instead of 12.5 m; 30 hp G Filtz-Arion)

The Bonnet-Labranche No 2A lot has been simplified; inter-wing ailerons have been added. (Courtesy of the Musée de l'Air et de l'Espace/Le Bourget-France)

No 3: In 1909 in St Die Emile Bonnet founded with Dutheil, Chalmers, and others the Société Aéronautique de l'Est, and the Avia Company, which built machines for SEA. Avia's chief engineer was Charles Roux, who is likely to have worked on the Bonnet-Labranche No 2, since No 3 featured many similar details. With the No 3 appeared the designation ABL (for Albert Bonnet-Labranche): it was a small biplane called védette militaire in the Avia catalogue (see Avia No 1); and another similar machine was built for the Russian Teretchenko. It had a biplane tail unit with central rudder, rectangular wings with interplane ailerons, as on No 2; a flat front elevator was rigged forward, also like No 2. The undercarriage was typically Voisin, as on both earlier Bonnet-Labranche designs; a 24 hp Dutheil et Chalmers drove a pusher propeller.

The Bonnet-Labranche No 3, also listed as "Avia védette militaire." Compare it with the ABL Nos 1 and 2. (Courtesy of the Musée de l'Air et de l'Espace/Le Bourget-France)

(Span: 7 m; length: 8 m; chord: 1.5 m; wing area: c 22 sqm; weight: 250 kg)

No 4: This monoplane built in the Avia workshops at St Die in 1909 flew at Juvisy. It had a simple half-covered rectangular fuselage with an Antoinette-style wing mounted on top, and inset rectangular ailerons at the tips. The tail was comprised of a long triangular fin and stabilizer, each fitted with a rectangular control surface. The undercarriage was similar to that of the Blériot XI, with the addition of long forward upward-curved skids. The uncovered forward fuselage carried the long copper-tube radiators for the flat-4 engine mounted high on the nose, probably a 40 hp Dutheil et Chalmers.

The first ABL monoplane, No 4. Note inset ailerons and high forward skids. (Author's collection)

(Span: 11 m; length: 10 m; 2.2 m diameter Avia propeller; 50 hp Dutheil et Chalmers)

(Span: 10 m; length: 10.75 m; wing area: 40 sqm; 40 hp Darracq)

By the end of 1910 the Avia company was nearly ended. The Bonnet-Labranche brothers had gone on designing their own monoplanes in a workshop on rue Lecourbe in Paris, with the assistance of Charles Roux, who was reported by the end of 1910 to be "adjusting" an ABL monoplane at Issy. The next ABL designs, Nos 6, 7, and 8, were variations of a quite successful earlier Avia monoplane.

No 5: This unsuccessful biplane was tested in 1910; it may have been also the Avia No 3, first flown at Issy in August 1910, in the presence of Charles Roux.

The ABL No 5 at Issy in 1910. (Courtesy of the Musée de l'Air et de l'Espace/Le Bourget-France)

The Bonnet-Labranche No 6 school machine; this photograph shows the 2-seater version. (Courtesy of the Musée de l'Air et de l'Espace/Le Bourget-France)

<u>No 6</u>: A school single – or 2-seater, with Blériot-style fuselage and inverted double-V mast. The main difference between No 6 and the Blériot XI lay in the undercarriage, a simple boxlike structure with 2 long skids across which lay the axle. The machine was offered with a 25 hp 3-cylinder Anzani, a 50 hp Viale or Gnôme; at least 2 were built, probably more.

(Span: 8.5 m; length: 8 m; wing area: 17 sqm; gross weight: 220 kg with the Anzani; top speed: 75 kmh)

<u>No 7</u>: A 2-seat racer (course deux places), similar to the previous model, though fitted with a 50 or 60 hp Anzani or a 50 or 70 hp Gnôme, it had a greater span, greater dihedral, and slightly flatter airfoil than No 6. At least 2 were built, probably more.

(Span: 9.6 m; length: 8.6 m; wing area: 20 sqm; gross weight: 280 kg with 50 hp Gnôme; top speed: 100 kmh)

<u>No 8</u>: A military 3-seater (militaire trois places), it was probably never completed. It was registered for the Concours Militaire in November 1911, but did not enter; moreover, the photograph of this machine in the Bonnet-Labranche catalogue is in fact of the 2-seater. In the first rendering the passenger sat behind the pilot and slightly higher; in the second, below him in the box of the undercarriage!

(Dimensions and engines as on No 7.)

Albert and Emile Bonnet-Labranche founded the *Revue de l'Aviation Illustrée* in 1908, and also the Aéro Garage Parisien, where they sold new aircraft and used spare parts. In 1910 they opened a flying school at Issy-les-Moulineaux (taken over by de Baeder and Duparquet in 1911-1912); another in Orléans at the Camp de Corcott; and a third in Oran, in Algeria; others were planned in many other cities. Janoir, a famous pilot who later built a large aircraft factory during WWI, was chief pilot for the Bonnet-Labranche monoplanes at Issy and Cercottes.

Bordier

A M Bordier was expected to build a full-scale aeroplane in 1909.

Borel

In 1909 Gabriel Borel and his brother began their interest in aviation and founded a flying school at Mourmelon. He collected a stable of young men who were to become famous on their own, including Antoine Odier, François Denhaut, Léon Morane, Jules Védrines, René Simon, and Raymond Saulnier. At first they sold Blériots and Blériot copies; Morane and Saulnier developed the little monoplane known first as Morane-Borel, which in various developments became famous in meets and races all over France. But in 1911 the Borel brothers stole a £1000 check sent to Jules Védrines, and their whole team abandoned them. Morane and Saulnier went on to develop the monoplane series known as Morane and Morane-Saulnier; their designs flew through World War II. They appointed Antoine Odier, who designed further monoplanes known sometimes as Borel – sometimes as Borel-Odier. Denhaut, the flyingboat designer, worked for the Borels, and his work was known as Borel-Denhaut; the work of Ruby was a single machine, the odd aéro-torpille Borel-Ruby.

Between 1910 and 1914 Borel designed a series of monoplanes, seaplanes, and flyingboats. In the meantime, the Borel firm also produced Morane-Saulniers; and during the course of WWI, Caudrons, Nieuports, and Spads as well. The complete series designation system for Borel is unclear.

<u>Borel-Moranes</u>: Based originally on the Blériot XI, to the design of which as well as of the early Moranes Raymond Saulnier had contributed heavily, the Borel-Moranes were very similar also to each other. Mostly 2-seaters with V-leg undercarriages and twin tailskids, they varied in several features:

    engines (usually Gnôme or Anzani)
    elevators, either oyster-shell-tip style or full-width with tip
      balances raked either forward or aft
    pyramid-shaped pylon for wing bracing
    double tailskids, either braced from the front, or long and

trailing, braced from behind

wing panels usually 11, 12, or 17 ribs long

undercarriage skids longer or shorter or absent (one model
    had no cross-axle)

fuselage covering, fully covered or partly, in various pro
    portions

cowling shape in front of the pilot

Some samples:

1910 (?): A light Blériot look-alike with 12 ribs/panel, a
Blériot XI rudder, tip elevators, and a single tailskid.

1911: In the Exposition, a 12-rib single-seater and a 17-rib
2-seater, each fully covered, with trailing skids, fully covered fuselages, and balanced elevators with back-raked balances; the latter appeared with a belly-pad under the center
fuselage. Also, an experimental all-metal fuselage with twin
cockpit cut-outs.

    For the Concours Militaire, Borel entered the Type
Militaire, a large 4-seater bearing the number 27, with tapered wings and a 140 hp Gnôme. The undercarriage featured 3 struts on each side and 2 pairs of wheels, and skids.
The pylon comprised 2 triangular frames; the fuselage was
half covered, and the tip elevators gave the appearance of
an enormous Blériot XI.

1912: In the Exposition, the experimental Obus (see below), and a 12-panel 2-seater with cut-out wing-roots, probably the model taken up by the military for school purposes.

    (Span: 9.5 m; length: 6 m; wing area: 14 sqm; empty
    weight: 245 kg; loaded weight: 430 kg; 50 hp Gnôme)

Also: Védrines' and Mestach's 12-rib single seaters with
wheel-skids, trailing tailskids, and forward-raked tip elevators. An 11-rib single-seater with back-braced skids, marked
VIII on the rudder. A pretty 2-seater with fully cowled
Gnôme and balanced elevators.

1913: A small fully-covered single-seater with twin skids,
nearly vertical and braced from behind: Daucourt used one
on 16 April to fly from Buc to Berlin. A 17-rib 2-seater with
no cross-axle: Daucourt flew a passenger in one on 30 October from Paris to Cairo.

Hydroaeroplanes: In 1912 and 1913 the firm built a variety of 3-
float seaplanes, some of which did well in the international meets
of the period. They varied in engine installation, size of crew,
and details of float attachment. Some samples:

*Right: Daucourt in his Morane leaving Paris for Cairo, 30 October 1913.
Note the twin skids, now-traditional Morane rudder shape, and separate trailing elevators. (Author's collection)*

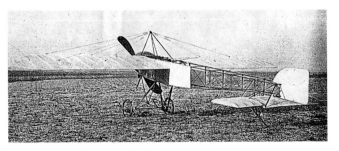

An early Borel, 1910. Note the single tailskid. (Author's collection)

*The Borel Type Militaire entered in the Concours Militaire of 1911. (Author's
collection)*

*Jules Védrines' Borel. Note the twin skids, tip elevators, and taller rudder.
(Courtesy of the Musée de l'Air et de l'Espace/Le Bourget-France)*

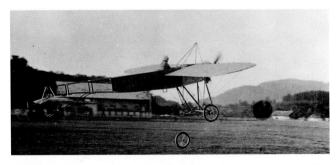

*Taddéoli at a tense moment in take-off at Bern, Switzerland. (Courtesy of the
Musée de l'Air et de l'Espace/Le Bourget-France)*

A 1912 2-seat hydro, the winner at the meet at Tamise. (Courtesy of the Musée de l'Air et de l'Espace/Le Bourget-France)

One of several Borel seaplanes of 1913. Note N-struts for float supports. (Courtesy of the Musée de l'Air et de l'Espace/Le Bourget-France)

1912: a 2-place machine with an 80 hp Gnôme, simple 4-strut float supports, and half-covered fuselage. A similar machine with double diagonal bracing at the feet of the float struts. Another 2-seater with cut-out sections in the leading edge wing-roots, and a low coaming aft of the rear seat; this may be the same as the winner at the Belgian meet at Tamise, painted with the race number 6. A 2-seater fitted with floats in addition to its regular wheels and skids, oyster-shell elevator surfaces, and a remarkably warped aft fuselage.

1913: A 2-seater for the Navy, with N-strut float supports, and a cut-out in the wing leading edge root. Chemet's 2-seater painted No 7 at the Paris-Deauville meet in August, with N-struts for float supports, and the top and bottom cowlings meeting in front in a horizontal line; and Chemet in No 10 (Type Tamise), perhaps the same machine as at Deauville, at Monaco; but he withdrew before the race began.

(Chemet's machine: span: 11.7 m; length: 8.5 m; empty weight: 540 kg; loaded weight: 920 kg; 100 hp Gnôme)

<u>Borel-Ruby</u>: Before the development of machine-gun synchronizers, designers had experimented with several generally unsatisfactory solutions; one was the pusher biplane with forward-

The Borel at Monaco. (Author's collection)

The cockpit of the Torpille looks small for both pilot and gunner/observer. (Author's collection)

The new Borel-Ruby Torpille at the Paris Exposition in 1913. (Courtesy of the Musée de l'Air et de l'Espace/Le Bourget-France)

mounted gun; another, less common and less satisfactory, was the so-called "torpedo" aeroplane with the propeller mounted behind the tail, like the Tatin monoplane. In 1913 Borel built such a monoplane, sometimes known as Ruby-Borel, sometimes simply as Ruby.

It had Borel warping wings, but the rectangular-sectioned fuselage was partly of metal, with a pointed nose and the aft fuselage sharply tapering to the propeller hub. The pilot sat ahead of the wing, with the 70 hp Gnôme inside the fuselage at his back, driving the pusher propeller mounted at the very tip of the rear fuselage through a shaft more than 5 m long, which may have caused problems. The gunner/observer sat in front with the machine-gun mounted on the cowl in front of him – sometimes replaced with a high windshield. Ports for cooling were let into the side of the fuselage aft of the motor. Vertical fins were set above and below the rear fuselage; the elevators trailed back in an arc behind the propeller, and together with the trailing wingtips, gave the machine a faintly bat-like appearance.

The Torpedo met with no success with the Army, nor did other efforts by Borel and Blériot to build monoplanes with forward-firing guns.

(Span: 9 m; length: 7 m; 70 hp Gnôme)

L'Obus (artillery shell): This handsome streamlined monocoque racing monoplane was shown at the 1912 Salon, and held the world's distance record from Vincennes to Biarritz. The fuselage was a wooden structure overlaid with very thin sheet-wood meant only for covering and not for strength. A distinctive feature was the bulbous cowling which surrounded the rotary engine completely down to the propeller hub, leaving only the bottom quadrant open; the formed sections were held together with 4 large flanges. A solid pyramidal structure in front of the pilot carried the top wing bracing; the wings were swept back, as were the fin and rudder. A smaller rudder was set underneath.

Monoplan Type Militaire: In 1913, another early effort to mount a forward-firing machine-gun, using a 2-seat box nacelle and a pusher propeller. The gunner and pilot sat side by side forward of the monoplane wing leading edge, sharing the cockpit space with a large cylindrical fuel tank and a smaller oil tank. A 4-legged pyramid above, and a tripod below, served to stay the wing bracing. The aft fuselage outrigger structure was of triangular section, with the single upper longeron attached through a bearing to the propeller hub. The undercarriage comprised 2 wheels and forward skids, and a pair of small skids set underneath the propeller.

(Span: 11.8 m; length: 7 m; 80 hp Gnôme)

Aeroyacht Type Denhaut I: This handsome biplane flyingboat was entered at Monaco in 1913, painted with the number 9. The upper wing had substantial overhang; outside the center-section, it was separated from the small triangular sesquiplane lower wing by struts at the leading edge only, the rest by wires for flexibility in wing-warping. The horizontal tail was fixed on top of the cut-off fin and rudder.

Aeroyacht Type Denhaut II: The wing arrangement was similar to that of Type I (perhaps the same machine, modified?), but with cut-outs in the small lower wings. The tail was new, with a distinctive long trailing point to the rudder, and the tip floats were of a different shape.

Aeroyacht Type Denhaut III: Clearly a development of Types I and II, this machine featured an even longer trailing rudder tip, longer lower wings, and conventional double-strut bracing – though still with wing-warping. It was powered with a 10-cylinder Anzani and competed in the Paris-Deauville meet in 1913, carrying the number 10.

The Borel Obus. Only the bottom quarter of the cowl is open for cooling. Note the simplified landing gear. (Courtesy of the Musée de l'Air et de l'Espace/Le Bourget-France)

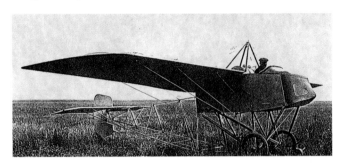

The Borel Monoplan Type Militaire. The top longeron attaches through the propeller hub. (Courtesy of the Musée de l'Air et de l'Espace/Le Bourget-France)

The Borel Aéroyacht Type Denhaut I, this one at Monaco in 1913. (Author's collection)

The Borel Aéroyacht Type Denhaut II. (Author's collection)

The Borel Aéroyacht Type Denhaut III, now a full biplane. (Bill Lewis collection)

(Span: 10 m; length: 7.8 m; empty weight: 300 kg; loaded weight: 580 kg; 100 hp Anzani)

Type Monaco: This interesting flyingboat also entered the meet at Monaco in 1913. It featured a short hull with the 160 hp Gnôme buried inside the hull, driving the 4-bladed pusher propeller through chains; 2 big cylindrical tanks were mounted above the hull under the wing; a streamlined cowl with an oval window on each side was set ahead of the 2 pilots. The aft fuselage, like the military pusher monoplane of the same year, comprised a triangular girder whose top longeron was fitted to the propeller hub and a bearing.

(Span: 15.4 m; length: 7.4 m; hull nacelle length: 4.5 m; empty weight: 750 kg; loaded weight: 1,320 kg; 160 hp Gnôme)

Borgnis et Desbordes de Savignon

After Achille and Paul Borgnis had left Firmin Bousson, they found another partner in Desbordes de Savignon, and built another triplane which may be considered a development of the second Bousson-Borgnis. It was of all-metal construction, built at Gennevilliers, with wings like those on the big Vaniman – they might have been built by Vaniman. There were no rear tail surfaces: steering was done with ailerons set on forward outriggers, and a forward elevator was set low ahead of the 4-wheel undercarriage.

(Span: l4.5 m; wing area: 80 sqm; gross weight: 570 kg; 28 hp 6-cylinder engine)

Modified, with new undercarriage and elevator moved to the rear, it was driven to Yffiniac on the northern coast of Brittany, where it flew and made a "memorable crash." Repaired, at the end of 1910 it was destroyed in a collision.

The Borel Type Monaco was basically a monoplane, like the 2 first Aéroyachts. The owners must have planned immensely long trips to use those fuel tanks. (Courtesy of the Musée de l'Air et de l'Espace/Le Bourget-France)

The first version of the Borgnis et Desbordes de Savignon; this picture was taken on 12 March 1909. (Courtesy of the Musée de l'Air et de l'Espace/Le Bourget-France)

Bothy

Léopold Bothy had worked in bicycles, and came to be interested in heavier-than-air machines. He got the Paris firm of Régy Frères to build his little monoplane patterned on the Demoiselle. The tail worked on a universal joint, but with an extra tailplane fitted on top of the outrigger, which unlike the Demoiselle's was made of 2 parallel booms strengthened with wires and a small mast. Bothy attempted flights at

Issy on 9 January 1910, and managed a hop. On 22 September he got off briefly, and then crashed, wrecking his aeroplane.

(Span: 7.9 m; length: 7.8 m; wing area: 20 sqm; gross weight less pilot: 260 kg; 30-35 hp V2 Anzani)

Boucheron

In 1910 *L'Aéronaute* printed a drawing and accompanying description of a 2-seat biplane with variable-size wings and a waterproof diamond-section fuselage for possible accidental water landings. 2 pusher propellers were mounted on outriggers aft of the wings, which were curved like a gull's. A small biplane elevator cell was set, as on the Voisin, on a curved extension of the fuselage. It is not clear exactly how the variable sized wing arrangement worked – or if in fact the machine was ever built.

(Span: 10.3 m; length: 14.6 m; 44 hp engine)

Boullay

This float monoplane was built by Mieusset, a noted automobile builder in Lyon, and tested on the Saône River on 24 Jan 1913, at which time the propeller was broken. It was powered by a 35 hp Boullay-Monin.

Bourcart

In 1908 JJ Bourcart from Colmar, a town then in Germany, built an unsuccessful ornithopter with tandem monoplane wings. 2 men stood up in tandem in a vertical frame beneath 2 pairs of horizontal flapping wings which resembled twin maple seeds. A Bracke, in his *Monographies d'Aviation*, reports the thing flew 200 m at an altitude of 1.5 m; he points out the need for practice for 5-6 weeks to learn how to operate it!

(Wing area: 16 sqm)

Bourdariat

In 1908 Edouard Bourdariat began at Tours the construction of a large machine which was not completed until 1910. The design seems to have changed along the way, and could have been labeled at different stages a monoplane, biplane, or triplane. The planned forward wing became a large forward elevator with swept-back leading edges and large dihedral, and a biplane cell was mounted amidships above the undercarriage. At the end of the long fuselage girder was set a rectangular tailplane, also with considerable dihedral, and a large rectangular rudder above and below. 2 wheels with skids carried the middle of the fuselage, and a third wheel supported the tail. A 4-cylinder inline engine drove 2 pusher propellers.

(Span: (forward wing) 9.5 m; (biplane pair) 7.5 m; (rear) 6.5 m; length: 10.5 m)

Bourgoin et Kessels

Bourgoin and Kessels' big machine, Aérobus, had been registered for the Concours Militaire in 1911, but it did not appear until July 1912,

The little Bothy monoplane of 1910. (Author's collection)

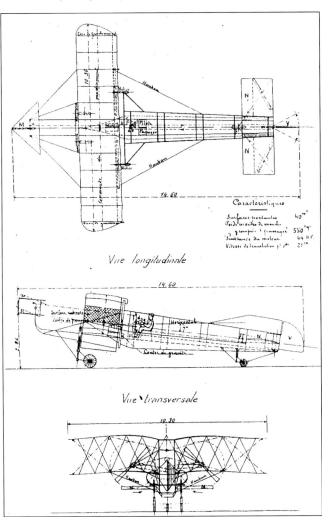

A contemporary drawing of the strange Boucheron biplane with variable-area wings. (Author's collection)

when it was introduced at the Vel d'Hiv, the famous Vélodrome d'Hiver, the winter cycling stadium in Paris. It was a huge uncompleted monoplane designed to carry 12 passengers in a boat-shaped hull slung between the great wing and the 4-wheel undercarriage. 2 engines sat on the rear axle driving 2-3.5-meter diameter tractor propellers through long diagonal shafts; a large fin and rudder hung at the rear between 2 shaft-controlled elevators.

(Span: 14 m; length: between 12 and 16 m; length of hull: 5.3 m; wing area: between 60 and 100 sqm; empty weight: 900 kg; gross weight: 2200-2600 kg; 2-125 hp (perhaps 200 hp) Dansette-Gillets)

In 1913 Bourgoin designed what he called a "parachute monoplane." The description, however, fitted the strange Lataste: horizontal and vertical propellers, a circular wing with variable angle of attack, 4 wheels and rudder. It is known the Lataste was built, but no other connection has been found so far between it and the Bourgoin.

Bourhis

A machine of this name went into a spin and crashed at the 1914 Concours de Sécurité.

Bourniquet

In 1909 at the age of 18 Robert Bourniquet built a Chanute-type glider; if he had not broken his leg during a test on the Buttes Chaumont, east of Paris, he would have remained completely unknown, like so many glider builders of the period.

Bousson-Borgnis

In 1901 Firmin Bousson built his first machine, described as a dirigible equipped with flapping wings. He was assisted – presumably unsuccessfully – by Achille and Paul Borgnis, and the 3 stayed together building kites and models; on 19 August 1908 they put out another complicated machine, the Auto-Aviateur. A tail structure of 4 uprights supported a high short upper wing with a longer lower wing close beneath it and shorter third wing below that; the floor of the tower held the pilot and the 34 hp Buchet driving a large 4-blade pusher propeller. A pair of long curved outriggers supported a pair of forward horizontal surfaces in tandem, the front single one a canard, the rear divided pair acting as a control surface; a large vertical surface between the outriggers served as fin. The machine was modified at least once; it may have been the second canard built after Santos-Dumont's.

In 1909 Bousson alone built a large triplane glider which succeeded in remaining for "one hour in the air, 200 meters high." The pilot sat low in an uncovered box frame fuselage fitted with a biplane tailplane with 2 rudders set between; control was through a large rectangular forward elevator.

Boutard

This attractive single-seater Taube-type may not even be French: a handsome three-view drawing from a German magazine is titled M-B Boutard.

(Span: 10.8 m; length: 8 m; what appears to be a Gnôme)

Boutaric

From an earlier model, Boutaric commissioned the firm of Labaudie et Puthet to build a tandem biplane with 2 propellers 2.5 meters in diameter driven with a double chain-drive at 600 rpm. The rear quarter of each wing was flexible, and ailerons were set ahead of the lead-

The first Bourgoin et Kessels design, perhaps as nearly complete as it ever got. (Author's collection)

The big Bousson-Borgnis canard, the Auto-Aviateur of 1908. (Peter M Bowers collection)

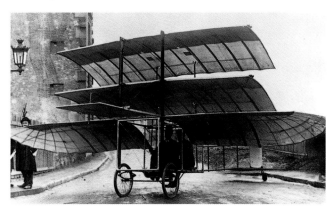

The Bousson-Borgnis firm followed the Auto-Aviateur with this big triplane glider in 1909; he claimed to have flown in it for an hour. (Courtesy of the Musée de l'Air et de l'Espace/Le Bourget-France)

The tiny-span Boutaric tandem biplane. The 2 forward surfaces were separately controllable as ailerons; perhaps they could be worked together to serve as forward elevators as well. (Courtesy of the Musée de l'Air et de l'Espace/Le Bourget-France)

ing edge. It was reported in 1909 variously to have flown on its first attempt, and never to have flown at all.

(Span: 6 m; length: 10 m; wing area: 36 sqm; 25 hp Anzani)

Boyenval et Jouhan

In 1904 Boyenval and Jouhan built a large sesquiplane glider at Dieppe; it was much photographed during its tests. The larger lower wing had significant dihedral; the shorter top wing had none. The pilot hung below the wings, which had a combined area of about 20 sqm.

De Brageas

Very little is known about de Brageas' first aircraft: it was developed by de Brageas, Bastier, and Sotinel in 1911 at Juvisy, and flown by Merle in October 1911. In March 1912 a second de Brageas monoplane, with a Darracq engine, appeared, and later in the year 8 monoplanes were reported sold to the Russian Army. By the end of the year 3 types were being described. The first 2 were a school machine and a touring machine; the third was larger, perhaps a 2-seater and probably of the same general appearance: rectangular wing with thick reflex airfoil, rectangular tailplane and 2 large elevators. The Nieuport-style undercarriage had the central spring leaf replaced by a flexible axle linked by streamlined struts to 2 spiral springs inside the fuselage. Below the pyramidal mast was a large windscreen which would seem to have largely obscured the pilot's view forward.

8 de Brageas monoplanes served in the Russian air service, fitted with 24 hp Darracq, 35 or 45 hp Anzani engines, and "Farman-like" undercarriages and clipped wings for use as penguin ground-trainers.

(School and touring machines: span: 8.88 m; wing area: 14 sqm; empty weight (with 30 hp Anzani): 220 kg; (with 40 hp Anzani): 245 kg)

(Third type: span: 11 m; length: 6 m; wing area: 18 sqm; empty weight: 320 kg; speed: c 80 kmh; 40 hp 6-cylinder Anzani, or 30 hp Anzani)

In 1913 de Brageas built another machine at Juvisy. It was a 2-seat pusher monoplane with a Canton-Unné engine, 2 tall radiators standing up on each side aft of the pilots, who sat side by side in a flattened streamlined nacelle. The tail was supported on an awkwardly shaped triangular-section framework.

Brazier

A photograph shows a tandem-high-wing seaplane glider set on 2 wide pontoons fore and aft; the pilot sat low under the single – (or twin?) boom fuselage, with flat vertical surfaces in front of him and behind.

Breguet

In 1906 Louis Breguet, his brother Jacques, and Professor Charles Richet designed and built a test model of a gyroplane, a sort of helicopter with wings. It was tested on an aerodynamic balance of their

A rare view of the underside of an early aeroplane: this de Brageas is clearly repairable. Note the reflex airfoil on both wing and stabilizer. (Courtesy of Harry Woodman)

The Brazier seaplane glider seemingly under tow. (Courtesy of the Musée de l'Air et de l'Espace/Le Bourget-France)

own design; the model was given by Louis Breguet in 1922 to the Conservatoire des Arts et des Métiers. It was followed by 2 full-scale machines.

Gyroplane Breguet-Richet No 1: The full-scale version was built and tested in 1907. It consisted of a 4-legged structure with a 4-bladed biplane set of rotors at the end of each arm. Wings were to be fitted, but did not in fact appear. Louis Breguet claimed that it lifted briefly, carrying its pilot. But Jean Boulet, helicopter historian, notes in his book *L'Histoire de l'Hélicoptère Racontée par ses Pionniers 1907-1956* that Breguet's assistants in these experiments later claimed that during the supposed flight they were in fact pushing upward on the helicopter framework to hold it up, rather than pulling it to hold it back, and concludes it probably did not take off at all.

(Rotor diameter: 8 m; total weight: 580 kg; 42 hp Antoinette)

Gyroplane Breguet-Richet No 2: In 1908 the firm built No 2, a monoplane with a pair of 4-bladed biplane rotors (the same rotors as in No 1?) below each wingtip. A long outrigger strut on each side below the lower wings had a wheel at each outer end,

A half-view of the Breguet-Richet Gyroplane No 1. If you look carefully you can make out the 4 arms emanating from the center, at right in photo, each arm with a 4-bladed rotor, each blade having 2 lifting surfaces. (Author's collection)

The Breguet-Richet Gyroplane No 2. This machine is also difficult to puzzle out from the photographs. It did not fly, either. (Author's collection)

and carried the lower ends of the long rotor axles; another supported the drive wheels at the center of each rotor. The wing had a single spar only, and was apparently arranged to have variable incidence. An awkward angular fuselage rested awkwardly on 4 wheels with a 5th to the rear, and a tall awkward rudder rose at the tail end with a long awkward tailplane beneath it. The pilot sat out in the open in front. A modification had a long covered nose extension to the fuselage resting on a tricycle undercarriage, and a second wing set between the 2 outriggers on each side. In this one both wings could pivot on their single spars. The machine never got off the ground and was abandoned.

(Rotor diameter: 8 m)

Gyroplane Breguet-Richet No 2bis: This version was built in 1908/1909, and was destroyed in its hangar during a storm before it could be tested. It was a handsome big biplane canard, with the front pair of wings of shorter span than the rear; both pairs featured the single spars and single wide struts of the No 2. On each side, between the inboard wing struts of both the front pair and the rear pair of wings, was fitted a pair of long crossed struts. At the center of each long X was the hub of a 4-paddle-bladed rotor, arranged to tilt back and forth, evidently for control and propulsion. The engine was set on the top of the fuselage amidships. The machine had the same tricycle undercarriage of the No 2, with the addition of wingtip wheels on the aft pair of wings.

Breguet-Richet No 3: Built in 1909, this was the firm's first aeroplane, and it was soon renamed Breguet No 1. It flew, and had an accident at Douai. It was a biplane with a big biplane tail cell, all surfaces with the same single spar and wide struts of the later Gyroplanes. The fuselage consisted only of a big open rectangular box like a box-kite with a small covered shoe-box for the pilot. The undercarriage consisted of a skid structure on each side, like the Wrights', with a single wheel underneath in the middle. Small wheels protected the lower wingtips; 2 rudders were set between the tailplanes. The big tractor propeller had 3 paddle blades.

(Span: 13 m; length: 10 m; empty weight: 500 kg; 50 hp Renault)

Modified with a lengthened top tailplane, twin wheels underneath, and a different wingtip wheel arrangement and shortened skids, the machine was painted with the race number 19 and flew and crashed at Reims.

Breguet No 2 (sometimes named No 4): This was rebuilt from No 1, above; it flew well. Simplified, it had a single rudder between the 2 tailplanes, and a simple 2-wheel undercarriage with a raised skid arrangement. The fuselage was slender and tapered back to the lower tailplane, while a V-outrigger supported the

The Gyroplane No 2bis, simplified somewhat from No 2. (Courtesy of the Musée de l'Air et de l'Espace/Le Bourget-France)

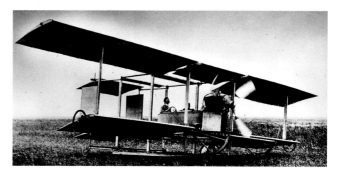

The Breguet-Richet No 3, renamed Breguet No 1. This one flew. (Author's collection)

73

upper, with a distinctive pair of vertical surfaces in the middle of each. The pilot sat aft, on top of the fuselage, behind 2 wide center-section struts. An enormous distinctive covered tailwheel brought up the tail. Rebuilt for the May 1910 meeting at Rouen, it now had a very slender "one-boom" fuselage with a cruciform tail attached with a universal joint. Most of the smaller vertical surfaces were removed.

(Span: 12.5 m; length: 8.5 m; wing area: 36 sqm; weight: 500 kg; 50 hp Renault)

<u>Breguet No 3</u>: The first really modern aircraft from the firm, it flew in April 1910 from Douai to Arras and back, but crashed some days after, and was totally destroyed. It had the tricycle oleo undercarriage and steel tube construction which appeared often on subsequent models. Small winglets were fitted to each side of the nose – "diffuseurs" – to balance the effect of torque; the single-bay wing-warping wings had a single wide strut between each pair. Odd 6-sided surfaces were attached to the tops of all 4 struts; a similar pair was attached between the undercarriage legs, and a wide fairing was attached to the nosewheel leg. The fuselage was long and boxy and fully covered; a high angular rudder was attached at the aft end. Between October 1910 and March 1911, paired undercarriage wheels appeared only on Gnôme-powered Breguets.

(Span: 12.5 m; length: 8.5 m; wing area: 36 sqm; weight: 500 kg; Gnôme)

After this, the numbering system went in 2 directions. Each aircraft was given a number corresponding to its place in the line since Aeroplane No 1. And each aircraft was given an additional designation, depending on the type of engine-bearer (for Gnôme, Canton-Unné, etc) and the particular Gnôme or Canton-Unné installed. Jean Devaux' table outlines the system:

Engine	Coding	Notes
Gnôme 50 hp	G, then G.1	
Gnôme 70 hp	G.2	
Gnôme 80 hp	G.2bis	
Gnôme 100 hp 9 cyl	G.2bis	
Gnôme 100 hp 14 cyl	G.3	
Gnôme 140 or 160 hp	G.4	
REP 50/60 hp	R.1	
REP 7- hp	R.2	
Renault 50/60 hp	L.1	for Louis Renault
Renault 70 hp	L.2	
Renault 100 hp	L.3?	no written proof
Chenu 40 hp	C.1	
Chenu 80 hp	C.2	
Canton-Unné 7 cyl	U.1	for Unné
Canton-Unné 9 cyl	U.2	
Dansette 100 hp	D.2	
Le Rhône 80	O.1	

A striking photograph of the Breguet No 2 in flight. The machine was sometimes named No 4. Note the elaborate undercarriage, and general configuration of Breguets for some time. (Courtesy of the Musée de l'Air et de l'Espace/ Le Bourget-France)

The 1910 Breguet No 3. Note the "diffuseurs." (Author's collection)

Sample designation:

Type U.2 No 45: U: engine mounting for a Canton-Unné
2: the 9-cylinder Canton-Unné
45: the 45th Breguet since No 1

The 149 different Breguet aircraft built before WWI can be identified with some 17 different engine designations and 149 individual numbers. A few examples follow:

<u>Type L.1 No 3</u>: L stands for <u>L</u>ouis Renault and the 1 for the 50/ 60 hp engine. This was a military design appearing in the Concours Militaire of 1911, which called for 3 seats: Breguet conceived of an officer/observer/gunner, a pilot/gunner, and a pilot mechanic facing aft to help the other pilot when he was shooting – hence the control column with wheels front and back! It was a neat single-bay single-spar biplane with long overhang, tricycle landing gear with a central skid and leggings on the forward strut. For economy, the 2 lower wings were interchangeable, the end struts attached at the very tip ribs.

<u>Type U.2 No 45</u>: Another military machine showing in the same Concours. A heavier aircraft than L.1 No 3, with an interwing

strut between the earlier 2, retaining the original wiring. 2 tall radiators stood up under the center-section; the nosewheel was now doubled.

Type U.2 No 87: The first Breguet seaplane appeared in 1912, similar to U.2 No 45, except that the lower wings had been replaced with panels identical to the upper wings; the 2-bay cell now had proper 2-bay bracing. The arrangement was soon abandoned. After this machine, seaplanes received the additional prefix H for Hydroaéroplane, at first with a number to indicate the number of floats. This latter was soon abandoned.

 (Span: 14 m; length: 11 m; wing area: 40 sqm; weight: 700 kg; 9-cylinder Canton-Unné)

Type G.3 (series number unknown): This 100 hp Gnôme single-bay biplane of 1912 was flown by the pilot Moineau, and featured the earlier uneven-span wings and non-symmetrical lower panels.

Type A.U.2 (number unknown): The A here stood for Aerohydroplane, and was abandoned after this remarkable and unsuccessful flyingboat named La Marseillaise. A French Navy officer had promoted the design for the use of the Navy in 1912-1913; a single machine was built and never flew. It was a tandem monoplane with the Canton-Unné amidships, driving a tractor propeller out on struts through a long drive-shaft. A typical Breguet cruciform tail brought up the rear of the hull, on which was built an almost automobile-style body with a rectangular radiator in front. The aeroplane had big sponsons amidships, and additional tip floats under the rearmost wing.

 (Span: 30 m; length: 7.5 m; weight: 1050 kg; 9-cylinder 100-120 hp Canton-Unné)

Type U.2 No 102: This 3-seater 2-bay single-spar biplane appeared in 1913. The 4-wheel landing gear was supported under the rear cockpit by a tall skid, keeping the cruciform tail off the ground. The fuselage was no longer a single boom aft, but consisted of 4 steel tube longerons supporting a structure faired out with stringers.

Type U.2 No 138: Similar to No 102, this new 1914 machine was a 2-bay 2-spar biplane, with 2 separate cut-out cockpits. The wing cell design was named "semi-rigide," and the wings still warped.

Type G.4 No 147: This handsome 2-bay 2-spar seaplane -it also flew as a landplane – competed in the 1914 meet at Monaco, its rudder painted with the number 21. It had a central float, 2 side floats and a tail float. Ailerons were fitted in all 4 wing panels.

In 1912 the Breguet Aeroplane Limited firm was established in England and built some 7 different designs, more or less similar to the

Breguet U-2; this may be the No 45 described in the text. (Courtesy of the Musée de l'Air et de l'Espace/Le Bourget-France)

A Breguet U-2 hydro, perhaps No 87. (Bill Lewis collection)

Above and below: Two views of the one-off and unsuccessful Breguet A.U.2 La Marseillaise. (Courtesy of the Musée de l'Air et de l'Espace/Le Bourget-France)

Breguet G-4, No 147, hydro. There is clearly no relation between the G-3 (in text) and the G-4, except for the engine. (Courtesy of the Musée de l'Air et de l'Espace/Le Bourget-France)

1912-1913 French Breguets, but differing slightly in such items as engine mounts and fuselage coverings.

Just before the outbreak of the War, Breguet had started 2 new aircraft and projected a third. The A-G.4 was a 160 Gnôme tractor; the A-U.3 was a 200 hp Canton-Unné tractor, and B-U.3 was a 200 hp Canton-Unné pusher (the A and B now used to distinguish similarly-powered machines only.)

Breton

This Demoiselle copy appeared at Juvisy in 1910. Breton may have been the name of the engine.

Du Breuil

The Marquis Picat du Breuil built headlamps for automobiles, using a constant-speed dynamo running on a gas made from oil; at least one of his dynamos was named La Patineuse (the skater); the name sometimes is sometimes erroneously applied to one of his aeroplanes.

He designed or sponsored 3, all built by Pouvarel, all odd and little publicized; all offered "an outstanding natural stability." The first was shown first at the 1911 Salon. It featured a semicircular wing formed with a steel tube leading edge filled with reed, the rest of the surface being formed of a loose piece of fabric, the whole thing set at an impressive angle of attack on a steel tube frame above the fuselage. The front of the 2-seated fuselage was streamlined like the front of a racing car, with the engine mounted low and driving a high-set tractor propeller through belts and a shaft. The radiator was made of tubes laid flat on the cowl.

The covered triangular-section rear fuselage was arranged to move fore and aft; a "lifting tailplane" was set at a large negative angle, and there was a "double-warping rudder." It rested on 2 main wheels, and its way through the night was lit with 2 large du Breuil headlamps. It was sent in 1912 to Juvisy, where a test-pilot named Koenig damaged it in February.

The Picat-du Breuil at the 1911 Paris Salon. Note the radiator tubing on the cowl, and the headlamps. (Courtesy of the Musée de l'Air et de l'Espace/Le Bourget-France)

A later du Breuil monoplane, with the same sagging fabric for wings. (Courtesy of the Musée de l'Air et de l'Espace/Le Bourget-France)

(Span: 9 m; length: 12 m; wing area: c 50 sqm; 70 hp Labor-Picker)

One, perhaps 2, other du Breuil monoplanes appear in contemporary photographs. A wing similar to that of his first machine was now set at the mid-position, with the same high incidence, the tips braced to the fuselage with struts. The fuselage was a box, covered in one version, uncovered in the other, with a small semicircular rudder above the rear end, a small rectangular elevator at the very rear, and a fixed – maybe warping – tailplane ahead of the elevator, again with the same high negative angle of his first machine. A double set of inverted V struts made up the pylon.

Briel

In 1909 a man named Briel was building an aeroplane at Lyons.

Bridoulot

In 1909 Bridoulot built a monoplane glider with a monoplane elevator and tested it near Bourg-la Reine and Fresnes, suburbs south of Paris.

(Span: 3.2 m; length: 2.4 m)

He was reported also to be working on an aircraft to be powered by an engine of his own design; it may not have been built.

(Span: 10 m; length: 7.8 m)

Brissard

This big monoplane being built by LA Brissard at Givat in northern France was intended by the designer to fly to the North Pole, but it had not been completed by 1 May 1914. The fuselage was nearly completely enclosed for the crew and an engine, which drove 2 propellers set in 2 large open tunnels attached to the fuselage sides. A completed model showed broad curved wings and a small curved tailplane and rudder set aft. The whole structure was gracefully faired together.

Brissaud

A Brissaud biplane from Nice was registered at the Monaco airshow of 1909; the design was patented, but it may not have been actually built.

Bronislawski

The so-called Bronislawski biplanes were in fact Henry Farmans modified with Boleslav Bronislawski's control mechanism. This consisted of small planes fitted between biplane wings and pivoting outwards; different shapes were tested, and the device was also advertised for monoplanes. The aim was to replace ailerons or wing-warping with the same efficiency but without the yaw, common to most early machines.

BRT

We do not know the names of the builders whose initials mark this odd biplane built and tested at Bethény before 1909. The uncovered rectangular-section fuselage carried a tractor engine and propeller at the front with the pilot seated aft of the lower wing trailing edge. The lower wing was mounted forward under the nose, and the upper wing very close above and behind it. A large cruciform tail unit was mounted on outriggers to the rear, supported on a pair of large semicircular

The big Brissard machine probably did not make it to the North Pole – it may not have been finished – but it was wonderful all the same. (Courtesy of the Musée de l'Air et de l'Espace/Le Bourget-France)

Bronislawski's Farman modified to take his experimental controls. (Author's collection)

The BRT biplane with its extremely close-spaced wings. (Courtesy of the Musée de l'Air et de l'Espace/Le Bourget-France)

hoops. Ailerons were fitted to the upper wing. The 2-wheeled undercarriage was high and fitted with 2 high skids curved forward.

Brulé-Girardot

In 1904 Girardot ordered a Wright-type glider built by d'Argent; perhaps he flew it, but he began to build automobiles in 1906 under the name first of GEM (Société Générale d'Automobiles Electro-Mécaniques); then, until 1910, under the name of CGV (Charron, Girardot, et Voigt).

A Brulé-Girardot biplane crashed during November 1911 at Issy; the pilot was named Roberts. The aircraft may have been a separate design, or a Voisin or other production machine given the names of its owners. A Brulé, perhaps the same one, was later an associate of Souchet.

A Brulé biplane appeared in *L'Aéronautique* for 1 March 1912, perhaps the same as the one described above. It had equal-span rectangular wings, an awkward uncovered rectangular-section fuselage, a large rectangular tailplane, and a rectangular rudder; a high under-carriage sported 2 pairs of wheels and skids. Large rectangular elevators hung from the top wing. It was reported to have flown well.

(Span: and length: 8 m; wing area: 25 sqm; empty weight: 250 kg; 30 hp Anzani)

Brunet

There is a photograph of a tractor machine of this name, dated 1910. The fuselage is a long uncovered box girder set between 2 pairs of rectangular wings, one at the very front and one at the very tail. A small oval rudder brings up the rear, with the pilot sitting just in front of it. A very long control rod connects him with the engine and its tractor propeller.

Bruyère et Sarazin

Both men started the construction of this monoplane in 1909; perhaps they finished it.

(Span: 12 m; 35 hp REP motor was planned for it)

Buchet

A helicopter of this name was reported built between 1906 and 1908.

Bueno et Demaurex

Bueno and Demaurex designed a biplane for Scott, a Swiss; it was built by Avia in July 1910, a big 12-meter span biplane with a wide rectangular-frame fuselage. A single tailplane lay across the top of the rear fuselage, with separate elevators on either side below it, and a small rectangular rudder perched at the tail end. The pilot sat at the very front, in front of the leading edge of the lower wing and the upper one directly above him. A 2-piece forward elevator was mounted on twin outriggers, and the 50 hp engine drove 2 pusher propellers through chains.

A model of another Bueno and Demaurex design appeared in a Bonnet-Labranche catalog, this one an odd monoplane with a second wing set immediately behind and slightly below the main wing, with a large independent aileron surface set on each side behind and below the second wing.. The fuselage was an untapered uncovered box, still with 2 pusher propellers on outriggers.

Bulot

Walther Bulot was born in Tournai, in Belgium, on 6 January 1874; he built at least 2 different designs.

1908-1909: His first aeroplane, which never flew, was shown at the air meet at Tournai in September 1909, a heavily staggered triplane with wings arched like a bird's, and a horizontal surface at the rear. A tall vertical surface stood in front of the tractor propeller; the fuselage was a high uncovered boxy structure set on 4 wheels. The pilot sat under the middle wing. In November 1909 it was entered in the Antwerp air meet, this time with only the first 2 of its triplane set of wings, a more conventional box

The Brulé biplane as it appeared in L'Aéronautique in 1912. (Author's collection)

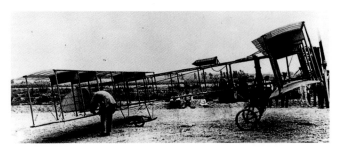

Another tandem biplane, the 1910 Brunet. The pilot's seat is just forward of the tail. (Courtesy of the Musée de l'Air et de l'Espace/Le Bourget-France)

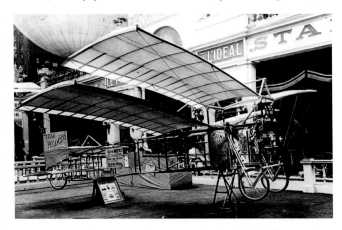

Walther Bulot's 1911 biplane La Mouette at the Paris Salon. The inscription on the rudder advertises Pegamoid, a contemporary covering material. (Courtesy of the Musée de l'Air et de l'Espace/Le Bourget-France)

fuselage which carried at least at one time the number 9 on the forward covered section. The rudder was moved to the rear, and the landing gear simplified to 2 wheels. In 1911 he had a biplane named La Mouette (the seagull), which he converted to a mono-plane in the same year. Perhaps La Mouette was the same aircraft as the biplane previous.

1911: Another Bulot flown at Tournai, this was a small mono-plane similar to the Demoiselle, with rectangular openwork fuselage, oyster-shell tip ailerons, and a conventional set of tail surfaces. 2 wheels were set on each side of the lower longeron at the pilot's seat.

(Wing area: 20 sqm; loaded weight, less pilot: 203 kg; 35 hp motor; it could reportedly take a 50 hp motor and carry 3 people)

Bunzli

There was a glider reported with this name.

C

Caille

Built at St Erme, a village in northern France, this probably unsuccessful machine was registered for the 1911 Concours Militaire, but was not finished before 1912. A 12 hp Chateau engine drove an 8-bladed propeller, soon replaced by a larger 2-bladed one.

Calvignac

The drawings of this monoplane appeared in the 15 September 1913 issue of *L'Aérophile*, showing a 2-seater with pilot and passenger sitting in tandem in front of the engine, which drove a propeller mounted on a ring around the fuselage. It may never have been built; the design is similar to that of the Bristol monoplane model tested by Eiffel in his wind tunnel.

Canton et Unné

Before they joined Emile Salmson, Canton and Unné designed and built their famous water-cooled radial engine, and 3 aeroplanes as well, all of the push-pull design. Their first machine was a triplane in tandem; to solve the problem of the gyroscopic effects of a single propeller, they used 2 counter-rotating propellers; but in order to avoid the dramatic possibilities of failure when the 2 propellers turned in the same plane, they mounted theirs at either end of the long rectangular fuselage. Their new 5-cylinder water-cooled radial was mounted flat inside the fuselage to drive 2 long shafts through a counter-gear. The machine was tested in 1909.

In 1910 Canton and Unné succeeded in actually flying a second machine, this one a monoplane with a cut-off fuselage, tail booms, and tricycle gear. The central section of the wing was built integral

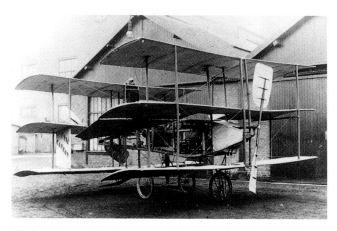

The first Canton et Unné aeroplane, their 1910 push-pull triplane. Note the flat-mounted engine amidships. (Courtesy of the Musée de l'Air et de l'Espace/ Le Bourget-France)

with the wooden fuselage, the 2 outer panels warping for control. Their engine (some accounts report the same one used previously) was mounted as before, the pilot seated behind it. Pedals operated the rudder, a lever at the left for wing-warping, and another at the right for the elevator. This extraordinary machine was tested as early as mid-January 1910; Canton flew it on 14 March, and other pilots took turns afterwards. On 8 June after a hard landing by Lhomme, the aeroplane caught fire.

(Span: 10.5 m; length: 8 m; wing area: 28 sqm; empty weight: 420 kg; 7-cylinder 90 hp Canton-Unné)

A third push-pull was similar to the second, but with a streamlined fuselage, and the propeller aft of the tail unit.

Capon

Nothing more is known about this small monoplane which flew in March and May 1911 at Issy.

Carlier

At least one design bore René Carlier's name, a wing-warping biplane which flew with the curious "birotatif" Ligez engine in the sum-

The second Canton et Unné push-pull, of 1910. (Courtesy of the Musée de l'Air et de l'Espace/Le Bourget-France)

mer of 1911. This 30 hp 3-cylinder radial was geared to turn in the opposite direction from its propeller.

(Span: 8 m; length: 7 m; wing area: 25 sqm; 30 hp Ligez bi-rotatif)

Carton-Lachambre

This firm remained one of the most famous balloon-builders in Europe before World War I, but they also built heavier-than-air machines: numerous Saconney kites for civil and military use; and some aeroplanes, at least a small biplane and a monoplane, designed by other people under the firm's name.

Castagne et Cambageon

A 2-seat biplane, built at Montpellier in 1911, crashed there on its first test in early 1912.

Casteljou

A builder or owner in 1908?

Cathelin

This 1909 Farman copy may not have been completed.

Caudron

Born in 1884, René Caudron grew up on a farm with his 2-year-older brother. Neither boy was interested in horses or in farming, but rather in the agricultural machinery of the farms around, and in bicycles and motorcycles. In 1908, out of the army and back on the farm, René heard of the Wrights, and he and his brother Gaston began in 1908 a big flying machine: the first Caudron was this 2-seat biplane finished in April 1909, designed for 2 small engines – one driving 2 tractor and the other 2 pusher propellers; but the engines did not arrive, and the project was given up and the airframe finished as a glider. Gaston mounted their horse Luciole and towed René in the glider some 10-15 m into the air.

(Wing area: 40 sqm; 2-30 hp Farcot engines)

Type A, No 1: The whole machine was redesigned smaller and lighter. A simple Anzani was now set on the lower wing beside the pilot, driving the pusher propeller through a chain. Wing-warping without ailerons, it flew, and was wrecked on its 9th flight. It was then rebuilt and modified, with the engine driving the pusher propeller directly, without chains. The tail booms ran back along the ground to a large tailplane and 2 small square rudders on top. It ran on 2 wheels fitted under the lower wing between the long forward skids.

(Span: 8 m; length: 8 m; wing area: 22 sqm; weight: 250 kg; speed: 98 kmh; 25 hp Anzani)

Type A, No 2: The 25 hp Anzani was now mounted on short struts above the lower wing in front of the pilot, driving the tractor propeller directly, without chains. Interplane ailerons were

The redesigned Caudron glider, Type A, No 1. This is the first version, with the propeller chain-driven. (Courtesy of the Musée de l'Air et de l'Espace/Le Bourget-France)

The Caudron Type A, No 2, with tractor propeller driven directly. In the background: perhaps No 1 modified? Note curved wingtips. (Author's collection)

fitted. The modifications were made in May 1910, and the overall configuration set the shape of the many later and more successful Caudron designs of World War I. Variations included raising the engine almost to the level of the top wing, squared-off wingtips or curved ones. At least Nos 3 and 4 were also Type A. Type Abis – perhaps including Nos 5-8 – was larger, with a 5-cylinder Anzani, and carried 1-2 people.

The Caudron firm became briefly associated with the firm SAFA (Société Anonyme Français d'Aviation), and the following designs were built under that name, partly sold to the school operated by CINA (Compagnie Internationale de Navigation Aérienne):

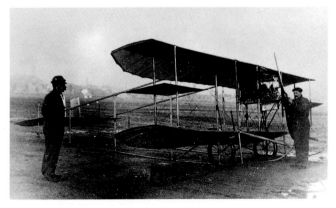
One of the last of the Caudron Type A series, perhaps No 6. (Courtesy of the Musée de l'Air et de l'Espace/Le Bourget-France)

<u>Type B</u>: a 2-seat version of Type Abis, it was Caudron No 9, and served for a long time.

In 1911 Caudron became independent again, and the subsequent catalog describes Type A and also another Type B, a 2-3 seater touring biplane which appeared in January 1911; it was No 9. By the end of 1911 21 Caudrons had been built, including some new types, all with equal-span wings; No 21 was a monoplane:

<u>Type N</u>: Caudron's first monoplane, designed for speed, flew first in December 1911. It featured steel-tube wing spars, wing-warping, a V-leg undercarriage, and a small rectangular rudder set on top of the tailpost.

(Span: 8.7 m; length: 6 m; wing area: 11 sqm; empty weight: 225 kg; speed: 120 kmh; 50 hp Gnôme; No 21 used a Y Anzani)

In the 1912 Salon catalog some other names appear:

<u>Type C and Type D</u>: 2 of each were built for the French army in 1911.

(45 hp Anzani or 50 hp Gnôme; Type D used the 35/45 hp Anzani and was slightly smaller)

<u>Type E</u>: A 2-seater for the Army – again, 2 built – perhaps more, for export.

(Wing area: 28 sqm; 70 hp Gnôme)

<u>Type Monaco</u>: This pusher seaplane with the race number 7 featured 3 big flat-bottomed Fabre floats fitted in front of the wheels, an Anzani engine; the pilot on a forward outrigger.

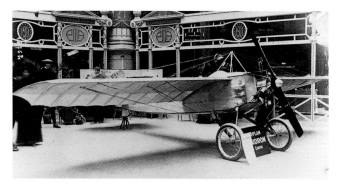

The little Anzani-powered Type N of 1911; the one pictured is No 21. (Courtesy of the Musée de l'Air et de l'Espace/Le Bourget-France)

<u>Type H</u>: This was a 2-seater pusher seaplane and landplane – not the Monaco pusher.

(Wing area: 35 sqm; weight: 380 kg; 60 hp Anzani)

<u>Type M</u>: A single-seater monoplane, fitted with a Gnôme – it appeared after Type N.

<u>Special Type</u>: A big 5-place design: unlike most of the other Caudron designs it featured a full-length covered fuselage, with

Caudron Type M of 1912, powered with a Gnôme. (Courtesy of the Musée de l'Air et de l'Espace/Le Bourget-France)

The Caudron Type Monaco of 1912. Note strut arrangement for attaching the floats over the wheeled undercarriage. (Courtesy of the Musée de l'Air et de l'Espace/Le Bourget-France)

a single rudder and Caudron-style wings and tailplane. It could be easily taken apart for transport. It crashed.

(Span: (upper) 15 m; (lower) 11.8 m; length: 7.5 m; wing area: 42 sqm; empty weight: 320 kg; speed, with Gnôme: 90 kmh; 70 hp Anzani or 80 hp Gnôme)

1913 brought a Type D with a larger Anzani, and some new designs:

Type F: A single-seater looper, flown by Chanteloup. The original pair of rectangular rudders was replaced by the raked triangular shapes which characterized the G-3.

Type G: A 2-seater, also with the new triangular rudder shape.

(Wing area: 30 sqm; weight: 350 kg; 80 hp Gnôme, 60 hp Anzani)

Type J: This was a 2-seater tractor, land – and seaplane, able to be carried on shipboard. Some J Types were sold to the RNAS in 1913, but the French Navy J Type was not built till later. 2 were flown from the cruiser La Foudre in 1914. Another, marked 6, flew at Deauville.

Type K: This was the big 2-seat pusher seaplane at Deauville in August 1913, powered by a 200 hp Anzani.

Type L: This was a side-by-side 2-seater seaplane pusher.

Type G 2: This pretty 2-seater appeared in Jan 1914.

(Wing area: 27 sqm; weight: 350 kg; 80 hp Le Rhône)

Type G 3: This most famous of all the early Wartime Caudron types first flew in May 1914.

The Special Type of 1912 (in one of the catalogs, it is listed as Type B Multi-Place). (Courtesy of the Musée de l'Air et de l'Espace/Le Bourget-France)

Chanteloup's single-seater Type F. (Author's collection)

One of the Caudron Gs sold to China, fitted only with wheels. (Author's collection)

One of 2 Type Js aboard La Foudre. This one has a hole in the top wing for the lifting hook. (Author's collection)

Above: Another J, No 6 at Deauville, powered with an Anzani, and displaying twin double rudders. (Author's collection)
Right: The big Type K at Deauville, with the new 200 hp Anzani. Note the elaborate strut arrangements for the tail. (Author's collection)

Caux et Camboulive

"Two young men from Calais" built an aeroplane at La Coquelle early in 1910.

Caye

Maurice Caye's monoplane might have been built from wrecked or damaged aircraft: it resembled the Borel-Morane monoplane. Photographs dated around April 1912 appear in rare private collections with no further information.

Cayol

A monoplane powered by a 50 hp Gnôme was being built – and perhaps designed – by Théodore Cayol at Aubagne, near Marseilles, during the summer of 1912. It was to have been flown by Lhoumeau at Miramas.

Cayre

In 1910 Edmond and Ernest Cayre built a monoplane on the aviation field of la Brague at Antibes, the same field where Fernandez met his death. Their high-wing monoplane resembled Fernandez' biplane with its front elevator and tail controls; it had 2 wheels with long skids, the engine mounted below the wing in front of the pilot driving a pusher propeller mounted on the trailing edge of the high wing. It was reported tested by Marc Pourpe in 1911; perhaps it never even flew.

(Span: 10 m; length: 10.7 m)

Cazalot et Prevot

A machine of this name was reported at Toulouse in 1909.

De Caze

Viscount de Caze undertook the design of his Helicoplane – what we would now call a convertaplane – early in the century. In 1902 he was working on a large 6-meter diameter turbine rotor, the blades alone having an area of 29 sqm. He subsequently joined his efforts at the Surcouf workshops with those of Dumoulin and Besançon, the famous editor of *L'Aérophile*. The rotor was later abandoned.

Construction started in 1912 at Lioré et Olivier, to be continued at the shops of Louis Clément. A narrow open fuselage of classic construction was set on 4 wheels; cruciform controls were at the front, and a biplane cell with 2 vertical surfaces at the tail. High above were fixed 2 wings in tandem, with double-curved surfaces, the tips linked with horizontal struts carrying ailerons. The total wing area was c 24

The de Caze, safely on 4 wheels on the ground. Note the 2 seats far apart. (Author's collection)

This is a Chinese G-2, this one with floats. Note the star under the wing. (Bill Lewis collection)

The Caudron G-3 of May 1914. (Author's collection)

sqm. A 50 hp Gnôme was mounted flat below the center of the fuselage driving 2 horizontally-mounted 4-bladed propellers, and a similar engine set ahead of the biplane tail drove a pusher propeller.

Ceita

A monoplane of this name was reported flown by Benoit at Juvisy in April 1911.

De la Celle

A Deperdussin modified with "an automatic stabilizer" was entered under this name for the 1914 Concours de Sécurité.

Certonciny et James

This 2-seat monoplane being built at Issy in 1912 may not have been completed; it was reported to have had ailerons and 2 propellers.

César

César, a Belgian, came to France like many other aviation enthusiasts of different nationalities to work with French designers, builders, and other workers. In 1910 he built what was probably his only machine, a tandem biplane with a pair of short rectangular wings at each end of a long rectangular uncovered box frame, the whole resting on a 4-wheel undercarriage. A pair of rudders was fitted between the aft pair of wings, and a pair of ailerons was set out in front on outriggers. A 50 hp 4-cylinder Prini-Berthaud sat on the trailing edge of the lower wing of the forward pair, driving a pusher propeller. Some photographs show the machine hung on 4 struts underneath a stubby cigar-shaped balloon; the combination was described as a "biplan mixte."

The tandem biplane César without its carrier balloon. (Peter M Bowers collection)

Chabeau et Biffu

An original design of this name was mentioned, without further detail, in 1908.

Champel

The wealthy amateur pilot Florentin Champel started flying in 1909, when he began flying his Voisin at Sartrouville, a northwestern suburb of Paris. He subsequently flew Henry Farmans; one of his machines was equipped with the automatic stabilizer of Bronislawski's, without ailerons. These aircraft were most of the time reported as "Champel biplanes," not "Champels."

But early in 1912 a Champel appeared which did not resemble a genuine Henry Farman. The vertical legs of the undercarriage sloped forward, and there were nose and tail elevators and 2 rudders with rounded leading edges. The engine was an air-cooled V Renault; the passenger sat on the lower wing leading edge with the pilot sitting on a seat overhung in front of him. Behind the passenger the Renault fuel tank was square and flat like a radiator; the upper wing was fitted with ailerons.

In the summer of 1912 appeared a new biplane, perhaps Champel No 4, featuring a shorter 4-blade pusher propeller, longer tail booms, a single large trapezoidal tailplane with 2 rudders below it, and both seats enclosed in a streamlined fabric-covered fairing. The wings may have been the same ones used on No 1. The landing gear was no longer based on the Farman. This machine is reported to have carried 852 passengers in 1912.

(Span: (upper) 16.6 m; (lower) 11.6 m; chord: 1.65 to 1.75 m; wing area: 42 sqm; empty weight: 500 kg; gross weight: 700 kg)

Champel's No 5 – perhaps a modification of No 4 with a shorter, fuller nacelle – appeared at the end of 1912 and was tested in mid-January at the Camps de Cercottes, near Orléans, and achieved a world record on 15 April, carrying 5 people including pilot Champel a distance of 250 m in 3 hr 1 min.

(Span: 12 m; 100 hp 12-cylinder Anzani)

The first distinctively Champel-designed aeroplane – though it has not moved far from the Farman influence. (Courtesy of the Musée de l'Air et de l'Espace/ Le Bourget-France)

Possibly Champel No 4, with the covered nacelle. (Courtesy of the Musée de l'Air et de l'Espace/Le Bourget-France)

Chapiro

The first Chapiro was a biplane copied from the Wright design and was tested by Guardt in 1909. It had castering front wheels and 2 pairs of wheels amidships, and ailerons linked together by thin spars. Unlike the Flyer there was only a single control stick fitted with a wheel. With a chain and long shafts the water-cooled inline Anzani drove 2 pusher propellers.

(Span: 12 m; length: 9 m)

The second, flown on one occasion by Hornstein, resembled a Farman more than a Wright. A single pusher propeller was set between the 4-boom tail structure, at the end of which was a single big tailplane with 2 rudders mounted below it. The pilot sat on the lower wing leading edge with the same wheel control as on No 1: pulling it back and forth moved 2 control rods to the forward elevator cell.

Charmiaux

A monoplane with this name was seen at Coudert in 1910.

Charpentier

The Charpentier seaplane existed in drawings only, which were published in 1909. To have been built at St Malô in northern Brittany, the big twin-float monoplane had spoon-shaped wings, no vertical surfaces, and a 50 hp engine driving 2 propellers with chains. The angle of attack of the wings could be altered either together or separately. The floats, each 5 m long, were actually completed in 1913.

Chassagny et Constantin

At least 3 aircraft bore Chassagny's name. The first was a copy of the Demoiselle, and the second was a small monoplane advertised in 1910 as "the lightest and cheapest." The latter was designed by Constantin, who also invented devices to improve the performance of all kinds of flying machines, like his cone added to the front of the Blériot XXIV; and his "deflecting surfaces," a kind of slots, on wing leading edges. The aeroplane was built at the Labaudie et Puthet workshops; it featured an all-covered fuselage, an air-cooled 3-cylinder Viale, a kite-shaped rudder, 2 long triangular tailplanes and a trapezoidal elevator brought up the rear. The wings warped. At the 1910 Paris Salon, the clear-doped Chassagny was sold without its engine for only 7,000F; it may have been the only one built. The pilot De Baleira crash-landed it in a yard on 12 November 1910.

The Wright-based Chapiro. (Courtesy of the Musée de l'Air et de l'Espace/Le Bourget-France)

Another Chassagny resembled the Nieuport monoplanes, but with a radial engine, V-leg undercarriage with a single long central skid with wheels set at the ends of a long cross-axle. The tail unit had a comma-shaped rudder, 2 long triangular tailplanes and 2 curved elevators at the rear; the wings warped. It was powered by an Anzani radial.

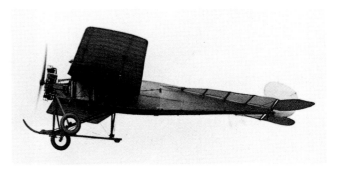

The second Chassagny monoplane, resembling a Nieuport. (Courtesy of the Musée de l'Air et de l'Espace/Le Bourget-France)

Chapiro No 2. (Courtesy of the Musée de l'Air et de l'Espace/Le Bourget-France)

Chaussée

A biplane built in Marters-Tolosane after 1909.

Chauvière

Lucien Chauvière made his fortune when he began building the first wooden Intégrale propellers for flying machines; he soon branched out into the aircraft subcontracting business; he also built a machine for Lescars in 1909. At least 3 machines carried his name; he was the builder of one and sponsor of the other 2. The first was a monoplane glider of the simplest design, built in 1909: the wing was made in 3 panels, the pilot hanging by his elbows from the center-section. 2 parallel tailbooms supported the fixed tailplane.

(Span: 9.5 m; length: 6 m: wing area: 17 sqm; weight: c 35 kg)

In the same year 2 powered aeroplanes appeared under Chauvière's name, a monoplane, probably designed by one of the Saulniers, and a biplane designed by the Spaniard Sylvio de Penteado. The first had a long uncovered box fuselage with a single motor far forward driving through a long shaft and chains 2 4-blade pusher propellers turning at only 800 rpm; they were mounted on outriggers at either side of the rear fuselage. 4 struts forward supported the broad parasol wing which had pointed wingtips.

(Span: 9 m; length: 8.5 m; wing area: c 20 m; empty weight: 430 kg)

De Penteado patented an aeroplane with "variable lift-power" in 1909, and had Chauvière build it. It resembled a biplane Demoiselle, with the wings sharply staggered: the forward tip of the lower wing met the trailing edge tip of the upper wing at joints made like propeller hubs, Chauvière's specialty! The lower wing warped for control. The pilot sat low in the openwork triangular fuselage frame, and the tractor engine was mounted just under the top wing.

It was claimed to have flown first on 16 December 1909, "flopping about" on each take-off attempt. Some references describe de Penteado as having had a second machine built at the same time.

(Span: 6.5 m; length: 8 m; wing area: c 22 sqm; empty weight: 320 kg; 24 hp 7-cylinder REP)

Chazal

Henry Chazal was involved in the construction of at least 4 aircraft and probably more, such as the Pacchiotti, a Gabardini, and the Marçay-Moonen; but it is difficult to say what exactly he contributed to the designs of such different machines.

Only a single monoplane carried Chazal's name, in large letters on the fuselage, Chazal-Gourgas; it was called L'Aiglon. The wings were thin and curved, with inset ailerons; a large trapezoidal rudder was set between 2 elevators, and triangular tailplanes on each side were set at a high angle of attack. The undercarriage consisted of 2 wheels at the tip of a lozenge-shaped frame welded to a central horned skid and attached to the fuselage by numerous struts. A wheel on a column operated all the controls; a substantial pylon supported the

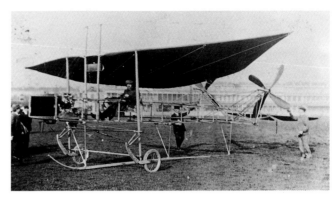

The first Chauvière powered aeroplane. (Courtesy of the Musée de l'Air et de l'Espace/Le Bourget-France)

The "variable-lift" Chauvière No 2. The circular "propeller-hub" joints at the wingtips would allow for warping the lower wings. (Author's collection)

wing cables. The engine was a 4-cylinder inline; the machine was tested at Issy in August 1911.

Chèdeville

Georges Chèdeville's first flight aboard a machine of his own design was recorded in 1909 at Flers, in Normandy. The monoplane is said to have flown 350 m at a very low level. It had built-in ailerons, a front elevator, and a fixed triangular tailplane. 2 long skids were part of the fuselage, the whole structure of hollow wooden struts.

(Span and length: 12 m; 35 hp Bénégent)

On 29 March 1911 Chèdeville started testing a new monoplane similar to the Demoiselle, with wing-warping but with a rectangular fuselage and a smoothly faired bathtub nacelle mounted between the wheels; the 60 hp water-cooled V8 was mounted at the level of the leading edge, along with its radiator.

Chepaux

Pascal Chepaux was only 18 when he built his first machine, a biplane with curved wings joined at the tips. The 20 hp motor was at the rear driving a 2-blade metal propeller; a unique biplane structure out in front was to work as elevator, ailerons, and rudder; the aircraft may not have been finished.

(Span: 7 m; length: 5 m; wing area: 25 sqm; empty weight: c 100 kg)

The handsome Chazal monoplane l'Aiglon. (Courtesy of the Musée de l'Air et de l'Espace/Le Bourget-France)

In 1910 or perhaps a little later, Chepaux and de Bussac built a monoplane, perhaps also uncompleted, copied roughly from the Antoinette. The fuselage was U-shaped in section, and stood high off the ground on a narrow-gauge undercarriage like the Antoinette's. The engine was a 6-cylinder de Bussac air-cooled radial with the cylinders grouped and staggered, with 2 opposed and 4 in a V around the egg-shaped crankcase.

Chesnay

The Chesnay monoplane was flown in 1910 by Million or Blanchard near Dijon. It showed Blériot-like wings, which may have been built at the Blériot factory, and a complicated undercarriage with 2 wheels and 2 central horned skids attached at the rear to work like a spring or shock-absorber. The engine may have been a radial, with one tank inside the fuselage and a second mounted below, just above the wheels; a third was hung from the top of the pylon, which was of the Blériot type, and the fuselage covered on the sides only. The tail was composed of a triangular fin and tailplane with triangular rudder and elevators; the skid was made of 2 long bows.

(Span: c 8 m; 50 hp Clerget)

Chevallier et de Clèves

A Blériot-type monoplane appears in at least one photograph labeled

The second Chèdeville, with wing-warping. (Courtesy of the Musée de l'Air et de l'Espace/Le Bourget-France)

Lechevallier; it may be another design by Yves Chevallier of CPC. Unlike the Blériot XI, the machine had long skids forward of the main wheels, and a rectangular rudder with the 2 aft corners clipped. Chevallier and de Clèves were the French representatives for the Labor firm.

Chevallier, Yves

Perhaps the same designer as the Chevallier above, this one designed and entered a remarkable pusher monoplane in the Concours de Sécurité in 1914. It had elliptical wings, a long flat triangular tailplane with no vertical surface; the engine was set amidships in the streamlined fuselage behind the trailing edge, the pusher propeller turning in front of the tailplane. 2 wheels and a short skid supported the aft end.

(Span: 8.25 m; length: 5.2 m; wing area: 10 sqm; weight: 110 kg; useful load: 90 kg; 12-15 hp engine)

Clément (Louis)

It is confusing to sort out Louis Clément's contribution to aviation design, since he is sometimes mistaken for Maurice Clément; or Maurice's father, Adolphe Clément-Bayard; and he often worked as a subcontractor for other designers (cf Albessard, Rossel-Peugeot, for instance). He was also the manager of a flying school at Bois d'Arcy, between Paris and Villacoublay near St Cyr, and was the French representative for the German firm Aviatik.

Since 1908 Louis Clément had pioneered oxyacetylene welding and metal construction for aeroplanes: he put together wings of 5-meter span weighing only 35 kg, and a 4.5-meter fuselage of only 30 kg; at the 1910 Paris Salon he showed an even lighter structure, a steel wing of 10 sqm weighing only 20 kg. In 1912 he was to build an all-steel Hanriot D IV which was lighter than the wooden original.

In 1911 he designed and built a series of biplanes based on the Aviatiks, which in turn were copies of the Henry Farman III. One of his biplanes entered the Concours Militaire. The upper wings were longer than the lower, which alone had dihedral. The machine had 3 rudders, a forward elevator, and a pusher Chauvière Intégrale propeller. The wings were built around 2 steel tube spars, one of which formed the leading edge; smaller tubes welded to the spars formed ribs, and the upper rib-tubes were longer than the lower, supposedly making the trailing edges flexible to absorb turbulence. Referring in 1913 back to the designs of 1912, Alexandre Dumas said about Clément's aircraft: "Outdated models, interesting examples of tube welding only."

(Span: (upper) 13.35 m; (lower) 9.35 m; chord: 2.5 m; length: 10.5 m; wing area: c 50 sqm; empty weight: 425 kg; gross weight (expected): 725 kg; take-off run: 40 m; 100 hp Aviatik)

Clément (Maurice)

Maurice Clément designed at least 2 aircraft. One was a curious tractor monoplane with low-set broad wing; the pilot sat underneath it between 2 large wide-set wheels and immediately behind a large fuel tank. The tail was supported on outriggers and a large tailwheel; the

The Chesnay appears here without its distinctive third tank. (Courtesy of the Musée de l'Air et de l'Espace/Le Bourget-France)

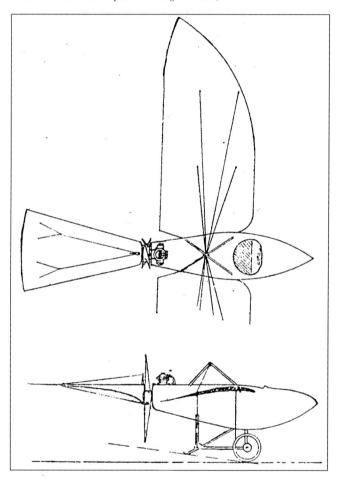

A contemporary drawing of the Chevallier monoplane of 1914. There seem no vertical surfaces aside from the fuselage. (Author's collection)

One of Louis Clément's big all-steel tube biplanes of 1911. (Author's collection)

front end terminated in twin skids each with a small nose-wheel. A 2-cylinder opposed engine was mounted on the leading edge. The other was an attractive Maurice Farman-type pusher biplane built by Letord and Niepce; it appeared at Issy in 1910, flown by François Parent, who passed his brevet test on 29 August 1910 on it. The machine, occasionally reported as a Poulain-Orange, seems to have been sold at the end of the year to the Morlat School at Pont Levoy. It had a single forward elevator, biplane tail cell with a single oval rudder set in the middle, trailing wheels. Ailerons were fitted behind the outermost wing struts; side-curtains were sometimes fitted here. One version had ailerons on the lower wings, an elaborate 4-wheel undercarriage, twin tailwheels, and a small uncovered box frame for the pilot and his passenger seated in tandem. It was first flown with a Clément-Bayard engine, and then with a 70 hp water-cooled inline Labor-Aviation.

The low-slung Maurice Clément monoplane, probably his first design. (Courtesy of the Musée de l'Air et de l'Espace/Le Bourget-France)

Clément-Bayard

Gustave-Adolphe Clément had made a fortune in bicycles, tires, and automobiles and their engines. In 1908 he had the Astra firm build him a dirigible, named for himself, and went on to build his own factory and 6 more dirigibles. He took the emblem of Bayard as his logo, and eventually added it to his own name. Victor Tatin, together with Professor Richet, did the first independent design for the firm Clément-Bayard: the handsome modern twin-boom monoplane bought by the Comte de la Vaulx.

<u>1909</u>: Demoiselle project – cf Santos-Dumont

The second M Clément, a very pretty biplane – a clear advance over his first design. (Courtesy of the Musée de l'Air et de l'Espace/Le Bourget-France)

<u>1910</u>: An ungainly big back-staggered triplane built in August-September, with high-set biplane surfaces both in front and behind. The engine was set on the rear of the lower wing between a pair of big side-curtains; it drove 2 pusher propellers through chains and sprockets like the Wright machines. The whole rig rested on 3 close-set wheels in front and a pair under the tail.

<u>1911</u>: A handsome shoulder-wing tractor monoplane with a long covered triangular-section fuselage, scalloped fin and rudder and tailplane, 2-wheel undercarriage and skids, rectangular wing with trailing edge and triangular-section fuselage – Clément-Bayard trademarks. Distinctive feature: automobile-type cowl and radiator, with propeller shaft at the very top – 55 hp Clément-Bayard motor and shaft, with side-louvers aft.

Also, at the 1911 Salon: what may be the same machine fitted with a high upper wing, the lower one dropped to midwing position.

The first Clément-Bayard machine after the abortive Demoiselle attempt. It would be interesting to see exactly how the engine and its chain drive connected to the horizontal pusher propeller shaft. (Courtesy of the Musée de l'Air et de l'Espace/Le Bourget-France)

<u>1912</u>: Another biplane (maybe the same one?) with unequal-span wings, uncovered rear fuselage, and a half-cowled (Anzani radial) instead of the internally-mounted one.

Right: The 1911 Clément-Bayard in flight. Note the high-set propeller shaft, driven by the Clément-Bayard engine mounted as shown in the next photograph. (Courtesy of the Musée de l'Air et de l'Espace/Le Bourget-France)

1912: Another monoplane typically Clément-Bayard, with skids ahead of the 2 wheels, and the fuselage triangular up to the very nose, where the bottom longeron cut upwards to the rotary engine, giving a resemblance to the REP monoplane. And yet another, like this one except with a simple V-leg undercarriage – exhibited at the 1912 Salon. And a military model with the skids and windows cut out under the wing, 1913; another monoplane with the REP-style nose, but a fully cowled Gnôme, heavier fuselage and rectangular tailplane in December 1913.

1913: A curious flyingboat: unequal-span wings, pusher propeller set between parallel tail booms and a typical Clément-Bayard tail; the fuselage nacelle built onto a wide flat pontoon-float, with large tip-floats under each wingtip. The 115 hp 4-cylinder Clément-Bayard in the hull drove the Chauvière propeller through shafts and gearing.

Military monoplane: a 2-seater.

(Span: 12.7 m; length: 9.8 m; wing area: 24 sqm; weight: 380 kg; speed: 90 kmh; 60/70 hp)

Military Biplane: also a 2-seater:

(Span (upper): 11 m; (lower): 7.8 m; length: 9.8 m; wing area: 28 sqm; weight: 400 kg; speed: 80 kmh; 40/50 hp)

Le Clère
A machine of this name, called Big Bird, was reported at Gonthier in 1912, made of metal and silk.

Clerget
Pierre Clerget is primarily associated with engines; he had been designing them since 1895, first alone, then with Clément-Bayard, then with Blin. He also built at least 2 monoplanes.

The first was also known as the Marquézy or CAM (Clerget-Archdeacon-Marquézy): Archdeacon provided the money for Clerget's design for Marquézy, and helped Clerget design a 4-cylinder inline aero engine. The machine had a long uncovered airfoil-shaped fuselage which was rectangular forward and trapezoidal aft, with a large

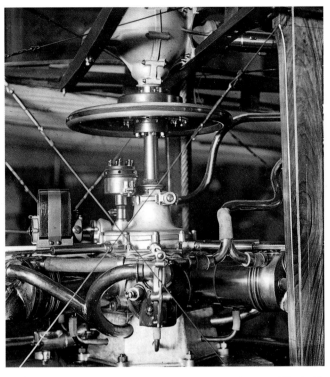

A good view of the water-cooled 55 hp Clément-Bayard mounted flat inside the C-B monoplane of 1911. (Peter M Bowers collection)

Perhaps the same monoplane with wing changes, and an upright-mounted Anzani instead of the buried Clément-Bayard. Note that the side louvers are still in place. (Courtesy of the Musée de l'Air et de l'Espace/Le Bourget-France)

One of several 1912 Clément-Bayard monoplanes, this one with the forward skids – which do not seem to have saved this landing.

Another C-B monoplane; the firm seems to have settled on a simpler and heavier design. (Courtesy of the Musée de l'Air et de l'Espace/Le Bourget-France)

rounded rudder. The water-cooled Clerget drove a tractor propeller through a long shaft. Marquézy stalled the machine in from 50' on 4 November 1909.

(Span: 9 m; length: 10 m; 50 hp inline Clerget)

From this engine Clerget developed first a 4-cylinder inline of 100 hp, and then a 200 hp V8. At the 1910 Salon a larger monoplane, similar to the earlier one, was shown with 3 dummies in French Army uniforms: the mechanic sat between the rectangular wings, the observer amidships, and the pilot at the rear in front of the large tail unit. The undercarriage was like the Hanriot's; a fuel tank hung below the fuselage amidships.

(Span: 11 m; length: 14 m)

Clerget never went back to aircraft, and is now more famous for his rotaries built as late as the end of the 20s, and for his heavy-oil aircraft engines.

Cluzan

In 1909 Cluzan designed and flew this large biplane at Tours, on the banks of the Loire; it seemed like a hybrid Wright/Curtiss, with a monoplane forward elevator and tailplane, and 2 small triangular rudders underneath the latter. The pilot sat forward of the radiator of the 4-cylinder inline Rolan Pilain engine. Completed on 27 November, the Cluzan had broken one of its wings by 17 December.

(Span: 10.3 m)

Coanda

Although Henri Coanda contributed largely to the various aircraft built under the name Bristol-Coanda in England, and went on to design a series of interesting machines afterwards in France, his name is best known for his discovery of the so-called Coanda Effect in fluid dynamics. But his most advanced and the most interesting aircraft designs were his 2 first, both unsuccessful. His so-called "jet engine" was installed in his sled, which appeared in the 1910 Paris automobile show, and in his first aeroplane, which appeared in the Paris Salon of the following year. In fact, similar powerplants were in both, neither of them jet engines. He had a 30 hp 4-cylinder inline Grégoire in the sled, and a 50 hp Clerget in the aeroplane: each was fitted with a 1-stage compressor set in front, ahead of the motor; the turbine pulled in air past the motor, mixed it with hot exhaust gases, forced the mixture through the long hollow fuselage, and expelled it from the tail.

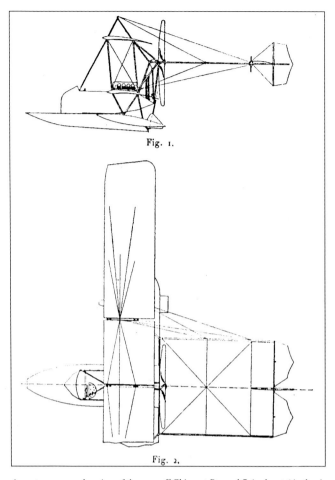

Fig. 1.

Fig. 2.

A contemporary drawing of the one-off Clément-Bayard flyingboat. (Author's collection)

The first Clerget monoplane. Note the drive-shaft inside the tapered nose; perhaps Clerget intended to cover it for streamlining. (Author's collection)

The second Clerget aeroplane; note the even longer drive-shaft. (Author's collection)

Left: The big Cluzan. (Author's collection)

91

No additional fuel was injected and burned. There is no record of the turbo-sled, built for the Grand Duke Cyril of Russia, ever having run. It was about 4.2 m long, cigar-shaped, with the driver at the wheel sitting in the tail end, and the same bucket-shaped front as on the aeroplane, housing the motor and the turbine blades.

Coanda claimed that with the "200 kg traction" he claimed for his power system, the aeroplane had actually taken off, but in actuality flames coming out the rear had ignited the fuselage, causing the machine to stall and crash, throwing Coanda out onto the ground with slight bruises. The incident was claimed as taking place in December, but no accident report appears in any of the European aviation journals for the entire month. Alfred Bodemer at the Musée de l'Air studied his design and concluded that compression ratio of the turbine could hardly have been more than 1:1, thus providing inadequate power for any kind of take-off.

But the structure of the aeroplane was fascinating: almost no struts or wires were used, the long upper wing and the short lower one, both plywood-covered, were supported by only 4 center-section struts that held the fuselage midway between them; the wings warped, but were otherwise unbraced. The fuselage was a ply shell with light formers and stringers to support its shape, flat on top and rounded on the sides and bottom. The pilot, sitting on top with side-mounted control wheels like the Antoinette, could draw down the trailing edge on one side to control roll, or on both sides at once, to reduce speed. The top wing had small fences below the leading edge to "canalize the air flow."

A small rectangular tailplane at a high angle of attack was set under the rear fuselage ahead of the cruciform tail, and the 4 triangular surfaces hinged to the 4 fins worked both as rudders and elevators.

The Coanda turbo-sled with a 30 hp Grégoire engine. (Drawing from Popular Mechanics of March 1911)

Right: The wooden mold for the making of the turbine for the Coanda monoplane. (Courtesy of the Musée de l'Air et de l'Espace/Le Bourget-France)

The first Henri Coanda aeroplane at the Paris Exposition of 1910. Note that each wing is attached in only 3 places at the center section. (Courtesy of the Musée de l'Air et de l'Espace/Le Bourget-France)

Above and right: Two views of the second Coanda design, his twin-Gnôme monoplane. The engine arrangements have no connection with his turbo design. (Courtesy of the Musée de l'Air et de l'Espace/Le Bourget-France)

(Span: 10.3 m; length: 12.7 m; wing area: 32.7 sqm; gross weight: 420 kg)

While Coanda seems to have been the first to build (but not fly!) the first reaction-propulsion full-sized aeroplane, he was not the first to propose the form of power. René Lorin described his aerial torpedo project of 1909-1912 in *L'Aérophile* in 1907-8, and again in 1909-10; Rankine Kennedy had written of it in 1909, A Budau in the same year; and as early as 1863-65 Charles de Louvrie described his Aéronave propelled by the burning of a hydrocarbon, "or, better, vaporized petroleum oil" ejected through twin tail-pipes.

In 1911 Coanda introduced his second design, similar to but also significantly different from his first. *L'Aérophile* of 1 January 1912 described the second machine:

> Pressing – and tactless – questions (about the earlier machine) were answered by a not-very-convincing explanation of the qualities of the turbine, and by the claim that the aeroplane had achieved test flights of up to 112 kmh. As in aviation nothing stuns, I approved without a word, though I decided to hold back until the proof of the experiments, which did not come. And the new machine, which appeared at the Concours Militaire (at Reims), where it raised some sharp dispute today, shows what remains... and what was given up. What was given up: the turbo-propeller ("turbo-propulseur" (sic)) and the wooden wing-skinning, as well as the wooden fences to ease the regular fluid flow. What remains: the aerofoil section, the structure, and the general shape of the fuselage. All very interesting, but built somewhat differently.

The fuselage of this second machine was fuller and more rounded than that of the first; only the front third was ply-covered. The cruciform tail remained, though without the extra horizontal surface. The top wing was of extremely high aspect ratio; only part was ply-cov-

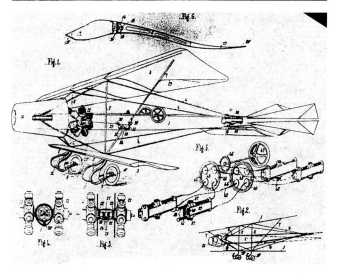

Constructional details of the second Coanda machine. Note reflex airfoil, among many other features. (Author's collection)

ered, to facilitate warping. The fuselage was set between it and the lower wing, now only a stub between the 2 pairs of tandem wheels, each pair housed in a large triangular cover. Only one tall strut on each side supported the wings.

The engine arrangement was unusual: 2 Gnômes were fitted into the nose, back to back, each facing outward, driving a single 4-bladed propeller through a differential gear-box. Coanda claimed that one engine could be cut in flight.

At least one drawing shows it with extended lower wing panels. There is no reliable evidence as to its flying.

(Span: 16.3 m; chord: 1.25 m; length: 12.5 m; gross weight: 1250 kg, with 170 kg of gasoline in the wings; empty weight: 470 kg; 1 pilot and 3 passengers; expected speed: 130 kmh; 2 70 hp Gnômes)

At the same time, Coanda shared with Ernoult the design of a racing monoplane built by Mélin. After the military biplane proved unsuccessful, Coanda went to work in England at Bristols, where he introduced many refinements to reduce drag, and shared design work on the various Bristol-Coanda aeroplanes. In 1918 he designed an advanced biplane for Delaunay-Belleville, which was destroyed in a crash.

Always busy with fluid-flow dynamics, he made important discoveries in this field, including what has been known since 1937 as the Coanda Effect.

Collin de Laminières
This machine was listed for the 1911 Concours Militaire, but it is not clear whether it was in fact entered.

Collomb
An ungainly 4-wheeled ornithopter was photographed at a transportation exhibit in March 1904, featuring a long triangular pigeon-tail and what appear to be trapezoidal outer wing panels. Perhaps these flapped.

The more familiar Collomb ornithopter was completed at Lyon in August 1909. A 40 hp motor in a 4-wheel frame was to pump vertically 200 times per minute a shaft on which a pair of hinged lattices pivoted. A rudder was at the rear. It did not fly.

(Span: 12 m; weight: c 250 kg)

Combes
A machine of this name was seen at Pertuis, in the south of France.

Compagnie Générale de Navigation Aérienne
This firm was formed in 1908 by Wilbur Wright and Lazare Weiller to build and sell the Wright aeroplanes in France. CGNA machines were built by the Chantiers de France shipyards in Dunkirk; the work was poor, with twisted wings and delayed deliveries. The engines were so-called 35 hp Wrights, but were actually designed and built by the French firm Barriquand et Marre. The first aeroplane was delivered to the Comte de Lambert in May 1909; the second to Paul Tissandier some days later; the third to the Army (the aircraft Eteré used for his experiments with automatic stability); the fourth to Eugène Lefebvre who was killed several days later testing another Wright built for Schreck. A still later machine, perhaps the sixth, was built for Baratroux, who put wheels on it in August 1909 and was able to take off without the catapult, but crashed it the following month at Juvisy. These aeroplanes were extremely unstable: Eteré reports in his memoirs that the elevator control had to be shaken several times per second.

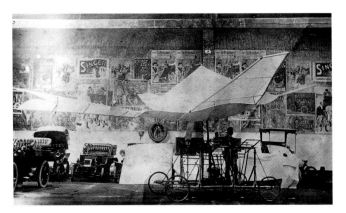

The Collomb ornithopter exhibited in 1904. (Courtesy of the Musée de l'Air et de l'Espace/Le Bourget-France)

THE "FLAPPING-WING" MACHINE, OR "ORTHOPTER," INVENTED BY M COLLOMB, THE EX-CYCLIST.

ANOTHER POSITION OF THE COLLOMB ORTHOPTER, WHICH WAS INTENDED TO "FLAP" 200 TIMES A MINUTE.

Two views of the second Collomb in action. (Author's collection)

(Span: 12.5 m; length: 9.3 m; wing area: 48 sqm; 35 hp Barriquand et Marre)

Construction of Wright aeroplanes in France was eventually taken over by the Astra firm after the bankruptcy of CGNA.

Compagnie Internationale de Navigation Aérienne
This short-lived firm was located primarily at Issy les Moulineaux in a large hangar. In 1912 they operated a flying school and did aeroplane repairs and construction under the guidance of the manager Charles

Roux. Some of the machines built at CINA and given the names of their designers were the Shigeno, and Filippi's Cyrnoptère; CINA also helped build some of the Sloan aircraft. They also built Excelsior propellers, and served as agents for Thomann, Goupy, and Caudron. They introduced a Blériot monoplane at the 1911 Paris Salon and flew at least 4 others in the school.

The firm was likely disbanded in 1913.

Comte, Gournay, Michaux

At the end of 1908, Captain Comte, Henry Gournay, and César Michaux built a biplane glider fitted with a tail unit and tested it on the dunes at Boulogne sur Mer in January, 1909.

Constantin

Constantin's Aéromobile was unique: a combined aeroplane and hot-air balloon. It was a monoplane with a 50 hp Gnôme, and constructed of "metal-liège" (cork-metal) an alloy of aluminum and magnesium. The large wings were to be filled with hot air. On each side of the fuselage small balloons could also be filled with hot air – the temperature of 4000° C is sometimes mentioned – designed as "montgolfières" to keep the whole thing up. It is likely construction began. It is unlikely that the Aéromobile was a success – a forerunner of the equally unsuccessful American Flying Pumpkin-Seed.

Constantin-d'Astanières

The young François d'Astanières designed in 1911 and patented in 1912 (Patent No 8486, 10 April), an automatically-stable monoplane; he entered a model of it at the 1912 Salon, looking for financial support. The patent included a forwardly-retractable landing gear, which seems not to have been used on the full-scale machine.

Louis Clément built the aeroplane at St Cyr, Bielovucic tested it in the summer of 1913, and Granel tested it further later that year. It was finally entered in the 1914 Concours de Sécurité as the Constantin d'Astanières, and may have included some of the safety features patented by Louis Constantin, such as concave leading-edge flaps (to increase the lifting depression above the upper surface), or inverted controls for the elevator (to reduce speed at landing even with the engine turning at full power).

A streamlined rectangular covered fuselage carried a 4-cylinder automobile engine aft of the cockpit driving through chains a high-set pusher propeller. The rear tail surfaces were standard in shape, but the forward elevator was mounted high on outriggers level with the high parasol wing; the two elevators could be worked together through moving the pilot's seat amidships. The wings pivoted on a longitudinal axis to absorb gusts, the wings being "slightly flexible" fore and aft.

Contal

During 1909 and 1910 Contal, the inventor of a motorcycle called the Mototri, tried to build a successful flying machine; "many previous attempts" are mentioned in the literature without further details. On 2 April 1910 he rolled out a monoplane he had built with Protin, but abandoned it shortly as being too complicated. The Protin-Contal had adjustable swept-back wings, a rear elevator, a 40 hp 4-cylinder inline

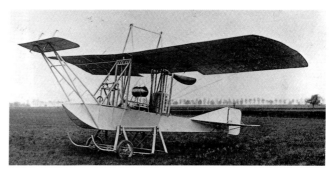

The remarkably ugly Constantin-d'Astanières safety plane: everything moved. (Courtesy of the Musée de l'Air et de l'Espace/Le Bourget-France)

A photo (from La Vie Automobile!) of the fuselage of the wildly experimental Protin-Contal monoplane. (Author's collection)

Dansette-Gillet engine driving 2 Lioré tractor propellers at 800 rpm. The controls worked by 2 levers, on the left for direction and on the right for warping. When both moved forward they controlled the elevator and the sweeping back of the wings; Contal could not make this system work properly.

(Span: 12 m; length: 9 m; wing area: 24 sqm; gross weight: c 400 kg; 40 hp 4-cylinder inline Dansette-Gillet)

In September 1910, still at Mourmelon and in front of the same green fabric hangar, Contal tested a more traditional design which might have had components of his earlier monoplane built into it. A narrow triangular fuselage was covered with sheets of mahogany; the 50 hp Gnôme overhung at the nose, the round top of which could be

A more conservative – and graceful – Contal design. (Courtesy of the Musée de l'Air et de l'Espace/Le Bourget-France)

covered by a long semi-cylindrical windshield. The rudder was nearly round and fitted with a small fin; the rectangular wings could be warped, with the front spars fixed through steel fittings to the top 2 ash longerons, and the rear spars hinged. The undercarriage was composed of 2 horned skids supporting the 2 wheels, attached to the upper longerons with 4 struts, and 2 diagonal struts attached to the lower longeron and joining the tips of the skids. The pilot sat with his legs extended so that he could set his back easily against the seat without having to be strapped in. In the review *Omnia* Henri Mignet wrote that this unusual position was "particularly appreciated by Americans."

Another Contal machine had an uncovered rectangular box fuselage, angular tail surfaces, and perhaps the same horned skids on the undercarriage. It had a water-cooled inline engine.

Contenet

This was a monoplane built by Odier-Vendôme in 1910, with a 4-cylinder inline engine.

Copin

In 1909 Georges Copin designed and built at Juvisy a "big and heavy" biplane with curved rear and forward outriggers, large rectangular forward elevator and large split rectangular aft elevator and small rectangular rudder; he got his brevet in 1909 on this machine also flown by Léon Morane and also known as the Popp-Copin. Richard Popp was a pioneer in the French automobile industry, and later claimed to have flown 300 m in the Popp-Copin on 21 November 1909.

Control was through a front elevator linked by a rectangular frame to 2 vertical bars on the lower wing leading edge; there was a rudder pedal, but it is likely there was no warping system nor ailerons unless they were joined to the rudder controls. The machine also appeared without the forward tail surface.

(Span: 10 m; length: 8 m; weight: 200 kg; 24 hp 3-cylinder Anzani)

In 1910 Copin was the assistant manager of the Borel flying school at Mourmelon, and in 1911 he built 2 monoplanes differing

Another Contal monoplane. Note additional rudder area added after construction. (Courtesy of the Musée de l'Air et de l'Espace/Le Bourget-France)

only in their engines. One is sometimes called the Copin-Révillard, but is likely properly to be Réquillard. Both aircraft were small, with triangular-section covered fuselages, in general arrangement similar to the Hanriot. A large curved triangle above the trapezoidal elevator served as the vertical surface. One machine had an 80 hp Gnôme with a 4-blade tractor propeller; the combination proved unsatisfactory and probably could not lift the machine. The other had a 50 hp water-cooled Chenu and an Intégrale propeller, with a triangular metal cowl like some of the Antoinette models, and with side radiators. Damaged in October 1911, it flew again in December when it achieved a speed of 110 kmh. Emile Védrines, brother of Jules, flew it in 1911 and 1912.

(Span: 9 m; length: 7.5 m; 50 hp Chenu)

The Copin photographed at Châlons in April 1912. (Author's collection)

The "big and heavy" Copin biplane of 1909. It seems to have flown very well. (Courtesy of the Musée de l'Air et de l'Espace/Le Bourget-France)

Corbadec

This was an ornithopter, with 3 wheels, bird-shaped flapping surfaces, and a front elevator.

Corignan

A Pierre Corignan is reported building a seaplane at Nice in 1910.

Cornu

Paul Cornu is often claimed to be the first man ever to take off vertically in a heavier-than-air machine. A modest retailer of cycles and cars at Lisieux in Normandy, he came of an air-minded family: his father had worked on the plans for a dirigible. In 1899, aged 18, he designed with his father a rotary engine and patented it in 1902. He also invented a steam tricycle, another gas engine, and a small car with 2 gas engines and no gearbox or differential.

In 1905 he started work on flying machines, and designed a balancing device for aeroplanes and a propelling device for helicopters. In 1906 he built a model helicopter consisting mainly of 2 horizontal propellers of the Renard type; on 4 October 1906 he managed hovering flights with a 2 hp model. By this time he had ordered a 24 hp Antoinette, delivered on 30 October.

Through vertical shafts and belts his engine drove 2 large spoked wheels less than 2' ahead of and behind the engine; a 2-blade propeller was fastened to each wheel, the blades built of spars and ribs and false ribs, all covered with fabric and mounted with substantial dihedral. At each end of the helicopter 2 similar blades were mounted as stabilizers. The pilot sat behind the engine on a 4-wheeled chassis.

The helicopter was finished in August 1907, and on the last day of the month hovered unmanned, with the engine turning at only 750 rpm and the propellers at only 70 rpm. Further tests were made starting in October in the former Duchesne-Fournet factory: of some 300 tries, only 15 were reported satisfactory. On 3 November 1907, with Cornu at the controls, the machine was said to have taken off and hovered at the height of one foot, engines turning at 850 rpm, gross weight 260 kg. On 26 March 1908 he was again reported to have flown at Coquainvilliers, near Pont Levêque, Normandy, this time in front of 200 people. As the wind was strong, Cornu asked one of his broth-

The Corbadec ornithopter. (Author's collection)

ers to secure the helicopter by holding it; it was claimed finally to have taken off with both men aboard, hovering in the gusts of wind with difficulty about 5' off the ground; the gross weight was then 328 kg. But Jean Boulet, famous helicopter pilot and author of *L'Histoire de l'Hélicoptère Racontée par ses Pionniers 1907-1956* claims the Cornu was not powerful enough even to hover, and notes in addition that there are no pictures of flight or even with spectators. Boulet notes further that when Cornu had flown a 13-kilogram model helicopter, he had arranged for a notarized document with 60 signatures to attest its flight, so he seems to have known about the need for documentation!

(Span of each rotor: 6 m; lifting area: 6 sqm)

Unable really to fly with his machine, Cornu began the design of a helicoplane, but lacked funds to build it.

De Coster

Charles de Coster's monoplane Flugi was shown at the 1910 Salon before it had been tested, and little was said about it afterward. It was a rough copy of the Blériot XI, differing mostly in the arrangement of the outer undercarriage struts; and in the fuselage, which was triangular and uncovered, forward, and triangular and uncovered aft. The

The Cornu helicopter safely on the ground. (Author's collection)

engine was a small 3-cylinder half-radial with a 2-blade Flugi-de Coster propeller.

The Spanish Villa-Nueva of the Quatro Vientos Museum is very similar to this machine.

(Span: 8 m; length: 8 m; wing area: 16 sqm; empty weight: 290 kg)

Couade

Couade, a captain in the artillery, built his monoplane in 1913 and flew it the following year.

Courrejou

This tractor monoplane is reported near Tours or at Pont-Levoy (Le Mans) in 1910. It had a triangular-section uncovered fuselage The pilot sat below the wing, the engine mounted on the center-section. A small rectangular rudder was set above a traditional tailplane and rectangular elevator.

Coursier

An aircraft of this name was reported under construction in 1907; in 1911 Coursier test-flew the de Dion Bouton at Chartres.

Courtet

The designer of this biplane was awaiting his engine in September 1910. Until then, perhaps, it was a glider?

Cousin

Dr Georges Cousin was known in aviation circles for his writing on aerodynamics based on the study of birds, and for one of his models. He also built 2 aircraft. The first was a glider designed and built in 1909, which crashed at Miramas on 2 April.

(Span: 8 m; length: 4 m; wing area: 14.6 sqm)

In 1912 he ordered his most famous model built, designed after a gliding bird, but resembling a dodo. In 1914 he had Jean de Serres build a short, bulky monoplane deep enough for the pilot to sit inside with only his head showing; the fuselage was covered with heavy 3 mm plywood. There were 2 small triangular tailplanes and a large S-shaped rudder. Only these parts and some wing ribs were done when the War broke out; it is likely the machine was a glider, and was designed with a deformable "penetration cone."

CPC

A man named Chevalier flew this Etrich copy at St Cyr in July 1912. Perhaps the first C stood for Chevalier – perhaps the Yves Chevalier who registered a monoplane with an elliptical parasol wing and swept-back tailplane at the 1914 Concours de Sécurité, and later completed it (cf Yves Chevalier); the second C may stand for (Louis) Clément.

Cussac

This machine was tried at La Vidamée.

De Coster's monoplane Flugi of 1910. Note the variation on the Blériot model. (Author's collection)

This particular Courrejou is marked Aéroplane Courrejou No 3 on the rudder; this might mean it was the third design of this man – or it might not. It is pretty, and looks light. The wing spars may run across the top of the wings, on the outside. (Courtesy of the Musée de l'Air et de l'Espace/Le Bourget-France)

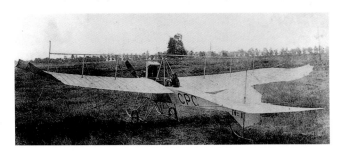

Clearly of Taube ancestry, this CPC is marked CPC No 1. Visibility forward would appear to be very poor. (Courtesy of the Musée de l'Air et de l'Espace/Le Bourget-France)

D

Danard et Nayot

This little biplane was completed and ready to fly in April 1912 at Juvisy; the pilot Trotton flew it in May and June. Its water-cooled motor drove a pusher propeller behind a fabric-covered nacelle mounted on the lower wing. Outriggers supported twin rudders and a single tailplane, and the 2 main wheels were set between twin skids.

Dardelet

A machine of this name was projected in 1909; all-metal, it may not have been built.

Daucourt et Pourrain

This machine, reported as a flyingboat, must have been amphibious or the report was in error, since it flew at Issy in 1911.

Dauheret

A helicopter...

Debort

In Limoges, in 1908 – perhaps even earlier – Serge and Jack Debort built at least 2 unmanned gliders, a monoplane and a biplane, both covered with paper. Their third glider, built in 1908/1909, was bigger and covered with fabric; towed by a car, it was probably manned.

The Debort No 3 was a wide-winged monoplane with an uncovered rectangular fuselage, high forward-tilting triangular fin and rudder, triangular stabilizer and one-piece trapezoidal elevator. The trapezoidal wings were braced from a high V-pylon, and the tail supported by a pair of trailing skids.

No 4 was a copy of the Demoiselle, with a large triangular fin and rounded rudder. The steerable tailwheel was connected to the rudder, and the 2 main wheels were fixed to an articulated axle, which was eventually broken. As on the Demoiselle, the wing-warping control was linked directly to the pilot's back. The machine was powered by a 20 hp Zedel water-cooled motorbike engine; it was tested on the Champ de Juillet on 10 July 1910, but was unable to fly until launched down a 15% ramp in September.

Debougnies

This monoplane glider was flown by Scrive, in 1911, in northern France. Debougnies was a Belgian designer/builder.

Decazes & Besançon

A helicopter of 1902. Another machine referred to as simply Decazes remains unidentified.

Deflers

A biplane belonging to the Société Française d'Aéroplanes in Savigny, near Juvisy, appeared under this name; it may have been a 1909 Voisin.

Defries

The biplane – a Wright type? – in which Lefebvre killed himself.

Delabrosse et Christollet

Tested in September 1910, this big and unsuccessful tractor was probably the first with variable-geometry wing. Each wing panel was a large semicircle of fabric stretched between the fuselage and curved leading edge spars which pivoted on vertical struts to vary the wing area: the span could thus be modified from 11 to 7 m. The long partly-covered triangular-section fuselage had triangular control surfaces at the rear.

Contemporary records show that Christollet was planning a machine called Abeille (bee), in 1909; this may have been the Delabrosse et Christollet – if, indeed, it was built.

The pretty Danard et Nayot biplane of 1912 poses on a roadway at Port-Aviation on 9 August. (Courtesy of the Musée de l'Air et de l'Espace/Le Bourget-France)

The third Debort. One hopes the swayback in the fuselage was intentional, but the general roughness of construction – note what appears to be a splice in the right-hand pylon post – suggests not. (Courtesy of the Musée de l'Air et de l'Espace/Le Bourget-France)

Delaisis

This monoplane had an automatic stabilizer and was completed at La Flèche, near Le Mans, in the summer of 1910.

(Span: 8 m; length: 9 m; weight: 350 kg; 45 hp engine)

Delalandre

A machine of this name but of unknown design was entered for the 1914 Concours de Sécurité – it was claimed to be automatically stable.

Delamotte

A glider of this name was tested at Juvisy in 1909.

Delasalle

Chanute-type gliders of this name were built by Louis Delasalle at Palaiseau, a western suburb of Paris, in mid-1911.

The unsuccessful Delabrosse et Christollet. The fabric semicircles which make possible the machine's variable wingspan show clearly in this photograph. (Courtesy of the Musée de l'Air et de l'Espace/Le Bourget-France)

Delaunay-Belleville

A 1908 project of this name, in association with Barbaroux, may have been a modified Wright. Delaunay and Belleville were later associated with the design of the WWI Coanda twin pusher.

Demazel

Lucien Demazel and his son Paul were in charge of the Demazel flying school at Issy in 1911, operating blue Caudron biplanes. The school became the Demazel and Sagitta Flying School, and in August 1912 were using Demazel biplanes equipped with 80 hp 6-cylinder radial Anzanis; a year later a civil machine with an uncovered fuselage, and a military 2-seater, Type M2, appeared as well; these latter 2 were Caudron biplane copies, also with radial Anzanis.

Démouveaux

In 1901 Démouveaux brought a giant glider to a great kite meet at the Parc des Princes in Paris. The pilot stood in the middle of the long front wing; a second long wing was set in tandem. The glider was wrecked on its first attempt, without damaging its pilot.

Denhaut

A long-time and very successful bicyclist, François-Victor Denhaut began in 1907 to build a series of gliders and test them. Interested in adding an engine, with the help of Bouyer, a local mechanic, he built a tailless canard biplane, the Denhaut-Bouyer-Mercier, in 1908. It featured ailerons between the 2 wings. The 20 horsepower his little engine could barely produce was not enough.

Denhaut then turned to designing a little racing biplane, with financial aid from a local enthusiast named Danton; it was built in 1910 by Espinosa, an early collaborator of Clément Ader's. It had a long thin triangular-sectioned fuselage, considerable back-stagger, and a Blériot-style landing gear; the top wing was more or less rectangular in shape. The engine was a 50 hp 6-cylinder fan Lemasson. This first Danton was bought by Victor Fumat; Denhaut contracted for 2 more, slightly different, with elliptical wings, one with a 25 hp Anzani and the other a 3 hp Viale, both 3-cylinder engines; but he sold his interest in them before they were complete.

Denhaut got his license in 1911 in a Fernandez biplane; and while chief pilot at Pierre Levasseur's flying school in 1911 he conceived of a new form of seaplane, this with a hull instead of floats. The hull was triangular in section, with the point at the top; a small forward

One of the school Demazels of 1911-1912 presents a clean modern appearance. (Courtesy of the Musée de l'Air et de l'Espace/Le Bourget-France)

The Démouveaux Aviator glider. (Author's collection)

The pretty little back-staggered Danton racing plane of 1910, designed by Denhaut. (Peter M Bowers collection)

Note the forward elevator and the hull shape of this first Denhaut flyingboat temporarily fitted with wheels: nearly flat on the bottom with only the shallowest step, and knife-edged on top. The machine still retained its forward elevator when this picture was taken. A larger step was soon added after the first hull had proved unsatisfactory. (Author's collection)

planing surface was placed close to the water under the bow. The lower wing was set above the hull, overhung by the upper wing. The 50 hp Gnôme, donated by Swiss engineer Jacques Donnet from his unused Blériot XI, was set between the wings with a pusher propeller. A temporary 2-wheel landing gear allowed the machine to take off from the ground; all of which worked well. On his first attempt to land on the water, Denhaut turned the machine over. The second machine had a pronounced step in the bottom of the revised hull, and no forward surfaces.

A Donnet-Levêque Type B. (Bill Lewis collection)

(First version: span: 9 m; length: 8 m; weight: 300 kg; Levasseur propeller; 50 hp Gnôme)

These trials interested the automobile manufacturer Henri Levêque, who put in some capital, and the famous pilot known as Beaumont – a navy officer whose real name was Conneau. Donnet and Levêque formed a new company with their name, Beaumont being the director, and took out a patent on the new flyingboat hull. Donnet-Levêque built several new flyingboats based on Denhaut's first 2, with 50, 70, and 80 hp Gnôme engines, and 2, 2, and 3 seats, respectively. All 3 showed their ancestry, with overhung top wings with cut-outs for the pusher propellers, high-set engines, and small triangular fins. The Type A was developed directly from the modified first flyingboat, with a more substantial hull, larger fin and rectangular rudder. The Type B had a still heavier hull and a rectangular rudder higher than the fin. The Type C rudder had a curved top, and was attached to a larger fin; the top wing was fitted with ailerons. One original Donnet-Levêque has been restored and is exhibited as a Type A at the Musée de l'Air et de l'Espace, but for some reason, with elements from several of these types. All 3 featured the characteristic upturned tail end to the hull, and wing-warping.

(Span: (50 hp) 9.5 m; (80 hp) 10.4 m; length: (50 hp) 8.8 m; (80 hp) 8.5 m; wing area: (50 hp) 17 sqm; (80 hp) 21 sqm; speed: (50 hp) 110 kmh; (80 hp) 115-120 kmh)

Shortly after, early in 1913, Denhaut left the firm and joined Borel, where he built Aeroyachts under the name Borel-Denhaut. Levêque continued to produce flyingboats under his name until Louis Schreck bought up the company, with Beaumont the director of the new firm, Franco-British-Aviation (FBA).

Denissel et Godville
A helicoplane of this name was registered at Monaco in 1909.

Deperdussin
The first aeroplane to carry the name of Armand Deperdussin carried the name of the painter-decorator Georges de Feure as well: it was built in 1910, and managed to fly only briefly, at Chambry. It was a canard because both Deperdussin and de Feure as well as their engineer Béchereau were interested in canard designs. The monoplane wing was braced with a forest of heavy struts. 2 propellers mounted coaxially were driven through a long shaft from a centrally-mounted water-cooled 4-cylinder inline engine, the forward end of which was covered with a curved screened hood – perhaps the radiator tubes? A small forward all-flying tail surface and forward rudder brought up the front end; the pilot sat in the extreme rear with a large control wheel. The machine was set on an awkward-looking 4-wheeled undercarriage.

Another de Feure-Deperdussin was hung from the ceiling of a Paris department store, and may have been only a big model. The pilot in this one sat on top, à la Antoinette, with control wheels on either side; the propeller was immediately behind him, with a high streamlined cowl in front. The wing was of broad chord cut out for

A Donnet-Levêque Type C. (Author's collection)

A Donnet-Levêque marked with the race-number 10; the hull resembles that of Type C, but this machine has ailerons. (Bill Lewis collection)

The first Deperdussin-de Feure canard. Note the coaxial propellers, and the centrally-mounted engine. (Courtesy of the Musée de l'Air et de l'Espace/Le Bourget-France)

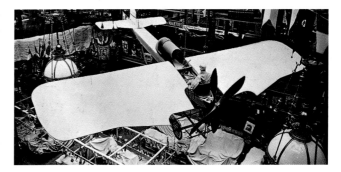

The second Deperdussin-de Feure canard, here on display in a Paris department store. But perhaps it is only a model. Again, note the coaxial propellers and mid-mounted engine. (Peter M Bowers collection)

the coaxial propeller. Both the forward vertical and horizontal surfaces were fitted with Blériot-like oyster-shell tip control surfaces.

Meanwhile Deperdussin was working on a series of small fast monoplanes, and also a series of fast monoplane seaplanes which would make him famous:

Type A, 1910: A long thin monoplane with a variety of complex undercarriages, a pair of tall vertical kingposts, and long triangular fin and stabilizer; 50 hp Clerget and a 3-cylinder Anzani. Some with uncovered fuselages were used for training by the Central Flying School at Point Cook, in Australia. Another, with a 4-cylinder Austro-Daimler, was shown at the Paris Salon in 1910. Others were used at the Deperdussin school at Reims.

Type B, 1910-1911: A 2-seater similar to the Type C, with small triangular fin and rectangular rudder, and a 50 hp Gnôme.

In May 1911 Deperdussin took out a patent on an engine arrangement featuring 2-100 hp Gnômes, one on each side of the front fuselage, combining in a gearbox to drive 2 contra-rotating tractor propellers. A photograph shows the device mounted on an airframe – it may not have been completed. The series continued:

Type C, 1911: This 1 – or 2-seater featured a long gently-curving fin attached to a rectangular rudder; 2 uprights still served as kingposts. The 70 hp Gnôme was partly cowled. It also appeared with 2 pairs of undercarriage wheels.

(Span: 10.5 m; length to tailpost: 9 m; 70 hp Gnôme)

Type D? a 2-seater.

(Span: 12.75 m; length (to tailpost): 10.5 m; 70 hp Austro-Daimler, 70 hp Panhard-Levassor, 100 hp Clerget, or 70/100 hp Gnôme)

Type F? a 2-3-4-seater.

(Span: 15 m; length (to tailpost): 12 m; 70 or 100 hp Gnôme)

Type Nardini, 1911: This 75 hp single-seater flown by and perhaps built for Nardini had deep cutouts at the wing-root trailing edges, and an angular extension forward at the wing-root leading edges. A rectangular cut-out in the fin allowed for movement of the one-piece elevator.

Type Concours Militaire, 1911: An Anzani-powered 3-seater similar to the Type Nardini, with a 2nd diagonal brace in the pylon structure. Another Type Militaire appeared at Reims in October 1911 with a Clerget rotary, and without the third pylon strut on each side.

Type Concours Militaire, 1911: A larger and heavier 3-place military machine with a 100 hp inline Clerget. The leading edge

Above and below: A single – and what was probably built as a 2-seater Deperdussin Type A, but which managed at least to seat if not to carry 5 people. Note distinctive twin uprights as kingposts. (Courtesy of the Musée de l'Air et de l'Espace/Le Bourget-France)

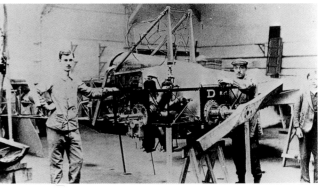

The 1911 twin-Gnôme installation in a Deperdussin fuselage frame, designed to drive counter-rotating propellers, one of which appears in this photograph. (Courtesy of the Musée de l'Air et de l'Espace/Le Bourget-France)

The Deperdussin Type C, with cowled Gnôme. (Author's collection)

extensions were omitted, the pylon consisted of 2 parallel verticals only, and a fuel tank with rounded ends hung under the fuselage.

Type ?, June 1911: Vidart was flying a smaller single-seater with a 2-triangles pylon, and a curved fin.

2-Seat Tandem (year unknown): 3 designs, one with a 70 hp Gnôme, one with a 50-60 hp Anzani, one with an 80 hp Anzani.

Type Meeting de Grenoble: Possibly a smoother version of Type B?

Type Militaire (year unknown): 2 single-seater designs, one with a 50 hp Gnôme, the other with a 80 hp Anzani.

Type Grand Prix d'Anjou, 1912: A 2-seater with separate cockpits, a 2-triangle pylon, scalloped trailing edges, large wing-root cut-outs, and wheels of large diameter. The angular rudder carried the number 22.

Type ?, 1912: G Busson flew this single-seater at Issy. It had the 2-triangles pylon, scalloped trailing edges, and a swelling aluminum coaming that almost surrounded the pilot.

L'Epervier, 1912: A military single-seater, with a 2-triangles pylon, a Gnôme in a horseshoe cowling, and what became a familiar Deperdussin trademark, 1-piece sculpted undercarriage legs. No 42, a Deperdussin number, was painted on the tail.

Type Militaire, 1912: A 3-place machine, perhaps the same as Type Militaire 1911, with the seats tandem in a wide bathtub of a coaming. The fin was small and triangular, the rudder a simple rectangle. The pylon was formed of a pair of triple struts.

The Deperdussin Type Concours Militaire of 1911. (Author's collection)

The sleek Deperdussin Type Meeting de Grenoble. (Courtesy of the Musée de l'Air et de l'Espace/Le Bourget-France)

Note the large wheels and wing-root cut-outs on the Deperdussin Type Grand Prix d'Anjou. (Courtesy of the Musée de l'Air et de l'Espace/Le Bourget-France)

Below: The Deperdussin Epervier of 1912. (Courtesy of the Musée de l'Air et de l'Espace/Le Bourget-France)

(Span: 12.5 m; length: 8.8 m; loaded weight: 930 kg; speed: 110 kmh; 100 hp Gnôme)

Type ?, 1912: a 2-place machine. The pilot and passenger sat in 2 separated cockpits, the wing-roots were cut out, and the trailing edges scalloped. (Perhaps Type M? Perhaps for Military?)

(Span: 10.63 m; length: 7.3 m; loaded weight: 550 kg; speed: 105 kmh; 70 hp Gnôme).

Monocoque, 80 hp Gnôme.

Type Record de Vitesse, 1912: Védrines flew this one for the speed record in January 1912. It had a monocoque fuselage, wing-root cut-outs and leading edge root extensions.

Type E, Ecole, 1912: a single-seater, the long box fuselage uncovered on top, a triangular fin and square rudder with rectangular cut-out for elevator movement, scalloped trailing edges, and a 2-triangles pylon. A similar racing version appeared with flatter airfoil section.

(Span: 8.85 m; length: 7.3 m; loaded weight: 300 kg; speed: 80 kmh; 30 hp Anzani)

Twin-boom pusher, Jan 1913 (model only): This was to have been a 2-seater, with pilot and passenger seated diagonally in the front of a blunt nacelle, with a pusher propeller at its rear. The twin booms were flattened versions of one of the monocoque

Two views of the model twin-boom pusher, designed by Deperdussin in 1913. (Author's collection)

Prévost's Deperdussin Monocoque Reims of 1913. (Courtesy of the Musée de l'Air et de l'Espace/Le Bourget-France)

This often-printed photo of what appears to a captured Deperdussin was in fact license-built in Russia. (Courtesy of the Musée de l'Air et de l'Espace/Le Bourget-France)

The 3-part elevator for the twin boom pusher – one of the few parts actually built. (Courtesy of the Musée de l'Air et de l'Espace/Le Bourget-France)

Deperdussins, and the wing panels seemed like standard panels. Parts of it were later built in the Blériot works.

Monocoque Reims, 1913: Prévost flew in R 2 in the Gordon-Bennett race, powered with a 160 hp twin-row Gnôme; the machine was built with both double and a triple kingposts. It had leading edge root extensions. The wings had slightly curved trailing edges and were narrower at the root than at the tip; there were substantial wing-root cut-outs.

(The single-seater marked with a German cross and the numbers 2-XIX was built, not by Deperdussin, but by Lebedev in Russia, under license. It was captured by the Germans.)

Deperdussin de Marc Pourpe, 1914: Similar in its forward coaming to Busson's of 1912, but without scalloped training edges. The

The Deperdussin de Marc Pourpe of 1914. Note the pilot's shoulder harness. (Courtesy of the Musée de l'Air et de l'Espace/Le Bourget-France)

The Type Mitrailleur of 1914. (Author's collection)

Lemoine's second experiment with a parachute; the experimenter is sitting under the fuselage in front of his parachute. (Author's collection)

twin triangles of the pylon were very high for extra strength in inverted flight, and curved at the top; a fingernail-shaped cowl covered the top of the Gnôme. A photo shows Silvio Petrossi, Italian stunt pilot, in a similar machine on the Christofferson wooden runway at Ocean Beach, California, in 1915.

Type Mitrailleur, 1914: This was a handsome 2 seater with separated oval cockpits set into the curved turtleback. The 100 hp Anzani was half cowled, and the undercarriage seemed heavier than other Deperdussins of the period. The tail surfaces were simplified and resembled those of the big seaplanes; the wing-root trailing edges were cut out. The Type Mitrailleur, 1914, was an experiment to test the usefulness of a machine-gun position where the gunner stood up right behind the propeller in an elaborate cage. At least 2 were built; Prévost tested one in February 1914.

On 11 February Lemoine tested a similar 2-seater, with the fin and rudder mounted underneath the rear fuselage. His passenger, Le Bourhis, tested a Bonnet parachute strapped to his back. And on 29 March, Lemoine, flying solo from the rear seat, tested another parachute carried in a package resembling a life raft strapped under the fuselage. The propeller he used showed an oddly-sculpted hub.

The seaplanes were equally famous:

1. No 11 at Deauville – a double 3-strut pylon, each float strut with 2 single diagonal braces attached at both inside and outside edges of the floats, big (1 or 2?) seat cockpit, monocoque fuselage, fully-cowled engine and big spinner. The triangular fin and rectangular rudder did not extend below the aft fuselage. (Type H?)

2. Tandem 2-seater with long double cockpit, long flat-sided fuselage, wing-root cut-outs, float attachments, complex 2-tiered assembly of struts with 2 horizontal bars above each float, 2-triangle pylon, small triangular fin and angular rudder with ver-

A close-up of the action in the Deperdussin Type Mitrailleur. The gunner is equipped with a safety harness, however inadequate it may be. (Courtesy of the Musée de l'Air et de l'Espace/Le Bourget-France)

The big Deperdussin at Deauville, painted 11, requires real horsepower at this stage. (Courtesy of the Musée de l'Air et de l'Espace/Le Bourget-France)

tical trailing edge. One flew at Geneva in August 1912; another – perhaps the same aircraft, flew in the same month at St Malô.

(Span: 12.5 m; length: 8.5 m; loaded weight: 640 kg; speed: 100 kmh; 80 hp Gnôme)

3. No 19 at Monaco, 1913 – tandem 2-seater with a single long cockpit, wing cut-outs, double 3-strut pylon, each strut float with 2 pairs of diagonal supporting struts, fin and rudder symmetri-

No 19 at Monaco; Prévost won the first Schneider Cup. (Author's collection)

cally above and below aft fuselage, full cowl and large spinner. A similar – the same? – machine flew in the Paris-Deauville race, carrying the number 4.

4. Shown at the 1913 Paris Salon, the seaplane featured a monocoque fuselage with nearly flat sides, a bathtub 2-seat cockpit, a 2-triangle pylon, fully-cowled engine and spinner, each float strut with a pair of diagonal supports. The fin and rudder were set symmetrically above and below the fuselage.

5. At Monaco, 1914 – flown by Prévost, this one featured simple N-strut attachments to the float centerlines, a 2-triangle pylon, and a single-seat oval cockpit in the monocoque fuselage. It carried the number 4.

6: Also at Monaco in 1914, a similar machine with a 4-strut pylon and rectangular rudder.

7. Type Tamise, in 1912, an odd 2-seater with flat sides but a fuller, more streamlined fuselage than the pre-monocoque fuselages, 2 separate cockpits in tandem, angular rudder equally above and below fuselage – with no fin! The float attachments were similar to No 2, above. In fact, this machine was built by De Brouckère, in Belgium, under license.

8. Again, with float attachments like No 2; fuselage shape also like #2; fin and rudder like #3; 2-triangle pylon. One photo shows it in front of yachts.

Dergint
An entry for the Concours de Sécurité, 1914.

Dernaut
A monoplane of 1908.

Deschamps et Blondeau
Owners of the Chantiers Navales de la Seine, these builders of motorboats in Monaco were reported to be building 2 aeroplanes in 1909, but the designer(s) of those machines is (are) unknown.

Desfons
Little is recorded of this twin-propeller seaplane which had front and rear elevators interconnected. A "cone redresseur" (conical stabilizer) was set in the middle to serve as parachute in case of accident.

Desfontaines
An unknown design built in Billancourt.

Desmonceaux, de Givray, et Gallisti
A glider with these names was built in 1908, to be tested in northern France.

Type Tamise. Note the untypical rudder shape – this machine was built by De Brouckère in Belgium under license. (Courtesy of the Musée de l'Air et de l'Espace/Le Bourget-France)

The Désusclade monoplane. (Author's collection)

Désusclade
In 1910 a Désusclade built a monoplane a little like a Nieuport with a Hanriot undercarriage.

(Span: 9.5 m; 30 hp 3-cylinder Anzani)

Detable et Tabary
Pierre Detable and his son worked with Tabary on the design and construction of several gliders, beginning in 1892. Most of them were models, but at least one them spanned 6.5 m with a wing area of 36 sqm, and was fitted with a 2 hp Herdtle-Bruneau engine in 1908; it was said to lack both tail and controls.

In 1912 the Detables planned an automatically stable aircraft, but lack of funds apparently prevented its completion. But a Detable was entered in the 1914 Concours de Sécurité as an "apparatus with stability-correcting planes." Available photos show a short-span tractor biplane with top-wing overhangs, side-curtains, a long uncovered fuselage. The "tailplane" was the full span of the lower wing and ran along the underside of the fuselage to the tail, where small elevators were mounted one on each side; a small rudder was fitted on top. But the odd feature of the Detable was the 2 fuselage-length half-conical surfaces set on each side of the long tailplane, with the points forward and the rear semicircular ends open. The pilot sat underneath the fuselage behind the axle.

Devaux

An unknown monoplane of 1911.

Dewailly et Vertadier

A design tried in 1911 – perhaps a model?

Dhumbert

The testing of this machine, design unknown, was mentioned as taking place in the Department of Isère.

Dinoird

Dinoird was one of the amateurs inspired by the success of Louis Breguet on the airfield of La Brayelle near Douai in northern France. He first built an unsuccessful biplane in 1910, and by the end of the following year had nearly completed an Antoinette copy with a fully-covered fuselage. The pilot sat aft of the wings behind a large fairing with 2 small mica windows.

(Span: 9 m; chord: 2.1 m; wing area: 18.9 sqm; length: 7.8 m; 50 hp Antoinette)

Another monoplane with Dinoird No 2 on the rudder, featured a sort of biplane tailplane, 2 small triangular fins above and below the uncovered aft fuselage, a high pylon, and a tailwheel.

De Dion-Bouton

Albert, Marquis de Dion, was one of the most famous names in automobile history. This tall commanding figure was associated with the small one of Georges Bouton; together they founded the famous car and motor company. In 1889, with Trepardoux, they designed and had built a rotary 4-cylinder radial motor, and later a series of more powerful inline aeromotors, more or less modeled on the air-cooled Renault: in 1918 the most powerful French engine was the experimental and unreliable 930 hp V-16 de Dion-Bouton. De Dion founded the Automobile Club de France in 1895; but also, much involved with aviation, he was one of the founders and first chairman of the Chambre Syndicale de l'Industrie Aéronautical which in turn created the Exposition de la Locomotion Aérienne, today the Le Bourget Salon International de l'Air et de l'Espace. His firm designed various kites and, eventually, 2 unsuccessful aeroplanes.

The first, a multiplane built by Corneloup, was shown at the 1909 Exposition in its uncompleted form; it is likely not to have been finished. The main structure remotely resembled that of the Wright Flyer, with twin rudders at the rear, a single small tailplane, and a triplane front elevator. There were no wings as such: on each side a frame stood outward at 30° dihedral, and at the end of each frame were 4 wing segments of about 3 meters in length. 4 pusher propellers were driven at 450 rpm by a de Dion-Bouton V8 mounted at the bottom of the central structure. The top plane of the elevator warped, the other 2 were fixed. Each of the 4 wing segments on each side could be inclined left and right. The take-off wheels were to be raised in flight, and skids were to be used on landing.

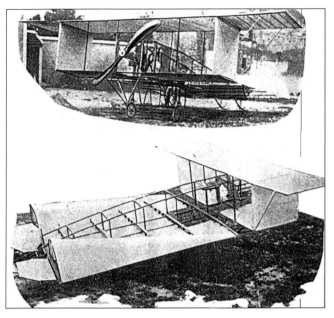

Two views of the Detable entered in the Concours de Sécurité. Note the odd half-conical surfaces aft. (Author's collection)

The Dinoird monoplane marked Monoplan Dinoird No 2. (Author's collection)

De Dion Bouton's second machine, first stage, under construction; the ailerons seem not to have been fitted so far. (Author's collection)

(Full span: 12 m; length; 9 m; total wing area: 62 sqm; front elevator span: 3 m; gross weight: 700 kg; 100 hp de Dion-Bouton V8)

The second de Dion-Bouton design was a biplane with a single front elevator, built at the Espinosa Avionnerie (SACAA). The fuselage consisted of twin booms each with 2 kingposts, the pilot sitting between them amidships; the wings were rectangular and of equal span, with ailerons mounted on square panels set between them; the tail was fixed at the ends of the outriggers. The 100 hp DDB V8 motor with a large radiator set on the leading edge of the lower wing

The big de Dion Bouton, second stage. Note the huge kingposts supporting the tail booms. (Courtesy of the Musée de l'Air et de l'Espace/Le Bourget-France)

drove, Wright-style, 2 4-blade pusher propellers. The machine was tested in 1911 at Chares by a pilot named Coursier. Photographs appearing in 1912 showed several modifications: the ailerons were now made part of the longer upper wings and the single tailplane was replaced with a biplane cell. Some said the machine was designed to test a new DDB 100 hp engine, and others said it could carry up to 10 people; on 2 August 1911 piloted by Champel, it leaped over a depression in the center of the field. De Dion compared his giant to the huge steamship Great Eastern, and admitted it changed form continuously as he worked on it.

(Span (upper): 18.5 m; (lower): 16 m; length: 15 m; wing area; 80 sqm; propeller diameter: 3.2 m; empty weight: 450 kg)

Domingo

The Aéraptère was one of the oddities of the 1914 Concours de Sécurité. Like several others in the competition it did not fly. Pivoted at the top of a pyramidal pylon set on a 4-wheeled frame was a large half-cylindrical tunnel, fabric-covered on the top, which could be adjusted for incidence. 2 semicircular flaps at each end allowed the pilot to regulate the amount of air circulating through the vault. A rectangular rudder was set at the opening and a hinged flap for elevator control was set below the center of the "wing." Huge unsupported coil springs ran between the wheels on each side, evidently to help in steering on the ground. The pilot faced 7 control levers mounted on the same axis in front of him; these worked the flaps, rudder, and the overhead vault. A marvellous exercise in coordination, and safe, as well.

(Length: c 10 m; height; c 8 m; 100 hp Anzani radial)

Domingo's Aéraptère, crew aboard, engine running. The elevator surface seems to be calling for a descent. (Author's collection)

The Aéraptère, now lightened by one crew member, tries it again. (Courtesy of the Musée de l'Air et de l'Espace/Le Bourget-France)

Dorand

Captain-Engineer (later Major) Jean Dorand was assigned in 1894 to the Etablissement Aérostatique at Chalais-Meudon, where he began the study of heavier-than-air machines: the Army was not satisfied with the achievements of civilian constructors, so Chalais-Meudon took the opportunity of having Dorand on the staff to study its own designs. In 1904 he wrote a report on manned kites, and so he began the construction of a steerable kite in 1908; he hoped to develop an automatically stable aeroplane.

When the powered machine was built, it was a huge quadruplane nearly 40' high, made from a giant triplane kite set over a fourth lower wing and a rudder. The pilot sat above and behind the 45 hp 3-cylinder Anzani all installed in a triangular frame hinged below the kite; by pushing or pulling on a control bar, the pilot could alter the kite's angle of attack. The big wood-framed 2-bladed Dorand propeller was fabric-covered and the pitch could be controlled by the pilot. Tested late in 1908, the machine was modified into triplane and then biplane configuration, but it was no more successful than before.

These experiments were kept quiet, but early in 1909 rumors began to spread about the "secret military aeroplane designed in Chalais and tested in Satory"; this led some historians to claim that the first Dorand was the first military aeroplane: it was built by a military officer and tested in a military establishment.

(Span: 11.5 m; wing area (as triplane): 90 sqm; gross weight: 500 kg; 45 hp 3-cylinder Anzani driving a 2.7-meter diameter Dorand-Renard propeller)

But Dorand was working along other lines as well, and more efficient ones. Though studying propellers, he was likely to have been involved in Gaudard's and Legrand's experiments on a Voisin. In 1910 at the military aviation laboratory at Chalais-Meudon he built his

One of the Dorand powered kites. Note the triangular frame with the engine and propeller attached, hinged to the main structure. It was Dorand's idea to swing this element back and forth for control – in this case, by control lines. (Courtesy of the Musée de l'Air et de l'Espace/Le Bourget-France)

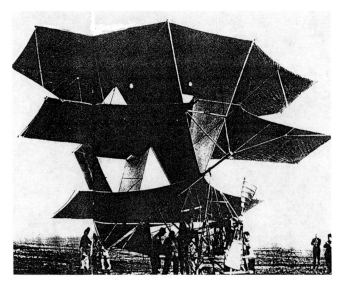

The Dorand as a triplane, retaining the swinging engine and control unit. (Author's collection)

Below: The big Dorand now as a biplane. (Courtesy of the Musée de l'Air et de l'Espace/Le Bourget-France)

Below right: Close-up of the business part of the Dorand biplane. Note the pivot on which the control unit swung. (Courtesy of the Musée de l'Air et de l'Espace/Le Bourget-France)

biplan-laboratoire. This, his most famous design, could be considered one of the most outstanding achievements of pre-WWI aviation. A classic biplane with staggered wings, forward elevators supported by skids as on the Maurice Farman, a tractor propeller and biplane tail unit, it was powered by a 60 hp air-cooled Renault. Dorand used it as a flying test-bed for wings and propellers, so it was constantly being modified. Basic equipment included a venturi to measure airspeed, a flexible engine mounting to study dynamometric balance, an electric tachometer, an hydraulic measuring-box, and various glass levels filled with tinted water to check speed, pitch, and roll – and a camera to take pictures of them all!

In 1912 Dorand designed his biplan de place forte (fortress biplane) similar to the laboratory biplane. The crew of 2 sat in a short covered nacelle behind a flat-mounted water-cooled Salmson driving a tractor propeller though a shaft. This aircraft was later equipped with a wireless set.

Dorand's most successful pre-War design was the 1913 armored biplane: at least 6 were built with the designation Do 1 on the rudder. The lower wing was slightly shorter and set forward of the upper wing, "to improve the lowering of pressure on its upper surface." The long covered fuselage had 2 cockpits forward, pilot in the rear. The biplane tail unit had 2 elevators and was fitted ahead of a large rudder. On one of the Do Is, Labouchère flew 18,000 km in 1913; early in 1914, a group of 6 led by Captain Leclerc flew 1,400 km in 6 stages: Villacoublay to Reims to Verdun to Chalons to Villacoublay to Dijon, and back to Villacoublay again, suffering only 2 "incidents."

The Do 1 was the forerunner of the 1916 Renault AR1s and AR2s; very precise data were made available by Dorand.

(Span: (upper) 12 m; length: 12 m; wing area: 50 sqm; empty weight without armor: 625 kg; weight of armor plates: 90 kg; gross weight: 1000 kg;; endurance: 4 hr; max speed: 108 kmh at sea-level, 100 kmh at 3000'; slowest speed: 55 kmh; ceiling: 8,400 m; climb to 4,500 m: 16 min; take-off: 90 m; land: 95 m; 10-cylinder 86.5 hp radial Anzani)

Dottori

The big Dottori biplane, built by Pouvarel in 1912, resembled the first de Dion Bouton. A triplane elevator cell was mounted forward, and a biplane cell at the rear, which could be tilted left and right. The pilot sat with 2 control wheels behind the 50 hp motor which drove,

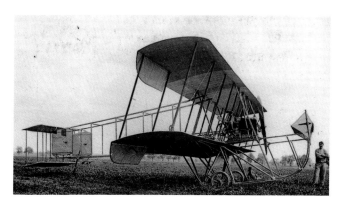

The Dorand biplan-laboratoire of 1912. (Author's collection)

Close-up of the Dorand biplan-laboratoire. (Author's collection)

Wright-style, 2 2-bladed pusher propellers. It was tested unsuccessfully at Issy.

(Span: 12 m; length: 11 m; wing area: 54 sqm; gross weight (including 120 kg for the motor): 450 kg; 50 hp Puvarel)

Doutre

Even though the Wrights had concluded that aeroplanes should be stabilized by direct pilot control, many French designers kept searching as late as 1914 for automatic stability. This fruitless quest led to various curious inventions as well as to the Concours de Sécurité of June 1914.

The Dorand Do 1 armored biplane of 1913; this one is marked Do 1 No 4. (Author's collection)

The only automatic stabilizer with any commercial success was invented by a lawyer, and was based on the pressure of the airflow against a steel plate. Doutre assumed the aeroplane flew level at a constant speed, and his device would counteract only gusts or engine failure. When the aeroplane slowed down, the stabilizer effected a nose-down attitude; and if the speed then increased dangerously it brought the machine back to a less dangerous course. The Doutre Stabilizer was claimed to have little inertia, and thus could respond quickly and accurately.

On 3 April 1911 the Société des Appareils Aériens (SAAD) Doutre was founded; Doutre contributed a Maurice Farman equipped with a Pharabet motor and the Doutre Stabilizer. The firm announced that it had sold 100 Stabilizers in 1913, but it was much more reticent about its own aircraft production; a sketch of a Doutre tandem biplane appeared in *Jane's All the World's Aircraft*, but it may not have been actually built. An aeroplane fitted with the Stabilizer was sold to Spain in May 1912; it was probably a Doutre. The firm offered designs of 1, 2, and 3 seats powered by 50 – or 70 hp Renaults; at the 1912 Exposition it displayed a 70 hp 2-seater with "long horns" fitted with a smoothly-faired nacelle.

(Span: (upper) 16.1 m; (lower) 13 m; length: 12.25 m; wing area: 50 sqm; empty weight: 600 kg (the stabilizer alone weighed 20 kg); speed range: 56-90 kmh; 50 or 70 hp Renault)

At the end of 1912 Doutre organized a flying school at Compiègne on the airfield of Corbeaulieu; Martinet and Legagneux were the managers and Didier the chief pilot. It is likely that not all the school's machines were Doutres. In 1913 the firm designed a lateral stabilizer which was tested by Didier; that summer 2 other Doutres were tested, one of them an aerobus for 3 or 5, fitted with a 100 hp 10-cylinder Anzani. One Doutre was flown with a radial engine, perhaps the same aeroplane that appeared in the Salons; its stabilizer had been lightened. The second was a military 2-seater with the pilot sitting at the rear of the nacelle; it was reported similar to the first one but without the horned skids; this one showed a wind-driven propeller set on the top wing.

Drouhet

A Drouhet biplane appeared at Issy in 1912.

Drzewiecki

A naval engineer and submarine designer, Drzewiecki was involved with aviation as early as 1904, assisting in the Archdeacon experiments on the sand dunes along the Channel, being one of the first members of the Commission d'Aviation of the Aéro Club de France, and having a glider built by d'Argent.

His most successful achievements in aviation, however, were not his flying machines but his propellers, the famous Ratmanoff Normale propellers – which did not carry his name. Drzewiecki built 2 unsuccessful tandem monoplanes, both designed to be automatically stable.

Doutre's Maurice Farman with his patented Stabilizer. It is visible under the nose of the nacelle, steel plate facing the air-stream. (Author's collection)

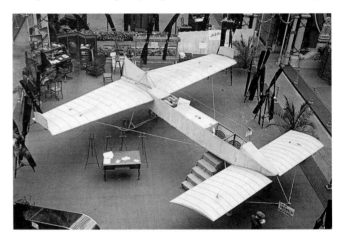

The first Drzewiecki canard at the 1912 Salon. (Courtesy of the Musée de l'Air et de l'Espace/Le Bourget-France)

The first was built by Ratmanoff and exhibited on his stand at the 1912 Salon. The shorter front wing (Eiffel airfoil No 8) with greater incidence (8°) had lift similar to that of the rear wing (Eiffel No 13bis, 5°). If the aeroplane reared up, the lift from the front wing increased more slowly than that of the rear, tending to right the aircraft. Climb and descent were controlled by varying the angles of attack; roll was controlled by differential variations. 2 rudders at the tips of the rear wings could also be operated as airbrakes. The forward undercarriage was fitted with a large shock-absorber sliding along the bottom of the fuselage. The pilot and passenger sat in tandem just forward of the water-cooled Labor engine, which drove a pusher propeller at the tail through a long shaft: the whole machine weighed 750 kg. It is likely that tests in Eiffel's wind-tunnel showed some lateral instability.

The second design was similar but better streamlined. A 2-seater for military use, it had the observer moved forward and the front wing raised above him for a better view. The pilot sat amidships with an 80 hp Gnôme at the tail; the undercarriage was simplified. This machine killed its military pilot, Captain Félix, during a demonstration for the Concours de Sécurité on 17 June 1914.

Dubois-Rioux

In 1912 Dubois and Rioux designed a machine meant to fly at 140 kmh and also to hover: they described it as an "invulnerable war machine." A very handsome as well as ambitious ornithopter, it was unsuccessful like all its predecessors – and its successors so far. The frame was all-metal, fabric-covered. A long narrow tailplane and elevator were mounted on the top of the rear fuselage, whic had a long nearly cylindrical shape; the rudder was set below the elevator. The wings had flexible tips and trailing edges, and were actuated by a 35 hp Viale mounted backwards at the nose. A large inertial wheel was to regulate the flapping movements.

(Span: 10.5 m; wing area: 15 sqm; empty weight: 360 kg; 35 hp Viale)

Dufour

Jean Dufour built at least one small biplane glider in 1908. It was very flimsy and loose, with a swallowtail tailplane and some sort of forward elevator. The airfoil section was flat.

His first powered design was based on the Blériot XI and built by Labaudie et Puthet. Sometimes described as an "ordinary monoplane," it had a classic fuselage of square section, and a long-legged undercarriage with skids ahead of the castered wheels. The long wings had rounded up-curved tips, and seemcd in the photographs never to be quite squarely rigged. A fixed tailplane was mounted on top of the fuselage ahead of the curved rudder, and an elevator was hinged at the stern. Dufour No 1 flew first on 27 March 1910, having been begun late in 1909.

(Span: 10.8 m; length: 10 m; wing area: 25 sqm; gross weight: 310 kg; a 45/50 hp Labor-Picker engine replaced the original 35 hp 4-cylinder Guérin)

Dufour No 2, completed by September 1910, was a biplane with a front elevator, monoplane tailplane and single rudder, and a 35 hp Gnôme. The top wing was of greater span than the lower, with ailerons set into it. The undercarriage was fitted with 2 pairs of wheels. This was probably the Dufour mentioned as being at the Garbero school in Antibes. It was reported that both Dufour aircraft had ribs made of frêno-liège (ash and oak).

A 2-seater is also mentioned in November 1911; it was either a new design or the old one modified. One journalist reported its roll-out in November 1911.

Duhany-Suthy

This was a biplane glider with tailplane on a long outrigger, and no vertical surfaces; it was described in 1909.

Dumas

Alex Dumas built 3-wheeled cars between 1899 and 1903 in the Paris suburb of Champigny, and then turned to aviation. In July 1910 the Société Générale de Fabrication de l'Aéroplane A Dumas completed its first and probably only production, the monoplane designed by

The Dubois-Rioux ornithopter. The range of movement of the wings may not have been designed to end at the ground. (Courtesy of the Musée de l'Air et de l'Espace/Le Bourget-France)

Two views of the first Dufour, the monoplane. Note fully-flying rudder and aft stabilizer. (Peter M Bowers collection)

Alex Dumas. Similar to the Nieuport, it had a rudder hinged at the stern and set below the tailplane. The wings were arched; the fuselage was all wood without wire bracing. The undercarriage had a central skid, as on the REP. A wheel controlled the rudder and elevators, and pedals the wing-warping cables. The machine was finally tested in August with a 40/45 hp Gyp engine.

Dumas is better remembered, however, for his articles on aeronautics and his famous yearly journal which succeeded de Gaston's.

(Span: 65 m; length: 8.6 m; wing area: 14 sqm; weight: 210 kg)

Dumont

The testing of this machine, design unknown, was reported as taking place at Pont de Briques, Department of Pas de Calais.

Dumontet et Talon

A monoplane of this name was built at Sai, in Normandy, in 1909, sponsored by G de la Nezières; no further details available. Since Sai, near Argentan, is also near Flers, it is possible that this aircraft may have been the Chèdeville.

Dumoulin

Dumoulin was a pastry-cook with little knowledge of either physical or aeronautical science: he devoted much of his small income to the development of ill-fated designs based on the flat cardboard roundels used under cakes – he threw them to make them fly.

In 1902 he worked with the Viscount de Cazes on a large helicopter rotor made of many thin blades; in 1904, in Agen, in southern France, in the hangar of the Comte de la Rochefoucault, he built a strange "tracteur pour la navigation aérienne." Above a high wooden frame was mounted a circular wing on a vertical axis; just below turned 2 Archimedean screws mounted side-by-side along horizontal semi-cylindrical cowlings. The wing turned on its axis, and the pilot sitting under a second fixed circular wing worked the screws himself. Subsequently – perhaps it should have been done earlier – he built models to study the gyroscopic effect of propellers, and built a propeller-driven bicycle. In 1911 he patented an "aéroplane gyropendulaire," and built a model of it – he called it Saturnian – in 1912, but did not complete it until 1921. It was based on a turning circular wing and 2 tractor propellers. Dumoulin died in 1923 age 57, always hopeful, always unsuccessful.

Duparquet

After founding a flying school with de Baeder, Duparquet built an automatically stable aircraft in 1911 or 1912. It was reported flown by Joanny Burtin, and eventually crashed in Evreux, Normandy.

Duray-Mathis

The automobile racer A Duray, in association with H Mathis, built a double canard biplane early in 1909; it was finished probably in late May. A 4-cylinder inline motor was set on the bottom of a high rectangular frame mounted on 4 wheels, and drove a large 2-blade pusher propeller through long shafts. The pilot sat above the engine on the lower wing; the forward biplane cell served as elevators, with the

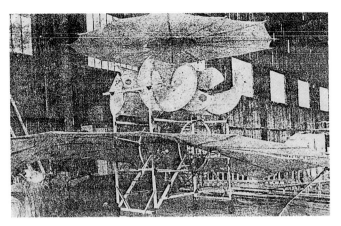

The Dumoulin "tracteur pour la navigation aérienne" of 1904. (Author's collection)

rudder fixed in front of everything. Ailerons, each pivoting around a central axis between the tips of the main wings, were actuated by pendulums. Nothing is known about its performance, if any. Duray went on later to fly Henry Farmans.

Dussot

Auguste Dussot's flyingboat had been entered in various competitions since 1910, but made its first and last official appearance in August 1913 at Deauville, flown under the number 13 by the young de Bosano. The aircraft was sometimes referred to by the latter name.

It was a 2-seater parasol monoplane with a long rectangular-section hull and slender tip floats. The Taube-shaped wing was braced from a pyramidal structure on top and was fitted with short deep ailerons. The Anzani, mounted behind and below the trailing edge, drove a 2-blade pusher propeller, and was equipped with a compressed-air-powered Gendron starter. On its first flight at Deauville, it "cavorted dangerously" and crashed, injuring de Bosano. Dussot later invented

The pretty but unsuccessful Dussot at Deauville in 1913. (Author's collection)

a parachute, but gave it up for lack of funds and went on to become a cycle mechanic.

(Span: 13.5 m; 100 hp radial Anzani)

Dutel

Dutel designed and built a monoplane for a tennis-racket manufacturer named Tunmer; it was Tunmer's only brief foray into aviation, and the so-called Tunmer machine was only briefly mentioned in February 1910. It is reported that Dutel had been interested in flying machines for 20 years. A 30 hp V2 engine drove 2 pusher propellers through a clutch and chain, and through an axle and pinions another tiny third propeller under the tiny rudder at the tail. One side-mounted wheel controlled the front elevator, and the other warped the wings.

Dutheil et Chalmers

These famous motor builders made a brief entry into aeroplane building. In 1909 they built a biplane similar to the Farman, but with triplane elevators and a single rudder between the tailplanes; ailerons were set between the wings.

The firm, wishing to produce copies of the Demoiselle, received a single example from Santos-Dumont, but did not carry through the project. This is the Demoiselle preserved and is now exhibited at the Musée de l'Air et de l'Espace at Le Bourget.

(Span: 10 m; length: 10m; 42 hp flat 4-cylinder water-cooled Dutheil et Chalmers)

Duvernois

A monoplane reported in Périgord.

E

Eparvier

H Eparvier was a manufacturer in Manthes, in southwestern France, who built 2 and perhaps 3 aircraft in 1909 and 1910.

The first was a large monoplane, designed probably in late 1908, with a long clear-doped fuselage uncovered in the middle, and a triangular fin and tailplanes. The undercarriage had castered wheels; the high-set tailwheel also trailed. A long streamlined tank sat on top of the fuselage just behind the pilot. The water-cooled 2-stroke 4-inline 40 hp Côte – sometimes a Prini-Berthaud – weighed 110 kg, the whole aircraft 350 kg.

A second Eparvier may have been a triplane that appeared in September 1909, powered with a Gnôme, but this may have been a wholly different aircraft.

The second monoplane – and perhaps the third Eparvier – was similar to the Hanriot, appeared at Ambérieu, near Lyon, in April 1910, and was still flying at the school 18 months later. The triangular fuselage was shorter than on the first design, completely covered; the undercarriage was made with 3 pairs of struts, 2 wheels and 2 long horned skids. The 50 hp engine was said to be Eparvier's own design, prob-

The first Eparvier; it resembles a large Blériot XI. (Courtesy of the Musée de l'Air et de l'Espace/Le Bourget-France)

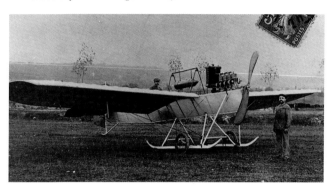

The second Eparvier, of 1910. (Courtesy of the Musée de l'Air et de l'Espace/Le Bourget-France)

ably the earlier Côte modified. The tank was hung under the Blériot-style pylon which braced the large rectangular deeply-curved wings. One 3-piece lifting elevator was mounted on the top of the rear fuselage just ahead of the trapezoidal rudder; there was no fin. The pilot sat well aft of the wings to balance the engine. Marius Lacrouze flew it in 1911.

D'Equevilly-Monjustin

The strange machine designed by the Marquis d'Equevilly, a navy engineer, is one of the most famous of the early oddities of aviation. Whatever the Marquis' source of inspiration and regardless of whether his machine flew, it was, as he said himself, simple and cheap. Designed in 1907 at Equevilly north of Paris, it consisted of a 4-wheel frame on which sat 2 vertical oval hoops into which were set 5 pairs of half-wings and one full wing, all of flat airfoil section. A 10 hp Buchet drove through a chain at 500 rpm a 2-blade tractor propeller. Various modifications were made to it in the course of its short life, including the addition of a sixth wing across the top of the hoops.

In June 1908 it was damaged in a fire at Carreau's garage where it was stored; it appeared again in November 1908 with narrower circular hoops and some 50 small wings arranged more or less horizontally inside. In this form it was tested at Issy at the end of November, when the wing frames were tilted back to give them all some positive angle of attack.

(Width: 5m; wing area: (lst version): 25 sqm; length: 2 m, with the propeller removed; gross weight: 140 kg; 10 hp Buchet)

The first form of the d'Equevilly-Monjustin, with 6 wings. (Author's collection)

The d'Equevilly-Monjustin with a 7th wing added on top; the wheels are turned sideways in this photograph to facilitate towing. (Courtesy of the Musée de l'Air et de l'Espace/Le Bourget-France)

Essort Aérien

A monoplane of this name at Juvisy was tested on 18 August 1912 by Couvert.

Etévé

The third Wright Flyer built by CGNA was sometimes known as the Etévé, named for the later famous Captain Etévé who built a special automatic stabilizer at the rear of the machine behind the rudder, linked to the front elevator. The rudder of this machine was marked CW3 (Chalais-Wright No 3, or the third Wright delivered to Chalais-Meudon) the very first serial number, on the tri-colored stripes.

Etienne et Cie

An aeroplane was registered under this name for the 1911 Concours Militaire; it may not have been built.

Etrich

3 Etrich Taubes were copied in France. The first was constructed in 1910 by a C Aman, whose name appeared on the tail. The second was a 2-seater built by Kerchone and Aman, also in 1910; an all-metal variant was built by Louis Clément in July 1911, powered by a 55 hp Aviatik.

(Span: 14 m; length: 9.5 m; 100 hp Aviatik-Rossel)

The third appeared under the names of Allard, a Belgian, and Carbonnier. It was painted with the name Le Vautour, and was distinguished from the first 2 by the small wheel at the end of each wing-skid. Aman flew in Wiener-Neustadt with another German pilot, Illner.

F

Fabre

Henri Fabre was born in 1882 to a family of wealthy ship-owners, and through his observation of birds and a small helicopter toy was

The 1908 version of the d'Equevilly-Monjustin, with more wings. Note tilted ring-frame. (Bill Lewis collection)

The 1910 Aman-Etrich single-seater. (Author's collection)

early attracted to the idea of mechanical flight. His father had objected to his studies, which seemed at the time a waste of effort and money, but after the boy had graduated from school he was free to do as he liked. He modified a small steamboat; and then, thinking a crash would be safer on water than land, planned and built a seaplane which he tested on the calm waters of the Etang de Berre, near Marseille, to measure wind speeds and the behavior of towed Hargrave-type kites. His boat was named L'Essor (soaring).

While in Paris Fabre had met Archdeacon, who in turn introduced him to other pioneers, including Gabriel Voisin. Fabre became the first customer of the new Blériot-Voisin firm, ordering further kites and a 15 sqm glider. Some of these he tested, mounting them on the mast of L'Essor, measuring lift and drag. He designed at this time his famous wooden truss girders, light and strong with very little drag, but complicated to build. In 1907 he tested a biplane-bladed propeller fitted at the top of a tall truss girder attached to his 14 hp Renault; the propeller had variable pitch and was driven by the car motor; it drove the car at 50 kmh. The top speed of the car with its standard drive was only 60 kmh.

Subsequent testing was done on floats, 2 long thin forms with foils, as on Forlanini's high-speed boats. Fabre planned a monoplane with these floats with a center nacelle for the pilot and engine. The drawings show that he planned to use the wing structure he was to use later, a single truss girder with trailing flat ribs and fabric attached with lacing.

The light Buchet V2 was not powerful enough, and Fabre designed a second machine and built it. This one had 3 flat floats, one at the tail and 2 in front. The fuselage was a rectangular frame with a triangular elevator and rudder at the rear and a pair of wings with marked dihedral in front. Above the front girder the pilot sat inside a tall triangular frame in a pin-jointed faired section; 3-12 hp Anzanis were mounted side-by-side driving through belts a single large tractor propeller. (The first trimotor?) Tested behind L'Essor, the machine was underpowered at 600 kg; it was abandoned after about 5 months' testing in the summer of 1909. The later Paulhan-Fabre used the frame from the second Fabre seaplane: a restored model of the trimotor, originally built by Fabre himself, is now owned by the Musée de l'Hydroaviation in Biscosse, north of Bordeaux on the coast.

Augustin and Laurent Séguin, inventors of the Gnôme engines, were distant relatives of the Fabre family, and Henri was eventually offered the use of the 50 hp Gnôme Omega No 2. In his memoirs, *J'Ai Vu Naître l'Aviation,* Fabre wrote that Augustin had once given him a small toy aeroplane, a little 40 cm monoplane designed by Lacoin, which flew and was perfectly stable; he was much inspired by it.

Fabre's third aeroplane was a small canard glider built for the Seguins and copied from this toy, with a covered fuselage, laced-up wing and elevator, and no rudder.

His fourth was a model for his next design; it was powered by one of the 12 hp Anzanis and a Chauvière propeller, built "to learn light construction." Evidently the lesson was not learned, for it was underpowered and failed even to skim, and it sank on 24 December 1909.

Fabre's 5th aeroplane was the famous canard seaplane, which he named Goeland (gull); the truss girders and ribs of taped hollow wood

Henri Fabre's unsuccessful trimotor hydro of 1908-1909. (From Les 3 Hydravions d'Henri Fabre)

The 3 Anzanis hooked together in the Fabre trimotor seaplane tested in 1909. (From Les 3 Hydravions d'Henri Fabre)

were fabricated by Espinosa, and the rectangular fuselage frame was built of ash by a mechanic named Burdin and 4 workmen at an autobody shop in Marseille owned by a man named Montel. The new floats weighed 30 kg each, with curved fabric-covered tops and flat plywood-covered bottoms. The wing fabric was coated with glue for waterproofing; the warping was controlled with pedals. Forward on the top of the top fuselage longeron, were mounted in a wooden frame a pair of rudders and a pair of horizontal surfaces; the whole frame together with the front float pivoted on the vertical support member. Only the top horizontal surface worked as an elevator. The Gnôme was mounted above the trailing edge of the wing, driving the pusher propeller aft of a large rectangular fin.

After careful taxiing on the lake at Berre, Fabre managed to lift from the water on 28 March 1910 at the harbor of La Mède, near Martigues. This was the first powered water take-off: the first by Glenn Curtiss took place on 26 January 1911. The Fabre machine was described variously as "aerhydroplane," "hydroaeroplane," or "hydroplane" – the final French term "hydravion" coming later after the term "avion" was commonly accepted. The original No 5 was destroyed, but 2 more were shown at the 1910 Exposition.

(Span: 14 m; length: 8.5 m; wing area: 17 sqm; gross weight: 200 kg; 50 hp Gnôme Omega – the 2d engine built)

The design was improved at the suggestion of Maurice Bécue, Fabre's pilot, in particular the control system. But in Fabre's 1911 model other changes appeared: the rudders were moved back under the wing, probably coordinated with the wing-warping, and were controlled by the pedals. The wings could fold. A single control lever now controlled the top forward surface. 2 small water rudders appeared at the back of the main float; the front float was fixed, with a smaller angle of attack. The machine was destroyed at Monaco on 11 April 1911.

Six Goeland types were begun, though only the first 3 were finished, and only one was sold. Fabre went on to build his floats at 100 francs each for Gabriel Voisin's canard seaplane; he also built Paulhan's "machines à voler." In 1914 he demonstrated his hydro-glisseur, a 3-float seaplane without wings.

In the course of the War he built 24 Tellier flyingboats. Shortly after the Armistice, Fabre went blind, but partially regained his sight when he was quite old: he died at 102.

De Fabrègue
This amateur builder constructed gliders in southern France in 1907-8.

Farcot
A helicopter named Libellule was shown at the 1909 Paris Salon, powered with a 10-cylinder Farcot rotary.

Farman, Henry
It is curious that among the most famous of the French pioneer aviators, Henry Farman and his brother Maurice, were the children of English parents; they grew up in Paris speaking little English, and Henry (who later sometimes spelled his name Henri), became a French citizen. His grave is in the cemetery of Passy, in Paris, and his stone is inscribed Henry Farman.

Both Henry and Maurice soon became interested in bicycling and both became skilled bicycle-racers. Henry and a third brother, Dick, opened an automobile dealership in Paris, but Henry was badly hurt in an car accident and shifted his attention to other things. He watched Voisin fly his gliders, and on 1 June 1907 ordered his first aeroplane from the Voisin firm after seeing the Voisin-built Delagrange No 1 in flight in March 1907.

HF I: His aeroplane was designed and built by the Voisins, and is described under their name.

HF Ibis: Voisin's modifications to the HF 1 are described under Voisin. But in November Farman himself modified it further: this was Henry Farman's first real design contribution. He rebuilt it as a triplane with the addition of a short high-set wing, 4

Fabre's 1911 Goeland at Monaco. (Courtesy of the Musée de l'Air et de l'Espace/Le Bourget-France)

The 1914 Fabre hydro-glisseur in action. (Author's collection)

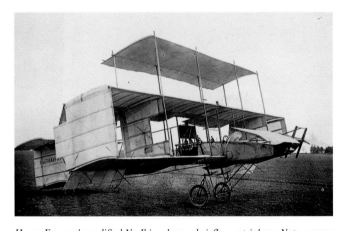
Henry Farman's modified No Ibis – here – briefly – a triplane. Note, among many things, the cut-outs in the inner wing-curtains, and the ailerons on all 4 wings. (Courtesy of the Musée de l'Air et de l'Espace/Le Bourget-France)

The Farman No Ibis in full flight. (Author's collection)

ailerons, the outer pairs of side-curtains with cut-outs to allow movement of the ailerons. It reverted to biplane configuration on 28 November with an enlarged tail cell; and then in December back to triplane, when it was sold to an Austrian syndicate where it was rebuilt once again as a biplane and Legagneux crashed it.

<u>Flying Fish</u>: In the meantime Voisin was building another machine initially designated HF II, although the Voisins took out a patent on it; it was never finished. It had 3 widely staggered rectangular wings with considerable dihedral, and 2 more in the rear. The long fuselage was rectangular in section and arched like an airfoil section. The nose was pointed: the engine would have been set back inside the fuselage. The purpose was to increase speed with more wings and less resistance from brace wires. Later in its unsuccessful life it was rebuilt with 2 sets of wings and a new tail. It may have been sold to a German Lieutenant Fritsche.

(Span: 6.25 m; length: 14 m; wing area: 25 sqm; empty weight: 600 kg; 47 hp Renault)

<u>HF II (Farman)</u>: In 1909 at Châlons, Farman built his second design: the II was a single-bay Gnôme-powered tractor biplane with heavy vertical struts through both leading edges down to the front of the double skid arrangement. The rear ends of the skids were attached to the lower outriggers with big flexible hoops, with a small pair of wheels behind them to keep the ends of the skids from digging in. A big biplane tail cell with huge rudders brought up the rear; there was no forward elevator. The completed aeroplane showed a simple triangular brace in place of the distinctive hoops. A handsome pair of photographs in *La Revue de l'Aviation* captions it Le Jabiru de Farman. He built No II and No III at the same time.

<u>HF II (Voisin)</u>: See the description under <u>Voisin</u>.

<u>HF No III</u>: Like the HF II, the HF III was Henry Farman's own design, and it was built in his new factory. It first appeared in 1909, a flimsy-looking 4-aileron biplane with a biplane tail cell and 2 huge rudder surfaces inside it; 2 tailwheels held up the heavy aft end. It was powered by a 50 hp Vivinus. A similar model went to Roger Sommer, with a Vivinus; the third, with a 50 hp Gnôme, went to George Cockburn and flew at Reims with the number 32. Farman flew his own Type III with the prototype 50 hp Gnôme at Reims, winning both distance and duration (180 km in 3:15).

<u>HF Type (?)</u>: Aircraft similar to the No III were built in some numbers, with many small and some large variations, for many purchasers – some were racing aircraft. The series could be distinguished from the earliest Farmans by the use of paired main wheels on a complex undercarriage structure, as opposed to the Blériot-style trailing wheels; long forward skids frequently extending back far enough for the machine to rest on; ailerons on

The Flying Fish under construction at the Voisin works. Note the airfoil-shaped fuselage and offset propeller blades. (Courtesy of the Musée de l'Air et de l'Espace/Le Bourget-France)

The Henry Farman II. Note the engine forward of the propeller, the minimal inter-wing bracing, and the distinctive initial hoops. (Author's collection)

The completed HF II, with the circular hoops replaced. Note the curious spinner around the engine and propeller. (Author's collection)

the top wings or on both wings. Except for No III itself, none had the Voisin boxkite tail cell; instead all had some combination of single or double tailplanes and single or double or triple rudders; most retained the forward single elevator on outriggers. Other production Type IIIs also used Panhard-Levassor and Gnôme engines.

The Henry Farman No III. (Peter M Bowers collection)

((Typically): span: (upper): 10.5 m; (lower): 7 m; length: c 12 m; wing area: 38 sqm; empty weight: 400 kg; loaded weight: 580 kg; speed: 60 kmh; 50 hp Gnôme)

<u>Russian HF</u>: Similar to No III with shorter skids behind the wheels, it was built in Russia in great numbers in different forms for use as trainers. The wings, at first covered only on the under surface with fabric strips applied to the tops of the spars, was later double-covered. Some had upper-wing extensions; some had small wheels fitted to the tips of the skids in front.

<u>Type de Course</u>: This light racing biplane appeared in 1910-1911.

<u>HF 2/2</u>: Henry Farman produced a pretty little parasol tractor monoplane at Mourmelon on 5 June 1910; parts of the HF II (Farman) may have been used in its construction. The high rectangular wing had ailerons and was braced to the V-leg undercarriage below and 2 inverted V posts above. The tail was of classical fin-rudder-stabilizer-elevator form – a very modern-looking machine.

(Span: 8 m; length: 7.1 m; wing area: 17 sqm; loaded weight: 300 kg; speed: 104 kmh; 50 hp Gnôme)

<u>HF ?</u> Another monoplane appeared in 1911, a 2-seater with rectangular wings set against the top longerons. One version had the long covered fuselage ending in a high rudder surface extending above and below the small tailplane; another had a conventional tailplane and finless rudder. The 4-leg 2-wheel undercarriage had short skids forward, sometimes with a pair of small wheels at each tip.

Right: The Henry Farman HF 2/2 of 1910. The designation system here seems to have changed radically. (Courtesy of the Musée de l'Air et de l'Espace/Le Bourget-France)

Henry Farman in his No III winning at Reims in 1909. (Author's collection)

Paulhan in his Henry Farman. (Courtesy Roger Freeman)

(Span: 10 m; length: 7.5 m; loaded weight: 285 kg; speed: c 100-110 kmh; Gnômes of 50-140 hp)

HF Type Coupe Michelin: This was a big 2-seat pusher with a long covered nacelle and a long top wing overhang with a single aileron set into the ends; the outer wing panels could fold down. The tailplane cell had 3 inset rudders, the third slightly forward of the other 2. On 18 December 1910 Farman flew it for a record time of 8 hrs 23 min.

(Span: 16.5 m; length: 11.67 m; 50 hp Gnôme)

HF 6 Type Militaire: In June 1911 Farman showed a pretty pusher 2-seat biplane with long upper wing overhangs with long hanging ailerons, an undercarriage with 2 pairs of twin wheels. The tail outriggers were not parallel, but came together at the single rectangular rudder and tailplane. The stubby nacelle was fully covered; it appeared with and without an awkward forward elevator outrigger structure.

(Span: 11 m; length: 9 m; wing area: 21 sqm; loaded weight: 550 kg; 50 hp Gnôme)

HF 10: A big 3-seat pusher without forward elevator built for the 1911 Concours Militaire, it appeared with and without wing stagger. It featured long wing overhang and 2 rudders. The pilot and passenger perched on a long forward rail.

HF 10bis: The big 3-seat pusher also built for the 1911 Concours Militaire had extreme wing stagger – the upper trailing edge was ahead of the lower leading edge. The parallel outriggers were very long, supporting a single high tailplane and 3 suspended rudders. Sometimes a third wheel was set with a third skid ahead of the main set. The pilot sat way forward in the uncovered nacelle, the 2 passengers behind him side by side.

The 1911 H Farman monoplane with the first version of its vertical surfaces. (Peter M Bowers collection)

The second version of the Farman monoplane. (Courtesy of the Musée de l'Air et de l'Espace/Le Bourget-France)

The Type Coupe Michelin. Note top wing overhang and ailerons. (Peter M Bowers collection)

Below: The HF 6 Type Militaire, with the Gnôme mounted behind the propeller. (Courtesy of the Musée de l'Air et de l'Espace/Le Bourget-France)

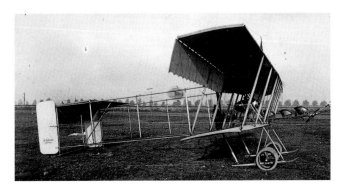

The HF 10, built for the 1911 Concours Militaire. (Courtesy of the Musée de l'Air et de l'Espace/Le Bourget-France)

The HF 10bis, with extreme stagger. (Courtesy of the Musée de l'Air et de l'Espace/Le Bourget-France)

(Span: 20 m; length: 10.95 m; wing area: 70 sqm; empty weight: 411 kg; loaded weight: 1000 kg; 75 hp Renault)

HF 11: Fischer flew this big 2-seat seaplane at Monaco in 1912. He sat out on an uncovered structure; the wings were overhung, and the outriggers came together at the high rectangular single rudder and tailplane.

(Span: 13.15; length: 8.3 m; 70 hp Gnôme)

HF 14?: Similar in design to the Type 6, it had the high rounded tailplane and single oval rudder which were to appear on many subsequent Farman aircraft. One was photographed with 4 passengers squashed in behind the pilot. This 2-seater saw military use, and was privately raced as well. One of these 1912 machines fitted with twin floats and a tail float flew at Deauville on 28 August 1913. In another in November 1913 Chévillard was the first to loop a biplane.

The 1912 HF 14 as a hydro at Deauville, in 1913. (Author's collection)

(Span: 13.75 m; length: 8.36 m; 80 hp Gnôme)

Le Babillard (chatterbox): This pretty machine was flown by Chévillard. It had the high rectangular tailplane and suspended oval rudder of the HF 14, a very short lower wing with unbraced overhang of the top wing. The undercarriage consisted of 2 wheels wide-set with a single high curved forward skid between them, and the pilot – perhaps with passenger behind him? – seated out in front on an extended seat frame.

The remarkable one-off Farman Le Babillard, with its simplified undercarriage. (Author's collection)

HF 15: Another 1912 design, this big 2-seater featured a long overhung top wing braced only with wires, and tail outriggers coming together at the single oval rudder and high tailplane.

The Bronislawski Henry Farman modified to demonstrate the Bronislawski stability system. (Author's collection)

(Span: 17.75 m; length: 9.81 m; 100 hp Gnôme)

HF 16: This single-bay sesquiplane was finished in 1912.

HF Type Répliable: a folding-wing biplane for the military, similar to Type 16.

Bronislawski: The engineer Bronislawski used his Type III (or IV?) in 1912 to experiment with his special stability system, a stack of 5 ailerons mounted between the wingtips. Later he used his Type VII to try out a similar arrangement, but with only a single pair of ailerons at the wingtips.

(Span: 13.75 m; length: 8.1 m; wing area: 35 sqm; empty weight: 250 kg; loaded weight: 660 kg; speed: 105 kmh; 100 hp Gnôme)

Above and right: two views of Henry Farman's 1912 amphibian, clearly passenger-carrying. (Courtesy of the Musée de l'Air et de l'Espace/Le Bourget-France)

<u>HF No ?</u> This pretty modern-looking 1912 design was an amphibian with a short sesquiplane wing set above the speedboat-like hull, and permanently-fixed wheels set at the tips; the long main wing high above. It could seat the pilot and 3 passengers behind him. The engine was half-sunk into the hull, driving the high-set pusher propeller through chains. A single high tailplane and 2 tall rudders below it brought up the rear, supported by a tall skid.

(Span: 13 m; length: 7 m; wing area: 37 sqm; weight: 350 kg; 80 hp Gnôme)

<u>HF 19</u>: The 19 flew as a hydro at Monaco under the number 2. The big Gnôme drove the high-mounted pusher prop through chains; the parallel tail outriggers supported a single high tailplane and 2 suspended diamond-shaped rudders. The hydro had 2 shovel-bowed floats and 2 bubble floats under the rudders.

(Span: 19.7 m; length: 9.87 m; wing area: 66 sqm; empty weight: 650 kg; loaded weight: 1250 kg; speed: 105 kmh; 160 hp Gnôme Double Lambda)

<u>HF 20</u>: similar to the HF 16, with differences in internal structure.

The HF 19 at Monaco. (Author's collection)

HF 22: At first a landplane, similar to the HF 16 and HF 20, it appeared at Deauville, but was not entered, and carried no race number. The 22 had a single high tailplane and 2 suspended rudders; 2 big shovel-nosed floats and a small one to hold up the tail.

HF 24: This curious biplane was shown at the 1913 Salon beside a Maurice Farman. The top wing was much longer than the lower, and the nacelle was attached to its underside, the rotary engine and pusher propeller at its aft end between the outriggers. The single rudder was oval, behind the single tailplane. The wheels were attached at the ends of the short lower wing.

Farman, Maurice

Henry's brother Maurice began as a balloonist, and took Henry up with him once. In 1909 he designed and built his own aeroplane:

MF 1: In December 1909 Maurice brought out his first machine, evidently having been designed with an eye on his brother's design and those of the early Voisins. It showed the split single forward elevator of the Henry Farman Ibis, the ailerons (lower wing only) of the later Ibis, the biplane tail cell with the 2 inset rudders of the same machine. The pointed nacelle was covered, like the Voisin, and on occasion featured end-plate side-curtains.

(Span: 11 m; wing area: 50 sqm; loaded weight: 580 kg; REP)

Type Coupe Michelin: Resembling a simplified development of the MF 1, this handsome aeroplane flew in March 1910 and towards the end of the year in the Coupe Michelin, showing what became for a while the Maurice Farman trademark: a forward elevator with curved tips mounted on large gracefully curved outriggers, 2 oval tailplanes and 2 rudders. 2 wheels supported the aircraft, with 2 small tailwheels at the rear. It first had equal-span wings with curved tips and side-curtains near the ends; then the upper wing was lengthened and the side-curtains removed. Ailerons were hung from the lower wings.

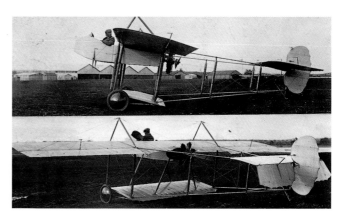

Two views of the HF 24; it had been shown at the 1913 Salon. This time, the Gnôme was mounted in front of the propeller. (Peter M Bowers collection)

Above and below: two views of the Maurice Farman No I, with and without some side-curtains, and single or twin rudders. (Author's collection)

Below: The MF Type Coupe Michelin. The tailbooms curve slightly inward toward the tail. (Peter M Bowers collection)

(Span: 11 m; length: 12.75 m; wing area: 50 sqm; loaded weight: 500 kg; speed: 80 kmh; 50 hp Renault V8)

MF ? This handsome staggered biplane appeared at the 1911 Paris Salon. Ailerons were set at the top wing trailing edge.

MF 2: Designed for the 1911 Concours Militaire, this big strongly staggered (30°) 3-place biplane had a biplane tail cell with the lower surface an oval. The uprights in the outriggers were staggered as well. A seaplane version of the Militaire, numbered 5, and flown by Renaux, flew at Monaco in March 1912.

(Span: 20 m (lower: 15.5 m); length: 13 m; empty weight: 689 kg; loaded weight: 1000 kg; 75 hp Renault)

A later version flew in 1913, also with staggered wings, uprights in the tail outriggers, but a forward-sloping set of tail posts.

MF 7: Model 7 flew in 1913, and the 7bis was produced in great quantities for the Armée de l'Air. It came in a variety of slightly different shapes: basically, a stubby covered nacelle, a single forward elevator mounted on the same curved supports as the Type 2, paired wheels and long skids, and tail surfaces similar to those of the Type 2. Some were built with the tail outriggers slightly bowed towards each other at the rear; some had rectangular tailplanes. The MF 7ter lacked the forward elevator.

(Typical specifications: span: 15.52 m; length: 11.52 m; wing area: 60 sqm; empty weight: 580 kg; loaded weight: 855 kg; speed: 95 kmh; Renault)

Renaux on the MF II on floats, at St Malô, on 26 August 1912. (Peter M Bowers collection)

The MF II with vertical uprights in the tailbooms. (Courtesy of the Musée de l'Air et de l'Espace/Le Bourget-France)

One of several versions of the MF 7bis. (Author's collection)

Below: Renaux at Monaco in a hydro Maurice Farman, possibly developed from the MF II. (Author's collection)

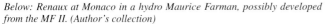

MF 10: This handsome big seaplane was shown at the 1913 Salon in Paris, the first Maurice Farman with the single low-set tailplane and 2 triangular rudders set on top. The top wings overhung substantially, and there was no forward elevator.

(Length: 9.68 m; Renault)

MF 11: Like the Type 7, the 2-seater 11 in its produced form, the 11bis, was the ancestor of hundreds of machines used by the Armée de l'Air in WWI. It was similar to the MF 10.

(Span: 16.13 m; length: 9.48 m; wing area: 52 sqm; empty weight: 620 kg; loaded weight: 945 kg; speed: 118 kmh; Renault)

Possibly derived from the MF 11 was a hydro numbered 17, piloted by Renaux at Monaco. It used 2 big floats and 2 bubble floats aft.

Farman, Henry et Maurice

Before the war, at least one aeroplane was designed by the brothers together, known as the biplan Farman Frères. It showed a single rectangular forward elevator mounted on straight Henry-style outriggers. An elevator was fitted to the upper of the 2 tailplanes, one oval and the other rectangular with rounded tips, and 2 rudders set between them. The wingtips were rounded. Fischer flew it, marked 12, at Reims in July 1910.

The brothers Farman later joined forces again in their design and production of the Farman F40 for use during WWI, a handsome machine resembling both its parents, in some versions with a polished eggshell nacelle.

Henry Farman died in 1958; Maurice died in 1964.

Farnier

The automobile-and-motor-builder Farnier had at least 3 and possibly 4 aeroplanes built to his designs. The first was a roughly-built monoplane constructed by the firm of Letord and Niepce, completed in late 1909 and claimed to have flown at Issy; this seems unlikely, as No 2 was described as "similar in all respects but lighter."

No 2 was also a monoplane, a large one, built by March 1910 by another car-body builder, Vinet, hence in Boulogne. The fuselage resembled that of the Antoinette, with the engine mounted above the undercarriage out in front; ahead of the wheels ran 2 up-curved skids, across the top of which sat a forward elevator. A tailwheel kept the large rudder off the ground, which was hinged to the trailing edges of 2 upper and lower fins. The rudder was controlled by a steering wheel turning, the wing-warping by the same wheel swinging from side to side, and the front elevator by pedals. Driven to Le Touquet, the machine was to have been flown by 2 specially-appointed pilots, but no successful flights were reported.

(Span: 9 m; length: 14.58 m; wing area: 19.8 sqm; span of front elevator; 3 m; gross weight: more than 520 kg; 50 hp 3-cylinder Anzani. The French magazine *L'Aéro* gives the first 2 dimen-

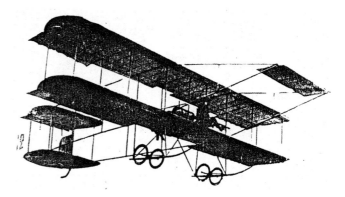

The aeroplane designed by both Henry and Maurice Farman. Note common elements. (Author's collection)

sions as 10 m and 11.6 m, respectively, possibly for the first machine, not the second)

The third Farnier was probably no more successful than the first 2. It was a large 3-seater "military" biplane built by Pelliat. The crew sat in a short fuselage at the rear of the lower wing trailing edge, and a Gnôme drove a large Pelliat Rationnelle propeller; the tail consisted of a biplane tailplane, 2 elevators and 2 rudders. There was no forward elevator. The wing trailing edges were flexible.

(Span: (upper) 12 m; (lower) 8 m; span of tailplane: 5 m; wing area: 50 sqm; empty weight: 400 kg; 50 hp Gnôme)

Fauber

A monoplane was reported under construction in 1907, to be powered by a 70 hp Antoinette engine.

Fauré

There were 3 Fauré monoplanes. One of them – the first? – was perhaps not finished: it seems to have been a graceful tandem built on a long flimsy-looking triangular frame; the broad wings reached barely beyond the edges of the frame. The next 2 were similar – perhaps they used the same broad monoplane wing braced with a structure of struts underneath like the Etrich Taubes, and odd twin-wheel tailwheel-cum-skid arrangement. One had an uncovered triangular fuselage and a "helical-pitch tailplane" which seems to have operated from a wheel mounted on the right side of the fuselage to warp and twist as for a regular rear elevator, and from a wheel on the left side to warp and

Perhaps the first Fauré – perhaps the first double-lifting fuselage? Handsome, though. (Courtesy of the Musée de l'Air et de l'Espace/Le Bourget-France)

twist as for a rudder. It was tested on 22 September, managed "a few straight lines" (but not necessarily in the air); it crashed 6 days later.

(Span: 14.5 m; length: 9 m; 70 hp Labor engine)

The other had a rectangular-section fuselage, covered in front, and looked remarkably modern.

Fauvel

In 1912 Charles Fauvel built a canard monoplane with 2 wheels under the nose and 4 more under the rear fuselage. The engine was set aft of the wing, forward of the rudder; the propeller rotated around the square-section fuselage.

(Span: 9.8 m; length; 9.2 m; 50 hp Gnôme)

In 1926 Fauvel returned to tailless designs, following in the footsteps of René Arnoux, with whom he later shared a patent on a flying wing.

Ferber

Captain Ferdinand Ferber was 36 when he read a report about Otto Lilienthal in the *Illustrierte Zeitung,* and realized the need of perfecting controlled gliding flight before going on with powered machines. His work falls into 3 periods: his first 4 designs were kite gliders, the last 2 of which were meant to carry a pilot – No 4 was a Lilienthal copy. Nos 5 and 6 reflected his discovery of the Wrights' work, and were Wright-type gliders; Nos 7, 8, and its twin No 9 were of more conventional tractor biplane design, but more primitive than contemporary designs.

No 1: Ferber built this one in 1911 and tested the full-scale version in Rue, a Swiss village where his family had an estate. It was lozenge-shaped, longer than wide, and was thought to descend too steeply.

(Length: 8 m; wing area: 25 sqm; weight: 30 kg)

No 2: In 1988 he was admitted to the Aéro Club of France, and built a second glider flown at Fontainebleau as a kite towed by a horse. It was also lozenge-shaped, but shorter than No 1, and proved unstable.

(Span: 6 m; wing area: 15 sqm; weight: 20 kg)

No 3: Developed from No 2, this glider was roughly triangular, with upturned tips for stability; it was tried at St Etienne de Tinée, but was unable to carry a man, much to Ferber's disappointment.

(Span: 7 m; wing area: 15 sqm; weight: 30 kg)

No 4: In 1901 Ferber got in touch with Gustav Lilienthal, brother of Otto, and Octave Chanute, and then built a Lilienthal-type glider with straight leading – and curved trailing-edges. It was

The second (?) Fauré. Note the little ears on the tips of the stabilizer – perhaps part of the "helical-pitch" tailplane. (Courtesy of the Musée de l'Air et de l'Espace/Le Bourget-France)

Another Fauré monoplane. It may have used parts from the previous one. (Courtesy of the Musée de l'Air et de l'Espace/Le Bourget-France)

The Ferber glider No 3. (Courtesy of the Musée de l'Air et de l'Espace/Le Bourget-France)

tested in 1901, flown with a pilot from a 5-meter scaffolding in Nice and again in the Alps at Bueil: it landed 15 m from the scaffolding, barely slowing the fall.

(Span: 8 m; wing area: 15 sqm; weight: 30 kg)

Ferber first learned of the work of Octave Chanute in an article in the *Revue Rose* dated 1 June 1901, which summarized a lecture given to the Royal Institution in London on 8 February 1901 by Professor GH Bryan, who was at the time a member of the Royal Aeronautical Society. Ferber delayed writing to Chanute until 10 November 1901, and then Chanute wrote him back on 24 November, mentioning the work of the Wrights. On 8 January Chanute sent Ferber the issue of the *Journal of the Western Society of Engineers* of December 1901, which contained Wilbur Wright's description of the brothers' work with the 1900 and 1901 gliders.

<u>No 5</u>: This was the second manned Ferber, a crude tailless biplane glider with a small front elevator. The pilot lay prone in a net suspended between the 2 lower wings; the panels were made of bamboo and tightened fabric: the pressure of the wind was meant to provide the necessary camber. Eventually a bamboo spar was added below the canvas.

He either modified his first machine or built others, all of the same general design. The first one had 5 equal bays between the wings; subsequent gliders had the center bay much narrower. The structure of the forward elevator varied, beginning with a single fore-and-aft rib, then going to 2, then using a single horizontal spar instead. The fabric was applied in different ways to the wings, and the shapes of the skids changed from machine to machine. Ferber called them all No 5.

The last ones had uplifted wingtips; triangular sails trailing back from the rearmost struts at the ends of the wings, supposedly to serve as rudders; and a rectangular horizontal tailplane on 2 floppy outriggers, and more ribs in the lower wing than in the upper. One of them was tested in September 1903 at Cape

Ferber's No 5 glider, first version. (Courtesy of the Musée de l'Air et de l'Espace/Le Bourget-France)

One of the later versions of Ferber's No 5 glider. (Courtesy of the Musée de l'Air et de l'Espace/Le Bourget-France)

Below: The Ferber No 5bis, one of the later No 5s with a Buchet engine, being tested on the swinging arm at Chalais-Meudon in 1904. (Courtesy of the Musée de l'Air et de l'Espace/Le Bourget-France)

Finisterre at Le Conquêt; another was tested on a whirling-arm machine on the estate La Californie at Nice. A 6 hp Buchet was fitted into No 5 which then became No 5bis, tested on the whirling arm and found to be underpowered even with 2 contra-rotating paddle-bladed propellers. The last one was tested in October 1904 at Chalais-Meudon. The Captain wrote that these tests "were completely useless, but drew public attention to aviation."

(Span: (lst version) 9.5 m; (second) 6 m; length: 1.8 m; wing area: 33 sqm; 6 hp Buchet)

In 1905 Ferber went back to help Archdeacon and Voisin handle their glider; in the same year he was assigned to the Centre Aérostatique at Chalais-Meudon, where he built another aerodrome – by which he meant a launching device. This was a wire bridle suspended from 3 towers; initially the wire was 25 m long, but it was later lengthened to 50 m. In the last of his books he established the famous Rule of 3 Vs: a lateral V (dihedral) for roll stability; a longitudinal V (positive angle of attack on mainplanes, negative on tailplane) for pitch stability; and a horizontal V (sweepback on mainplanes) to reduce drag. He wrote that any aeroplane designed with the 3 Vs would be automatically stable.

No 6: When Ferber arrived at Chalais Meudon in May 1904, he ordered his 6th design built in Marseille by his mechanic Marius Burdin. It was tested and modified at Chalais-Meudon. It was similar to No 5 with narrower wings and a long tailplane mounted with negative angle of attack. It was tested on the lengthened aerodrome with and without the front elevator mounted as on No 5bis between 4 struts attached to the wing leading edges. His 26-year-old daughter flew No 6 as a glider free of the wire bridle, and with the 6 hp Buchet and the contra-rotating propellers. On 27 May 1905 Ferber managed what is sometimes improperly referred to as the first powered flight in Europe – but he did not actually take off, only sliding along the wire and then gliding away. Photographs of further such flights show twisting and distorted wings and wildly waving jibs.

The 6 hp Buchet weighed nearly 90 kg with all its equipment; in 1904 he had ordered a slightly lighter and more powerful 2-cylinder engine of 12 hp which he tested over a long period. Never satisfied with it, Ferber finally ordered a 24 hp water-cooled Levavasseur Antoinette V8, but geared it to be transverse in the airframe with the drive to be taken from the middle of the crankshaft; but unfortunately for Ferber, Colonel Renard, the Director at Chalais-Meudon, died in 1905, and his successor was not much interested in aircraft "which had not yet proved capable of flying." He saw no point in waiting for the Antoinette, thinking the Peugeot would do.

No 7: Ferber planned to test the Peugeot on his No 7 at the start of July 1906; he was running it on a propeller test-vehicle in August, a 4-wheel frame powered by the propellers which were of wood, skinned with imitation leather and tested at Meudon. The machine was damaged.

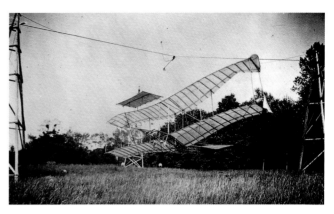

The Ferber No 6 attempting to take off from a wire in 1905. (Courtesy of the Musée de l'Air et de l'Espace/Le Bourget-France)

No 8: By the summer of 1906 Ferber was asking for a 3-year leave, and by late in the summer he joined Léon Levavasseur to work on aeroplanes at the Antoinette company. When he left Meudon, his No 8 was complete and awaiting its engine, a special V8 made with 2 V4s on either side of a vertical propeller

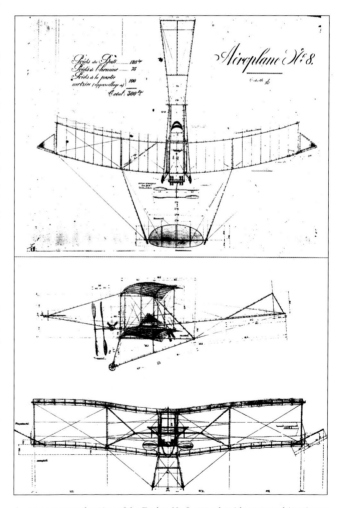

A contemporary drawing of the Ferber No 8; note the side-mounted Antoinette and the contra-rotating propellers. (Courtesy of the Musée de l'Air et de l'Espace/Le Bourget-France)

shaft and its 2.5:1 reduction gear. Though it belonged to the Army, Ferber could have got permission to test it; perhaps he never intended to do so. In November 1906 it was taken outside from the dirigible shed where it was being kept, to make room for a dirigible; on the night of 19-20 November it was completely destroyed in a storm.

No 7 is rarely mentioned or described, apparently confused with No 6 or No 8: it may have been the machine shown in photographs with the Peugeot V2 and odd horizontal ailerons pivoting outside and around the front tip wing struts, and captioned Ferber No 8. This machine is likely to be No 7; No 8 was a more conventional-looking biplane than his earlier designs, with a front elevator, a long triangular rudder fixed to a long fan-shaped tailplane similar to that of No 6, bicycle-style undercarriage, wingtip skids, and the same floppy construction of his earlier designs. The Antoinette drove 2 contra-rotating propellers out in front. The wings curved slightly backward (the third V) and did not warp: roll and direction were controlled by 2 jibs.

<u>No 9</u>: With Levasseur at Antoinette, Ferber worked on the great Levavasseur Monoplan de Villotrans powered with a 100 hp Antoinette. Photographs show both men working next on models of the Antoinette IV, but it is clear that things did not go well between Ferber and Levavasseur or the other partners in the firm who were more interested in building automobiles. Ferber and Levavasseur rarely agreed on what was to be done, and Ferber worked more as an accountant than as an engineer in the company. Eventually the firm built Ferber's No 9, also known as the Antoinette III, a slightly altered version of his No 8; in it he made several take-offs and short straight-line flights at Issy in July 1908.

(Span: 10.5 m; length: 9.5 m)

In August Ferber was by error posted for punishment in Brest; the day he had to leave, his mechanic Legagneux won fourth prize for the 200-meter flight at Issy. The aeroplane was then moved to Normandy with the rest of the Antoinette company, and on 19 September Legagneux wrecked it in a crash. From Brest, Ferber was awarded Brevet No 5bis, and he ordered his No 10 from Burdin in Marseille. In the meantime he bought a Voisin with a 50 hp Antoinette and began a new career as a pilot under the name of F de Rue, from the name of the village where he had made his first experiments. In the morning of 22 September 1909 he made a rough landing in his Voisin at Boulogne; he was taxiing fast when the wheels went into a ditch, and the left wing hit the ground and the aircraft turned over and broke up. Ferber was thrown out, but the engine fell onto his stomach. At 10:30 Ferdinand Ferber was dead. He had often said he wished to be Minister of War.

Fernandez
Antonio Fernandez was born in Aranjuez, in Spain, in 1876; 33 years later he moved to Nice and set up as a ladies' tailor. An automobile enthusiast, he soon developed an interest in aviation. He designed 3 aeroplanes:

The power installation for the Ferber No 8. The unit is hung from 4 cables, perhaps to test thrust. (Courtesy of the Musée de l'Air et de l'Espace/Le Bourget-France)

Ferber No 9 in flight at Issy in 1908. (Courtesy of the Musée de l'Air et de l'Espace/Le Bourget-France)

<u>No 1</u> resembled a Wright, but with short flat planes set between the wings, a 24 hp Antoinette with 2 propellers made of steel tubes and oval aluminum paddles; it was launched by catapult but achieved only a few brief glides over the grass. It had been built at Verany's in Nice, and was tested first on 10 April 1909 on the estate of La Grimaude, at Antibes.

<u>No 2</u> was a biplane designed around the frame of No 1 with 4 wheels. The Antoinette this time drove a single large pusher propeller through a chain and shaft. The twin rudders differed from the Wright design, and the Wright aft fuselage outriggers were replaced by single spars, one bent up over and the other down around the propeller disc. It flew first on 10 June 1909; it was reported that Delagrange had flown it on straight-line flights at Issy, but a few days afterwards it was entered at the competition

at Béthény; on that occasion it was unable to fly twice over the starting line. Its most interesting feature was the handlebar used for control: the handles of it could be pushed together or pulled apart. One of the 10 men who worked on it was Louis Lefebvre. It crashed shortly after the meeting at Reims.

(Span: 8 m; length: 10 m; wing area: 28 sqm; empty weight: c 300 kg. These same figures also appear for the Fernandez No 4.)

No 3, named Aéral, was a good copy of the Curtiss pusher of the period. The monoplane front elevator was set as high as the top wing; both wings had trailing triangular ailerons covered with the same flap of fabric that covered the wings themselves. Pierre Levasseur, much later the builder of the Nungesser and Coli Oiseau Blanc, saw the Fernandez at the 1909 Paris Exposition and bought the manufacturing rights; François Denhaut got his license in one of these in 1911.

(Span: 9.55 m; length: 9.2 m; wing area: 24 sqm; top speed (reported but highly unlikely): 100 kmh; 42 hp water-cooled ENV)

On 6 December 1909, Fernandez took off in No 3 even though an elevator cable was damaged. The mechanic, Fighiera, wanted to take time to repair it, but Fernandez, in a hurry, repaired it with his handkerchief. After some satisfactory flying, the aircraft dived into the ground, and Fernandez became the third aircraft casualty in France, after Lefebvre and Ferber.

Filippi

M Filippi owned the Cyrnos firm, in which he built a propeller called the rotary wing. He went on to build a helicopter consisting of a triangular 4-wheel frame, carrying a 200 hp Clerget V8 at the bottom with 2 horizontally-mounted chain-driven propellers. The unsuccessful machine was built by Malicet and Blin, and was shown at the 1912 Exposition under the name Cyrnoptère.

A second Cyrnoptère design had a different frame with 3 wheels; the floor-mounted engine drove through a shaft and bevel gears a horizontal shaft with vertical propeller-shafts at either end, also driven through bevel gears.

Some of the Filippi-designed propellers turned as high as 2300 rpm.

Fillon

In 1909 Eugène Fillon tested a strange glider at the Sables d'Olonne on the western coast of France. A high rectangular uncovered fuselage carried a large wing on the top surface, and a long narrow tailplane with rudder at the same level; the pilot sat at the front end.

(Span: c twice the length; length: c 5 m; weight reported as 25 kg – perhaps it should have been 125 kg)

The second Fernandez aeroplane, with a single propeller and 4 wheels. (Courtesy of the Musée de l'Air et de l'Espace/Le Bourget-France)

The Fernandez Aéral, in good times. (Courtesy of the Musée de l'Air et de l'Espace/Le Bourget-France)

The wreck of the Aéral. (Courtesy of the Musée de l'Air et de l'Espace/Le Bourget-France)

Florencie

Florencie was the first to order an aeroplane from the Voisin firm after they had set up alone in 1906. He had invented an ornithopter, but had little idea of how to build it; it was a monoplane with roughly bird-shaped wings containing slatted shutters. A small forward elevator surface was matched with small horizontal and vertical tail surfaces in the rear. It was unsuccessfully tested hanging from a cable at Massy-Palaiseau, south of Paris.

(Span: 15 m; wing area: 35 sqm)

The second Florencie, probably designed by Gabriel Voisin and sometimes incorrectly reported as Florenty, was a tractor biplane with a 24 hp Antoinette motor. It was tested for the first time at Juvisy on 16 September 1909.

Fouin

This name was associated in 1911 with an ornithopter.

Fouquet

Fouquet ordered a biplane built by de Pischoff et Koechlin in 1909, almost identical to the Lejeune, built by the same firm. It was an equal-span biplane, with a centrally-mounted engine driving 2 pusher propellers on Wright-style outriggers through chains and enormous sprocket wheels. It had tandem-wheel undercarriages, a biplane tail cell with a single rudder in the middle, ailerons set out ahead of the outer pair of interplane struts. The Fouquet was supported at the wingtips by curved skids, where the Lejeune had wheels; the Fouquet had a forward biplane elevator with side-curtains at the ends, and the Lejeune had 2 pairs of cells side by side with no vertical surfaces. The Fouquet used a 50 hp Antoinette, and the Lejeune used a 3-cylinder 12 hp Buchet. On 12 August Fouquet rolled 80 meters, hopped, the engine stopped abruptly and the machine came down hard on its undercarriage, which gave way: the aeroplane was destroyed. By October he had rebuilt and modified it twice, and made several hops with it.

Franchault

At least 3 aeroplanes were built and probably designed by Franchault. The first was an awkward open-work biplane with tailplane and front elevator mounted high at the level of the upper wing. It was said to have taken off on 17 December 1910, but it never really flew.

(Span: 10.5 m; length: 9.5 m; 60 hp Dansette-Gilet)

The second was a monoplane with a slight resemblance to the Caudron biplanes; 2 high inverted Vs at the front formed the undercarriage and the wing pylons, and the 2 pilots sat in a short nacelle. It was flown by Loctin in May 1913, and was sometimes referred to as the Franchault-Loctin; Loctin may have been Franchault's financial partner.

(Span: 10 m; length: 7 m; wing area: 20 sqm; empty weight: 300 kg)

Franchault built his third design, a biplane with very short lower wings, shortly before the War. The radial engine was partly covered by a streamlined cowl, and the fuselage was covered only at the front end. It had a high angular rudder and no fin; the undercarriage had 2 wheels and heavily-braced skids.

Franco-British Aviation Company, Ltd

In November 1911 the Société Anonyme des Chantiers Tellier failed, and in January 1912 Louis Schreck joined the aviation section into a company called the Société Anonyme des Anciens Chantiers Tellier (former the Tellier works) at Longuenesse; he bought the Tellier patents and continued to sell Tellier monoplanes. Early in 1912 a Tellier monoplane was reported with a 50 hp Chenu engine, and up to 7 were reported built by May 1912. The question remains as to how many were built after Schreck took over the firm, and who exactly was re-

The graceful Florencie ornithopter. (Courtesy of the Musée de l'Air et de l'Espace/Le Bourget-France)

The de Pischoff et Koechlin-built Fouquet biplane of 1909. (Courtesy of the Musée de l'Air et de l'Espace/Le Bourget-France)

The first Franchault, of 1910. (Courtesy of the Musée de l'Air et de l'Espace/ Le Bourget-France)

The second Franchault, the rakish 1913 monoplane. (Courtesy of the Musée de l'Air et de l'Espace/Le Bourget-France)

sponsible for the later machines. It is possible that the Chenu-powered machines may have been earlier Telliers retrofitted.

Then in April 1912 Schreck formed the Société Anonyme des Chantiers Tellier pour la Construction des Monoplanes. After the accident in which pilot Marc Pourpe was hurt in a Tellier monoplane, Schreck hired Louis Gaudard as chief designer. 2 of his designs appeared at the 1912 Paris Salon, under the name D'Artois – these are described under that name. A year later, in May 1913, this new firm merged with the Société des Hydroaéroplanes Levêque – the remains of the Donnet-Levêque firm – to form Franco-British Aviation (FBA), also under Schreck. FBA then held the patents to flyingboats designed by Tellier, Levêque, d'Artois, and the manufacturing rights to those designed by Curtiss. Their aim was to produce the best possible flyingboats for England and for France.

The early FBA boats were similar: 2-seaters; single-bay wings with top wing overhang and large cut-out for pusher propeller; lower wings in separate panels set above the hull; pairs of interplane struts with outboard diagonal bracing struts; slender arched aft hull with the tail surfaces set above the tip; awkward angular rudder set on top of the tailplane; sharp upward curve in forward hull to meet the top deck; rotary engines; large streamlined tank under top center-section. Some are described below:

No 26: as above.

No 27, Type Schneider: painted with the number 7, it flew at Monaco. It had a sharper bow than No 26.

No 28: this one was larger, with 2 wing bays, and a curved rudder above the tailplane.

More FBA flyingboats were built and copied during the War than any other type; the French Navy often referred to them as Schrecks.

Fumat

Victor Fumat's monoplanes were mentioned between 1910 and 1912; they were perhaps all the same machine. The front end resembled a Blériot XI, but the fuselage was very short, with the tailwheel fitted just below the pilot's seat. The rear fuselage consisted of a single long spar carrying a long triangular fin and tailplanes, a small elevator and a Blériot-like rudder.

(Span: 8 m; length: 8 m; wing area: 16 sqm; 25 hp Anzani))

The third Franchault, a business-like biplane. (Courtesy of the Musée de l'Air et de l'Espace/Le Bourget-France)

FBA 26. (Bill Lewis collection)

FBA 27 – note differences in hull shape. (Author's collection)

FBA flyingboats under construction at the FBA works, January 1914. (Bill Lewis collection)

One of the Fumat monoplanes. (Peter M Bowers collection)

The Gabardini flyingboat of 1912. (Courtesy of the Musée de l'Air et de l'Espace/Le Bourget-France)

G

Gabardini

Though a Milanese, Gabardini designed and had built 2 aeroplanes in France. The first, a small often-modified tractor named Le Monaco, was a monoplane with an all-covered fuselage with triangular section aft, a triangular tailplane, and a Morane-style undercarriage. It was seen in April 1911 flying at La Brague, near Antibes, with a large numeral 10 on the rudder, piloted by Gibert or Desbrouères – the latter sometimes referred to as the builder as well as the designer. It is likely that the machine was built in Marseille by Deschamps et Blondeau. It was later reported flown by Chavagnac at Milan in January 1912. Still later, developed into a Nieuport-style design, it was flying in 1914-15.

A later Gabardini design was the curious monoplane flyingboat built by Sevon et Lavignon (other sources describe Henri Chazal as pilot and builder) in 1912. It was tested, unsuccessfully, in the harbor at Monaco. The hull was short and streamlined, cut off abruptly at an angle aft of the wings. An uncovered framework to the rear supported a small elevator and a large rudder forward of the tailplane. The motor was buried in the hull and drove a tractor propeller mounted high above the nose, through a pair of shafts at right angles: at rest the tips of the propeller were in the water.

Gabelle, Hauguet, Riard et Martin

A 6-meter span biplane glider made from bamboo and carrying the weight of these names, was built at Le Havre in 1910.

Galvin

Little is known of the aeronautical work of Clément Galvin of Lyon, who nevertheless designed one of the most advanced, if not successful, seaplanes of his time. His first design was a small biplane with a 12 hp Anzani: tested in 1909, it did not fly. His second was a monoplane mentioned briefly in the late fall of 1911.

The third was the seaplane tested and probably not flown on the Saône River in October-November 1913. It had a highly-streamlined fuselage of circular section with a blunt round nose: the engine was mounted as on the Gallaudet seaplanes in the fuselage behind the wings, with the propeller turning amidships on a ring. The lower wing was set below the fuselage, the upper at shoulder height; the machine rested on a wide central float and 2 small tip floats, and the bottom of the fin was attached to the tail of the main float. The pilot sat on top, level with the leading edge of the top wings. A blurry photo shows it taxiing at high speed, the ring removed from the propeller, leaving a gap more than 2' long; it has French colors on the rudder.

Gambier

This was a Blériot-type monoplane built after 1909, with a 5-cylinder Anzani. A triangular tailplane was set underneath rear fuselage.

Gangler

Eugene Gangler's monoplane is visible in the background of a photo of the first Avia at the 1909 Paris Exposition, and it was shown at the Paris Salon of 1910. It had a streamlined covered fuselage with a centrally-mounted engine driving 2 pusher propellers on outriggers aft on each side. The wing, in 2 separate elliptical panels, was set slightly above the fuselage, with warping tips which could be pulled

The mid-engine, mid-propeller Galvin seaplane. (Courtesy of the Musée de l'Air et de l'Espace/Le Bourget-France)

down together "to form a parachute" and thus make the machine "absolutely safe." A cruciform tail brought up the rear. Though an obliging journalist wrote that "this interesting machine reserves surprises," the Gangler was unsuccessful. It greatly resembles one of the experimental – and unsuccessful – variants on the first Koechlin monoplane.

(Span: 11.3 m; wing area: 27 sqm; 40 hp engine)

Garaix, L

At the end of the summer of 1910 in Montélimard in southeastern France, an L Garaix was reported to have built a monoplane, first towed by a car and later fitted with an engine driving a tractor L Garaix propeller. The control device for lateral stability was fastened to the pilot's back; the wings had a slight dihedral. L Garaix may have been some relation to Victor Garaix.

(Span: 8 m; length: 5.6 m; propeller diameter: 1.2 m; 8-10 hp motor weighing 70 kg)

A 1911 postcard photo shows a biplane under construction; the text on the back describes a visit to L Garaix' workshops with the biplane under construction!

Garbero

Some of the pre-1919 aeronautical activities on the French Riviera centered on Joseph and Hector Garbero. After building an unsuccessful box-kite design, they bought Wickman's Blériot XI at the end of April 1909, and modified it with a biplane tail unit: a single tailplane with high angle of attack was set below the fuselage, and a back-staggered pair of elevators on top, forward of the rudder.

In 1911 Casimir Garbero and his brothers founded an Hanriot school at Antibes, while helping other designers with construction. They built a monoplane sometimes referred to as the Garbero-Bécue, designed by Maurice Bécue, formerly Henri Fabre's pilot. It was actually a 2-seater Hanriot modified with a 60 hp 6-cylinder radial Anzani. Jean Bécue, Maurice's brother, crashed it at the end of April 1911; a second similar machine was later built and flown successfully. In 1912-13 they modified and flew another 2-seater Hanriot with twin floats and another Anzani: it was damaged and repaired in January 1913.

Garnier

In 1910 Léonce Garnier, a garage mechanic from Biarritz, designed and built with the assistance of his mechanic Hourdebaigt a monoplane which he named Olga. It was made from parts of a Blériot XI fuselage, tail and undercarriage, but featured rectangular wings with a heavily-cambered leading edge and a Darracq motor. This is likely the same machine in which Leforestier was killed during an airshow at Huelva, in Spain.

Garros et Audemars

While working at the Moisant International Aviators' Flying Circus, Roland Garros and his best friend Edmond Audemars decided to build a Gnôme-powered Demoiselle; both had learned to fly on the little

A striking view of a striking aeroplane, the unsuccessful Gangler of 1910. (Author's collection)

The L Garaix under construction. (Author's collection)

Santos-Dumont monoplane built by Clément-Bayard. They planned to improve on the design by fitting a 50 hp Gnôme. John Moisant allowed them to return to France for that purpose, upon their agreement that the new aeroplane would be called the Baby Moisant.

They bought black fabric, went back to Paris, and worked with their mechanics and Arnold Clément-Bayard on a Demoiselle copy, with a metal-tube fuselage. Studying the machine before its first flight, Santos-Dumont recommended shortening the tail by 80 cm; this was not done, and Garros could not prevent the aeroplane from going into a steep climb, stall, and ensuing crash. A second machine with the engine moved forwards was not properly trimmed, either, and also crashed. They then abandoned the project; but the violin-shaped seat meant for 2 passengers was retained and appeared on later Morane-Saulnier Type Gs.

Gary

A 1909 project.

Gasnier

One of the most famous of the French pioneers, René Gasnier won the Gordon-Bennett trophy in his balloon in 1906. In 1908, near Angers on the Loire, he designed and built a small biplane which succeed in making short hops on 17 August 1908.

No 1: This machine resembled a Voisin with a short nacelle and forward elevator. A 50 hp Antoinette of 1907 vintage drove an all-metal pusher propeller designed by Gasnier himself. The non-warping wings had considerable dihedral; the single tailplane was supported on a pair of castering tailwheels and the front elevator could be tilted to work as a rudder. The machine was tested at Rochefort sur Loire, and it was badly damaged on its first day.

<u>No 2</u>: This was No 1 rebuilt, shortened by a foot, and featured a rudder and 4 ailerons. He managed some short flights on 9 September, but the machine was still tail-heavy. Gasnier increased the angle of attack of the new tailplane and flew steadily on 17 September, but unfortunately a wire came loose and was ripped away by the propeller, and one wing was torn off.

<u>No 3</u>: This Gasnier had straight wings, a forward elevator in 2 parts on each side of the nose; the elevator and the ailerons were worked from a single control stick. He completed the machine on 23 September 1908, but he was beginning to suffer from the disease which was later to kill him, and the tests were stopped. This machine has been preserved with its original 1907 Antoinette, both restored in 1986 by the Angers chapter of the Ailes Anciennes, under the direction of its chairman, Christian Ravel. Seen today, the wooden construction seems thick and heavy.

(Span: 10 m; length: 9 m; height: 3.25 m; wing area: 35 sqm; gross weight: over 400 kg; 50 hp Antoinette)

As Chairman of the Aéro Club d'Anjou, which was founded in 1908, Gasnier with his brother Pierre organized the famous Circuit d'Anjou. He died on 3 October 1913, aged 39.

Gassier

The Gassier monoplane commonly referred to as the Sylphe was actually designed and built by 4 men, Messrs Hamelis, Delamare, Mathieu, and Gassier. A high rectangular wing fitted with large drooping ailerons sat on top of an uncovered triangular fuselage with 2 large semicircular frames surrounding the pilot and the engine; the

The first Gasnier under construction. (Author's collection)

The Gasnier ready for flight. (Author's collection)

The forward elevator of the Gasnier No 3 under reconstruction at the Musée de l'Air et de l'Espace. (Author's collection)

Right: The nacelle of Gasnier No 3 before reconstruction at the Musée de l'Air et de l'Espace. (Author's collection)

The Gassier Sylphe. There seems to be a great deal of structure in it. (Courtesy of the Musée de l'Air et de l'Espace/Le Bourget-France)

pusher had a forward elevator coordinated with the aft one, and an oval rudder. The Sylphe made its first taxi runs on 16 February 1911, and its first flight on 11 April at Juvisy. Although designed to carry 2, it could barely lift the pilot alone, with its over-heavy fuselage. Only the propeller survives today, in the possession of the Gassier family.

(Span: 12 m; length: 11 m; wing area: 30 sqm; empty weight: c 450 kg; speed: c 80 kmh; 50 hp 4-cylinder inline inverted Grégoire-Gyp)

Gaudard

Louis Gaudard was an electrical engineer who began his aeronautical career as an instructor with Ferdinand Ferber at the flying school of the Ligue Nationale Aérienne, flying a Voisin; Igor Sikorsky was one of their students. In 1909 he worked with Jean Legrand to work on Legrand's modified Voisin; it was tail-heavy and crashed in 1910.

In 1911 he rebuilt it as an observation pusher; Legrand may have helped with the redesign and with the subsequent monoplane. Its un-equal-span wings had large cutouts for the pusher propeller; mounted below the lower wing was an enclosed nacelle with rectangular windows. A Blériot-style undercarriage supported the front end, and the rear ends of the lower outriggers supported the tail, featuring a single large rectangular tailplane.

Some months later at Alaise, in eastern France, Gaudard built a "rigid trussed-beam monoplane." The tail, and the high wing fitted with big rectangular trailing ailerons, resembled those of the biplane. The pilot sat in a light structure set below the wing, slightly ahead of and below the passenger, who could rest his head on the leading edge. A 50 hp Gnôme was mounted aft of the pusher propeller; the aircraft sat on 2 wide-set pairs of wheels. It was flying at Juvisy in October 1911; shortly afterwards Gaudard went to work for Jean Legrand, whom he eventually left for Louis Schreck to design the d'Artois pusher biplanes.

Gaudard's "rigid-trussed-beam monoplane" of 1911. (Courtesy of the Musée de l'Air et de l'Espace/Le Bourget-France)

(Span: 9 m; length: 8 m; wing area: 18 sqm; gross weight: c 300 kg; speed: c 95 kmh; 50 hp Gnôme)

Gauthier

The wings were described as made from "franco-liège."

Gavault

The Gavault monoplane appeared at Issy in February 1912. The wings were deeply arched with no dihedral, set on the top of a large rectan-

The 1912 Gavault. As with the Gassier Sylphe, there seems a great deal of heavy structure here. (Courtesy of the Musée de l'Air et de l'Espace/Le Bourget-France)

gular-section uncovered box. The water-cooled engine sat on the floor at the nose, driving through chains (one crossed, similar to the Wright), 2 tractor propellers mounted on outriggers on each side; the pilot was seated immediately behind it. Out in front was a curious triangular cell with curved sides, serving apparently as a forward stabilizer. Another just like it was fitted aft of the wing inside the fuselage, just ahead of a conventional set of tail surfaces.

Gayot

A monoplane of this name was reported at Orléans in 1912.

Genuel, Chaboussant, et Giraud

A glider?

Gérard

A project, complete or incomplete, in 1909.

Géraud

Regarding the machine designed by Joseph-Albert Géraud of Brou, all we have is the term "Le triomphe Géraud" from 1907.

Germe

The first of the 2 Germe pusher biplanes was clearly inspired by the Wright Flyer and was reported first flown at Issy on 11 August 1909. It had a 4-wheel undercarriage and 3 triangular fins mounted between the forward biplane elevators; 2 separate high rectangular rudders were set on parallel outriggers. The Anzani motor was set on the lower wing leading edge. It drove a single 4-bladed pusher propeller of 3-meter diameter, formed of 2 2-bladed propellers set back to back, through 2 shafts and a diagonally-mounted belt. Ailerons were fitted to all 4 wings.

(Span: 12 m; weight: 400 kg; 50 hp 3-cylinder Anzani; propellers by Petit-Conchia)

The second Germe was tested at La Brayelle, near Douai, in September 1910. The forward elevators were gone, and there was a tiny tailplane and rudder; ailerons appeared only on the top wings. The same engine in the same place now drove a single pusher propeller with a shaft and chain. It was reported crashed on its first flight in February 1911; the engine used may have been a Grégoire-Gyp, replacing the Anzani.

In 1912 Germe was still offering to build fuselages, monoplanes, or biplanes on request.

Gibert

In 1910-11 Louis Gibert was a famous pilot flying Blériots, and later, REPs; in 1912 at La Brague on the French Riviera, he struggled vainly to fly the Gabardini Monaco, and also tested the Blinderman-de Mayeroff monoplane sometimes referred to as the Blinderman-Gibert. Sometimes Gibert's name was attributed to various experimental aeroplanes, even though he himself was only the pilot: hence the inclusion of his name in this list.

The first of the big Wright-based Germe biplanes. Note the heavy belting for the propeller drive, and the double tip ailerons. (Peter M Bowers collection)

In 1912 he tested and probably flew a canard amphibian monoplane reported to be of his design; but it may have been confused with a design of another engineer, Gilbert. The Gibert should properly be called Chéramy-Gibert, built in partnership with Chéramy, a Swiss from Lausanne, whose function was perhaps to provide funding. The aeroplane was a 2-seater with triangular-sectioned fuselage and flat top deck, triangular elevator and rudder. The undercarriage included floats and castering wheels. Rudder control was by a foot-bar, and the elevators by a wheel on the starboard side or the fuselage. The machine was being completed at Chateaufort early in 1912 and was reported flying at Juvisy in November 1912.

(Span: 8 m; length: 12.5 m; 70 hp Gnôme)

Gilbert, E

Eugène Gilbert was one of the most popular French pioneers, famous for his flying the fast Deperdussin in the 1913 Gordon-Bennett race, and afterwards. His name is otherwise connected with a curious tricycle-geared tailless monoplane early in 1908. A high-set wing with S-curved leading edges had a kite-shaped fin above it; the pilot sat below it on a bicycle seat above and aft of the wheel; a bird-neck and bird-beak arrangement over the 2 front wheels supported the forward control surfaces operated by a steering bar. It was tested, presumably unsuccessfully, on a road near Paris in January 1908.

(Span: 4 m; length: 4 m; 4 hp motor)

In 1908 Gilbert joined with Louis Besseyre, an automobile racer, to build at Clermont-Ferrand a large monoplane with a wide triangular-sectioned fuselage, and a rough steel-tube framed undercarriage with 2 small wheels forward. The gull wing lay on the fuselage deck. Power was to have been a 100 hp 2-cycle V8 mounted in front, driving a 2-bladed tractor propeller; Besseyre was killed in an automobile accident in 1909, and the unfinished monoplane was probably abandoned.

Early in 1912 Gilbert had a canard monoplane built and then housed in Anzani's hangar at Issy. The long rectangular uncovered fuselage had a forward elevator at the very nose, with a pair of vertical rudders set one on either side of the nose behind it. The whole front end was supported by a Blériot-style crossed-cane skid. The wings at the rear were highly arched, with thick leading edges and general

Eugène Gilbert's 1912 canard. Note the heavily arched airfoil with thick leading edges. (Courtesy of the Musée de l'Air et de l'Espace/Le Bourget-France)

Blériot outline, with a large rectangular cutout for the pusher propeller; 2 vertical fins formed the undercarriage struts for the 2 wheels.

By this time Gilbert had flown the Sommer, and was regularly a Morane pilot. In 1913 he had a seaplane built by Morane and Saulnier; probably Gilbert helped with the design, which resembled a Henry Farman and was different from other Morane-Saulnier designs.

Gilbert, O

In 1909 Octave Gilbert built a biplane glider based on the Wright design, with a single large rudder and large forward monoplane elevator. All surfaces consisted merely of fabric stretched over a frame outline. The pilot lay prone in netting slung between the wings, which had only 4 flat crosspieces for ribs in each panel – no camber at all. The undercarriage was made from 2 bicycle wheels and forks.

Gildorf

Chauvière built a machine of this name in 1909, probably a monoplane glider.

Gilly

The Gilly triplane was tested by Guercin in August 1909. It is reported to have had a wing area of 100 sqm, and was powered by a 100 hp motor driving 2 propellers.

Giraud-Pastorino

In 1909 Giraud and Pastorino had a small monoplane built at Marseille, patterned after the Demoiselle. Its wing area was about 10 sqm, and it was powered by a 10 hp engine.

Givaudan

Claude Givaudan was born in 1872 and received his balloon brevet in 1911. He became a builder of small 3-wheeled vehicles and went to work for the Vermorel automobile and engine company at Villefranche. There he designed and built his first aeroplane, sometimes referred to as the Vermorel monoplane. The pilot sat in the middle of a long uncovered triangular girder set on 4 wheels. At each end was a large cylindrical drum, each with a smaller concentric drum inside con-

Octave Gilbert's glider. (Courtesy of the Musée de l'Air et de l'Espace/Le Bourget-France)

Octave Gilbert aboard his glider. (Courtesy of the Musée de l'Air et de l'Espace/ Le Bourget-France)

nected to the outer drum with 8 vanes for lift and stability. Each double drum could pivot: the front for altitude – and the rear for directional control. The arrangement was meant to be proof against side gusts in the air: it was certainly safe in this respect, since it never got off the ground. The engine was mounted just forward of the pilot, and drove a tractor propeller through a long shaft.

(Wing area: 15 sqm; 40 hp Vermorel engine)

A subsequent version was sometimes known as the Vermorel triplane, having 3 small extensions fitted to each side of the forward drum, and single ones at each side of the rear drum.

(Span (drum diameters): (front) 2.8 m, 1.5m; (rear) 2.4 m, 1.3 m; length of drums: (front) 1 m; (rear) .8 m; length of fuselage: 7 m; wing area within drums: (front) 19 sqm; (rear) 14.8 sqm; wing area of winglets: (front) 11 sqm; (rear) 8.7 sqm; weight: 360 kg; 50 hp Vermorel V8, modified by Givaudan)

Givaudan was vice-president of the Aéro Club de France when he died in 1945.

Givray et Galeotti

In 1908 these 2 builders attempted to fly an ornithopter of their own design.

Gobbi

This name is mentioned in 1914 – it may have been the Italian aircraft.

Golant

JP Golant was named in connection with a monoplane with a 6-cylinder Anzani at Pithiviers, some time after 1909.

Goldschmidt

This was a handsome monoplane resembling the Hanriot, with deeply arched airfoil, 4-legged undercarriage unlike the Hanriot's 6-legged gear, and a Gnôme mounted precariously high on the nose. One photograph is dated April 1911.

Goliesco

Though built and patented in France, this large and unsuccessful bird-like monoplane was designed by a Rumanian ordnance officer Goliescu (spelled Goliesco in France). It featured a large central uncovered box on which were mounted inverted spoon-shaped wings and a large tail unit. The airframe was made of hollow wooden spars and struts, and the machine was built at Espinosa's Avionnerie, the Société de Construction d'Appareils Aériens (SCAA). The upper surfaces of the wings were smooth, but the undersurfaces were covered with a scaly

The graceful Goldschmidt monoplane. (Courtesy of the Musée de l'Air et de l'Espace/Le Bourget-France)

Above and below: two views of the first version of the Givaudan tandem-drum machine. (Author's collection)

membrane; each wing had spoilers and was pivoted for automatic stability. Elevators and rudder were set on the nose, and another set on 2 single booms at the rear. The whole machine rode on 3 wheels.

(Span: 10 m; length: 6.8 m; gross weight: 425 kg; 25 hp 4-cylinder inline Buchet, driving a propeller designed by Goliesco and built by Georges et Gendre)

Gonnel

This strange design by Arthur and Georges Gonnel was completed and tested by Pappaert at Juvisy in March 1911; it is unlikely to have flown. A square-sectioned uncovered fuselage sat on 2 wheels; the engine was set inside just over the wheels and drove a tractor propeller through a shaft. Above the fuselage, extending its whole length and about as wide, was a long covered boxlike frame, with fabric-covered extensions down each side, making rudimentary wings or fins. The underside of the box was left open, in which the air stream was to "induce a lifting reaction which ought to make it fly."

The machine was to be operated from roads: it was named Uniplan.

(Span: 3.2 m; length: 7 m; height: 3.33 m; wing area: 34 sqm; gross weight: c 300 kg; 30 hp Velox Suer)

Goulois-Crépin

This biplane with a 30 hp Dutheil et Chalmers appeared at Douai in 1910.

Goupy

Goupy started with 2 triplanes, and then moved on to a very successful series of biplanes. The system of lettering/numbering may have been clear and complete at the time, but much of it has since become mysterious or downright missing.

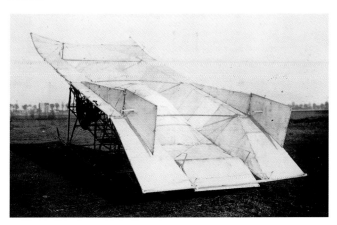

Above and below: two views of the Gonnel Uniplan. If it was meant to run on roads, there seems no indication of steering, either of the main wheels or of the tailwheel. (Courtesy of the Musée de l'Air et de l'Espace/Le Bourget-France)

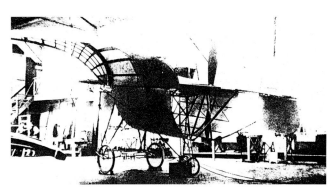

This photo of the Goliesco is light-struck, but gives a good sense of the grace of this seemingly awkward-looking monoplane. (Author's collection)

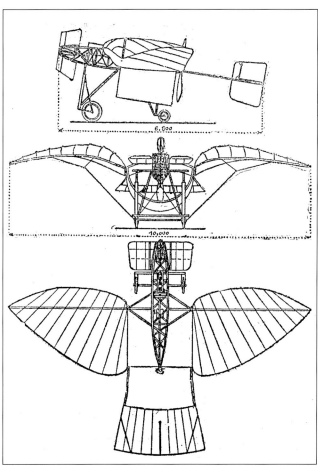

A contemporary Romanian drawing of the Goliesco. (Author's collection)

Type 1: Goupy's 2 triplanes were built by Voisin, perhaps using one of their standard fuselages, a long arched box framework. The tail was a box structure with double vertical and horizontal surfaces with a third tailplane set in between. The lower wing was set against the lower longeron, the middle wing against the upper, and the top wing supported by 4 light vertical struts. The first version showed side-curtains between the 2 middle pairs of struts, and a rectangular rudder set behind the tail. The second, 1bis, showed side-curtains à la Voisin outboard, half-curtains inboard. A third version had these taken off, and a rudder added between the aft end of the fuselage and the upper stabilizer.

(Span: 7 m; weight: 650 kg; 50 hp Antoinette)

The second appears to be a whole new machine. It was under construction in 1909, often appearing in photos taken in the Voisin factory. This one looked more substantial, with heavier struts inboard. The lower wing was fixed below the fuselage; side-curtains were fitted between the outer pairs of struts; and the elevators protruded through the big vertical surfaces.

(Span: 7.5 m; length: 9.8 m; wing area: 44 sqm; speed (planned); 54 kmh; weight: 650 kg; 50 hp Antoinette)

Type 2: Resembling a 2-bay heavily-staggered biplane Blériot XI, this Goupy had been designed by Goupy and the Italian Lieutenant Calderara, and built in the Blériot factory; it flew in March 1909. The fuselage, tailwheel assembly, rudder, undercarriage (here fitted with skids), cloche, and perhaps the seat may have been purchased from Blériot. The lower wing was set below the fuselage; small "aileron" surfaces protruded from each side of the nose, rigged to operate differentially, and there were no aileron or elevator surfaces otherwise. On one version the struts between the 2 tailplanes were filled in. One Type 2 was painted with the numeral 14 and had undercarriage skids and a tailskid. Another was flown by Ladougne at Reims in 1910; it had short forward skids and a tailwheel, and a modern-looking fairing between the top tailplane and the aft fuselage.

(Span: 6.09 m; length: 7.01 m; wing area: 22 sqm; weight: 250-290 kg; 24 hp REP and a 4-bladed propeller)

This same machine modified, or a new one, also had a 4-bladed propeller, and the tailplane-struts were sometimes filled in like side-curtains. The ailerons and the elevators were of the oyster-shell tip design, fitted to all 4 panels and both tailplanes.

(Span: 6 m; length: 7 m; wing area: 26 sqm; loaded weight: 290 kg; 25 hp Anzani)

In 1910-1911 appeared a series of Goupy racers and at least one Type Militaire, usually with forward skids and Gnôme engines. In 1911 appeared some larger versions, 2-seaters, with Gnômes, shorter lower wings, and diagonal brace-struts for the overhanging top wing.

Type Concours Militaire: This big 3-bay sharply-staggered biplane was shown at the Concours in 1911. It featured double wheels, twin skids, and retained the Goupy biplane tail cell with oyster-shell elevators and Blériot-shaped rudder. The aft fuselage was uncovered; elaborate shock absorbers and undercarriage supports ran up beside the nose. One version had 2 concentric propellers and doubled skids.

The first Goupy design was this Voisin-built triplane, variously modified along the way. (Author's collection)

The second, Goupy No 2, in full flight. The lightness of the structure shows clearly in the original photograph, where the horizontal segments of the 4 longerons are warped and uneven. (Peter M Bowers collection)

The big Goupy Type Concours Militaire of 1911, still with wingtip ailerons. (Bill Lewis collection)

(Span: 14.2 m; length: 10.6 m; wing area: 56 sqm; empty weight: 500 kg; 75 hp Chenu)

Type X-II: This 1912 design was a pretty 2-bay heavily staggered 2-seat biplane, but this time with ailerons set into all 4 wing panels; a simple single horizontal tailplane rested on the aft end of the covered fuselage. It appeared with a variety of simple tail surfaces – a common one consisted of a simple square rudder and triangular fin fixed on top. The simplified 4-legged undercarriage had twin skids and twin tailskids. The lower wing was set below the fuselage.

The 2-seater Goupy Type AA. This model features inset top-wing ailerons. (Author's collection)

Type A: A 50 hp Gnôme biplane, similar to the Type X, but with overhung top wing and diagonal struts, and ailerons on the top wing only. The tailskid was single.

Type AA: Similar to the Type A, but with an Anzani engine. This 2-seater appears often in photographs of military line-ups.

Type B: Also similar to the Type A, this version was sometimes set, wheels and all, onto 2 forward floats and a tail float to make a hydro. Both land and sea versions used either an 80 or a 100 hp Gnôme.

Type B.1: Similar to the previous types, this 3-seater was shown in the December 1913 Salon, fitted with a 100 hp Gnôme.

(3-seater: span: (upper): 12.4 m; (lower): 10 m; length: 9 m; 100 hp Gnôme)

Also in the Salon: a pretty single-seater biplane of very modern appearance, with curved ailerons on the top wings only and a neat installation of the 80 hp Gnôme in a horseshoe cowl.

(1-seater: span: (upper): 8.5 m; (lower): 7.2 m; length: 9.2 m; 80 hp Gnôme)

Type M: For some reason, this later machine reverted to the Blériot-style undercarriage, seemingly mated to a Type AA or B. A single diamond-shaped rudder was fixed precariously on its corner above the standard tailplane. One of these was used by Madame Cayat de Castella for her parachute jump on 17 May 1914 at Nevare. The lady was strung horizontally under the fuselage aft of the undercarriage, perilously close the ground, strapped into her parachute.

Gourvène
A biplane of 1912.

Goyard-Aillaud
Two Goyard-Aillaud monoplanes were built and tested in 1910. The first, the Colibri, resembled a Demoiselle, with flat wings and a flat-twin Clément – Bayard; it crashed on 28 May. The second was built partly from steel tubing; it had upward-curved wingtips and skids fitted above the wheels in case these should break off. The engine was the same 35 hp Clément-Bayard used in the first machine; control was through wheels set as on the Antoinette on each side of the fuselage. It was tested in September.

Gramaticescu
This odd monoplane was designed by George Gramaticescu, a Rumanian. Unfortunately he died of pulmonary tuberculosis before the machine could be built, and his mother Emilia undertook to have it built by a French team led by the pilot Maurice Herbster in France. The first – and only – machine was completed and flown on 30 April 1914 at La Vidamée. A second machine was planned, but the correspondence about it is incomplete, and its fate is so far unknown.

The streamlined fuselage was covered, and the undercarriage resembled that of a Morane. The wings were of surprisingly wide chord, more than 2 m, and the front half of the airfoil was twice as thick as the trailing section, resulting in a pronounced step in the lower surface. But as originally designed, there was to have been a second full-span wing of slightly shorter chord fitted just behind and below the main wing, leaving a slot between them.

(Span: 8.5 m; length: 7 m; wing area: 25 sqm; 50 hp Anzani)

Right: The odd Gramatisesco monoplane. Note the striking airfoil section. (Courtesy of the Musée de l'Air et de l'Espace/Le Bourget-France)

Grapperon

In 1911 the former cycle champion Grapperon was testing a monoplane reportedly of his own design at Lèvesville la Chenard in Normandy. It was a Blériot copy – perhaps made from a Blériot XI airframe – with a Labor-Aviation motor and an Hanriot-style undercarriage.

Grégoire-Gyp

Grégoire owes more of his reputation to his fast cars built between 1900 and 1922 than to his brief efforts in aviation.

Grégoire 1909: He designed and built a monoplane powered with a motor of his own design; it was tested at St Chéron des Champs, about 15 km from Chartres, at the end of September. Grégoire himself was at the controls, seems to have been surprised at the take-off, and broke a wheel on landing. It was then shown at the 1909 Paris Exposition with a sale price of 1000F.

A rectangular uncovered fuselage carried a triangular tailplane and elevator and a long triangular rudder at the rear. The design featured a heavy tubular spar in 2 parts, connected in the middle with the equivalent of an automobile differential; through his steering wheel the pilot could twist the 2 rectangular wing panels to produce different angles of attack and so control bank. Pulling the wheel back and forth changed the angle equally for both at once; the wings were detachable and could be moved bodily back and forth (on the ground) to allow for variation in loading according to whether or not a passenger was carried. Steering was done with a rudder controlled through the pilot's back-rest. It first flew on 6 November 1909, piloted by the student pilot de Lailhacar.

The 1911 Grapperon was a real Blériot XI look-alike, except for the landing gear and the skids. (Courtesy of the Musée de l'Air et de l'Espace/Le Bourget-France)

The first Grégoire of 1909, with a double-strut pylon, tailskid, and long curved forward skid. (Courtesy of the Musée de l'Air et de l'Espace/Le Bourget-France)

(Length: 11 m; wing area: 22 sqm; gross weight: 300 kg without pilot; 40 hp water-cooled Gyp)

Grégoire-Gyp 1910: One of these monoplanes was a cross between the Hanriot (undercarriage) and the Antoinette (wing, tail, long covered fuselage, side-mounted control wheels, tail surfaces). It sat tail-high on its wheels and long forward skids, a very graceful machine. Another, perhaps a version of this one,

The modified Grégoire at the Salon of 1909, with revised landing gear and tail support. Note the same striped awning canvas used for the sling seat in both versions! (Courtesy of the Musée de l'Air et de l'Espace/Le Bourget-France)

had a slightly heavier-looking fuselage and modified rudder, and sat back on its tailskid. And still another, powered with a 40 hp Grégoire-Gyp engine, was a still closer copy of the Antoinette, with a simplified V-leg undercarriage and Blériot-style pylon. The control wheels were set halfway down outside the fuselage sides.

Gregory

A Gregory machine was entered in the Concours de Sécurité in 1914.

Gremaud

The American Mrs J Dunbar commissioned and took delivery of this approximate Blériot XI copy in 1910; it was built at Montpélier.

Groffaud et Jolly

The Belgian Groffaud and his partner Jolly built a moto-aviette (a flying motor-bicycle) in 1913 and tested it in France: it was reviewed frequently in sport journals of the period. A small monoplane with a triangular-sectioned covered fuselage and tractor propeller, it was set on a sort of bicycle frame with the pilot on a saddle between the wheels. A motor was to have been fitted.

Gron

Built or building – or perhaps just reported – in 1909.

Groos

In 1909 at Vannes, Brittany, a lieutenant engineer of this name tested an aeroplane said to be of his own design.

Guédon

A monoplane of this name was built by Vinet-Boulogne, to be shown at Lille in March 1910.

Guée

In Nice in 1908 a man named Guée tested a monoplane model under Ferber's "aerodrome" pylon; by early 1909 he had built a biplane glider which was intended to be powered. It was a simple equal-span biplane with rectangular wings and a tail on a single outrigger. Between the wingtips were ailerons, each with small triangular vertical surfaces both above and below, apparently to act as rudders, turning while the ailerons moved up and down.

Guercin

A Rochet-Schneide truck engine of 80 hp powered this triplane at Le Roux in 1909.

Guigardet

A monoplane of this name was reported at Carpentras, in southeastern France.

Guillaume

After working as one of Jean Legrand's pilots, Camille Guillaume de Mauriac experimented with parachute jumps. In 1913 he built a Blériot XI copy, with an uncovered fuselage and a 3-cylinder Anzani. Some

The 1910 Grégoire-Gyp with Hanriot-style undercarriage. (Courtesy of the Musée de l'Air et de l'Espace/Le Bourget-France)

A still later Grégoire-Gyp with a completely different landing gear. (Courtesy of the Musée de l'Air et de l'Espace/Le Bourget-France)

The Guée, evidently in this picture still a glider. (Author's collection)

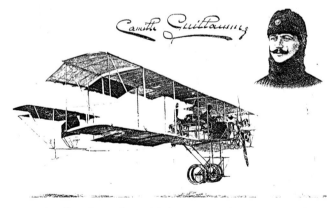

The push-pull Guillaume, his modified Voisin. Note the nose-over wheels under the propeller shaft behind the engine. (Author's collection)

reports say the machine was built to test a new Dangy-Baillet parachute, but it is more likely that test was made by another pilot with another aircraft.

One of his more technical experiments was his modified Voisin, rebuilt with ailerons, an altered undercarriage with 2 pairs of trailing wheels, and 2-100 hp Gnômes, one driving the usual pusher prop, the other, in front, driving a tractor. 2 tiny wheels were set under the nose; perhaps de Mauriac feared a nose-over with his heavier engine installation.

Guillebaud

It is difficult to trace the work of Charles Guillebaud, since his name was spelled in various ways from 1908 to 1912 in journals and on postcards: Guilbaud, Gillebaud, Guilbeau, or even Guisbaud. And he worked in Rouen as well as Le Havre, along the Seine; moreover, the published descriptions of his machines were generally highly whimsical! But all these names were probably the same man, and the machines the same machine.

Guillebaud's single tandem monoplane was called Armorique, after the ancient name for Brittany; it was designed in 1908 and probably tested as late as 1910. The designer meant to build an amphibian which would descend slowly and safely in case of engine failure: built of "artificial bamboo," the machine was very light. The 2 wings were separated only by their own chord's width, each with significant dihedral rising from the keel of the triangular hull and then curving gracefully downward at the ends. A long tail-boom carried the tail, a long tapered cruciform box open at the back end. The tractor propeller was set at the tip of the pointed nose; the machine stood poised on 4 small wheels.

(Length: 13 m; gross weight: 220 kg; 11 hp motor)

Guillebaud later founded a flying school in Rouen; it is reported that early in September 1910 he managed to fly 10 m before crashing in an aeroplane powered by a 25 hp Anzani – probably not the Armorique but a Caudron. In 1911 he claimed to be designing an all-metal machine "to be outstandingly quick," with a lifting surface of 30 sqm, but nothing further was heard of it, or of Guillebaud.

Guillemin

Tetard flew a machine of this name at Mourmelon in May 1910; Guillemin either designed it or owned it.

Guinard

In 1909 at Limoges an accountant named Guinard built an ornithopter to be fitted the following year with a 10 hp motor. And in 1912, pho-

The first Guyard, a seemingly clumsy Demoiselle copy. (Courtesy of the Musée de l'Air et de l'Espace/Le Bourget-France)

The Guillebaud amphibian, ready for flight. (Courtesy of the Musée de l'Air et de l'Espace/Le Bourget-France)

The strange Guinard monoplane still inside its hangar, pilot ensconced in the aft fuselage. The tail surfaces seem made of a single sheet of material. (Courtesy of the Musée de l'Air et de l'Espace/Le Bourget-France)

The Guinard just outside its hangar. More fuselage covering has been added, and the position of the main wheels has been changed. The rudder still seems small. (Courtesy of the Musée de l'Air et de l'Espace/Le Bourget-France)

tos captioned with the name Guinard show a curious and very sophisticated parasol monoplane, partly built. The pilot sat towards the tail of a chubby streamlined covered fuselage supported on 4 small wheels. The engine drove 2 small 3-bladed propellers, which were preceded by a small horizontal surface. Guinard's special interest seemed to be in airfoil sections: both the wing and the propeller blades were composed of separated wide ribs, apparently uncovered: each rib resembled a small boat upside down.

Guyard

The first Guyard, a straight Demoiselle copy, appeared in 1910 and was tested in Madagascar. The 3 tail booms were thick and awkward-looking; a tiny diamond-shaped cruciform tail pivoted at the point of the tail booms, and a supplementary triangular fin was set on top half-way back.

Another, later, Guyard. Several contemporary aeroplanes shared the inverted-U undercarriage frames. (Courtesy of the Musée de l'Air et de l'Espace/Le Bourget-France)

The second, entirely different, was tested at Issy in April 1911 and was flown the following month. The overall appearance looks crude, although it was reported to be "very well finished." The triangular fuselage was almost completely sheathed with sheets of citron wood; the rectangular monoplane wing with noticeable dihedral was mounted slightly above the fuselage under a high Blériot-style pylon. A small rudder was fitted at the tail, and long triangular tailplanes carried the elevators. The distinctive undercarriage was built on 2 arched wooden struts and a cross-bar; the trailing wheels were at the end of short skids. The early descriptions of the Guyard No 2 mention a 4-cylinder 40 hp inline Labor-Aviation motor with radiators alongside the fuselage like the Antoinette; but photographs show the same aircraft with a 50 hp radial Anzani, and the arched undercarriage legs of the Vendôme and other contemporary designs.

(Span: 10.8 m; length: (Labor) 9 m; (Anzani) c 8 m; wing area: 15.5 sqm; empty weight: (Labor) 245 kg; (Anzani) 225 kg)

The Guy et Bollon glider. It looks flyable. (Author's collection)

Guy et Bollon

Guy and Bollon together built a large 10-meter span monoplane glider in 1910, in the Alps. A short triangular-sectioned fuselage carried a forward monoplane elevator and a short monoplane tailplane with long fin and tiny rudder. The wings were flexible, consisting of a single central spar below to which only 5 ribs were attached; ailerons were hinged to the trailing edges. It ran on a single-track undercarriage.

Guyot

The name Guyot was carried by various French builders, and it is difficult to separate them. The name appears alone for some machines, and with other designers/builders for others.

A man of this name ordered a Wright early in 1909 at Nantes, on the Atlantic coast. Shortly afterwards Albert Guyot, a famous automobile racer from Orleans, started flying a Blériot and even traveled to Russia with Louis himself to demonstrate the line. Albert Guyot's son stated that the 2 entrepreneurs "flew little but spent lavishly for various entertainment so that they had not enough money to travel back to France." After Guyot's death, his son reported, his widow destroyed most of his archives and personal papers "to take revenge on this unpleasant man."

Guyot, Boeswillwald et Stahl: The first monoplane of this name appeared at the Semaine d'Aviation de Touraine in the first week of May, 1910, a Blériot copy of 8-meter span, with the rear fuselage triangular in section and with a 4-cylinder inline water-cooled Labor-Picker engine with its radiator slung horizontally underneath. 3 monoplanes of this type were reported flying.

Guyot, Boeswillwald and Villem: It is known that it was Albert Guyot who was associated with this project, as it most likely was with the previous design. The GBV was a 2-seater monoplane also known as the Villem-Guyot. It was said to have been finished in early March 1911 at the Camp de Cercottes, near Orléans.

Guyot-Cellier-Jaugey: Guyot (perhaps it was Albert) and Cellier formed the Société d'Etudes d'Aviation, for which in 1909 Jaugey built them a small tractor biplane which was then entered in the 1909 Monaco meet. The wings were short and rectangular, with 2 rounded ailerons set outside the outer interplane struts. A monoplane elevator in halves was set on each side of the long propeller shaft just ahead of the wing leading edges. The pilot sat high above the long rectangular fuselage frame with the engine almost in his lap, a pair of vertical radiators standing one on each side of the drive-shaft. The tail resembled the Voisin's, with the

A good view of the Guyot-Cellier-Jaugey of 1909. Note the long forward extension shaft. (Peter M Bowers collection)

rudder between the 2 tailplanes. 3 wheels on a steel-tube framework supported the machine, 2 forward and one aft; 2 tiny wheels kept the tail off the ground. It may not have flown.

(Weight: 260 kg; 36 hp Mors automobile engine)

Guyot et Verdier

Guyot and Verdier were manufacturers at la Souterraine, in midwestern France, and built at least 2 biplanes, the first finished by the end of 1908. It was a tractor with front elevator and a tailplane at the far rear, with a large rectangular fin and rudder set immediately aft of the wings between the outriggers. The center-section of the top wing was bent slightly upward above the 40 hp flat twin engine on the lower wing, which drove an Antoinette-style propeller. 2 ailerons were hinged between the 2 outer struts at the leading edges of the wings.

The first Guyot-Verdier, the tractor biplane, of 1908. (Courtesy of the Musée de l'Air et de l'Espace/Le Bourget-France)

The second machine was finished in February 1910, and was taken to the hippodrome la Guéridière at Dorat, near Clermont-Ferrand in mid-France. A large pusher biplane probably developed from the first and unsuccessful design, No 2 had a 60 hp ENV V8, and ailerons set into the upper wing trailing edges. The tailplane and inset elevator were fixed aft of a very large rudder. During the trials the engine was moved forward, and the metal propeller changed for a wooden one designed by Guyot, which broke soon after. The aeroplane had a wing area of 40 sqm – some said 50 – and was flying "fairly well" over Juvisy by June 1911. It was entered in the Concours Militaire of 1911.

H

Hanriot

The first Hanriot was shown at the 1909 Paris Salon, underpowered with a Buchet engine. It was the clear forerunner of most of the subsequent Hanriots, with long uncovered fuselage, the monoplane wing rectangular. The stabilizer was set on the top of the aft fuselage, with a small triangular fin below and a small triangular rudder aft. The wheels, each with its long skid, were attached with the typical Hanriot

The first Hanriot, already showing the beginnings of the familiar trade-mark undercarriage. (Author's collection)

The 2 Hanriots at the 1910 Brussels show – note the wheeled vehicles in the background. (Courtesy of the Musée de l'Air et de l'Espace/Le Bourget-France)

4-strut arrangement, the rear 2 coming together above the fuselage to form the pylon.

A 1910 version flew at Reims, perhaps with the same fuselage and engine. An extra pair of landing gear struts were added forward; the whole tail structure was now mounted on the top of the fuselage; and kingpost was set onto the rear fuselage with a tailskid set underneath. A similar Hanriot was photographed with a different vertical fin and rudder, with the tailplane set again under the fuselage.

Also in 1910, on 16 January at the Brussels IXième Salon de l'Automobile, de l'Aéronautique, du Cycle et des Sports, 2 new Hanriots were shown, each with the now-typical long covered fuselage, rectangular wings, and 6-legged undercarriage. One featured 2 kingposts and a single long fin and trapezoidal rudder; the other had the V-pylon and a forward kingpost, and a small pointed rudder fitted to a peaked fin. Both had control wheels on each side of the cockpit.

The same year, a prolific one for the firm, appeared the Grand Monoplan with 2-3 seats; perhaps it was designated Type II. Also offered for sale was the Libellule (dragonfly), a smaller single-seater with a 45-50 hp Clerget, also with the pointed fin and rudder. A similar machine with a 50 hp Clerget and rounded wingtips and a trapezoidal pylon was marked VI. One of these was reworked for Pequet with a Gnôme and different undercarriage legs.

In 1911 the firm built a military version, with rounded wingtips, a single seat and a 4-legged undercarriage. A second military type

The Type VI. Would that designations could all be so clear. (Courtesy of the Musée de l'Air et de l'Espace/Le Bourget-France)

was entered in the Concours Militaire; this one had a big 100 hp Clerget, 2 pairs of close-set wheels in a 6-legged structure, and could seat 3 to 5 people. The pylon was of the familiar trapezoidal form, but with an inverted arch for the rear support.

After the Concours, Ponnier, a designer for Hanriot, bought out the firm, which took the name of the new owner. The Ponniers will be described under their own name, though some of these also appeared in later Hanriot catalogs.

But the name Hanriot had not disappeared: for the 1913 Concours de Sécurité he entered a "natural stability" aeroplane. This odd design featured several sets of adjustable surfaces mounted high on an awkward frame structure, itself running on 4 wheels. The outcome of all this is not known. And during World War I, the Hanriot firm was re-formed and went on to build a long series of successful aircraft.

Hans

An owner or designer in 1908.

Hansen

An owner or designer in 1908.

Hayot

From 1909 to 1914, Captain Hayot worked at refining his basic design for an automatically stable aeroplane, and designed 5 awkward tandem machines.

The first, a multiplane built by Chauvière and tested near Beauvais during the spring of 1909, was described as being equipped with 5 groups of 3 small planes, 2 each at front and amidships, and one at the rear, all above a long fuselage. But when it appeared, it showed 2 groups of 4 planes forward, linked by a long spar to 2 other groups at the rear, with a pair of ailerons on each side of the fuselage at the middle, and a biplane rudder fitted ahead of an elevator at the rear. Each group of 4 wings was fitted so close together that the leading edges of the second set were just behind the trailing edges of the first. The pilot sat behind the rear group; a mechanic sat between the en-

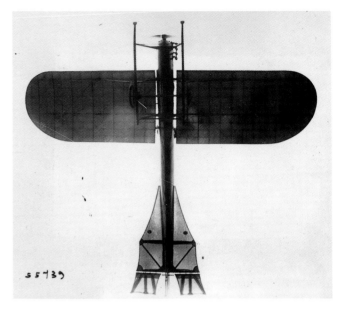

A Hanriot from below – a Spitfire of its time, at least in appearance. (Courtesy of the Musée de l'Air et de l'Espace/Le Bourget-France)

The 1911 military version with the 4-legged undercarriage. (Courtesy of the Musée de l'Air et de l'Espace/Le Bourget-France)

The Hanriot entered in the Concours de Sécurité of 1913. (Courtesy of the Musée de l'Air et de l'Espace/Le Bourget-France)

Left above: The big tandem Hayot multiplane under construction. The photo shows the divided tail surface in the foreground, preceded by the 5 sets of small triplane wings going forward to the nose. (Courtesy of the Musée de l'Air et de l'Espace/Le Bourget-France)

Left: The Hayot as it finally appeared; the fuselage may have remained unchanged. (Author's collection)

gine and the radiator, mounted above a Blériot-style undercarriage just ahead of the first wings. The engine drove 2 tractor Chauvière propellers through a long shaft. Little more is known about this huge set-piece: Goffin's flight tests were apparently unsuccessful.

(Span: 4 m; length: 10.6 m; height: 6 m; 60 hp 6-cylinder water-cooled Dutheil-Chalmers)

The other 4 designs were all 2-seat tandem-wing monoplanes; the high parasol rear wing was set close behind the high parasol front wing, at a lower angle of attack. All 4 had rear monoplane elevators and single rudders. The positions of the wings in these 4 designs moved further and further forward, the pilot always below the rear wing and the passenger/mechanic below and to the rear of the forward wing. Descriptions of Hayot's device remain unclear. The wings were mounted on frames which oscillated freely fore and aft on the sides of the fuselage to damp oscillations of the machine between 2 stable positions. It appears that the inventor was pleased with the lack of sensitivity of his controls, and that he continuously increased the power of his machines from 50 to 100 hp, at the same time reducing their weight.

(Data for the 1913 design under construction in 1914: span: 13 m; length: 8.65 m; wing area: 35 sqm; empty weight: 550 kg; 100 hp engine)

Hekking

In September 1909 at Le Havre Raymond Hekking built a glider of 7-meter span and 25 sqm wing area; it is said to have "flown into the wind."

Helliot

A designer or builder in 1908.

Henry

A postcard shows this pretty canard monoplane with (presumably) M Henry at the controls. The wings resemble those of the Blériot XI, with a pair of castering wheels set under the wing, and pusher engine. The fuselage was long and covered and tapered, with small rectangular rudders above and below the nose, and a forward elevator. It is not clear what supported the front of the machine while it was on the ground.

Herbster

A man named Herbster, probably Maurice, Henry Farman's mechanic, had a glider built by Dargent in 1904.

Herve

Herve had a glider built in Rennes in 1909, featuring a single spar with large feathers "on 1/3 of the length," and an elevator. It was 3 m long.

Right: The 1908 Hervieux seems to have lacked rudder control. (Bill Lewis collection)

One of Hayot's later safety monoplanes. (Courtesy of the Musée de l'Air et de l'Espace/Le Bourget-France)

The Henry canard. (Author's collection)

Hervieux

In October 1908 at le Havre, Léon Hervieux built a big monoplane with broad rectangular wings with drooping tips and a broad flat fantailed horizontal surface. A large rectangular vertical surface was fitted under the middle of each wing, perhaps to resist side-slipping.

(Span: 10 m; weight: 100 kg; an 18-24 hp motor)

HF-BV

Hartmann was an infantryman of the fourth Regiment of the line, who with the Vicomte Bernard de Virel had a biplane built by Servais in 1909 at the workshop in Auxerre in central France. It had a "monoplane-in-tandem" tailplane, warping wings, and 2 counter-rotating propellers driven by a 40 hp Grégoire-Gyp.

(Span: 12 m; wing area: 54 sqm; weight of airframe alone: 90 kg; 40 hp Grégoire-Gyp)

Hartmann was not exactly a newcomer: he had been involved in aeronautical research for some time previously, although without much success. In particular, with a man named Hofman he had patented a control system with 2 steering wheels on a single post, one for rudder and elevator; and the other immediately aft of it, for the roll-control surfaces.

Hornust

In 1908-09, a man named Hornust had a glider built at St Piat, near Mainlenon near Chartres, with wings shaped like those of a bird, but with ailerons. Captive flights were planned for the beginning of 1909, and powered flights to follow.

(Span: 12 m; length: 3.8 m; wing area: 27 sqm)

Huet, Grazzioli, et Lombardini

In 1913 Grazzioli was reported to be flying a new monoplane of his own design from the new airfield at Pontlieu, in addition to working at the Brulé-Souchet flying school. The Grazzioli monoplane was in fact designed by René Huet of Le Mans, with contributions from Grazzioli and Lombardini. It resembled the Nieuport II, powered with a 60 or 100 hp 6 – or 10-cylinder radial Anzani. The undercarriage featured 4 vertical struts, 2 wheels, and short skids; a Blériot-style double-curved skid supported the tail.

I-J

IAL (Imbert and Latour)

Early in 1909 Imbert and Latour publicized the beginning of their aircraft work at Le Vesinet, near Paris. They built a tractor monoplane with rectangular – slightly drooping – wings, a long uncovered box fuselage with a long rectangular rudder set on top and a rectangular elevator surface pivoted behind it. The pilot sat inside the fuselage behind the wing. A water-cooled straight 4 engine was set out ahead level with the wing.

Illinschulz

The description of this machine in *L'Aéro* in 1910 suggests an attractive streamlined design: the fuselage covered with veneered wood had the shape "of a bird or a fish," the tail ended like the flat point of an arrow, with a triangular elevator. The wings were covered with fabric on top and veneer below, and their incidence was controllable with foot pedals. The undercarriage consisted of 2 wheels in front which castered, and one behind that did not. It was flown by Nourry at Issy in 1910.

(Span: 8 m; length: 7 m; wing area; 18 sqm; weight empty: 350 kg; an Illinschulz propeller of 2.3 m diameter and 1.8 m pitch)

The IAL monoplane of 1909. (Author's collection)

Jacob et Audenis

In 1909 Jean Jacob and Charles Audenis, both about 20 years old, began building a Henry Farman copy at Lyon. The rectangular forward elevator was connected with the rear elevator which had a bean-shaped rudder set below it. The pilot sat on a wooden frame forward, as on the Farman; the 2-wheeled undercarriage had a wide track.

Upon their graduation with their baccalaureates, their fathers gave them a bright new 50 hp Gnôme, with which they were flying in 1910.

Jacquelin

Like many former bicycle racers, the world champion Edmond Jacquelin turned his attention to aviation: his imagination in this new field, however, brought him little success. His first heavier-than-air design was nicknamed "les cinq doigts de la main" (the 5 fingers), and "le pied de nez" (a rude gesture); it was probably the monoplane built in 1908 or 1909 at Trignac, near St Nazaire, and sponsored by the Société Géographique de St Nazaire. In 1909 he had a man named Moles in Montières-les-Amiens, in northern France, build an ornithopter with several pairs of wings, apparently capable of hovering; but by June 1910 it was not yet completed.

Also in 1910, Jacquelin purchased the one-off Voisin tractor biplane and modified it: he took off the wing curtains and converted the biplane tail cell to monoplane form, set directly on top of the end of the fuselage frame; 2 lozenge-shaped fins were set on the tailplane. He added 2 pairs of flaps, one on each side of the fuselage: in each

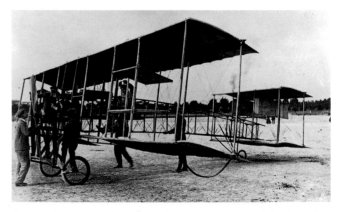

Jacquelin's Voisin as he began to modify it. Compare this with the photo of the original Voisin tractor, under Voisin; also with the following photo. (Courtesy of the Musée de l'Air et de l'Espace/Le Bourget-France)

Note the continuing changes made to Jacquelin's Voisin. (Courtesy of the Musée de l'Air et de l'Espace/Le Bourget-France)

pair, the upper apparently moved only down and the lower up, to work both as spoilers and as rudders. Steering was done with a massive wheel nearly 1 meter in diameter; a passenger sat behind the pilot in the uncovered fuselage, and in front a 3-cylinder air-cooled Anzani drove a 2-blade tractor propeller. The fate of this machine is not known, but in 1911 Jacquelin was appointed a mechanic at Blériot, and shortly after, invented a tricycle street-sweeper.

Janicot

In March 1909 at Limoges, Janicot and Delbrel built a light biplane glider weighing only 25 kg; it was "broken by a gust" while being flight-tested for the first time by a young man named Cadillat. In the same year Janicot began a monoplane with Mouricot; it was not finished by September, at which time it was still awaiting its engine. The machine, called Le Barbichet (little dog), had a square-sectioned fuselage tapering to the rear, 2 castering wheels, and a 2-piece rear elevator. It may never have even been taxied.

(Span: 8.6 m; length: 6.5 m; wing area: 18 sqm)

Janin (Jeannin?)

A machine of this name was reported in 1908. (Jeannin was the German designer of several Taube aircraft.)

Janoir

An important subcontractor during WWI, Janoir had begun his career as a pilot with several aviation firms like Bonnet-Labranche and Deperdussin; he also worked with Guérin and Corneloup. At the end of 1911 he was reported to be building a monoplane of his own design at the Camp de Cercottes, near Orléans. Janoir was said to be the manager of the ABL flying school at Cercottes, flying an ABL monoplane with a 50 hp Viale.

He worked in Russia from 1914 to 1915 with Wladimir Lebedeff, building Deperdussins and probably some Lebedeff designs; returning to France, he built Spads, including the Type XII, and prototypes of his own curious flyingboats.

JAP

Although the JAP monoplane was not French – it was a British-built copy of the Blériot XI, powered by a 40 hp JAP motor and built by JA Prestwich in London for HJ Harding. It began with ailerons, which were soon replaced by the Blériot wing-warping arrangements; we are including it here, since it was often referred to in French aviation journals in 1910. It still exists, and can be seen in the Science Museum, in London.

Below: The JAP monoplane: the first version had ailerons. (Courtesy of the Musée de l'Air et de l'Espace/Le Bourget-France)

Jeanson-Colliex

If the amount of information about this monstrous double biplane flyingboat is in proportion to its size, it is not because the aircraft was successful. It was well publicized in aviation journals, even at the end of 1914, a time of secrecy and censorship; but then as now some of the most publicized designs were the least successful.

Maurice Colliex began as a draftsman for the Voisin company, and became a friend and collaborator of Gabriel Voisin. He started the construction of this aeroplane in mid-1912: one might wonder at its similarities to another giant machine, the Icare, built by Voisin. The Jeanson-Colliex was built around a large hull shaped like a speed-boat, built by the boat-builder Despujols, with a cut-off stern and a step midway back. Inside the hull, designed to accommodate 10 people or the corresponding weight of armament, were mounted side-by-side 2 200 hp 6-cylinder inline water-cooled Chenus, which together through a reduction gear and concealed chains or shafts drove a single 5-meter diameter 2-blade pusher propeller.

The high-aspect-ratio wings were arranged in 2 biplane cells: the main set was mounted over the sternpost, fixed on booms; and the forward set was braced like a set of jibs from a bowsprit. Ailerons were fitted only to the top rear wing. The elevator and twin rudders were mounted behind the rear cell; wingtip floats were set under the lower rear wings.

The flyingboat was launched on the Seine at Triel, upstream from Meulan, west of Paris, in 1913; it was demonstrated in 1914 in front of the Commission de Sécurité at Triel. It is reported to have made "some flights" between Triel and Vaulx-sur-Seine (Meulan), where the river is straight for almost 4 km. Other sources report earlier flights of 10 km between these same places, but these seem unlikely, and were probably taxiing trials up and down the river from Triel. Photos dated February 1914 show several modifications: 3 rudders, shorter struts for the wing floats, longer spans for both sets of wings, a more streamlined fairing added to the stern.

This version was photographed taxiing at high speed, pushing a big foaming bow wave. And one photograph shows it in flight.

(Span: rear set, 24 m, with rows of 7 and 9 interplane struts; increased to 27 m (rows of 9 and 11 struts); wing area, longer span: 145 sqm; length overall: 16 m; length of hull: 7.7 m increased to 8.6 m; hull width: 2.6 m; empty weight: c 3700 kg; gross weight (2 pilots, 2 mechanics, fuel for a 13 hr flight to maximum range of c 1500 km): 4300 kg; 2 200 hp Chenus)

Joliot (Julliot?)

Using information from Gabriel Voisin, André Joliot like many other amateurs built an unmanned biplane glider in 1907; in 1908 he was listed as constructor or owner of an aeroplane. Early in 1910 he announced that he had designed a monoplane to be built by Lebaudy, but nothing more was heard of it after that. Joliot was an engineer for Lebaudy.

Jorwitz

A man named Guy Jorwitz was mentioned as having his name on a flying machine in 1908.

Above and below: two views of the Jeanson-Colliex flyingboat. (Courtesy of the Musée de l'Air et de l'Espace/Le Bourget-France)

Jourdan

Photographs of this ungainly machine from April 1910 to March 1912 show a wide variety of alterations: evidently the designer remained unsatisfied. The Jourdan appeared first at the field at Juvisy in the spring of 1910. On top of an uncovered box frame was mounted the most striking feature of the design, a large open-ended conical barrel with the large opening in front, 2 m in diameter. Inside at the forward end was set a 70 hp Gnôme driving a tractor propeller. A long deeply curved rectangular wing on each side made it into an ungainly monoplane, with a triangular tailplane at the rear, set at a high angle of attack. The pilot sat below, between the twin paired wheels of the 2-skid undercarriage; his control stick with horizontal steering wheel directed the rudder, rear elevator, and wing-warping. The machine was tested, unsuccessfully, during the rest of 1910; in November it was reported the wings could warp from 14° to 7°.

Early in 1911 Bobba continued to try to make the machine airworthy, and during the summer it was modified heavily: the tailplane

An intermediate version of the Jourdan of 1910, with the full cone-shaped barrel, rectangular wings with trailing ailerons, and the pilot seated below. (Peter M Bowers collection)

was now rectangular, and new wings were squared off, with trailing ailerons. Since the kingposts had disappeared, the barrel was now mounted level with the wheels, with an open-frame fuselage arranged at the back of it, with the pilot sitting inside it just aft of the rear end of the barrel. The reporters called it a helicoplane. In March 1912 Jourdan modified it again. The barrel was cut in half longitudinally to make a lifting vault on top of the fuselage, which consisted of the mating of the sections of the first and second frameworks together, with the addition of a second seat in front of the pilot. The wings were changed again, now warping, with raked tips. A small fin was added and 2 of the wheels and the skids deleted. In this form it managed to fly early in 1912.

(Span (last version): 14 m; length: 10 m; weight: 500 kg; 70 hp Gnôme)

But Jourdan, now without further funds, abandoned his work. It is reported that he was hired by another aviation firm, but he was found apparently murdered on the morning of 15 July 1912; but he may have committed suicide.

Juge et Rolland

In 1908 JJ Juge and Paul Rolland began the construction of a large ornithopter which attracted some attention; built mainly of steel tubing and covered with silk, it had a streamlined fuselage on 3 wheels with wings high enough to beat: they were bat-wing-shaped, with 6 or 7 flaps on each leading edge. The tail could be castered by "reflex movements of the pilot." The flaps were to be actuated through connecting rods and an endless screw powered by the 20-24 hp motor, which was inside the body hidden under an aluminum fairing. But Juge and Rolland never had the money to purchase the engine.

(Rotor span: 11.5 m; weight: 30 kg; 20-24 hp motor which was never installed)

Juvigny (or Javigny?)

This shapely canard monoplane may have been built for the 1914 Concours de Sécurité, but was not fitted out in time to participate.

The aft end of the Juvigny canard. The drive chain is not installed in this picture. (Courtesy of the Musée de l'Air et de l'Espace/Le Bourget-France)

A later version of the Jourdan, now with new wings and only half the overhead barrel. This may well have been the final version. (Courtesy of the Musée de l'Air et de l'Espace/Le Bourget-France)

The huge Juge et Rolland ornithopter. (Author's collection)

The fuselage seems to have been covered with ply veneer; both wings and forward surface were rectangular and back-swept. The wings had ailerons set into the trailing edges, and the forward surface had triangular panels hinged on its trailing edge. A water-cooled inline motor was at the very rear of the fuselage driving a 2-blade pusher propeller through a chain. Behind the propeller, pivoted at the top end at the hub, was a large rectangular rudder. 2 main wheels were close together on either side under the leading edges, and 2 nosewheels were paired under the nose.

(Span: c 9 m; length: c 7 m)

K

Kapferer

Graduate of the Ecole des Mines, collaborator and nephew of Henri Deutsch de la Meurthe, Henri Kapferer was well known as a balloonist; but it was he who in 1904 suggested to his uncle that he should sponsor research into heavier-than-air machines, and his suggestion was followed by the creation of the Prix du Kilomètre, which was won by Henry Farman on 13 January 1908. Through the support of men like de la Meurthe and the banker Lazare Weiller, the powers of money stood guarantee for the new industry.

Henri Kapferer is not included in this section as a constructor but as a buyer and enthusiast: he had 4 aircraft built, but none of them were of his design. With Léon Delagrange, the first client of the Voisin brothers' aircraft manufacturing firm, he ordered a Voisin biplane late in 1906. Though warned to use a light motor of at least 40 hp, he fitted to his new machine a heavy and useless 20/25 hp V8 Buchet. Tested unsuccessfully on the Sartrouville grounds on 1 March 1907, the machine was abandoned.

His 3 other aircraft were built at Astra, de la Meurthe's new company. All were tandem monoplanes: the second was marked Astra on the rear of the fuselage, and the third was marked Kapferer-Paulhan, as the first should have been also, since both had been designed at least in principle by the young Louis Paulhan from an earlier model built by Paulhan and Burdin, and perhaps Peyret; a photo shows Paulhan and Peyret holding up a large tandem model with twin pusher propellers.

Kapferer-Paulhan No 1 (or Kapferer-Astra): A tandem with the tail unit set on long outriggers, one set above the other. It had a short deep fuselage with mica panels set into the sides of the circular open cockpit just ahead of the leading edge of the rear wings, which were set at the same height as the front pair and with reduced angle of attack. The spars were fitted into special aluminum boxes inside the fuselage. A small forward elevator was set between the front wings and the engine, and a cruciform tail was mounted on a universal ball joint. The covering was varnished parchment. It may not have been completed in this form.

(Spans: 10.85 m; length: c 6.5 m; wing area: 30 sqm; gross weight: c 400 kg including 10 liters of gasoline; 35 hp REP)

Kapferer-Paulhan No 2 (or Kapferer-Astra): This one resembled the first, less the twin outriggers, and may have been the same airframe.

Kapferer-Paulhan No 3 (or Kapferer-Astra): A long Langley-type tandem, with a long narrow rectangular fuselage, clear-doped, on a Voisin-style undercarriage with 2 trailing wheels forward and a third wheel under the tail. A 35 hp semi-radial REP drove a tractor 4-blade metal propeller; 2 small square rudders were set at the tail, one above and the other below, with an elevator

The tandem Kapferer-Paulhan No 3. The 2 men plus the 35 hp REP proved inadequate to get the aeroplane into the air. (Author's collection)

The nacelle of the Kapferer Voisin. Note the sandbags to prevent it tipping backward on the trestles. (Courtesy of the Musée de l'Air et de l'Espace/Le Bourget-France)

Assembling the Kapferer Voisin on the field. (Courtesy of the Musée de l'Air et de l'Espace/Le Bourget-France)

The Kapferer-Paulhan (Kapferer-Astra) No 2 – perhaps No 1 without the tail outriggers. Note the small numerals 1 and 3 painted above the wing roots: presumably 2 and 4 are on the other side, and all 4 panels may be the same. (Courtesy of the Musée de l'Air et de l'Espace/Le Bourget-France)

hinged at the rear. The thin wings showed a "quadruple curve" and a high angle of attack, the forward set higher than the rear. Tested in the summer of 1908, the machine may not have been able to take off. It is possible that all 3 of these machines were developments of the same single airframe, Kapferer No 1.

(Spans: 8.6 m; length: 11 m; wing area: 32 sqm; 35 hp REP)

Kaspar

Apparently a copy of the Demoiselle, but built of bamboo and steel tubing, it was finished in December 1909. Kaspar was a German.

Kassa

The Pole Josef Kassa started his aeronautical studies in France in 1910. In Paris he designed 3 aircraft, Ery 1, 2, and 3; at the time this last

The first Kassa, with double tailplane. (Peter M Bowers collection)

machine was flying near Paris, there were reports of a 50 hp 2-seater being built in Russia.

All 3 were of the same basic design: a triangular-section uncovered fuselage of wood; the undercarriage was made on a large inverted U, similar to that on the Vendôme monoplanes; the wheels were set in slotted frames which came forward into curved skids, from the ends of which heavy springs ran back to the arch to provide shock-absorbing. The inner ends of the 4 wing spars curved upward to form an unusual wing pylon.

The first one was likely to be the "monoplane of Mayeroff and Blinderman," flown by the latter at Nice in April 1911 and later crashed by Lecomte. The fuselage was covered only around the cockpit; there were 2 tailplanes slightly staggered, the upper one with a curved airfoil set on the fuselage top, and the lower consisting of 2 elevator flaps hinged underneath the aft end of the fuselage. The tail may have been copied from Garbero's modified Blériot XI.

(Span: 10 m; length: 9 m; wing area: 20 sqm; 50 hp 5-cylinder Viale)

The second, rather similar but with a better finish, may have been built at the Ateliers Aéronautiques de l'Est at St Die. The somewhat shorter fuselage carried long triangular fin and tailplanes with rectangular rudder and elevators; the down-curved wings of the first design were replaced by rectangular panels with slight dihedral and large angle of attack. The engine was the same 5-cylinder engine, perhaps a Viale.

The third, also known as the Blinderman-Gibert, was flown in 1912 at Chateau Fort, near Buc. The tail surfaces were now swallow shapes, with rounder control surfaces. The triangular section of the aft fuselage became polyhedral forward.

Kaufmann

Son of a wealthy Paris banker, Paul Kaufmann built 4 monoplanes between 1909 and 1911.

No 1: An odd tractor monoplane which appeared in 1910: the fuselage consisted of 2 thin parallel outriggers supporting a rect-

The second Kassa. (Courtesy of the Musée de l'Air et de l'Espace/Le Bourget-France)

The first Kaufmann monoplane. (Courtesy of the Musée de l'Air et de l'Espace/Le Bourget-France)

angular tailplane with 2 rectangular rudders below it. The pilot sat amidships between the booms and on top of the wing. Below him the axle was supported at the end of 2 parallel triangles. A single skid reached forward, and 2 others supported the tail. The wing was rectangular with a highly-arched airfoil. It did not fly.

(Span: 6 m; length: 6 m; wing area: 12 sqm; gross weight: 200 kg; 24 hp 3-cylinder Anzani)

No 2: It was finished early in 1911 and tested unsuccessfully at Issy. The pilot sat on the lower boom of the triangular fuselage frame behind the motor. The drooping wings were again deeply arched with thick leading edges; the panels were nearly square and set at a nearly 30° angle of attack. They were designed to warp, but only upward, to reduce lift but not increase drag at the same time. The tailplane and elevators were swallowtailed in shape.

<u>No 3</u>: Tested during June 1911, it flew in August; it was a rough copy of the pigeon-tailed Blériot. The horizontal tail surfaces resembled those of No 2 and were set at a high angle of attack; the rudder, well aft of the tailplane, was similar to those used on the ACRs and the Thomanns, and like them was made of steel tube with bronze bearings. The whole machine may have been built of welded steel tube, either by Thomann or more likely, by Roux. The bent-wood tailskid and undercarriage may have been built by Blériot, and the wheels were faired with fabric on the outsides. The wings curved downward slightly "to improve the return to level flight after a bank"; Kaufmann seem to have believed that lift resulted from air pressure underneath the surfaces. A small flat fin was added aft of the rear cockpit. A later version of No 3 with 12-rib wings was described with a 50 hp Anzani; it was the first of the Kaufmann aeroplanes to fly.

(Span: 10.6 m; length: 7.6 m; 50 hp 6-cylinder Anzani)

<u>No 4</u>: This was the last of his designs, shown under the placard Type de Course at the 1911 Salon, with a triangular rudder and reduced angle of attack on the tailplane. The wings were long, and tapered to pointed tips, curved down like a bird's. A contemporary drawing shows still another wing arrangement, with gracefully upswept tips. The fuselage was narrow, with a wide-set undercarriage. A double-looped skid Blériot-style held up the tail. This machine may never have been tested at all.

Slightly reminiscent of the Demoiselle, Kaufmann's second design. (Peter M Bowers collection)

The third Kaufmann. Note the covered wheels, slightly gulled wings, and narrow-bladed propeller. (Courtesy of the Musée de l'Air et de l'Espace/Le Bourget-France)

Below: The fourth Kaufmann. Note the drooping wings and the covered wheels. (Courtesy of the Musée de l'Air et de l'Espace/Le Bourget-France)

(Span: 11.6 m; length: 7.6 m; empty weight: 280 kg; payload: 180 kg; 90 hp 6-cylinder Anzani)

In 1913, Kaufmann graduated from the Ecole d'Aéronautique at about 24, and was appointed engineer by Louis Clément. He volunteered in WWI and flew Voisin bombers; in the course of the War he was wounded, and his aeronautical career was ended.

Kluytmans

The big Kluytmans biplane was built by Voisin and appeared at Reims in the summer of 1909: it had features of the Wright, but bigger. A biplane front elevator was mounted with curved struts onto the leading edges of the wings; 2 wheels and a skid fitted with a front roller resembled the undercarriage of the first version of the Antoinette IV. The engine, probably an Antoinette with its copper-tube radiator, was on the lower wing to the right of the pilot, driving twin pusher propellers, and a second seat was attached on the center-line. The 2 curved rudders rested on a single castering tailwheel.

Koechlin

Paul Koechlin designed and built his first aeroplane, a little biplane completed in May-June 1908; it was sometimes referred to erroneously as the first de Pischoff and Koechlin design.

Koechlin No 1: It comprised 2 biplane cells connected like those in a box kite, with struts at the corners; unlike a box kite, the horizontal surfaces were broken at the center-lines, making shallow hexagons spanning c 3 m each; the aft cell had side-curtains. The pilot lay prone between them on a sort of hammock, his face immediately behind the 17 hp Dutheil et Chalmers 2-cylinder motor in front. 2 bicycle wheels in front and 2 castering tailwheels at the very end supported the machine on the ground. There seemed no provision for cushioning the shocks of landing – but this in practice made little difference.

In 1908 and 1909 Koechlin joined forces with de Pischoff, and built aeroplanes for other people, and their own much-modified de Pischoff et Koechlin.

The Kluytmans. (Author's collection)

The Koechlin No 1. The pilot lay in the hammock aft, encased in the hoop; his throttle control is suspended beside him. (Courtesy of the Musée de l'Air et de l'Espace/Le Bourget-France)

The de Pischoff et Koechlin tandem monoplane of 1908. (Author's collection)

The tandem revised, or a new machine: the de Pischoff et Koechlin. (Courtesy of the Musée de l'Air et de l'Espace/Le Bourget-France)

De Pischoff et Koechlin monoplane: In 1908 the team designed and built a tandem monoplane with the second wing close behind the first, and a little shorter. A horizontal tail surface brought up the rear, along with fins above and below, and rectangular rudders for each one. The thin streamlined rectangular body was supported in front by a Blériot-style undercarriage, and behind by a large tailwheel. A separated pair of forward elevator surfaces protruded from each side of the nose, and another pair of small trapezoidal surfaces aft, forward of the tail. It is reported to have hopped once, for 500 meters, on 29 October 1908, at Villacoublay.

(Spans: 6.3 m, 5.3 m, 3 m; wing area: 25 sqm; 20 hp Dutheil et Chalmers)

Either this same machine or a development appeared the same year. One of them seemed to have the same basic structure less the middle wing and the extra forward and aft surfaces: it made a very pretty conventional-looking monoplane. Another had a water-cooled flat twin engine set amidships, driving 2 tractor propellers on outriggers aft of the wing.

Then Koechlin went off on his own and designed the monoplane which he developed steadily until 1911.

The basic design had a rectangular wooden fuselage covered with ash-and-mahogany ply, avoiding the need for wire bracing and turnbuckles The trapezoidal wings were formed on 2 steel tube spars, with wooden ribs, and aluminum sheeting; they were said to be very rigid. The tailplane was triangular, with a warping trailing edge; the vertical surfaces consisted of a square rudder and triangular fin, with another fin below which developed into a second rudder. Both mainwheels and the tailwheel castered; 2 skids were later added in front. A steering wheel and tilting column controlled the rudder and elevator, and the ailerons were linked to the pilot's back, though the first version had neither wing-warping nor ailerons but probably un-

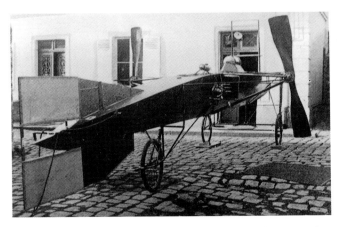

The twin-outrigger version of the de Pischoff et Koechlin under construction. Note wide propeller blades. (Courtesy of the Musée de l'Air et de l'Espace/Le Bourget-France)

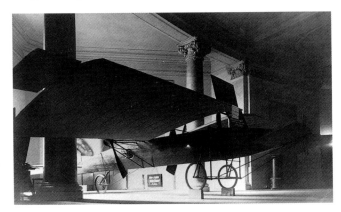

The completed twin-outrigger de Pischoff at the 1908 Paris Salon. Note the new wingtip aileron surfaces. (Courtesy of the Musée de l'Air et de l'Espace/Le Bourget-France)

der-surface spoilers; small ailerons appeared first on the trailing edges and then at the wingtips to pivot on the front spar.

The basic Koechlin monoplane. This one had small trailing ailerons. (Peter M Bowers collection)

The first Koechlin monoplane flew first at the end of 1909; at the subsequent Salon its varnished ply skin drew favorable attention. At least 2 monoplanes were flying by the end of 1909, one built for Koechlin, the other for de Nabat. Others may have been built in 1910; on one of the first a Mrs Niel became the first woman to receive her brevet on a monoplane. In 1910 Koechlin offered a monoplane to the Army; in 1911 the Army ordered one, fitted with a 70 hp Gnôme: it may have been the same one. 3 variants were offered in 1910; they may not have been built.

Type A: a single-seater.

(Span: 8.5 m; chord: 2.5 m; wing area: c 17 sqm: empty weight: 260 kg; speed: c 70 kmh; 20-28 hp Grégoire-Gyp or Anzani)

Type B: similar but "stronger": more powerful, with a 40 hp Grégoire-Gyp.

Type C: a 2-seater.

(Span: 11 m; wing area: 25.2 sqm; 50 or 70 hp Gnôme or similar engine)

In 1911 Pivot joined Koechlin; the Pivot-Koechlin, or Pivot, resembled the Deperdussins and was built by Audineau; it was similar to the previous monoplanes but more streamlined, with a radial engine and smaller trapezoidal rudders. The thin fuselage was faired out around the engine and pilot with round metal sheets ending in a cylindrical cowl for the engine, a Gnôme or Rossel-Peugeot. The undercarriage was simpler than that used on the Deperdussins, with castering wheels and diagonal skids attached under the nose. The earlier pylons had disappeared, replaced with 4 long struts to brace the wings, attached to the wings and the undercarriage. The wingtip ailerons were actuated by movement of the pilot's body.

A 3-seater version was mentioned, with 2 seats side-by-side behind the pilot: this was probably the one referred to as the Type Militaire. The Pivot was often described as the fastest machine of its time: 1911.

(Span: 10 m; length: 7.8 m; wing area: c 17 sqm; speed: c 110 kmh)

From 1911 to 1913 Koechlin built racing cars with underslung chassis, but they failed to achieve their expected performance.

De Korvin

Only a few rare notices and even rarer photographs remain of the aeronautical efforts of the Chevalier de Korvin. In 1907, with the Russian military attaché in France, Rebikoff, he began work on an 8-wing flying machine with a 60 hp Antoinette V8; the wings were said to be "workable." In 1911 appeared a photograph of a second machine, resembling a heavy Demoiselle. 2 ailerons or small wings were hinged to a lower spar; wingtip skids held the machine level on the

A Koechlin of 1910, this one with tip ailerons. (Courtesy of the Musée de l'Air et de l'Espace/Le Bourget-France)

The Pivot-Koechlin, still with wingtip ailerons. (Courtesy of the Musée de l'Air et de l'Espace/Le Bourget-France)

ground. The motor was set ahead of a cut-out in the leading edge of the wing, driving 2 tractor propellers; 2 streamlined tanks were fixed to the top of the wing. The tail was cruciform, the surfaces seeming to move independently.

Rebikoff continued to appear in the aviation journals flying a Morane-Saulnier.

L

Labaudie et Puthet

Labaudie and Puthet had a workshop where they primarily built flying machines designed by inventors who themselves lacked the tools, skills, or manpower to realize their ambitions. In addition to these outside projects, Labaudie and Puthet built first a series of biplane gliders, and later a powered monoplane. The first of these was tested in 1908 by various people, including M Fafiotte, editor of *L'Aéro*; it was towed behind Jean Dufour's Rochet-Schneider automobile. The gliders soon acquired "front wheels and a rear skid," and an elevator so as "to take off while rolling."

At the end of 1909 the 2 builders were preparing their first powered design for its first trials, a monoplane called La Comète, probably designed by Piau; it was tested at St Cloud beginning 6 November. They also built the Boutaric biplane and Jean Dufour's first monoplane. All their constructions featured wing ribs of frêno-liège (ash and oak). One of the monoplanes was a Darracq-powered Demoiselle copy. Their firm was disbanded in July 1910.

Lacaille et Lemaire

In 1910 Lacaille and Lemaire built "a monoplane glider which could be disassembled."

Lachassagne

In 1913 an associate of Léon Levavasseur, Adolf Lachassagne, built a strange tandem aeroplane described as "automatically stable." The front pair of wings carried 2 counter-rotating propellers and featured variable incidence. The propellers were described as either tractor or lifting, depending on the angle of the front wings; the rear wings pivoted on each side of the fuselage to control roll. Lachassagne borrowed various engines which he described bitterly, much later, as not working.

Ladougne

At the end of 1911 André Ladougne left the firm of Ambroise Goupy, where he had been a pilot, to become a builder himself. He designed 2 small monoplanes inspired by the fastest Nieuports, both named La Colombe (dove). The first was a single-seater which flew for the first time at Juvisy on 1 January 1912, and was reported to be "the quickest aircraft ever seen there." The rectangular fuselage was narrow (.68 m at the widest), but very deep (1.5 m at the cockpit); the section decreased quickly aft of the cockpit. The top longerons were straight, the lower ones bellied down. As on the Nieuports, the wings were trapezoidal with the same double-curved section. On the triangular tailplane were 2 elevators with distinctive inwardly-curving ends; the large rudder had a similar shape. The rear legs of the 4-leg undercarriage curved out in front to become skids. The machine was flown first with a 28 hp 3-cylinder Anzani and achieved 96 kmh; refitted with a 50 hp Gnôme it reached 120 kmh.

(Span: 8.6 m; length: 7.1 m; wing area: 16 sqm; empty weight (Anzani): 230 kg; (Gnôme): 260 kg)

The second Colombe was built for the 1912 Circuit d'Anjou, a more powerful and slightly larger tandem 2-seater.

(Span: 9.7 m; length: 7.6 m; wing area: 17 sqm; 75 hp 6-cylinder Anzani)

The 2 aircraft had similar shapes and were similarly constructed: the wings were built on shaped spars fitted to the fuselage through 8 cm tubes; the first 3 ribs were of ash, the others poplar. The whole airframe was covered with varnished fabric. Control was through a single lever or an oscillating bridge; rudder pedals were retained for those who were accustomed to using them.

Bobba and Divetain, also former Goupy pilots, flew the 2 Colombes; Divetain crashed in the 2-seater in the Anjou contest. After the accident, Ladougne gave up his firm and joined Bobba in Italy, where together they formed a new company to build monoplanes copied from the Moranes and Morane-Saulniers.

Ladougne's pretty and fast monoplane La Colombe. (Peter M Bowers collection)

Lagasse

A machine of this name was reported at Toulouse.

De Lailhacar

This high-wing monoplane is said to have been designed by the Spaniard Jacques de Lailhacar, but was built in France by Berthaud. The deep rectangular uncovered fuselage rested on the axle of the 2-wheel undercarriage; long skids stood out in front, and 2 shorter skids at the rear. The 50 hp 4-cylinder inline water-cooled Prini-Berthaud was set on the top of the nose, with the wing aft of the radiator at a high angle of attack and slight anhedral. The large rectangular elevator was hinged above the stern, behind a large rudder pivoted the flat deck. A control wheel was mounted on an inclined column; photos dated 5 March 1910 show the column tilted back but the elevator down. The monoplane was said to have flown first on 6 March 1910.

(Span: 10 m; length: 11 m; weight: 300 kg; 50 hp Prini-Berthaud)

Lalouette et Maillaud

The helicopter built by Lalouette and Maillaud may not have been expected to fly, but only to test a rotating lifting surface. The pilot and the 50 hp water-cooled inline engine sat on a wooden grid; the engine drove a 2-blade paddle propeller of some 4 meters in diameter, somehow geared. An interesting feature of the design was that the pitch of the rotor could be controlled: a large wheel was centered on the rotor shaft, probably mounted on a screw thread. In turning moved up and down the shaft, raising and lowering a pair of vertical rods attached to the paddle leading edges, thus altering the angle of attack of the blades. No other surfaces were fitted; the motor seems to have been controlled by a foot pedal. The device is said to have risen 2' on 26 December 1912.

The de Lailhacar monoplane of 1910. (Courtesy of the Musée de l'Air et de l'Espace/Le Bourget-France)

Laminne

This was a big 4-wheeled biplane at Verlaine in 1909.

(Length: 13 m; wing area: 60 sqm; 60 hp Vivinus)

Lamotte

Victor Thomas Lamotte had been studying aviation in Nantes since the beginning of the century; in 1909 he also designed a glider described as a "trimonoplaneur," with 2 monoplane surfaces in tandem and a third mounted above.

Lamoureaux

Lamouroux was a mechanic at Narbonne on the Mediterranean coast, near the Spanish border. He is reported in 1909 to have built – perhaps not designed – and tested a monoplane on the parade ground of the 80th regiment of the line. It had ailerons on the trailing edges of the wings and a swept-back tailplane with 2 elevators; both elevators and rudder were controlled through a steering wheel, and the ailerons by moving the column on which the wheel was mounted.

(Span: 8 m; length: 7.5 m; 35 hp Anzani)

Landeroin et Robert

Introduced at the 1914 Concours de Sécurité, this bizarre machine was meant to be automatically stable. It was built at Pierre Levasseur's factory around what looked like a Morane-Saulnier fuselage, at the rear end of which was set a trapezoidal rudder and a semicircular elevator on each side. These were the only familiar features. The rest was a tandem monoplane with one pair of straight rectangular wings mounted far back at the top of the fuselage; the front pair was swept back from a straight center-section which was mounted precariously out in front of the engine and propeller, the whole thing braced with curved struts over and around the propeller, down to the undercarriage; one ran all the way back over the top to the tailpost. Ailerons were set into the inner sections of the trailing edges of the front wings. A 3-skid addition was made to the undercarriage.

(Span: 10.5 m; length: 8 m; wing area: 23 sqm; empty weight: 500 kg; 70 hp Le Rhône)

Apart from its wings and overhead bracing, the Landeroin et Robert 1914 entry for the Concours de Sécurité seems a very straightforward design. (Courtesy of the Musée de l'Air et de l'Espace/Le Bourget-France)

Landron et Cornet

This seems to have been some sort of autoplane. Perhaps Landron was the same designer as Landeroin?

Lane

There were at least 2 Lane monoplanes, the first resembling the Blériot XI with a 30 hp NEC motor; the second resembling the Blériot XII.

De Langhe

The name of Charles de Langhe appears in several places, sometimes in connection with a Tambarly (who may have drawn the plans), sometimes with a Corville – the latter a monoplane built by L Patte. It had the inverted U undercarriage shared by several contemporary builders, like Vendôme; a long triangular covered fuselage, Blériot-style wings (perhaps purchased from the Blériot firm), and a trapezoidal pylon for the wing-bracing.

(De Langhe-Corville – span: 8.5 m; length: c 10 m; wing area: 16 sqm; speed: 70 kmh; 3-cylinder Anzani)

Lanzi et Billard

The dart-shaped La Flêche (arrow) was built by Espinosa at his Avionnerie (SACAA). It was tested unsuccessfully in the summer of 1910, and was known only as one of many oddities of the period. It is likely, however, that the machine was built earlier in 1910 or even in

Charles de Langhe's slender monoplane. (Peter M Bowers collection)

1909, and modified at Espinosa's. It resembled exactly a folded paper dart mounted on a 4-wheeled undercarriage; 2 small surfaces were set behind the tractor propeller. Semicircular ailerons were fitted on the trailing edges of the wings, a trapezoidal tailplane set on the extended upper fuselage longerons, with small elevators at the end.

It appeared later with a motor in a covered box-mounting in the nose, with a small streamlined tank above it. The front undercarriage legs are heavier and braced to the nose; the rear ones sport spring shock-absorbers. In the photo taken at Espinosa's and described in the 1910 *Jane's* as "completed in August 1910," no engine is visible, no tank appears, the front and rear undercarriage legs are connected, and the shock absorbers are in front.

(Span: 6 m; length: 8 m; empty weight: 290 kg)

Lartigue

Maurice Lartigue's biplane glider was mentioned briefly in the pre-War aeronautical reviews: it was a simple design even for 1912, with rectangular wings and a biplane forward elevator cell. His younger brother Jacques-Henri became a famous photographer and painter, and took many photographs of the happy life of the somewhat eccentric Lartigue family, showing rubber-powered models and a good many elementary gliders built under Maurice's direction and tested on the sloping hillsides of their estate at Rouzas, in the Auvergne. Little success but much enjoyment! The designs were monoplanes or biplanes, made with rough wooden frames and covered with bedsheets: they seem all to have been christened with Maurice's nickname, Zyx.

Lassagne

Lassagne's biplane was reportedly being built for Cornet, an automobile racer, and was to be tested at Juvisy in June 1910; no information is available as to the results. It was a pusher biplane with biplane forward elevator, hanging ailerons, and an undercarriage whose wheels could be raised to allow landing on the skids alone. Control was through a vertically-set steering wheel.

(Span: 8.3 m; length: 9 m; wing area: 24 sqm; empty weight: c 200 kg; 35 hp radial 4-cylinder Miller driving a 2 meter diameter Intégrale propeller)

Lasternas

At Douai in 1909 a science teacher named Lasternas designed a biplane, seemingly similar to the Voisin. The wings, slightly swept back, had flexible trailing edges and showed side-curtains; the airfoil section was said to be "that of a bird." A biplane forward elevator regulated pitch, and a warping tailplane controlled roll. A 40-50 hp motor drove 2 pusher propellers through chains.

(Span: 13.75 m; chord: 2.3 m; span front elevator cell: 4.5 m; 40-50 hp motor)

The next Lasternas biplane we hear of was built in 1911, with his associate, Lepers. The wings were trapezoidal, the upper longer, braced together as "an American girder" (Warren truss?). A covered

One of the first versions of the Lanzi et Billard La Flêche. (Courtesy of the Musée de l'Air et de l'Espace/Le Bourget-France)

Laughing mechanics towing La Flêche at Juvisy. Note castering rear wheels, partly turned. (Author's collection)

The Lartigue glider Zyx rises, with the Lartigue family and friends in attendance, September, 1910. (Author's collection)

cockpit was set on the lower wing. The front monoplane elevator was braced with an assemblage of spars and was connected with the rear elevator, itself set at the ends of the tail outriggers. The top wing had ailerons, and the wing itself was reported to have had flexible trailing edges in addition. The frame was of both wood and metal.

(Span: 11 m; length: 12.5 m; main wing chord: 2.37 m; wing area: 34 sqm; empty weight: 320 kg; 50 hp Gnôme driving a 2.35 m diameter Intégrale propeller)

Lataste

If more than one poor and heavily retouched photograph had survived, this machine might be classed with the Domingo, the d'Equévilly-Justin, and the Givaudan as one of the most famous curiosities of the pre-War period. The so-called Aéroplane Gyroscopique, built of metal and covered with fabric, appeared in 1909-1910: it featured a long uncovered tapered frame with a propeller at each end; each propeller had 2 semicircular blades like sections of archimedean screws, and turned the same way. Above the frame was a flat rotating circular surface, probably mounted on a swivel joint. This surface and the propellers were driven through a long horizontal propeller shaft and planetary gears; the shaft ran through a cylindrical fuel tank inside the fuselage. The machine was mounted on 4 wheels with the pilot sitting among them, holding tightly to a steering wheel, which perhaps controlled the rotating surface high above him.

(Length: c 7.5 m; diameter of the disc: c 6 m)

Latopp

The French magazine *L'Aéro* claimed in an early issue that Latopp had tested "a flying apparatus" at St Martin de Crau, near Istres, on 22 December 1908. His machine is said to have flown 32 seconds, powered by an engine fueled on glycerin. It may have been a model and not a full-scale aeroplane.

Lautard

The young Lautard is reported to have built his eighth glider in the shape of a triangle when he was only 16. These gliders may not have been manned.

Lavesvre et Veillon

The November 1912 issue of *La Technique Aéronautique* described this monoplane as a larger copy of the Demoiselle, with a braced Taube-shaped high wing with swept-back, almost transparent, warpable wingtip trailing edges. The tailplane was triangular, as was the fuselage section. Mounted on 3 wheels, the top longeron of the fuselage was horizontal, and the 3 tail outriggers were mounted on the hub of the pusher propeller, which itself was driven by an 8-cylinder bi-rotating Burlat of 60 hp: the rotating cylinders turned at 900 hp, half that of the propeller shaft which rotated in the same direction. The motor was set in a heavy bearing behind the pilot and his passenger who sat side by side in the open under the wing.

Lavezzari

One of the earliest pioneers in northern France, Lavezzari was the chairman of the Aero Club at Berck, a Channel coast resort town. He tested his gliders on the dunes there at the turn of the century: one was a tailless hang-glider built in 1903 with triangular bat-shaped wings; another, also a tailless hang-glider with triangular wings, was built in 1904, probably based on a Lilienthal design.

(Span (No 2): 6 m; length: c 3.6 m; wing area: 37 sqm; gross weight: 37 kg)

Lazard et Lemoine

A photograph shows the little parasol monoplane flying near Pacy sur Eure, Normandy, in an airshow in September 1913. It was a 2-seater

Right: The Lavezzari hang-glider, probably the 1904 version. (Courtesy of the Musée de l'Air et de l'Espace/Le Bourget-France)

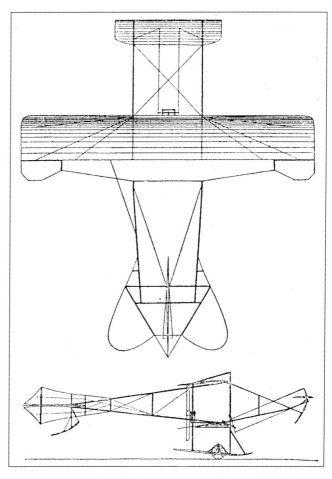

A contemporary drawing of the Lasternas et Lepers biplane of 1911. (Author's collection)

The Lataste Aéroplane Gyroscopique was actually built. (Author's collection)

with a wide covered box-like fuselage with a Blériot-type rear skid and a tail similar to that on the Nieuport monoplanes. The 4 vertical struts of the undercarriage rose above the cowl to act as cabane struts, and a 50 hp 3-cylinder Anzani was mounted up between the high rectangular wing and the fuselage.

Lebeau

A machine of unknown design was built under this name at Rosières in 1912: Rosières is a very common village name.

Leblic

E Leblic flew his small metal tractor biplane over Issy in 1912. The rectangular wings with scalloped trailing edges warped; the trapezoidal rudder hung below the rectangular horizontal tail surfaces, which were supported at the ends of a pair of V-shaped outriggers. The undercarriage used 2 wide-set wheels with skids, and a third skid at the rear.

(Span: 8.6 m; length: 6.5 m; empty weight: 300 kg; 50 hp motor)

Leclerc (Le Clère or Leclère?)

In 1912 it was reported that a Docteur Leclère or Leclerc had "a huge bird of metal and canvas," probably built by a M Gonthier at Mareuil, near Riberac, near Dordogne, east of Bordeaux. It was a large monoplane with a streamlined clear-doped cylindrical fuselage, an air-cooled engine, and high wing pylons shaped like 2 large letter A's; the cockpit was well forward underneath them. The rectangular tailplane rested on the top of the fuselage, with a rounded rudder set between 2 elevators. The machine ran on castering front wheels with a third immediately aft of them and a long tailskid behind that. It is shown also in a slightly different form, with larger nose, shorter pylons, and a second cut-out, this time for a water-cooled motor.

Lecoeur

In 1912 Gaston Lecoeur was said to have built a biplane of his own design for the British chapter of the Laviator Club, and also a 2-seater monoplane, probably for the Laviator Club of the United Kingdom. Nothing further is known about either, except that the Laviator flying school advertised its 50 and 70 hp Blériots, and so it is possible the monoplane was a Blériot assembled by Lecoeur.

The first version of the Leclerc monoplane of 1912. (Courtesy of the Musée de l'Air et de l'Espace/Le Bourget-France)

George Lazard, smiling, on board his 1913 monoplane. It seems barely big enough for 2 seats. (Author's collection)

Above and below: two slightly different versions of the 1912 Leblic. (Courtesy of the Musée de l'Air et de l'Espace/Le Bourget-France)

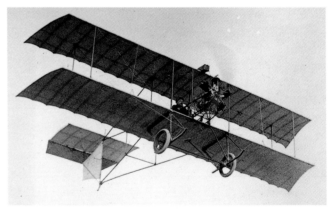

Lecomte

Early French aviation is studded with Lecomtes, and it is not always easy to keep them distinct. In 1911 a Lecomte was registered for the Concourse Militaire, but the firm exhibited only the model of a military aeroplane at the Paris Salon: it was described as having a monocoque fuselage, but in fact the slender frame was sheathed in plywood. It is not certain whether the full-scale aeroplane was ever built. But in a photograph taken at the Ateliers Aéronautiques de l'Est appears the fuselage of just such a wood-covered monoplane with nicely tapered rounded fuselage and high V-legged undercarriage with long skids forward.

One Lecomte was Henri, the son of the colonel who commanded the 41st Territorial Regiment at Nancy, in the east of France. In 1911 the Lecomtes bought the building and tooling of the disbanded Avia company to establish the firm known as Ateliers Aéronautiques de l'Est (Eastern Aeronautical Workshops, or AAE).

In 1912 Henri Lecomte moved to Varengeville, near Luneville near Nancy, where he also founded a flying school; by the end of the year he is reported to have built at least 3 monoplanes, one of which was a side-by-side 2-seater, and the other 2 were single-seaters; one of these, powered with a 3-cylinder Viale, resembled a Blériot, with a curved cane tailskid so large as to keep the fuselage nearly horizontal on the ground. The main 2-wheel undercarriage was low, with a third wheel forward. The long triangular tailplane surface reached forward along the uncovered sides almost to the cockpit; 2 trapezoidal elevators were accompanied by a small trapezoidal rudder. What was possibly the third machine had a long covered diamond-section fuselage with a small angular rudder and large trapezoidal tail surfaces set slightly ahead; the wings were long and tapered, with scalloped edges and tips.

On 8 January 1913 Henri Lecomte crashed on take-off; afterwards, nothing more was heard of the aeroplane, the man, or the company.

Other Lecomtes were also in the news: one crashed Blinderman's monoplane, the Kassa Ery, at Nice; another fought during WWI in the Aviation Militaire and later went to the United States.

(Span: 12.6 m; length: 8.6 m; wing area: 22 sqm; chord: 1.6 m; 25-30 hp 3-cylinder Viale)

Lecoq-Monteiro-Aillaud

A series of monoplanes under these names (sometimes reported as Monsèvro-Allaud) were introduced from 1910 to 1913; the first one was tested by Collardeau, and had wings "which recalled Ader's Avion." A photograph in a 1910 issue of *La Revue de l'Aviation* showed Collardeau in a clear-doped LMA monoplane, seated in a closed box to which the bat-shaped wings were attached directly; they curved downward and may have been swept forward. The tailplane was shaped like a bird's, and there may have been no rudder. A 3-cylinder engine, probably an Anzani, was fitted at the forward tip of a pin-pointed fairing.

During the 1911 Salon the firm's catalog showed 2 much more advanced machines, single – and 2-seaters at 50 hp; and 3 and 4 places at 100 hp. The photographs show a handsome long-winged monoplane with dihedral and raked wingtips. The engine was fully cowled, with 4 exhaust pipes showing under the cowl. 2 small wheels were set at the ends of a long axle, with a central single skid.

In May 1912 Lecoq and Monteiro were flying another monoplane powered by a 3-cylinder Viale. It had marked dihedral and drooping triangular wingtips; the airfoils were developed from the first bat-like machine. It sat long-legged on wide-set wheels and skids.

In 1913 they were testing a similar monoplane numbered 4bis. Lecoq also worked with Théodorescu.

Leduc

A machine of this name was mentioned in 1908.

One of Henri Lecomte's single-seat monoplanes. (Courtesy of the Musée de l'Air et de l'Espace/Le Bourget-France)

Perhaps the third Lecomte: little in common with the design in the preceding photograph. (Courtesy of the Musée de l'Air et de l'Espace/Le Bourget-France)

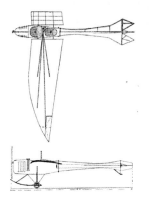
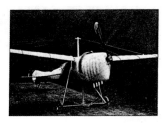

Monoplan L M A. 1 à 2 places, 50 HP. **12,000**
Monoplan L M A. 3 à 4   »   100 HP. **18,000**
Moteur en plus au choix du client
Train d'atterrissage breveté S. G. D. G.
pouvant s'adapter sur tous les
Appareils **2,000**

N. B. Les Appareils L M A sont tous munis de la poutre centrale
et du train d'atterrissage L M A breveté S. G. D. G.

Illustrations from the 1911 LMA catalog showing their new offerings. (Author's collection)

This appears to be a revised version of the first LMA aeroplane, with true tail surfaces. Note the hinged triangular wingtips. (Courtesy of the Musée de l'Air et de l'Espace/Le Bourget-France)

A slightly later model of the LMA. Note side radiators for the water-cooled engine. (Courtesy of the Musée de l'Air et de l'Espace/Le Bourget-France)

Lefebure

An ornithopter of this name was completed in 1911, with a span of 9 m and height of 4 m.

Lefebvre

At the end of 1909 *L'Aéro* published a brief notice in which a Lefebvre, "34 years old, 60 kg, at the end of his resources because of aviation experiments," was looking for a pilot's job. This was doubtless Louis Lefebvre, who had by then left Fernandez for whom he had worked as a mechanic. Subsequently he became known for founding at Rouen a company to build his own design, La Mouette (gull); but his career was actually more important than this suggests.

In March 1910 Lefebvre was working on a large monoplane of 17-meter span, reportedly to have featured bat-shaped wings, which he may have begun much earlier. Also in 1910 he and his brother Philippe, an accountant, organized a company in Rouen to build La Mouette; the firm was shortly afterwards disbanded and re-formed in 1911 with a new title, La Société Nouvelle pour la Construction de l'Aéroplane La Mouette. The aeroplane was described as a "double monoplane" with telescoping wing panels: the span could vary from 6 to 10 m. The machine was shown at the Brussels exhibition in 1910.

(Span: 6 to 10 m; length: 8.5 m; gross weight: 400 kg; 35-40 hp motor)

But in April 1911, La Mouette was described in *L'Aéro* as a stagger-wing biplane. It had a covered rectangular-section box fuselage, and triangular vertical fins and tailplanes. The lower pair of trapezoidal wings were fixed to the top of the fuselage, and the top pair, of the same size and shape, were higher and forward, with more dihedral. Between the 2 main spars of the top wings ailerons could slide in and out at the tips, operating independently and actuated by cables, sheaves, and cogwheels, controlled by 2 levers to the right of the pilot.

(Span: 8 to 12 m; wing area: 28 to 33 sqm; length: 9.6 m; gross weight: 520 kg; 50 hp Clerget)

The LMA 4bis. (Courtesy of the Musée de l'Air et de l'Espace/Le Bourget-France)

The big Lefebvre machine for the 1911 Concours Militaire. (Courtesy of the Musée de l'Air et de l'Espace/Le Bourget-France)

The same year, 1911, at Chartres, Sadi-Lecointe was testing another Lefebvre, this one a monoplane, a big 3-seater, for the Concours Militaire. The rectangular fuselage was completely covered, and the tail surfaces were large. It is likely there was no elevator, the control being accomplished by varying the wing incidence: the wings were of very high aspect ratio, rectangular in shape, built around 4 spars. The ailerons were trapezoidal surfaces hinged along the wingtips.

(Span: 17 m; length: 12 m; wing area: 55 sqm; 50 hp V8 ENV)

There was also a La Mouette V mentioned in 1912, powered by an 80 hp Anzani.

Leflot

This was the first aeroplane built by the firm of Lioré.

Leforestier

The photograph of G Leforestier's No 1 shows a large frail triangular box-kite arrangement set diagonally on edge above a 4-wheeled cart with a small motor and tractor propeller inside it. From the sides of the kite protruded each side a large triangular wing, seemingly formed of fabric stretched across the frame outline. A later machine by this designer was much more polished, a Blériot XI copy, with a chopped-off rectangular rudder, a pair of long thin skids forward, and a single pylon coupled with a single inverted V.

Léger

In 1905 Maurice Léger had Ouvière from Marseille build a huge ill-fated helicopter at Monaco; Léger means light and the machine was sometimes erroneously ascribed to a builder named Light, with contemporary English captions showing this name. A half-scale model was built first, with a 140-volt 40-ampere electric motor on the ground, and a connecting cable. At a power setting of 5.6 kw, it lifted first 85 kg as a test-load, and then later it lifted Dr Richard, manager of the oceanographic center at Monaco. The spoon-bladed aluminum propellers were 6.5 m in diameter, and the empty weight of the model was 110 kg.

The full-scale machine appeared shortly after, an enormous construction for the period. A 4-legged pyramid stood on 2 huge skis, the 2 coupled Antoinette engines mounted on the top, driving 2 contra-rotating propellers made of fabric-covered frames. The pilot and his passenger sat on the base with twin steering wheels. A biplane tail unit was fixed within the diameter of the rotors. This monument to human great expectations was destroyed on its first test.

(Length: c 12.5 m, same as rotor diameter; height: 10 m; chord of rotors at tips: 3.5 m)

Legrand

One of the most interesting and productive of the early French aeronautical engineers was Jean Legrand, but today his work is largely forgotten: it exists now in the form of poor postcards of 2 of his achievements, a brief note left by his daughter at the Musée de l'Air, and the texts of various lectures published in *La Revue Technique Aéronautique*. There is enough left to show clearly his scientific reasoning and brilliance – even though he never designed or built an aeroplane. He modified either one or 2 Voisins to clarify why an aeroplane flies.

In May 1909 he bought de Caters' Voisin, and, associated with Louis Gaudard who brought with him a 50 hp Gnôme, made endless modifications designed by Legrand and built by Voisin. It is likely Legrand flew a second Voisin built especially for him: he fitted a dynamometer to the propeller; he also tried a magnetic tachometer, a Bourdon speed indicator, and an incidence meter designed by Arnoux for automobiles. The experimenters broke a lot of wood in the course of their trials. Noticing that oil sprays appeared only on the upper rear surfaces of the wings, he realized that lift was produced by a reduc-

Leforestier No 1. Note the big pulley on the drive-shaft. (Courtesy of the Musée de l'Air et de l'Espace/Le Bourget-France)

A later – and better informed – design by Leforestier. (Author's collection)

The half-scale model of the big Léger helicopter. (Courtesy of the Musée de l'Air et de l'Espace/Le Bourget-France)

Right: One of the huge blades for the Léger helicopter under construction. For scale, note the size of the man in the background. (Courtesy of the Musée de l'Air et de l'Espace/Le Bourget-France)

tion in pressure above the wings and not by increased pressure below. He recommended ailerons to replace the wing-warping which tended to weaken the structures, and had his own aircraft modified with 4 ailerons on the top wings.

He was granted 3000F on behalf of Major Renard by the Société d'Encouragement pour l'Industrie Nationale, a group founded by Nadar, alias Félix Tournachon, and used it to have a new set of wings built by Voisin (some say a whole new aeroplane) with a span of 9 m instead of 10.5, a chord of 1.75 m instead of 2: the modified biplane could fly at 62 kmh. He removed the lower tailplane and increased the span of the upper. To improve lateral stability, he shortened the wing curtains, though without apparent effect. He further modified the Voisin as a triplane and as a quintuplane, and then modified it further to carry a crew of 2 with a forward-firing machine gun, and even altered it to carry 2 push-pull Gnômes. The triplane spanned 7 m with unchanged wing area, and was flown successfully by Camille Guillaume de Mauriac in 1910-13, and by Verrier in April 1911. Legrand is reported to have also modified Wrights, Blériots, and Voisins by reducing the angle of attack, but found they glided too fast or too steeply. He may have helped with the design of the Gaudard monoplane; eventually he abandoned his aeronautical research for want of money.

Legras

A biplane of this name was entered for the Concours de Douai in 1909.

Legraton

A machine of this name was mentioned in 1908.

Lejeune

A biplane said to be designed for Louis Lejeune was built by de Pischoff and Koechlin in 1909, almost identical to the Fouquet, built by the same firm. Both were equal-span biplanes, with a centrally-mounted engine driving 2 pusher propellers on Wright-style outriggers through chains and enormous sprocket wheels. Both had tandem-wheel undercarriages, biplane tail cells with a single rudder in the middle, ailerons set out ahead of the outer pair of interplane struts. The Fouquet

Above and below: Variations on a theme: the Legrand Voisin. (Courtesy of the Musée de l'Air et de l'Espace/Le Bourget-France)

A 1911 Legrand modification to his Voisin: to triplane configuration. (Author's collection)

was supported at the wingtips by curved skids, where the Lejeune had wheels; the Fouquet had a forward biplane elevator with side curtains at the ends, and the Lejeune had 2 pairs of cells side by aide with no vertical surfaces. The Lejeune also featured aileron cells. The Fouquet used a 50 hp Antoinette, and the Lejeune used a 3-cylinder 12 hp Buchet.

(Span: 6.5 m; length: 5.04 m; wing area: c 20 sqm; gross weight: 175 kg; 12 hp Buchet)

The Lejeune of 1909. Note the big pulleys on the 2 propeller shafts. (Author's collection)

Lelièvre

Lieutenant Lelièvre's stubby monoplane was built by Vendôme and resembled a radial-engined Aeronca C-2. The wing was mounted on the top of the short covered fuselage, with the engine set almost at ground level driving through a chain the tractor propeller mounted slightly forward of the leading edge. The pilot sat inside the fuselage under the wing, entering through one of 2 small side doors. A large triangular tailplane, large elevator and rudder surfaces brought up the rear. 2 large spoked wheels were fitted, one on each side of the cabin, and the machine rested on a long tailskid immediately behind the pilot. The monoplane flew frequently at Issy late in 1912 or early in 1913; it crashed in August.

Lemaire

In 1907 Jules Lemaire, a wine-dealer in Bonneval, built an ornithopter. Each elliptical surface was supported by a single kingpost and many guy-wires. A central pylon braced the whole thing, and a thin outrigger carried a tall triangular rudder surface; there was no place for any engine. Lemaire was the first in his village to own an automobile, and later he bought his own Blériot XI, which he wrecked while trying to fly solo.

Lemaitre

This biplane appeared at Juvisy in 1910. It had a long upper wing with S-shaped dihedral at the tips ending in wingtip ailerons; and a shorter lower wing with little gap. Elevator surfaces were set out ahead of the tractor propeller; curved arches supported the undercarriage.

Lemaitre, Maucourt, et Legrand

Associated with Maucourt, Henri Lemaitre and Gaston Legrand built a monoplane they called Hirondelle (swallow); some sources report 3 separate Hirondelles, and there do appear variations from picture to picture. But others report a Lemaitre monoplane uncompleted at Juvisy in May 1910, a Lemaitre et Legrand flying at La Vidamée (Chantilly) early in 1911, another finished in July, and still another flying at La Vidamée at the end of the year.

Whether one or 3, the basic design had a flat-decked fuselage of triangular section. The wings warped, and were set on the deck ahead of the cockpit; the trailing edges were longer than the leading edges. The machine stood on a 4-legged undercarriage with 2 wheels and skids, and a pyramidal skid in front of the rectangular tailplane and its triangular elevators. A semicircular rudder was fitted to a triangular fin. A 40 hp 4-cylinder inline Labor-Aviation motor drove a 2-bladed Normale propeller; the radiators were attached to the forward sides of the fuselage, which was covered only on the bottom from the pilot seat aft. Construction was of both wood and metal.

(Span: 9 m; length; 7 m; wing area: 16 sqm; empty weight: 240 kg)

Lepers

This machine was on the list for the 1911 Concours Militaire.

The Vendôme-built Lelièvre. Note the vertical bracket to support the drive chain from the rotary. (Courtesy of the Musée de l'Air et de l'Espace/Le Bourget-France)

A very poor photo of the Lemaire ornithopter. (Author's collection)

The Lemaitre wings must have required some difficult woodworking. (Author's collection)

One of the Lemaitre-Maucourt et Legrand Hirondelles of 1912. (Courtesy of the Musée de l'Air et de l'Espace/Le Bourget-France)

Lepin

A biplane of this name was entered for the Concours de Douai in 1909.

Leray

Georges and René Hugues designed and built at least 2 aeroplanes at Lamalou les Pains, near Montpellier on the Mediterranean coast: the first, in 1908, was a little 10 hp triplane with close-set wings attached to a long boom on top of which was set the pilot's chair. The tail consisted of a biplane cell with 2 small back-slanting rudder surfaces. The second, advertised in October of the same year, was a monoplane, to be tested on the Plaine de Corbillon.

(Monoplane: span: 6 m; length: 7.45 m; wing area: 32 sqm; 10 hp Hugues)

Leroy et Marzollier

Either at a meet titled Nantes Aviation, or under the firm name of Nantes Aviation, these 2 men from Nantes showed their glider on 14-21 August 1910 – perhaps they flew it. It might have been meant to have developed into a powered aeroplane, with its long uncovered trapezoidal-sectioned fuselage, trapezoidal wings with the spars on the upper surface, ailerons attached to the trailing edges, classic tail surfaces, and a forward elevator.

Lescars

Chauvière built this otherwise unknown design in 1909.

Lesna

This machine, design unknown, was operated at Issy in 1911, powered by a Rossel-Peugeot. Lesna was also a Blériot pilot.

Lesquins

Lesquins was probably one of the numerous modelers or woodworkers or cabinet-makers who became briefly involved with aviation. In 1910 he was reported to be building spare parts for undercarriages,

The tiny Leray triplane of 1908. The engine is between the pilot's feet – but where are his controls? (Courtesy of the Musée de l'Air et de l'Espace/Le Bourget-France)

A poor photograph of the Leroy et Marzollier monoplane of 1910. (Author's collection)

and an "automatically stable" biplane spanning 9 m which was "to be covered with fabric in December." In November he was building a 4-wheeled monoplane, with a 25 hp Anzani driving a Chauvière propeller through a long shaft, and "wings above," with variable incidence. It had elevators fore and aft.

Letord and Niepce

Letord was first associated with Niepce, and the firm did wooden

Another Blériot XI copy, the Letord et Niepce. Skids added. (Courtesy of the Musée de l'Air et de l'Espace/Le Bourget-France)

models, some of which were built for Chalais Meudon; by 1905, civilians interested in having their flying machines built were being referred to Letord and Niepce; probably Letord himself never designed an aeroplane. In 1909 the firm built a monoplane for Lunel, sometimes referred to as the Lunel machine. It was based on the successful Blériot XI, and first flew at Issy on 9 November 1909. The rudder was a small rectangle mounted aft of the rear end of the fuselage, and the triangular tailplane carried small elevators. The Blériot-style undercarriage carried 2 long horned skids out in front.

(Span: 9.6 m; length: 8.5 m; gross weight: 350 kg; 3-cylinder Anzani)

In 1910 their pusher biplane appeared at Issy, with a big biplane tail cell set on outriggers, and a third tailplane surface set on top of the outriggers ahead of the cell. The machine rested on a pair of castering wheels forward and a tailwheel aft; oval skids protected the rounded wingtips. It was seen with and without side-curtains between the outermost interplane struts; once it carried the name L Barnavon on the panels.

Letord remained a subcontractor for other firms after the start of the War, and the aircraft carrying the Letord name were designed by Jean Dorand after 1913.

Leuilleux et Babry

In 1908 Leuilleux was mentioned with a man named Fardel as a builder; the following year he was associated with Babry, and was reported testing at Lille a machine which had been without its motor for a long time.

Levasseur

Pierre Levasseur, later famous for designing Nungesser and Coli's Oiseau Blanc, began his career before WWl as a builder of propellers. He also built several aircraft not of his own design, such as the Landeroin and Robert. One machine was offered under the Levasseur name after 1910, but it was in fact the Fernandez biplane No 3, to which Levasseur bought the manufacturing rights.

On 3 January 1912 he crashed at Fécamp in a seaplane of his own design, and his mechanic was drowned. His pre-WWI aircraft production was limited, probably no more than 3 biplanes; during the War he made his fortune building Spads and Breguet XIVs.

Levavasseur

Born 8 December 1863 at Mesnil-Auval (Manche), Léon Levavasseur began his engineering career by building electrical equipment. He was not yet interested in aviation when he reorganized the powerplant in Algeria owned by Jules Gastambide, who became his financial partner and signed a contract with him for the construction of an aeroplane in August 1902. In October he began the engine, working for 3 months at 14 hours a day, and finished it with the help of his brother-in-law Charles Wachter and the 4 Welferinger brothers. The 82 hp V8 weighed 100 kg. General André, Minister of War, gave him 20,000F from his "secret funds" to develop his first aircraft.

Aéroplane de Villotrans: In March 1903 Levavasseur began construction of his first flying machine in a workshop on the rue du Bas Rogers in Puteaux, and he assembled it after 14 July in the park of Mellon Castle at Villotrans (Oise), with the help of the Welferingers. The huge monoplane had high arched wings which ran back to form a horizontal tail without either rudder or fuselage; the structure was of wood and metal girders, and the airfoil

Above and three below: four views of the Levavasseur Aéroplan de Villotrans in varying stages of construction. Note that the wing structure consisted of 4 long curved built-up spars, each panel cross-braced by 4 rectangular girders on top. Fabric was laced across the undersides of each panel. The push-pull propellers were set at each end of a nacelle built inside the wing. (Author's collection)

was formed only from the tightened fabric. The 80 hp Antoinette engine between the wings drove 2 4-bladed propellers made of wood and stiffened with wire, each 3.6 m in diameter. The front tractor propeller turned at 800 rpm and the rear pusher at 1000 rpm. The machine was fitted with 25 cm wooden wheels rolling on U-sectioned wooden rails, soon replaced by iron ones. At about 36 kmh some lift was felt, and on 29 September 1903 the machine left its rails and was wrecked, the pilot unharmed: it is possible that the Aéroplane of Villotrans had actually made a short hop. The pilot was Charles Wachter, sitting under the wing and below the engine; it was ironic that Wachter should be the pilot of the first of the Antoinette designs and later lose his life in the crash of one of the last.

(Span: 18 m; length: 15 m; wing/surface area: 108 sqm; 80 hp Antoinette)

After these efforts Levavasseur abandoned the machine, and with Gastambide he concentrated on the engine, then named Antoinette, which was subsequently used successfully in Antoinette automobiles and motor-boats. In 1904 and 1905 he developed V engines of 8, 16, and 32 cylinders (the last only on paper), ranging from 24 to 100 hp.

During this time Levavasseur met Ferdinand Ferber, who ordered a 24 hp engine; together they began the study of heavier-than-air flying machines. In 1904 Levavasseur built a small wind tunnel, probably the first in France, though it could accommodate only model parts. His future career was inextricably linked to the firm of Antoinette, which he and Ferber founded together.

Levêque

Henri Levêque was first associated with Donnet, building flyingboats designed by Denhaut; when Denhaut left Donnet-Levêque, the firm kept building designs derived from Denhaut's, but known as Levêques. One of the Salmson-powered Levêques (the Levêque-Salmson) painted with the number 15 flew at Deauville in August 1913; a Gnôme-powered machine, No 6, flew in the same meet.

(Span: 12.7 m; length: 8.3 m; empty weight: 630 kg; loaded weight: 1000 kg; 110 hp Canton-Unné)

Louis Schreck bought up the company and with his own firm, les Ateliers d'Artois, formed a new one, the Franco-British Aviation Company, known as FBA; and during the War he built flyingboats in great numbers.

Levy-Gaillat

The strange Levy-Gaillat machine was still being worked on in 1908; no information is available as to its further history. A 20 hp de Dion-Bouton driving a tractor propeller was fitted into the front of the short fuselage, the whole engine arranged to turn right or left, presumably for directional control. The machine sat on a 4-wheel undercarriage. A monoplane wing with no dihedral and a flat airfoil sat on top of the fuselage; immediately above was pivoted a large rectangular flat surface: changing its angle of attack was meant to control pitch.

The Levêque-Salmson with the race-number 15 at Deauville in 1913. (Author's collection)

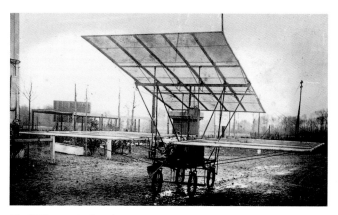

The 1908 Levy-Gaillat. The top surface seems adjustable, perhaps for control. (Courtesy of the Musée de l'Air et de l'Espace/Le Bourget-France)

(Span: 6.5 m; wing chord: 2 m; wing area: 43 sqm; gross weight: 650 kg; 20 hp de Dion-Bouton)

Leyat

Marcel Leyat built mainly biplane gliders, a few of which were later fitted with motors. His first was built in May 1909 and was shown in 1910 at the Grau air meet near Istres in southeastern France. In September Leyat and Lindpainter were reported testing "a new biplane racer" at Mourmelon; it featured a Wright-style undercarriage (with wheels), a long pointed uncovered nacelle, ailerons set between the wingtips, and a curved tailplane mounted on outriggers to the rear.

In 1911 Leyat came up with another biplane glider set on 2 skids, with a warping tailplane inside a box-like outrigger. Aileron surfaces were hinged to the top of the upper wing, with a secondary set of surfaces hinged in turn to the top of the first. It was reported to have taken off from a rail at 30 kmh-probably catapulted – and to have flown for 800 m at a height of 50 m. A 50 hp Gnôme was fitted as an experiment at the end of July. In this configuration it was probably the "biplane with a lifting tail" mentioned in 1912.

(Span: 16 m; length: 11 m; wing area: 49 sqm; weight: 500 kg; 50 hp Gnôme)

In the same year Leyat also built a glider, of wing area 18 sqm mounted on a single 1.2 x 5.2 m float, to be towed by a speedboat.

The Leyat biplane fitted with a Gnôme. (Courtesy of the Musée de l'Air et de l'Espace/Le Bourget-France)

LG

It is not clear who the builders were (perhaps Levy-Gaillat?). The LG biplane was being finished in January 1911 at Montélimard to be tested the following April. The wingtips were curved upward, and it had a biplane forward elevator.

(Span: 7 m; length: 5 m; wing area: 28 sqm; 8-10 hp motor driving a 1.2 m diameter LG propeller)

Linzeler

The biplane designed by Linzeler was built by Desplanches in 1908, and was to be tested at Vernouillet, probably the town near Paris. Mounted on 3 wheels, it had a biplane front elevator and full tail unit.

(Span: 11 m; length: 8 m; gross weight: 400 kg; 45 hp 4-inline Linzeler)

Lioré et Olivier

Fernand Lioré began his aircraft designing with Witzig and Dutilleul in the Witzig-Lioré-Dutilleul (WLD) company; in 1909 Lioré designed a monoplane with 2 tractor propellers driven by a single motor. This machine was completed and tested at the end of the summer, shortly before the 1909 Salon where it was shown in the WLD display. In its first form it had 4 wheels on a single axle and a long skid forward, a long uncovered fuselage with fin and rudder set on top of the aft end.

(Span: 9.5 m; length: 8.2 m; wing area: 23 sqm; loaded weight: 380 kg; 30-40 hp Grégoire-Gyp)

The second version, now known as the Lioré et Olivier, had the same narrow rectangular uncovered fuselage now mounted on 2 castering front wheels and a castering tailwheel which was steered by foot pedals. The tail unit was cruciform and mounted on a universal joint; the wings were rectangular with rounded tips, and the trailing edges were hinged to the longerons. The nose-mounted engine drove through chains and gears 2 tractor propellers, each on an outrigger on each side, turning in opposite directions. The propellers were pressure-fitted to their shafts, and clutches allowed their disengagement; a special device cut the engine if a shaft or chain should break.

(Span: 8.57 m; length: 9 m; total area: 22 sqm; weight: 350 kg; 30-40 hp Grégoire-Gyp driving 2 2.25 m diameter Lioré propellers)

On 4 January 1911 Lioré and Henri Olivier formed the first Lioré and Olivier company; the LeO firm came much later. With a capital investment of 250,000F of which only 50,000 were in cash, the firm was founded for making models, wooden automobile bodies, plywood,

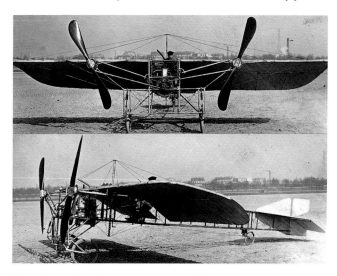

The twin-propeller Lioré et Olivier. (Peter M Bowers collection)

wooden steering wheels, entire aeroplanes, and aeroplane spares – and for selling or purchasing or renting "any kind of aviation machinery."

In 1911 the firm also built (and perhaps also designed) the handsome Balsan monoplane.

Liurette

Two photographs show this clumsily-built semi-biplane apparently in Africa, in front of a grass-thatched hut, several black onlookers, and a determined-looking Britisher in his pith helmet in front. For some reason he is holding up a dead buzzard. A Gnôme is mounted on the leading edge of the lower wing; both wings droop badly at the tips. A large fabric-covered cone is set out in front on 4 curved outriggers. The purpose of it all is unknown.

Lods

This steel-tube monoplane was seen at Nice in 1910.

Loisel

Jabiru is the name of a large African bird: Loisel, a former member of Archdeacon's Syndicat d'Aviation, chose it for his first design in 1908. Except for the name, nothing further is known of Jabiru No 1, except that it was probably an ornithopter.

Loitron et Delage

This 1909 biplane glider had wings consisting of 2 sheets of fabric tightened between 2 frames and simple ribs. Inter-wing ailerons were hinged between the front outer struts; the tail rested on a pair of thin outriggers joined at the stern. The tailplane, thick and short, was mounted on the upper outrigger, the rectangular elevator below the lower one. The pilot sat under the lower wing on straps, between the 2 close-set wheels; his head and shoulders protruded through the wing. Designed to be towed by a car or launched on a slope, it was said to be able to glide for 100 m.

This Belgian may have been Gustave Delage.

(Span: 7.35 m; wing area: 20 sqm; loaded weight: 110 kg)

Lonnet

This aeroplane mentioned in 1908 may actually have been a Donnet.

Loubéry

This monoplane rolled out in July 1911 and was much modified in August; since it was tested at St Cyr and was powered by a 60 hp Aviatik engine, it was most likely built by Louis Clément. The long fuselage of inverted U cross-section was uncovered at the rear; ailerons were fitted at the trailing edges of the wing, and a split pair of elevator control surfaces were set on either side of the single forward landing gear wheel. The feature of the design was a pair of propellers mounted on either side of the fuselage with another engine set crossways between them; the plan was apparently to produce sideways motion.

The Liurette, complete with feathered friend. (Courtesy of the Musée de l'Air et de l'Espace/Le Bourget-France)

The twin-engine 3-propeller Loubéry biplane of 1911. (Author's collection)

Lucas-Girardville

Artillery Captain Lucas-Girardville was one of the 3 pilots to be trained by Wilbur Wright at Auvours according to the agreement signed by Lazare Weiller; but he was apparently too old to learn to fly the difficult Wright biplane at the school.

In 1910 he completed a huge military aeroplane developed from models tested at the Eiffel Tower and the Renard wind-tunnel at Chalais-Meudon; it used 2 gyroscopes to control stability. Kept very secret, it was referred to as the Enigma or the Gyroscopic Spinning-Top – but more often, probably, La Baignoire (bathtub). A patent dated 1907 was finally registered in 1910.

It was a high-wing monoplane spanning about 15 m, with rectangular panels of strange airfoil section attached to each side of a large circular surface; and comprised as well 2 forward engines but only one 4-bladed propeller. Some of the controls were manual, others actuated automatically by the gyroscopes. The slatted ailerons were

The big Lucas-Girardville of 1910. It was wrecked before actually taking to the air. (Courtesy of the Musée de l'Air et de l'Espace/Le Bourget-France)

managed by the pilot, the biplane set by one of the gyroscopes; the other was for the elevators. Each gyroscope weighed 5.8 kg and was driven at 12,000 rpm by the engines – and in flight, by wind-driven propellers. The mechanic sat between the engines; there was accommodation for 2 others as well. Loaded, it weighed c 1200 kg with a wing area of 50 sqm.

In June 1910 it was moved from Chalais to the Vincennes parade field; on 11 June it crashed while taxiing, and poor Lucas-Girardville was injured. In 1912, unfazed, he designed an experimental helicopter: we can only hope he was more successful with this one.

Ludwig

Ludwig exhibited a complex helicopter at the Société des Ingénieurs Civils in 1897. It featured 2 flapping wings, 2 rotors, and 2 propellers for horizontal motion.

Lumière

A "large military biplane" was tested under this name at Issy in 1910. Lumière may have been the pilot as well.

M

Mabelly

In 1908-09 at Aubais in the south of France near Sommières, Mabelly showed a flying machine said to be part aeroplane, part helicopter.

Maglione

An unknown flying machine of this name was mentioned as being at Miramas, in the summer of 1912.

Magnard

Apparently this was a glider – nothing further is known.

Maigrot

This biplane was built by Dutheil et Chalmers in November 1909 and fitted with a special 8-cylinder engine; it may have been the Dutheil et Chalmers exhibited at the Paris Salon of 1909.

Maillot

In 1884-86 Maillot built a large kite of 72 sqm surface, probably of his own design; he was working at the same time with the Marquis de Dion. Several years later he rolled out an ornithopter at Sanarpont in northern France: he had registered the design in 1910 with the Société de Navigation Aérienne. It was man-powered through foot pedals; more power was provided by 2 men, Cailleux and Lenormand, rowing together. In 1911 he contributed the airframe of a machine similar but with warping wings to the military aeronautical center at Vincennes.

Mainguet

Henri Mainguet built this 10-passenger tractor monoplane, La Dorade (sea-bream), in 1910 at Chartres; it appeared for the first time on 21 May. Guppy-shaped, it featured the pilot's windshield set low in the

The 1910 Mainguet was designed to carry 10 people. It flew, but probably without the full complement. (Author's collection)

nose of the all-covered fuselage, the engine set out above and above him. The passengers sat in the enclosed cabin with mica windows which made up the bulk of the streamlined guppy fuselage; aft, it tapered down to a long sweeping horizontal tail. No vertical surface appears to have been fitted. The oval somewhat drooping wings were mounted at a very high angle of attack, and had wheels set below the tips; the whole machine was resting on a long skid with 2 trailing wheels forward and one under the rear of the cabin. The engine seems to have been a 40 hp 3-cylinder Anzani. With a higher-powered engine, Mainguet at first succeeded at first only in running into the trees, and later in some prolonged hops.

Malecot

A so-called "mixte" appeared under this name in 1908: a dirigible combined with an aeroplane.

Mallet

Always grumbling but never unpleasant, the artist Maurice Mallet founded the Ateliers Aéronautiques Maurice Mallet in 1891 to build gas balloons; in 1904 he commissioned himself a glider from d'Argent. As public interest in heavier-than-air machines grew, he began to describe himself as a constructor of flying machines "of any shape and any kind." He built the first Maurice Farman.

In 1908 with the Comte Henri de la Vaulx he founded the Zodiac Company to build dirigibles; in 1910 the firm was constructing aeroplanes. In the same year Mallet designed a model of a glider shaped like a bird; mounted on floats it was tested at Evian on Lake Geneva.

Malloire

A flying machine was reported tested in 1913 near Bar-le-Duc, in eastern France. It was described as having "allocaves and allogones" wings (different curves? different angles?).

Mamet

A well-known pilot and former mechanic of Louis Blériot's – he had worked for Blériot since 1907 – Julien Mamet introduced a monoplane of his own design in 1911 intended to fly around the world; it was also registered at the Concours Militaire of 1911. The machine resembled the Antoinette rather than the Blériot, though slightly smaller. The pilot sat behind and slightly higher than his passenger in a long Antoinette-style fuselage with a flat rectangular tank in front of him as a windscreen. The wing panels were rectangular at the fuse-

The handsome 2-seat Mamet of 1911: some of its ancestry is very clear. (Courtesy of the Musée de l'Air et de l'Espace/Le Bourget-France)

lage, but the trailing edges then angled forward to elliptical wingtips. The machine sat tail high, on a third wheel trailing behind the forward pair; a semicircular elevator was hinged to a rectangular tailplane; the rudder was a large polygon. Though the aeroplane was registered for the Concours Militaire with a 100 hp Gnôme, it appeared in photographs dated October 1911 with a 60 or 80 hp radial Anzani.

(Span: c 12 m; empty weight: 570 kg; apparently a variety of engines)

Marcal

This was an ill-fated glider called the Homoplane.

De Marçay-Moonen

In 1911 the Army expected that most aeroplanes most of the time would be ferried from place to place by road, towed by trucks or carried by rail in crates; they were therefore especially interested in machines that could be disassembled and later quickly put back together.

Designers worked to develop ingenious ways of doing this, but the Baron Edmond de Marçay and Moonen avoided the problem entirely by having the wings fold without unrigging them. A kingpost on each side of the fuselage slanted outwards toward the top, serving as anchor for the wing bracing – and warping-wires, and as the vertical pivot around which the butt of the rear spar could swing. Each panel then swung around back and down along the sides of the fuselage, which was triangular in section to accommodate them there.

The first de Marçay-Moonen was shown at the 1911 Exposition and had a triangular-section covered fuselage, the wings with rounded tips folding with all 12 rigging points per wing intact. The undercarriage was a simple structure of straight steel tubes and an Antoinette-like skid forward; 2 tailwheels held up the rear, with its lifting triangular tailplane and half-round elevators. The rudder was balanced, a comma, with no fin. The pilot sat aft of the trailing edge and the passenger sat forward of the leading edge; the cowled motor was mounted far forward.

In 1911: the first de Marçay-Moonen showing its folding wings. (Courtesy of the Musée de l'Air et de l'Espace/Le Bourget-France)

(Span: 13 m; length: 12 m; wing area: 20 sqm; empty weight: 450 kg; gross weight: 600 kg; 50 hp Gnôme)

Sadi-Lecomte flew a second type in the summer of 1912, this one with most of the fuselage uncovered, the tailwheels gone, and a small wheel fitted to the end of the forward skid. The Gnôme was now uncowled.

In 1912 the firm was reported building a single-seater, L'Abeille (bee), at the Camp de Châlons, while another 2-seater was being tested at Villacoublay.

In 1913 Bielovucic flew a de Marçay-Moonen seaplane under the race-number 18 at Monaco. Another single-seater, it had trapezoidal wings with squared-off tips, an uncowled 100 hp radial Anzani, and rectangular elevators. The twin front floats curved up in front; the rear one resembled that on a Tellier.

In 1914 the firm designed and built their only biplane, probably to enter the Concours de Sécurité. It was a double biplane canard, the fuselage uncovered, supported by a high tricycle landing-gear; the top rear main wings were longer than the lower and carried ailerons. The engine mounted at the rear end of the fuselage drove a tractor propeller at the front end through a long drive-shaft.

De Marigny

An "articulated" multiplane of this name was to be built in 1909 with a "new" motor. It was possibly an ornithopter.

Marin la Meslée

In 1909 the engineer Marin la Meslée tested a 25 kg biplane glider at Paris-Plage, on the Channel. He was related to Edmond Marin la Meslée, one of the highest scoring French aces of WWI.

Marque

This was a monoplane with Morane-like wings and undercarriage, Blériot XI-style fuselage and rudder and horizontal tail with tip elevators. It carried a sprung tailskid aft, a single skid forward, and a 4-strut pyramidal pylon above.

Martin

In 1909 Martin, a clock-maker from Orleans, built a monoplane of 8.1-meter span. It was claimed to be foldable "owing to its construction of hinged panels"; when last heard of, he was looking for an engine to rent for it.

Martinaisse

One photo shows this odd pusher monoplane outside a hangar marked REP. The long rectangular wings lacked dihedral, but the inner panels were hinged at the center-line, presumably for lateral control, since otherwise there was only a forward biplane elevator cell. The pilot sat in a low-slung car, and the rest of the airframe was a long uncovered overhead beam. The engine was set into the rear of the car, driving a 4-bladed propeller through chains, or perhaps a belt.

A later model of the de Marçay-Moonen. The spinning Gnôme shows clearly. (Courtesy of the Musée de l'Air et de l'Espace/Le Bourget-France)

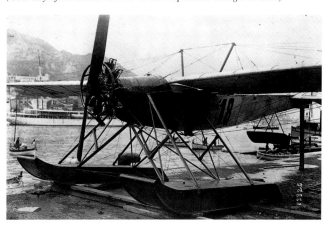

Bielovucic's big de Marçay-Moonen seaplane at Monaco. (Courtesy of the Musée de l'Air et de l'Espace/Le Bourget-France)

A poor photograph of the de Marçay-Moonen canard of 1914. (Author's collection)

The Martinaisse shows off its hinged inner-wing panels. (Author's collection)

Martinet et Legagneux-Riffard

In 1912 Robert Martinet and Georges Legagneux, founder of the Compiègne flying school at Corbeaulieu, had a torpedo monoplane built under the direction of Marcel Riffard. It was a pusher, with the propeller aft of the tail unit and the motor buried inside the streamlined fuselage. Riffard, later to become the designer of the famous Caudron-Renault racers of the 1930s, swore that "before one year" the machine would achieve at least 200 kmh. The all-metal machine was not completed, though some reported it as having been tested on the ground.

De Mauriac

This name may have been associated with the work of Legrand.

Maurice

A machine of this name was registered for the 1911 Concours Militaire.

Maurin et Willaume

Associated with another builder, Willaume, Louis Maurin built 2 monoplanes at Nice, called Niçois I and II. The first was a tiny machine resembling a rowboat set on 2 wheels, with a propeller fitted to the very bow. The rudder and curved elevator were fixed at the end of a 3-spar outrigger, fabric-covered. The wings, to which the undercarriage was attached, were nearly flat, with a large angle of attack.

(Length: c 4 m)

His second machine was less simple and bulkier, with a low-set triangular covered fuselage. A heavy water-cooled inline motor set behind its radiator drove a tractor propeller; the pilot sat in a bucket seat high on the rear fuselage behind the wing. Small ailerons were set into the outer trailing edges of the thick rectangular wings. A 2-piece rectangular tailplane pivoted on top of the aft fuselage; the rectangular rudder was fitted well behind. The machine was said to have made "bright flights" at the field at La Brague.

(Span: 9 m; length: 7 m; 45 hp inline Clément-Bayard)

Mazoyer

In St Etienne, near Lyon, Marius Mazoyer created the firm Metalloplan which offered spare parts and bearings for aeroplane builders. He specialized in metalwork, and also walnut propellers priced at only 125F. This low price angered his competitors and drew attention to his firm. He built one Metalloplan monoplane at the end of 1910; it was offered for sale at only 8000F, 1/3 the going price of the 25 hp Blériot XI, "after a flight of 10 km in closed-circuit." It was flown early the next year by Burrel, and crashed, badly, on 10 January. The aircraft was very similar to the Blériot XI, but with a double tailskid and 2 long trailing rectangular elevators.

(Wing area: 25 sqm; 25 hp Anzani)

Right: Mazoyer's one-only Metalloplan, an advanced-looking but unsuccessful machine of 1910. (Courtesy of the Musée de l'Air et de l'Espace/Le Bourget-France)

The Maurin et Willaume Niçois 1bis readied for take-off. (Peter M Bowers collection)

Note the minor differences between this 1909 Mazoyer and the Blériot XI. (Courtesy of the Musée de l'Air et de l'Espace/Le Bourget-France)

Mélin

Designed by Ernoult and Coanda and assembled by Berthaud in Lyon in 1912, the Mélin monoplane resembled the early Nieuports. The rare photographs are slightly different from the builder's descriptions; it is not certain that the projected variants were all built. The frame was made up of pressed steel strips; the single wing spar was a steel tube, and the ribs were pressed by the Arbel company. The rectangular fuselage was covered in front with steel sheets, and 3-millimeter armor plates were options for military variants. The wings were fabric-covered, except at the roots, which had transparent panels let in. The airfoil was the Eiffel No 8 section.

There were no bracing pylons, the landing and flying wires being attached directly to the upper and lower longerons to save weight and drag. The first descriptions did not include a vertical rudder, but only 2 shark-like fins, and ailerons which were hinged only to lift and act as spoilers for both glide and roll. Later descriptions mentioned "conjugated ailerons made with metal plates." Photographs show a more conventional tail; the ailerons do not show. The 2 wheels were set at the bottom of a single vertical leg which may have carried a shock-absorber.

(Single-seater – span: 9 m; length: c 6 m; wing area: c 14 sqm; empty weight: 260 kg; gross weight: 420 kg; 50 or 80 hp Gnôme)

(2-seater, perhaps not built – span: 11 m; length: 7 m; wing area: 18 sqm; empty weight: 320 kg; 80 or 100 hp Gnôme)

A photograph shows what is perhaps a later version of the first design, a handsome 50 or 80 hp Gnôme monoplane with an all-covered fuselage, a long-chord stabilizer and the 2 shark-teeth fin and rudder. There was a single pylon, the wings warped, and the undercarriage resembled that of the Antoinette.

Later Mélin worked out a much more advanced design, also perhaps never built: a large flyingboat with a pair of biplane wings set on top of the hull at each end; a glassed-in cockpit was in front, and a row of circular windows along each side. A pair of contra-rotating propellers was mounted on a pylon above the hull amidships; wingtips floats were attached to the tips of both lower wings, all of which were designed to fold.

Meugniot et La Clémendière

An "automatically stable" biplane was reported under construction at Arc les Gray in eastern France in May 1911; 3 years later another machine also designed by Meugniot was registered for the 1914 Concours de Sécurité. This one was to be trimmed by varying the angle of attack of the wings, which were mechanically joined; it might have been the same as the first machine, modified.

Michaud

A machine of this name was reported at Issy in 1913.

Mieusset et Monin

In 1909 Monin designed a helicopter which was built in Lyon by the automobile-builder Mieusset. 2 contra-rotating 6-bladed rotors turned at the tops of 2 axes about 1.5 m apart. The blades could be controlled for incidence; they totaled 9 sqm in area, and turned slowly. Separate plane surfaces of c 1.5 sqm each were set at the corners of each of the 2 axes, adjustable for control in flight. The 35 hp motor contributed to the gross weight of 360 kg.

Milord

In 1909 in Lille, Vinet-Boulogne built a monoplane for Milord's garage, probably powered with a 50 hp Gnôme. A forward elevator was built in 2 halves.

(Length: 7.5 m; chord: 2.5 m)

Moisant

John Moisant was American, born of French-speaking Canadians. He was about 40 when he went to France to learn how to fly, and in 1909 he designed the first of 2 curious aeroplanes. It was an all-metal sesquiplane, the upper wing of long aluminum sheets with 6 rolling chordwise corrugations, each supported by a rectangular chordwise plate underneath. The center-section ran back and became the tail with a nicely rounded elevator at the end, and an oval rudder with a large round hole in it underneath. The whole assembly was mounted on 5 struts above the streamlined boat-like fuselage, in turn made of steel sheets in case of accidental landing on water. A short stub wing helped

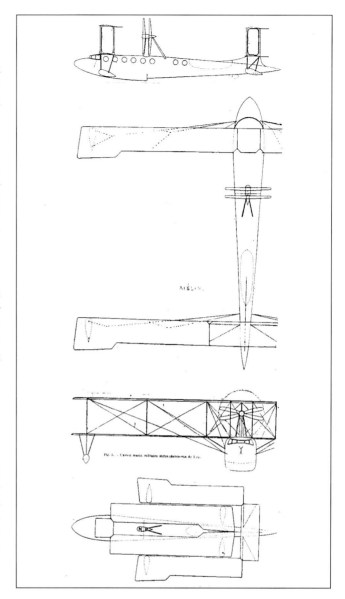

A contemporary drawing of the remarkable Mélin tandem biplane flyingboat. (Author's collection)

support the upper wing and the spidery 2-wheeled undercarriage, and a tailwheel on long legs kept the end of the machine off the ground. A forward elevator was controlled with a long rod. It was not successful, having a tendency to turn over on the ground, though a note in *Popular Mechanics* for September 1910 reports several short flights. It was painted red and known as L'Ecrevisse (crayfish).

(Wing area: 24 sqm; empty weight: 250 kg; 50 hp Gnôme)

Using parts from this ambitious design he built a second, more conventional monoplane, apparently retaining the fuselage and tailwheel. Conventional monoplane wings were mounted at deck-level, the undercarriage was simplified and attached directly to the fuselage, and a large teardrop-shaped fin and rudder assembly was mounted at the very stern. Painted black, it was called Le Corbeau (crow), and

This view of John Moisant's L'Ecrevisse does not show its most remarkable feature, its corrugated surfaces. (Courtesy of the Musée de l'Air et de l'Espace/Le Bourget-France)

did little better than his first effort. Both machines may have been built at Clément-Bayard. He later backed 2 of his pilots, Roland Garros and Edmond Audemars, who wanted to build a Gnôme-powered copy of the Demoiselle: it was hoped it would be known as the Baby Moisant. Also in 1911 his firm built a Farman-type pusher biplane with one rudder set ahead of the 2 on the trailing edge of the tailplane.

He returned to the United States and founded the Moisant International Aviators, a traveling flying circus, and was killed on 31 December 1910 while practicing for an air meet in New Orleans.

His brother Alfred founded his own flying school, and in 1914 built at least one Morane-style monoplane of his own design for another American, Harold Kantner; powered by a 50 hp Gnôme, it was called the Bluebird.

Molon

In 1911 2 monoplanes with this name appeared; the first, a single-seater, resembled the Blériot XI but with trapezoidal wings with wire trailing edges, a more rounded rudder, and elliptical tailplane with standard elevators. The fuselage was completely uncovered. The second monoplane may have been a 2-seater, otherwise similar to the first.

Moncher

A machine was described under the name of Guy Moncher.

De Monge

Although Vicomte Louis de Monge de Franeau was Belgian, his name is included in this book because he was often associated with French design projects: he entered a modified Deperdussin – a parasol – in the 1914 Concours de Sécurité; it was built by Debrouckère. He financed French designs during and after WWI. He built, and probably designed as well, a series of racers after the War. His 1914 entry in the Concours had been rebuilt the previous year; it appeared with a standard Deperdussin fin and rudder, as well as a tall rectangular affair with a balanced rudder. The undercarriage was fitted with 2 pairs of wheels and a single skid.

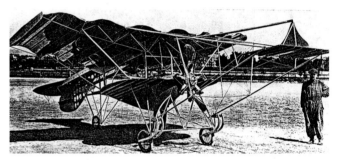

This view shows clearly the structures of the Moisant L'Ecrevisse of 1909-1910. (Author's collection)

The Moisant Le Corbeau, showing more than a family resemblance to his first design. (Author's collection)

The single-seater Molon monoplane of 1911. Note the heavy undercarriage structure. (Courtesy of the Musée de l'Air et de l'Espace/Le Bourget-France)

Monnier-Harper

A tractor monoplane seaplane of this name appeared in 1912 – perhaps it was an amphibian with curved gull-shaped wings and twin floats.

Montel

This was probably an aircraft built by Odier and Vendôme and tested in Marseille. It had 2 pusher propellers, tricycle undercarriage, a forward elevator, and 4 ailerons.

(Span: 11 m; length: 11 m; wing area: 44 sqm: gross weight: 500 kg; 18 hp Turcat-Méry engine)

Montéry

In 1910-11, L Montéry opened an "aérodrome-garage" near Châlon sur-Marne, describing himself as a constructor; he may have only repaired or modified other people's aeroplanes. One monoplane was introduced as his design, but it was a Blériot XI powered with a 25 hp flat-twin Dutheil et Chalmers set just aft of the undercarriage, in the same way that the small Anzani had been mounted.

Montgolfier

Between 1910 and 1913 Raymond de Montgolfier followed, though less successfully, in the footsteps of his aeronautical ancestors. Photographs suggest he built at least 4 different aeroplanes.

1. A Demoiselle copy, with 3 tiny trailing wheels, the wings almost flat and with a high angle of attack, and 2 small rudders above and below a rounded tailplane and elevator. It is reported to have been built at the shops of Louis and Laurent Seguin, inventors of the Gnôme rotary engines, and de Montgolfier's cousins. It had a non-Santos feature of a fabric fairing on each side from the wing trailing edge root up to the upper fuselage beam. But the machine was fitted with a 3-cylinder Anzani or Viale – why not a 50 hp Gnôme instead, if the Seguins built it? The aeroplane was taken to Issy in May 1910 and damaged there on 1 June by Lt Bier; it was flown again early in September by one of the Bonnet-Labranche brothers.

2. This was generally called the Raymond de Montgolfier No 1, a huge twin-float seaplane, the monoplane wings slightly upcurved and with a high angle of attack. The pilot sat in the short uncovered fuselage with the 45 hp water-cooled V4 Mors automobile engine which drove 2 propellers, one at each end. The tail was comprised of 2 triangular rudders and a triangular elevator, and was braced by uncovered tail booms. Since Montgolfier was too short-sighted to fly himself, the first runs were made by Almyre Janvier; on 13 July 1910 in one of the first tests, it taxied into a fisherman's pole and the starboard wing and tail unit were torn apart.

(Span: 16 m; length: 15 m)

The de Monge entry in the 1914 *Concours de Sécurité*; its resemblance to a *Deperdussin* is not accidental. (Courtesy of the Musée de l'Air et de l'Espace/ Le Bourget-France)

One of the first of the Montgolfier aeroplanes, the Demoiselle copy. Note the differences from the original. (Courtesy of the Musée de l'Air et de l'Espace/ Le Bourget-France)

Raymond Montgolfier's unfortunate second machine before its terminal accident in 1910. (Courtesy of the Musée de l'Air et de l'Espace/Le Bourget-France)

Montgolfier's all-blue monoplane of 1911. There seems hardly ground clearance for the propeller. (Courtesy of the Musée de l'Air et de l'Espace/Le Bourget-France)

3. Sometimes called R de M No 2, it was tested at Bron in November 1911. Built at the shops of Jacob et Cathelin, it was covered with sky-blue fabric, and with its long fuselage resembled a shorter-legged REP. It was powered initially with a 24 hp air-cooled flat twin Coudert Aérien, and later re-powered with a 70 hp radial Anzani and equipped with floats to be tested on the Lake of Paladru. There, at the end of 1911 or early in 1912, Montgolfier is said to have crashed with his mechanic "in a floatplane of his own design" from a height of 6 m.

4. A "new Montgolfier monoplane" was reported at the end of July 1912, to be flown for the first time on 10 August 1912. It was similar to the previous machine, and may have been the same aeroplane with changes: the rectangular wings had more camber, and used wing-warping; a 3-legged pylon above the fuselage replaced the inverted V mast of No 2. Janvier earned his brevet No 1195 on this aeroplane. The machine was sometimes referred to as R & M No 3, but no markings showed on this or any of Montgolfier's other aircraft.

(Span: c 11 m; radial engine, probably Anzani)

Monthier et Calamard

They designed the Sporta monoplane with triangular-sectioned fuselage and cruciform tail; it flew for the first time on 16 January 1911 near Grenoble.

Morane-Saulnier

Raymond Saulnier's early designs are described in the section under his name. In 1911 he and his friends Léon Morane and Gabriel Borel joined to form a new firm, La Société Anonyme des Aéroplanes Morane-Borel-Saulnier, and built the Morane-Borel monoplane flown by Jules Védrines in the Paris-Madrid flight of 21-26 May – and in several other meets as well; and a 2-seater.

Morane-Borel: This was a single-seater similar to the Blériot XI, but with a simple V-leg landing gear with a small skid at each wheel, a tall double tailskid aft, elliptical wingtips and a high rectangular rudder; the tailplane was fitted with tip elevators. The aft fuselage was sometimes left uncovered.

(Span: 9.3 m; length: 6.9 m; wing area: 14.5 sqm; top speed: 111 kmh; 50 hp Gnôme)

A 2-seater was entered in the 1911 Concours Militaire; it was similar to the single-seater, but with a larger multi-strut 4-wheel undercarriage, and a tall angular rudder. The fuselage was short in proportion, with the rear section uncovered. At least once it was fitted with a pair of small wheels forward.

On 10 October 1911 the firm changed its name to Société Anonyme des Aéroplanes Morane-Saulnier, and showed 4 new monoplanes at the 1911 Exposition:

PP: a single-seater with a simple V-leg landing gear, tip elevators fitted to the tailplane, with the wing trailing edge raked forward and the wingtips raked forward as well, built for Maurice Tabuteau for his Pau-Paris flight of 1912 (hence PP).

(Span: 9.2 m; length: 6.12 m; wing area: 14.9 sqm; empty weight: 280 kg; speed: 114 kmh; 50 hp Gnôme)

Type A Ecole: part Morane, part Borel, apparently a single-seater with a Borel-type undercarriage with a pair of wheels on each

The Morane-Borel, similar to the Blériot XI. This is Védrines on 9 August 1911 in the Coupe Michelin race. (Peter M Bowers collection)

The 1911 Concours Militaire 2-seater Morane-Borel. (Author's collection)

side, and a cowling extension over the top of the engine. 2 Morane-Saulniers, perhaps Type As, were delivered to the Army in 1912.

Type B Ecole: a tandem 2-seater similar to Type A Ecole.

(Span: 10.2 m; length: 6.12 m; wing area: 16 sqm; empty weight: 325 kg; 80 hp Gnôme)

Type C: a single-seater with a 4-wheel undercarriage of steel struts.

(Wing area: 14 sqm; 35 hp engine)

Type HS Ecole: a 2-seater with a 4-wheel undercarriage with wood struts.

(Wing area: 16 and 18 sqm; 50 hp Gnôme)

Hydro Canard single-seater: not finished.

(Wing area: 16 sqm; 70 hp engine)

Design built for Rebikoff: a 3-seater.

(Wing area: 21 sqm; 70 hp engine)

Type TB (Torpille-Blindée): a streamlined armored military 2-seater with separated square cockpits, rounded all-steel-covered fuselage, and a 4-wheeled undercarriage. A Donnet-Levêque marked with the race-number 10, the hull resembles the The nose was faired in and there was a series of circular cooling holes cut around the propeller shaft.

(Span: 11.2 m; length: 7.5 m; wing area: 28 sqm; empty weight: 375 kg; 80 hp Gnôme)

Type Renault: a very pretty racy-looking 2-seater at the 1912 Paris Exposition, featuring a V-leg undercarriage and separated seats.

(Wing area: 20 sqm; 80 hp V8 Renault)

Type Canton: a 3-seater.

(Wing area: 21 sqm; 90 hp Canton)

Type J: a 2-seat touring monoplane.

(Wing area: 15 sqm; 80 hp Gnôme)

Type K: a racing hydro monoplane with a huge engine.

(Wing area: 15 sqm; 160 hp Gnôme)

Type Garros: In 1912 the firm built a small monoplane for Roland Garros, who flew it from Tunis to Sicily, and then in stages to Rome. A similar but slightly larger machine followed it, also for Garros, and fitted with floats for his Monaco attempt in 1913. Later in 1913 Morane-Saulnier built 2 more monoplanes for Garros, and in one of them he flew from St Raphael in France to Bizerte in Africa. Work on these monoplanes culminated in the Types G (2-seater), and H (single-seater).

Type G: This straightforward 2-seat monoplane set the standard for many of the following M-S designs. The wing was untapered, and the tips raked forward. The undercarriage was of simple V-design with a V-brace to the center of the axle. The engine was half-covered in a horse-shoe-shaped cowl. An Ecole version with a 3-cylinder Anzani had skids and a support structure under the propeller. Several 3-float seaplane versions were built and raced. There were 2 versions of the basic G – the GA and the GB:

(GA: span: 14 m; speed: 12-124 kmh; 60 hp Gnôme, 60 hp Le Rhône)

(GB: span: 16 m; 60 hp and 80 hp Gnôme, 80 hp Le Rhône; speed: 123-125 kmh)

Type G Parasol: The first Morane parasol, it was a 2-seater based on the Type G.

The Morane-Saulnier Type TB with its Gnôme fully cowled. It appeared unfinished with a slightly different cowling in the 1911 Paris Salon. (Peter M Bowers collection)

The 1913 version of the Type Garros which Garros used at Monaco in 1913. (Courtesy of the Musée de l'Air et de l'Espace/Le Bourget-France)

The Morane Type G 2-seater: the basic Morane monoplane. (Peter M Bowers collection)

The Morane Type G parasol. (Courtesy of the Musée de l'Air et de l'Espace/Le Bourget-France)

(Wing area: 16 sqm; 80 hp engine)

Type E: a single-seater.

(Wing area: 14 sqm; 80 hp Gnôme)

Type M: an armored version of the G, with a flat disc covering the engine in front.

(Span: 10.4 m; length: 6.3 m; weight: 490 kg; speed: 122.3 kmh)

Type WR: a 2-seat armored version of the Type G was built for the Russian navy; it featured wing-root cutouts, an elongated nose, and odd glazed panels on each side, protruding out like radiators. The Type VR was similar.

(Wing area: 18 sqm; 80 hp Gnôme)

Type H: a widely-used single-seater resembling the Type G; perhaps it preceded it. Grahame-White license-built them in England. Several 3-float versions were built as well.

Another M-S monoplane appeared in 1912, with the trapezoidal-tapered wings of the much later Moranes and Nieuports.)

Type K: a hydro.

Type O: Similar to the Type H, it was built for the Monaco rally; flown by Roland Garros in the London-Paris race, it featured a reflex airfoil section.

Type L: This 2-seater (sometimes a single-seater) parasol with warping wings appeared in 1913; it was similar to the earlier monoplanes. A somewhat later wartime development, the Type LA, had ailerons.

Demoiselle: The firm attempted in 1913 to build a commercial variant of the successful Santos-Dumont machine; it was a side-by-side 2-seater, with a Gnôme engine mounted low in a ring cowling and Morane-Saulnier wings and tail surfaces.

Type M: This was a single-seater monoplane which appeared in 1913.

A flat plate over the front of the engine marks the military Morane Type M of 1912. (Author's collection)

The 1913 Morane Type L parasol, this one with warping wings. Access to the front cockpit looks very difficult. (Courtesy of the Musée de l'Air et de l'Espace/Le Bourget-France)

Type N: This was a 1914 racing design.

(Wing area: 11 sqm; 80 hp Gnôme)

Type Biplan: a Farman look-alike seaplane which flew at Monaco, with Morane-Saulnier painted on the nacelle.

The Morane H, a single-seater resembling – but perhaps preceding! – the Type G. (Courtesy of the Musée de l'Air et de l'Espace/Le Bourget-France)

The Morane-Saulnier Demoiselle, with 2 seats and cowled Gnôme with chain drive. (Courtesy of the Musée de l'Air et de l'Espace/Le Bourget-France)

This Morane-Saulnier seaplane, clearly so marked on the nacelle, is often confused with a similar Farman. Here it is flying at Monaco, carrying also the inscription Le Rhône. (Author's collection)

Moreau

Albert Moreau was a salesman of printing equipment and the father of 6 children; most of his modest income was spent on the design and construction of one of the most famous pre-WW1 designs, the Aérostable. With his brother André he had started in 1902 with models of gliders, observing the reflexes of flying pigeons.

He was inspired by de Perthuis' theory of pendulum stability when he built his first powered machine in 1909. It was a monoplane, with a steel tube fuselage; the wing rested on the open – frame fuselage, and a large triangular tail surface give the plan view the appearance of a pigeon. Within the fuselage frame the pilot and passenger seat, side by side, encased in an aluminum car, was suspended from a fore-and-aft pivot. The aeroplane could fly normally with the car locked; when it was free to swing, the elevators were engaged and moved automatically to counter the swing. The pilot still controlled roll with a hanging control stick, and turn, with rudder pedals. On 22 September 1913, flying for the H Bonnet prize which stipulated that roll controls were not to be used, Moreau flew keeping his machine

The Moreau Aérostable. (Bill Lewis collection)

A close-up of the passenger unit of the Moreau. (Author's collection)

The military Aérostable at the 1913 Salon in Emaillaite. The placard reads Appareil Invisible. (Bill Lewis collection)

level with the rudder only. Alex Dumas said the Moreau was "a shoal of ingenious systems"; he also said that in rough air the device did not work well because of its inertia. Moreau had to install a pneumatic shock-absorber to damp the oscillations. If the engine cut out, the car could be locked quickly to allow a shallow dive. Reports state that Moreau intended to build a much lighter machine at the beginning of 1911.

(Span: 12 m; length: 9 m; wing area: 25 sqm; empty weight: 500 kg; 40 hp engine driving a 2.4 m diameter tractor propeller at 900 rpm)

The second Moreau appeared in April 1912 as a military 2-seater. It was shown at the 1913 Salon with a transparent skin made of light fabric doped with Emaillite, but was not flown this way.

(Span: 14.15 m; length: 9.3 m; wing area: 32 sqm; empty weight: 510 kg; top speed: 95 kmh; low speed: 67 kmh; rate of climb: 100 ft/min)

The military machine was tested by the Etablissement Aéronautique de Chalais-Meudon, Lt Saunier flying as passenger with Moreau; the tests resulted in a contract for further testing. The machine was shown at the 1914 Concours de Sécurité; shortly after, during a test flight, the elevator collapsed and Moreau tried to land in a street in Melun, but hit a pole and was killed.

Mounier

In Alaise, in 1912, Mounier finished his monoplane. The pitch was controlled through varying the incidence of the wing; the tail was mounted on 3 2-meter-long outriggers, and the 2 rudders were set below the wing itself. A one-cylinder motor drove a 2-bladed tractor propeller. The machine sat on 3 castering wheels.

Moutatet

A biplane seaplane of this name was tested in Algiers in 1909.

(Span: 11.5 m; 60 hp Mutel)

Mullot

The brothers Mullot built 2 early aeroplanes. The first was a handsome low-wing monoplane with considerable dihedral, the 4 wing spars on the top surface and the ribs nearly flat; large ailerons were hinged to the trailing edge. It had an uncovered box-frame fuselage, a large free-standing scalloped rudder, and a long triangular tailplane and rear elevator.

A single photograph titled "La Ferté Alais – Biplane des Fils Mulot" shows a Farman-like machine with a small biplane forward elevator cell mounted high on forward outriggers; free-hanging ailerons hinged to the front outermost interplane struts; twin small rudders and 2 wheels. The tips and trailing edges of all the surfaces were deeply scalloped.

N

Nau

Two monoplanes are known to have been designed by Robert Nau. If the "Nault from Paris" was indeed Robert Nau, then he was also responsible for the Nault ornithopter.

The Mullot aeroplane. Note its similarity to the Leroy et Marzollier. (Author's collection)

A poor copy of the postcard showing the Mullot biplane, similar to a Farman. (Author's collection)

The first big Nau monoplane. (Peter M Bowers collection)

The first monoplane appeared in 1909, a big one, with rectangular wings set low on the forward fuselage: their angle of attack at the roots was less than at the tips. The top longerons of the uncovered fuselage ran back and out to become the tailplane. A high bridge structure served as pylon on top; the whole machine sat on 2 castering wheels, and high on a small tailwheel. A 3-cylinder Anzani was mounted at the level of the lower longerons in front. The aeroplane was not successful.

The second Nau. Note design features in common with No 1. (Peter M Bowers collection)

The second was probably little better than the first, though it was claimed to have flown at Juvisy in 1910. The long tapered fuselage was covered on the sides only halfway from the nose; a strange cruciform tail unit with a round rudder and triangular fin was supported at the aft end. The thick wings were much shorter than on the first design, and were set higher on the fuselage; each panel had a small kingpost at mid-span and was braced to the same bridge pylon as before. The elaborate 2-wheel under-carriage was of steel tube and fitted with long skids..

(Span: 13 m; length: 12 m; wing area: 24 sqm; 60 hp Renault)

Nault

In the summer of 1908 an unknown "Nault from Paris" tested an ornithopter monoplane at Brest. The pilot sat behind mica windows in a streamlined fuselage, clearly anticipating high speeds. This Nault may well have been Robert Nau, whose designs appeared the following year but whose name was listed among owners and builders of 1908.

Nicolas

François Nicolas' 1909 – and only – design was sponsored by the small hunchbacked Marquis de Salamanca, under whose name it was frequently described. An automobile-body-builder in Biarritz, Nicolas based his monoplane on the Antoinette, but made his even bigger. The triangular-section fuselage was long and slender, about one meter deep. Fully covered, it carried a long triangular tailplane and elevator. The rectangular wings were deeply arched in section and were sup-ported by 6 kingposts and a forest of brace-wires. Mounted high at the roots, they drooped towards mid-span and then rose again at the tips. Tiny triangular ailerons drooped at the trailing edges. The nar-row landing-gear was comprised of an inverted U arch which sup-ported a pair of wheels and skids, and the elevator was separated from the tailplane by a wide gap. The aeroplane is unlikely to have flown.

(Span: 14 m; length: 12 m; wing area: 35 sqm; weight: 450 kg; 50 hp 3-cylinder Anzani with a Bonnet-Labranche propeller)

Nicolas' grandson was once Deputy Secretary of the Aero Club of Biarritz.

Right: One of the first Nieuport II monoplanes. Note the differences between these 3 photographs. (Author's collection)

Nieuport

The first company founded by Edouard Nieuport, formerly de Niéport, was a small firm producing spark-plugs and magnetos for automobile engines. Early interested in heavier-than-air flying machines, he also furnished some of the electrical equipment for the Antoinette engine fitted to Henry Farman's Voisin when it flew on 13 January 1908, the year in which he founded his first – and unsuccessful – aeronautical company. From his racing cycle experience, he was interested from the beginning in streamlined shapes. At first he thought aviation could be nothing but a sport, and he sought always for speed.

At the end of 1908 he built his first aeroplane, with the help of his brother Charles, the Swiss Jacques Schneider, and his grandpar-ents' money. His monoplane, powered with a 20 hp 2-cylinder water-cooled Darracq, had an abbreviated deep fuselage which almost com-pletely protected the pilot from the airflow. The tail was supported on outriggers. Completed and flown in 1909, it was destroyed by a Seine flood.

In 1910 he built another monoplane, this one with a full clean deep fuselage completely covered with fabric, the pilot sitting so low

The first Nieuport of 1909. (Author's collection)

Still another variant of the Nieuport II theme. (Courtesy of the Musée de l'Air et de l'Espace/Le Bourget-France)

that only his head was exposed. The fuselage was built of wooden frames and longerons which were cable-braced (no piano-wire), its shape determined from tests with a piece of soap towed in the Seine behind a motorboat. A semicircular tailplane was fitted in front of a complicated tail consisting of a horizontal surface and 4 fixed small vertical surfaces, the whole thing swiveling to serve as both elevator and rudder.

The 2-spar thin tapered wings caused little drag: they were braced on each side by only 4 cables, 2 of which were used for warping. The undercarriage became a Nieuport trademark, made with a short central metal skid supported by 2 V-struts of metal. A wheel was fitted at each end of a leaf spring laid across the skid. On the ground the machine sat level, but waddled at take-off. The engine was a 28-32 hp air-cooled flat twin designed by Nieuport; at 1,200 rpm it was powerful enough and the aeroplane streamlined enough to provide a top speed of 80 kmh.

Before the end of 1910 the complex tail unit was altered, and with the semicircular tailplane, 2 small semicircular elevators, and the famous Nieuport rudder, it was used in slightly differing forms through 1917. A delta tailplane with 2 small elevators was tested, but not developed. The controls were a stick controlling the elevators and the rudder, and foot-pedals for wing-warping: Nieuport thought if the aeroplane tilted to the left, the pilot would naturally lean right, pushing the right-hand pedal to bring the machine level.

The little single-seater was known as the Nieuport II; it was to be developed into a variety of both land – and seaplanes, and provided the basis for the later 1915 Nieuport scouts and fighters. On 11 May 1911 Edouard Nieuport broke the world speed record at 119.7 kmh with only 28 hp. The next month he achieved 145 kmh with an 80 hp Gnôme, and in 1913 he still held the world speed record with 2 passengers.

The successful Nieuport II was to be built in impressive numbers, and in several variants:

Another version of the Nieuport II. (Peter M Bowers collection)

<u>IIN</u>: With the original Nieuport engine.

<u>IIA</u>: With the 40 hp Anzani.

<u>IIB</u>: A 2-seater with the 20 hp Darracq.

<u>IIC</u>: With Gnôme engines of 50, 70, or 100 hp.

<u>IIIA</u>: This 2-seater was powered by a 40 hp Anzani.

<u>IVG</u>: This model was a similar to the Type II, but larger, a single, 2-, or 3-seater, powered by a Gnôme. The first Nieuport sea-

The Nieuport IIN with the Nieuport engine. (Peter M Bowers collection)

plane was developed by the firm in 1912 from a Type IVG, to which were fitted 2 main floats said to have been designed by Gustave Delage. They were of a thick T-section with a maximum depth of 52 cm. The first variant of these floats had only one step; later and longer ones had up to 3. They all had little winglets on their noses which prevented pitching into the water. A third small float, streamlined and of circular cross-section, was attached under the tail. On later types in 1913, the rudder was raised to keep it out of the water.

The Nieuport seaplanes had one cockpit for 2 or 3 people, and longer wings than the landplane versions. They were sold to private owners and to the French Navy. They all used rotary engines of 80 to 100 hp: Le Rhônes, Gnômes, or Clergets.

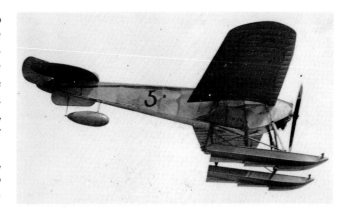

The Nieuport IVG hydro. (Author's collection)

IVM: A slightly-modified Type IV, with 3 seats, the military Type IVM won the first military contest ever held, in 1911. This type was later sold to the armed forces of Britain, France, Italy, Sweden, and Russia. With the Blériot XI it was the first aircraft involved in a war, in Italy, in 1911. The armored version saw service in France as late as 1915. Though fast, these later Type IVs, in 1912-1913-1914, climbed at less than 2 m/sec at their best, and provided poor downward visibility: attempts were made in 1912 to improve the view by reducing the wing chord on each side between the fuselage and the first wing rib. One such was shown at the 1913 Paris Salon and flown by Espanet at Reims in 1913. It had a smaller wing and a fully enclosed 50 hp Gnôme – a beautiful aeroplane.

The Type IVM Concours Militaire 2-3-seater of 1911. (Peter M Bowers collection)

VI: The second seaplane design, Type VI(?), retained the shape of the IVM, but had 2 cockpits in tandem for the pilot and observer, and a small fixed vertical fin in front of the rudder. These were powered with either the 100 hp Gnôme or the 80 hp Le Rhône, and could stay aloft for three hours. Produced in smaller numbers than the IV-series, they saw service mainly with the French and British navies, some as late as 1917.

Espanet's 50 hp Gnôme Nieuport IV. (Peter M Bowers collection)

Below: The Nieuport VI tandem seaplane. (Peter M Bowers collection)

(Length: 6.8 m; wing area: 12.4 sqm)

X: The 2-seat X, and the XI, were entirely different machines, both monoplanes. The XI was designed for cavalry support and dirigible interception, but they proved unsuccessful. They had untapered wings of different spans, larger elevators and simplified undercarriages.

(2-seater, passenger in front): span: 12.3 m; length: 5.8 m; wing area: 14.1 sqm; weight: 401 kg; speed; 115 kmh; 80 hp)

The Nieuport X 2-seater. (Courtesy of the Musée de l'Air et de l'Espace/Le Bourget-France)

XI: This monoplane came in single – and 2-place versions, each with a choice of engines.

(Single-seater: span: 9 m; length: 6.49 m; wing area: 14.5 sqm; weight: 270 kg; speeds with 50-60-80 hp: 110-115-120 kmh)

(2-seater: span: 8.9 m; length: 5.84 m; wing area: 14.1 sqm; weight: 270 kg; speeds with 50-60-80 hp: 109-115-124 kmh)

The Nieuport XI, not the WWI scout biplane! (Courtesy of the Musée de l'Air et de l'Espace/Le Bourget-France)

They were fast, with the 100 hp Gnôme (145 kmh with 2 men), and climbed at 2.2 m/sec. On one of these machines, equipped with long wings and without armor, Legagneux broke the world altitude record and reached 6,160 m in 1913.

It is likely that the sole pre-War sesquiplane designed by the Nieuport firm for the 1914 Gordon-Bennett Cup, and eventually developed into the fighter series of 1915, was directly descended from the Type Léger, the light cavalry monoplane.

Very little is known about a third seaplane design from the Nieuport firm. Built in 1912-13, it was a large sesquiplane with a short central fuselage for a crew of 2 or 3, and a 110 hp Salmson engine installed as a pusher. The tail surfaces were mounted at the ends of 2 long booms fabricated of compressed paper. The machine was reported to have been an armored design for military use only, eventually to mount a forward-firing machine-gun. Only one was built and flown.

The twin-boom Nieuport hydro made of compressed paper. (Courtesy of the Musée de l'Air et de l'Espace/Le Bourget-France)

(Span: (upper) 15 m; (lower) 7 m; length: 7.5 m; wing area: 40 sqm; speed: 110 kmh)

After the death of Edouard Nieuport in September 1911, and Charles' fatal crash in 1913, the company was eventually taken over by Henri Deutsch de la Meurthe, who saved it from bankruptcy in 1913, even though it was then the third largest aircraft firm in the world, by the start of the War behind only Blériot and Farman. The company thus was able to survive the 1918 cancellation by the Army of its production contract for the Nieuport monoplanes. These machines were reliable but by that time inefficient, and the Army ordered the Voisin biplane instead.

Though there seem no accurate figures on the production of the pre-War Nieuport monoplanes, it is safe to assume that about 150 of them in one form or another were built, including

The one-off Nieuport-Dunne flying wing of 1913. (Courtesy of the Musée de l'Air et de l'Espace/Le Bourget-France)

Prince de Nissole's own design. (Peter M Bowers collection)

those built during the war as trainers for the Nieuport Company's own flying school. Nieuports were built under license by Macchi in Italy and by the Nieuport subsidiary in England.

The firm became interested in the tailless Dunne designs, and Commandant Félix was sent to England to evaluate the Dunne. He was impressed, and in 1913 flew one back to Villacoublay to demonstrate. At an air meet at Deauville, Félix thrilled the crowd by getting out and walking on the wing while flying solo. The French firm took out a license and built at least one, but the Army was not interested further.

The first of the Nieuport sesquiplanes was the Model X, built in 1914; Patent No 477.457 was taken out on 30 Jan 1915, and called for a ball joint for the attachment of the lower wings to allow for incidence adjustment. The resulting semicircular fittings for the outboard struts remained in production even though the original design intent was never implemented!

De Nissole

Prince de Nissole designed an Albatross for Zodiac. He also designed and built a curious monoplane with elevator surfaces like sesquiplane wings below the main wings, with the pilot sitting in an uncovered fuselage with cruciform tail and tailwheel. Ailerons were attached to the trailing edges, like the Antoinette IV, and small hexagonal surfaces were fitted on each side between the wings and the ailerons

(Length: 9 m; wing area: 16 sqm; weight; 320 kg; 25 hp Anzani)

Noël

At least 3 Noëls were involved in pre-WWI French aviation. André Noël was an oft-publicized Blériot XI pilot; Jules Noël was a pilot for Roger Sommer and was killed in a Sommer on 9 February 1911; and Louis Noël was a designer and builder.

While still flying his Blériot, André was reported building an "extra rapide" monoplane; and at the end of October 1910 he claimed

The first (1911) Noël biplane. (Courtesy of the Musée de l'Air et de l'Espace/ Le Bourget-France)

a top speed of 100 kmh with a 5-cylinder 50 hp Anzani in his new machine, Le Moineau (sparrow). At about the same time, Alessandro Anzani is reported to have bought from a Noël – very likely André – a shed at Issy "with everything locked inside."

Before becoming a Sommer pilot, Jules had built at least 3 aeroplanes of his own at Carignan, in the south of France. A postcard dated 1910 shows his No 3, a monoplane with an uncovered rear fuselage, and Blériot-style kingposts; the undercarriage consisted of 2 vertical struts side by side with a long cross-axle, the whole wire-braced.

(Empty weight: 210 kg; 25 hp Anzani)

The first aeroplane designed by Louis Noël (sometimes mistakenly called Paul Noël) appeared in 1911; completed in April, it was flying in June. An unequal-span biplane with an all-tubing airframe for disassembly, it had an uncovered box fuselage with a rudder hinged at the tail and a huge tailplane set ahead of it. After brief testing at the end of June, the Anzani was replaced with a Viale – itself an Anzani copy – and the balance was changed. Later a Gnôme was installed.

The 1914 Noël. (Courtesy of the Musée de l'Air et de l'Espace/Le Bourget-France)

(Span: (upper) 12 m; (lower) 8 m; length: 9.5 m; wing area: 32 sqm)

Louis Noël's next design, also in 1911, was based on the Caudron, with rectangular wings and 2 small triangular rudders set below a large tailplane with an elevator hinged at the rear. There were flaps set between the wings, perhaps for roll control. The pilot sat in an uncovered nacelle behind the tractor engine.

In 1912 Louis was also reported as flying the Paumier biplane, which he may have helped design or build, since his first known biplane and the Paumier were similar. In 1914 he showed another Noël biplane, this one designed with a man called de Rue, who was in fact Captain Ferdinand Ferber. The large covered nacelle sat 2 in tandem, and was set between the large unequal-span wings. Large ailerons were fitted to the upper wings, and drooping panels were set inboard of the ailerons as air-brakes for landing. The rectangular tailplane was mounted above the rudder, the whole assembly attached to the wings with a Farman-like set of tractor outriggers. The machine sat high on 2 pairs of wheels, and the tractor Gnôme was nicely cowled.

(Span: (upper) 15 m; length 9.5 m; empty weight: 450 kg; 80 hp Gnôme)

Jules Noël's designs are likely to have been more numerous than these; he was frequently mentioned between 1908 and 1912 as an enthusiast of flying machines, but not as a pilot. In 1912 he founded a small automobile company that continued until 1925.

Nord Aviation

Fernand Scrive and his son organized a flying club called Nord Aviation, which published aeronautical articles in 1908 and 1909. The school carried on many manned glider experiments; several of these biplane gliders were shown at the Paris Salon of 1909, both with the top wings horizontal and the lower wings angled sharply up; they flew in public at the 1909 air meet at Tournai, in Belgium. The most famous was designed by Scrive, with a short top wing and a much larger lower wing. The tail unit had a tiny tailplane and a large vertical fin with triangular trailing edge; the whole unit was set on a single thin boom braced with a kingpost. The pilot hung by his elbows beneath the wings. The glider was later modified with a different tail and 2 small wheels forward, with a skid at the trailing edge of the lower wing. The glider was sometimes referred to as the Scrive-Van Damme, for the pilot.

(Span: (lower) 8.5 m; wing area: 24 sqm; length: 7 m; weight: 25 kg)

Another was designed by Didier Scrive and Marcel Coquard, and was similar to Fernand's except with equal-span wings. The tail was cruciform and set on a shorter outrigger; the initials SG were painted on the rudder.

The Scrive glider of 1909. (Author's collection)

(Span: 6.5 m; wing area: 26 sqm)

Another machine spanned 5 m with skids underneath: the pilot was to pull up his legs above the skids for landing.

Norrep-Lau
This firm built at least one Nieuport copy, one with an Edelweiss radial engine. "Norrep" is Perron, reversed.

O

Obre
While Emile Obre was working as a mechanic in Morteau, he learned of the aeronautical experiments of the Wrights and Santos-Dumont, and he was attracted to the new sport; by 1908 he had designed his first aeroplane.

1. It was a monoplane with a fuselage of uncovered steel tubing, perhaps suggested by the REP designs. The engine was mounted behind the leading edge of the wing, and drove the tractor propeller through a long shaft; the pilot sat behind the engine. At the rear, functioning as extensions of the 2 upper longerons, were the tailplane and elevator; a long rectangular rudder was set below, hinged to the castering tailwheel. 2 short semicircular wings were fitted to either side, with a longer-than-wide rectangular panel formed with an reverse-curve airfoil section fixed high above.

(Wing area: 38 sqm; 3-cylinder 30 hp Anzani)

It was soon modified, with an extended fuselage and a triangular elevator hinged to the very stern. The rudder had a new cut-out on its leading edge, and the wings were longer with pointed tips. On 18 January 1909 it was damaged at Issy.

Below: The first version of Obre No 3, in 1910. The reflex airfoil has been abandoned. (Courtesy of the Musée de l'Air et de l'Espace/Le Bourget-France)

The Norrep-Lau Nieuport copy, with the Edelweiss engine. (Courtesy of the Musée de l'Air et de l'Espace/Le Bourget-France)

Emile Obre's first aeroplane. There seems no inter-wing bracing other than the 6 struts. (Author's collection)

The second Obre. Note reflex airfoil contours. (Author's collection)

2. The second aeroplane designed by Obre was designated No 3, equally unsuccessful, also tested at Issy in the summer of 1909. It was similar to the Henry Farman III, with a biplane forward elevator and biplane tailplane with a single rudder between. Ailerons were set into all 4 wing panels; the airfoil section was a gentle reverse curve similar to that on the odd upper panel of his first machine. It stood on 2 wheels under the engine, and 2 tailwheels at the tips of the tailplane. The engine was a 4-cylinder inline water-cooled model, possibly a 40 hp Chenu.

3. The next Obre machine was a tractor monoplane ordered by the Comte de Noue and built at the shops of an automobile-builder, Bottiaux. It was sometimes described as the de Noue monoplane designed by Horber or Herber, an error for Obre. The fuselage was long, a very thin box, covered only amidships. The warping wings were rectangular with square tips and a good deal of dihedral; there were 2 rectangular tailplanes close together at the same levels with a triangular fin and small rudder on top. The undercarriage comprised 2 Blériot-style legs, with 2 extra S-curved skids; a castering tailwheel brought up the rear. A flat-twin engine drove the tractor propeller through a long shaft. It first flew on 6 April 1910; Obre's license received on it was dated 19 July 1910; and De Noue crashed it 9 days later at an airshow at Rennes, in Brittany. A slightly different version had a

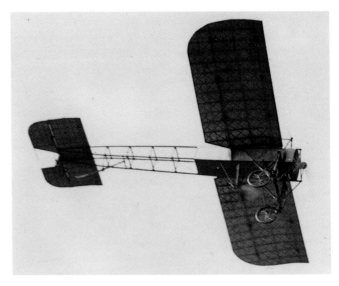

Obre No 4. Note inner-wing or covering bracing pattern. (Courtesy of the Musée de l'Air et de l'Espace/Le Bourget-France)

tall Blériot-style pylon instead of a single tall inverted Y; the skids had disappeared.

(Span: 11 m; length: 10 m; wing area: 21 sqm; gross weight: 300 kg; 50 hp flat twin air-cooled Darracq)

4. The last Obre was based on the Blériot XI, this time with a 50 hp Gnôme. The fuselage was covered from the nose to the back of the cockpit; small triangular fins with a single tall rudder were set above and below the rear of the fuselage, with a large split elevator and rectangular tailplane carried by a long skid. The wingtips were curved at the trailing edges, clearly distinguishing this machine from de Noue's. It was flying at Issy in 1911; Obre had flown it in several shows, showing little skill as a pilot.

Olivier

A balloon-glider combination appeared under this name in 1884; and the name appears again in 1912.

Above and left: two views of the Ouarnier biplane showing typical pre-WWI structural details. (Author's collection)

Ouarnier

This was a Caudron copy with a 50 hp air-cooled Renault: a large fan was mounted in a housing immediately behind the engine. 2 small square rudders pivoted above a large cut-out in the large rectangular tail; there was a tailplane but no fins. It was tested at La Vidamée in July 1911, and was reportedly being rebuilt in October.

Outrey

A glider of this name was built in 1908 at Compiègne, spanning 5 m and reported towed by a car. The machine was probably unmanned.

Ouvrière

A native of Marseille, Ouvrière seems to have begun by building gliders in 1908; the following year he was building the helicopter for Léger.

P

Pacchiotti

During the summer of 1910 Henri Chazal built a large tractor monoplane for Pacchiotti. It resembled the Blériot XII, but with a front elevator and a rectangular lifting tailplane set on top of the rear fuselage. The long rectangular rudder hinged on the sternpost was painted PACC 1 in bold capital letters. The wings had triangular ailerons partly set into the wingtips.; the propeller was set on the leading edge, chain-driven from the engine below. The undercarriage consisted of 2 castering main wheels and a fixed tailwheel. Pacchiotti took his monoplane to the airshow at Vichy in 1910 and flew it.

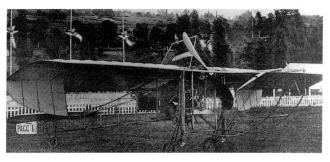

The Pacchiotti monoplane of 1910. Note the distinctive trailing ailerons. (Courtesy of the Musée de l'Air et de l'Espace/Le Bourget-France)

(Span: 9 m; length: 12 m; wing area: 25 sqm; empty weight: 500 kg; 40 hp water-cooled ENV V8)

Pajot

A glider with feather-like sections comprising the monoplane wing and monoplane tailplane – there was no vertical surface. Sliding the feathers into each other on one side or the other was to provide control; the whole thing could be folded together on the ground, supported by a 2-wheel undercarriage.

(Span: 10 m; wing area: 18 sqm; empty weight: 220 kg; loaded weight: 350 kg)

In 1926 there appeared a Pajot-designed lightplane, a pretty monoplane with a strong family resemblance to the earlier design.

Papin et Rouilly

In 1911 A Papin and D Rouilly patented their Gyroptère and built it in 1913 and 1914. The first (if unsuccessful) air-jet helicopter, their

Above and top of next page: three views of the remarkable Papin-Rouilly helicopter, showing the contours of its single rotor and the pilot's controls and swiveling cockpit; and what turned out an unsuccessful attempt to fly it on Lake Cercy. (Peter M Bowers collection; and Courtesy of the Musée de l'Air et de l'Espace/Le Bourget-France)

machine was based on the sycamore seed, which falls, turning, a one-bladed rotor. Slightly to one side of the axis of rotation was mounted a rotary motor on its back, which drove a turbine to draw air in and force it out the length of the single long airfoil-shaped blade, exiting through a nozzle at the trailing edge of the tip. The blade would turn rapidly, and the gyroscopic force of the motor would lift the blade into a positive angle of attack. Centered on the axis of rotation was the drum in which the pilot sat; it was mounted on ball-bearings and was centered against 4 horizontal rollers. The pilot controlled a separate swiveling air-duct to keep his drum-shaped seat from moving with the blade, and to provide forward thrust in flight.

Beautifully built, with compound curves and a smooth sweep of its blade, the Gyroptère was not a success. It was tested in 1915 on Lake Cercey, near Pouilly-en-Auxois in eastern France. Lead was fitted to improve the balance and increase the rpm; on 31 March it achieved 47 rpm, but was wildly out of balance, and the blade smashed repeatedly into the water, damaging itself and shaking up the pilot. The last photographs show its wing still intact.

(Length: 14 m; empty weight: 380 kg)

Parent

Of the 2 Parent brothers, one worked at Hanriot in 1909-1910; this may have been François, pilot of the first Poulain-Orange, and likely a relative of the car-builder DFP (Doriot, Flandrin, et Parent). In any case, one of the brothers was associated with a Hanriot copy built in 1910. Only the first half of the long square-section fuselage was covered, and the wings were braced from a Blériot-style pylon. The pilot sat at the trailing edge in a seat high in the fuselage, using a large steering wheel and foot pedals. The 2 elevator control levers were mounted on top of the fuselage behind the pilot. Radiators were

mounted vertically on each side, and a tiny tank hung from the cross-bar of the pylon to feed the motor by gravity. Later a very similar machine – perhaps the same one with a more rounded nose – was flown at Issy by Ernest Lhoste.

(Span: 12.5 m; length: 10 m; gross area: 32 sqm; 70 hp Labor-Aviation)

The very similar Poulain-Orange had a different engine and tank, and was fully covered: it may have been designed or built by Parent. At the end of 1910, François Parent was flying his own monoplane at Issy, showing it at some small airshows.

In 1911-12 Parent worked with Bruneau and built a very different-seeming aeroplane. Though unsuccessful, it suggested some of the streamlined designs of the 1930s and even later. The monoplane wing, unbraced, probably extended through the fuselage, the pilot's cockpit right in the middle of it; the second seat was well aft of the trailing edge. The outer panels were of greater chord and had a dihedral angle; tiny ailerons were set into the tips. The covered fuselage

The 1910 Parent, resembling the contemporary Hanriots. (Courtesy of the Musée de l'Air et de l'Espace/Le Bourget-France)

was deep at the stern, and flat-sided; there was no fin, and the rudder was hinged directly to the fuselage. Inadequate horizontal surfaces rested on top. The motor was fully cowled, with the rectangular radiator lying back at more than 45° from the motor. A 2-wheeled undercarriage was supported by 2 pairs of forward-inclined struts; 2 skids ran forward. The effect was of a rather angular 1930s racing plane. Parent and Bruneau were privates in the army at the time the machine was tested.

(Span: 9 m; length: 9 m; wing area: 22 sqm; 50 hp water-cooled V8 Vivinus)

Pasquier

In 1908 Pasquier, a former bicycle-racer, began building a biplane with a simple tailplane at Saint Hilaire-le-Grand, near Châlons-sur-Marne. The 60 hp engine of his own design was to drive 2 propellers, and weighed only 88 kg. The machine was probably not completed. He became a Blériot pilot.

(Wing area: 40 sqm; gross weight; 400 kg including pilot)

Passerat et Radiguet

Automobile-body makers and propeller-makers since 1909, Passerat and Radiguet introduced their monoplane at the 1910 Exposition in Paris. It resembled a Blériot XI with a stalky 4 parallel-strut undercarriage supplemented with Blériot-style looped bamboo canes for a skid. Oyster-shell wing-tip ailerons were fitted. The engine was a 4-cylinder radial Berthaud.

By 1911 Berthaud had built a copy of this machine, very likely of metal, referred to as the Moreau-Berthaud Sylphide. At the same time Passerat and Radiguet announced they had registered a design to compete in the 1911 Concours Militaire, but this machine never appeared.

Paulat

Emile Paulat was building a high-wing monoplane at Marseille in the summer of 1910. It was reported to have automatically-controlled ailerons and a fuselage made of "hammer-wrought steel plates." It may not have been completed.

It is hard to believe that this Parent machine came only a year after the one in the preceding photograph. (Courtesy of the Musée de l'Air et de l'Espace/Le Bourget-France)

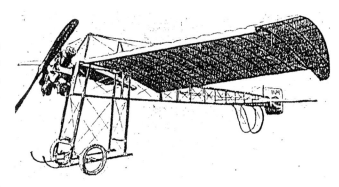

The 1910 Passerat-Radiguet with wingtip ailerons. (Author's collection)

(Span: 9 m; length: 12 m; gross weight: 490 kg; 40 hp 4-cylinder Turcat-Méry)

Paulhan

Although as a pilot the greatest prize-winner of his time, Louis Paulhan was a relatively unsuccessful constructor; his aeronautical work ended before World War II.

During his military service from 1905 to 1908, he was assigned to Chalais-Meudon, where he worked with Ferdinand Ferber. With Louis Peyret he built a series of large tandem monoplane models which marked the start of his career. At least one of them was about 4 m in span, the 2 pairs of wings with arched dihedral; 2 pusher propellers were mounted on outriggers between the wings. A forward elevator sat high above the boat-shaped hull.

He became the captain of Surcouf's dirigible Ville de Paris, and was a major contributor to the design of Kapferer's Astra monoplanes, the second of which resembled closely his big model. And his models won him a prize: a complete Voisin airframe. He christened it Octavie III; it was the first Gnôme-powered aeroplane to fly.

In 1910 he started his aeroplane-building business in association with Henri Fabre, and in February 1911 built his "machine à voler" (flying machine); it was similar to the earlier Fabre seaplanes, but a biplane. Fabre girders were used as leading edges to which the wing coverings were laced, with battens loose in pockets every few inches; 2 more, but covered over, were used to carry the forward elevator and aft tailplane. 4 single struts separated the upper and lower wing girders. Shorter Fabre spars were used as leading edges of the other surfaces. A streamlined aluminum nacelle was supported between the wings and carried 2 pilots. Long skids ran forward from between the pairs of wheels up to the forward elevator, which was split right and left and could be moved differentially, giving the effect of ailerons. Paulhan rigged his machine with cables instead of wires, and claimed to have assembled it slack so that rough air would not throw it out of alignment.

(Span: 12.2 m; length: 8.5 m; wing area: 30 sqm; gross weight: 610 kg; top speed: 80 kmh; 50 hp Gnôme)

A second biplane followed it, this time with no Fabre girders at all: the wings had steel tube leading edges and main spars, and pairs of thin interplane struts braced both. 2 thin booms supported the front elevator, and a second pair supported the tail. Otherwise it was similar to the first biplane, though seemingly with a wire trailing edge and fixed ribs; it retained the aluminum nacelle. Paulhan flew it in March 1911 at St Cyr. It was easily disassembled for transport.

A third one followed, this time with a single boom replacing the pair of tail outriggers, and a slightly different rib arrangement. Paulhan flew this in May 1911.

A big triplane was shown in March 1911 at the Concours Militaire, where it achieved no success at all. Although resembling the earlier biplanes, it was quite different in construction. It was a 4-seater designed with the assistance of Antoine Odier, and was built mainly of metal. The 2 spars in each wing were made of 3 tapered tubes screwed together, and the ribs were metal blades protected from corrosion. Assembly was done with collars, clamping bands, and bolted brackets: no welding was used. The machine rested on 2 double pairs of wheels, each double pair with a long skid between them, tipped by another pair of small wheels. The wingtips were fan-shaped with 8 hinged ribs which served as ailerons. 2 semicircular rudders flanked the tailplane, whose trailing edge was linked to the forward elevator. The pilot and 3 passengers sat side by side in 2 rows in the aluminum nacelle which was referred to as "the wooden shoe" because of its shape. The controls consisted of a rudder bar and a vertical lever hanging from the upper wing.

(Span: 13.8 m; length: 10.2 m; wing area: 63 sqm; empty weight: 711 kg; gross weight: 1050 kg; Gnôme (at the Concours); a 60 hp air-cooled V8 was subsequently fitted)

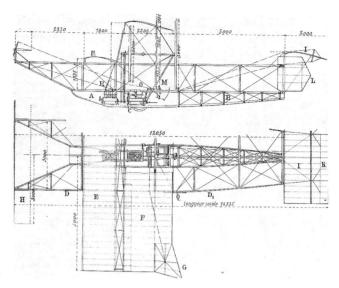

A contemporary drawing of the 1910 Paulat back-staggered amphibian. The engine buried low in the hull drove 2 counter-rotating propellers of different sizes through belts. This machine is not the one described in the text, and may not have been built at all. (Author's collection)

Louis Paulhan (L) and Louis Peyret (R) with their big model with twin pusher propellers on outriggers between the wings. (Author's collection)

The first version of Paulhan's biplane, with Fabre-type spars with the fabric laced to them. (Author's collection)

The second version of the Paulhan biplane, with standard spars. (Courtesy of the Musée de l'Air et de l'Espace/Le Bourget-France)

The fate of Paulhan's machines à voler is not clear. The triplane flew first at St Cyr where Paulhan had his school and his hangar; the biplane is likely to have been used there as a trainer. But the triplane was still in use in 1912 and was reported sold to a Marchenay School at Juvisy, to be flown by Camille Guillaume de Mauriac. But photographs showing it in flight or even with the motor running are very rare. Paulhan then sponsored the construction of Victor Tatin's Aérotorpille.

Paulhan's firm also license-built 2 Curtiss designs, the Triad amphibian, and the F-Boat. 2 Triads were entered at the Tamise meeting in Belgium, piloted by Barra and Mollien. The Paulhan-Curtiss Triads were 2-seaters, with a forward elevator mounted over the front of the main float.

The Paulhan, folded. Note the basic rigid wing frame; all the rest flexed and folded. (Author's collection)

(Span: 8.75 m; length: 8.3 m)

The Paulhan-Curtiss F-Boat included many Curtiss-built parts. Paulhan himself flew it on its first test in France on 29 December 1912 at Bezons, on the Seine. It differed from its American cousin in having a flexible, rather than a hinged, elevator surface; a single diagonal strut supported only the leading edge of the wing overhang, rather than the pair used in the American version. At least 4 of the French-made boats were sold to Italy.

Two views of the Paulhan triplane of 1911. Note the control stick dangling from the top wing over the cockpit, and the 8-wheeled landing gear. (Courtesy of the Musée de l'Air et de l'Espace/Le Bourget-France)

(Span: 10 m; length: 8.5 m; gross weight: 500 kg; Curtiss OX5)

During World War I Paulhan was assigned to service in the Balkans, where he was credited with 2 victories in air combat.

Paumier

Emile Paumier is one of the few pre-War French home-builders whose work survives: his last aeroplane was donated to the Musée de l'Air et de l'Espace and is currently on exhibit. His first machine was built at Lemerle, rue Croix Nivert, Paris, not far from the airfield at Issy, to which it was driven at the end of 1910.

The long square fuselage was uncovered and untapered at the tail, and was set slightly above the lower wing. A small flat twin was mounted in a short nose; the tail surfaces were all large rectangles mounted on top of the fuselage with elevators at the tips of the tailplane. The rectangular wings were set at a high angle of attack and had large hanging ailerons. A pair of main wheels were supported by a maze of struts, and short skids protruded forward. Paumier and his mechanic Hébert modified the aeroplane a few weeks after its appearance, probably at Héritier's workshop: the nose was lengthened and the engine increased from 20 to 50 hp, the top wings were lengthened and the angle of attack reduced. Further changes included the use of an even larger motor.

(Span: (upper) 10.5 m; (lower) c 5 m; wing area: 23 sqm; gross weight: 350kg; 20 hp flat twin Dutheil et Chalmers, then a 50 hp Anzani, then an 80 hp Anzani)

The second Paumier was introduced as No 2, but often referred to as No 3; it had the same fuselage with an even larger Anzani, and a second rudder fitted below the tailplane. New and longer equal-span wings with high aspect-ratio were built.

(Span: 11.8 m; length: c 7.5 m; 100 hp 10-cylinder Anzani)

Paumier was assigned to Mourmelon for his military service in 1912, and was allowed to fly his biplane, provided cocardes were painted under the wings. In 1914 the Army commandeered the motor, and the aeroplane never flew again, finally to be donated to the Musée de l'Air. Paumier began home-building again in the late 1950s.

Péan

In 1908 Péan de Saint Gilles tested unsuccessfully a big tailless monoplane at Bagatelle; he claimed to have based the design on Vuia's principles. The gull wing was set high on an openwork box frame wider than it was long; the airfoil section was flat. The pilot sat low in the middle of the frame behind the motor, which drove 2 small counter-rotating propellers through belts. The machine sat on a pair of bicycle wheels with a tailwheel behind the pilot's seat.

(Span: c 10 m; wing area: 28 sqm; gross weight: 250 kg; 12 hp Buchet)

The Paulhan-built Curtiss Triad. (Courtesy of the Musée de l'Air et de l'Espace/ Le Bourget-France)

The Paulhan-Curtiss F-Boat. The additional strut to the lower wing, and the simplified cowl are some of the differences from the American version. (Courtesy of the Musée de l'Air et de l'Espace/Le Bourget-France)

The rather uncompromising Paumier in flight. (Courtesy of the Musée de l'Air et de l'Espace/Le Bourget-France)

Pégase

This triplane by an unknown builder appeared at La Seyne in 1909.

Pelletier et Sergeant

This was a biplane at Juvisy which in 1910 was awaiting delivery of a Labor-Picker engine.

Pelliat

Pelliat is better known for his series of Rationnelle propellers than for his aircraft, but he did build one or perhaps 2. In 1910 he completed a Blériot XI copy powered by a 28 hp 3-cylinder Viale; the trapezoidal wings warped, and had squared-off tips. It was flown at Issy in November 1910 and was at that time referred to as the Pelliat-Viale; it was later flow at Saint-Samerin. In 1911 a large monoplane under Pelliat's name with a 60 hp ENV and a Rationnelle propeller was seen in the Clément-Bayard hangar; it is not clear whether this was a second machine or the same one.

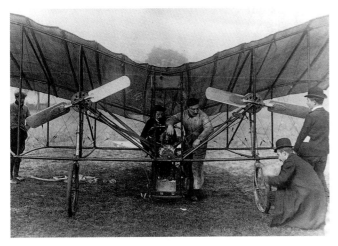
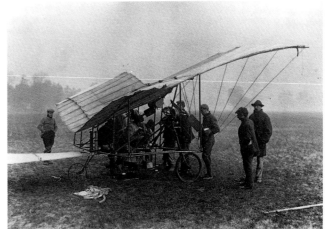

Since the configuration of the Péan monoplane is hard to take in from one angle alone, here are 2. It is interesting to see how many early experimenters used the 12 hp Buchet, clearly too small. (Courtesy of the Musée de l'Air et de l'Espace/Le Bourget-France)

(Span: 8.7 m; length: 8.6 m; wing area: 17 sqm; empty weight: 230 kg)

Perrin et Bethenot

This Wright copy was to have had a single pusher propeller, though no engine seems to have been fitted. In October 1909 it was towed like a glider – perhaps at Lyon.

Perron

A biplane named Lis with a 50 hp Anzani appeared at Issy in 1911.

Perrot et Duval

A seaplane named La Mouette (seagull) was registered for the 1912 meet at Monaco where it was to be flown by Taddeoli; it was reported crashed on Lake Geneva in March 1912.

Petit-Conchis

Armand Petit-Conchis was one of the many subcontractors who furnished parts and propellers to aircraft builders in 1908. At the end of the year he was building a copy of a Wright fitted with a tail and wheels for the Société des Elèves-Ingénieurs Industriels de France (association of students in engineering schools). Another machine, or perhaps the same one, with the same name was registered for the 1909 contest at Monaco, powered by a Farcot engine.

(Wing area: 42 sqm; 30 hp 6-cylinder motor)

Peyret

Captain Ferdinand Ferber tested a tandem monoplane glider with this name at Chalais – but it may have been only a model. It had a triangular-section fuselage girder and a forward elevator. Peyret may also have designed a model from which Louis Paulhan designed the Kapferer aeroplane built by Astra.

Philippon

One of the more audacious designs of 1913, this tandem monoplane was designed "to be flown like a bird." There was no tail nor rudder of any kind; 3 steering wheels allowed the daring aeronaut to vary the incidence of the ailerons (small surfaces set between the pairs of monoplane wings) together, to control pitch; or separately, to control yaw; to increase the wings' angles of attack to slow down and nose up on landing, like a bird; to move the wings bodily fore and aft to control pitch. The wonder was it took only 3 control wheels. A long open box sat on 3 wheels, the pilot ahead of the motor, which drove a pusher propeller aft of the rearmost wings through a diagonal shaft and Cardan joints.

(Span: 5.44 m; length: c 8 m; wing area: 16.2 sqm; 100 hp ENV V8)

Piau

In 1909 Charles Piau had a tractor aeroplane built by Labaudie et Puthet, powered by a 15 hp Zedel motor, to be flown by Alfred Gauthier. This or another monoplane built by the same firm was tested at the end of 1909; yet another (or the same) monoplane called La Comète also built by Labaudie et Puthet was tested at Juvisy in May 1910.

An unfortunately dark picture of the tandem monoplane by Philippon. The pilot and engine are in the middle, and the pusher propeller is at the far left. Small tilting control surfaces are visible high up between the wings on each side. (Author's collection)

(The first Piau): span: 10 m; length: 8 m; wing area: 36 sqm; 25 hp motor)

Pichou

Alfred Pichou studied flying machines from 1872 to 1912, and the result of his efforts was his Autoaérienne with lifting surfaces made like paddle-wheels fitted parallel to the direction of flight. The position of the paddles varied through gears according to the rotation of the wheels.

Picot et Christophe

In 1909 2 infantrymen of the 156th Regiment assigned to Toul, in the eastern part of France, built a glider spanning 5 m with a wing area of 19 sqm. They intended to fit a pedal-powered propeller.

Pierlot

A machine of this name was built in 1910, perhaps by Espinosa.

Piffard

This large pusher biplane had its forward elevator mounted on outriggers; another set of outriggers supported the high-set horizontal tail. The most striking feature of the Piffard was a pair of arched structures incorporating high curved skids and the 2 main wheels; a third wheel was set forward on a separate structure. A pair of copper-tubing radiators was mounted above and forward of the ENV engine and its pusher propeller. A biplane elevator cell was set high on 3 pairs of outriggers. The machine may not have been completed.

Piquerez

Charles de Piquerez was an explorer who asked de Pischoff and Koechlin in December 1908 to build him a large biplane which he claimed to be his own design, though it included construction details which had appeared earlier in their work. It appeared, unsuccessfully, at Issy-les-Moulineaux in April and May 1909. The long thin streamlined box fuselage was fully covered, and carried biplane tail cells at each end; the equal-span rectangular wings were set nearly amidships, near the engine, which drove 2 pusher propellers on outriggers at each side of the rear fuselage. Small wingtip panels could be warped upward, perhaps to serve as ailerons or rudders. The aft tail cell had side-curtains, but seemingly no moving vertical surfaces. The machine sat on pairs of castering wheels both fore and aft; the pilot was above the front pair, and the passenger was well behind him, between the wings.

For all its size, the Piquerez was an oddly graceful looking machine; it was driven to Chartres for testing in June 1909, where it crashed on its first flight in July. A 50 hp Dutheil et Chalmers replaced the 40 hp one, and as a monoplane it hopped briefly on 27 August and crashed again. The single wing was braced with twin masts, the 2 biplane tail cells were replaced with single horizontal surfaces, and the aft pair of wheels became a single wheel.

(Span: 10.8 m (some sources say 14); length: 10.6 m; total area: 78-80 sqm; gross weight: 600 kg; 40 hp Dutheil-et-Chalmers)

Above and below: Two views of the Piquerez biplane of 1909. The radiator seems to have changed position between the times of these 2 photos. (Courtesy of the Musée de l'Air et de l'Espace/Le Bourget-France)

De Pischoff

Alfred de Pischoff was born in Austria of French parents; by 1907 he had moved back to France and had designed and had built a biplane glider like Ferber's, which he had intended to power with a 25 hp Anzani.

De Pischoff No 1: In 1907 he designed a small biplane with the same Anzani and had it built at the Chauvière works; it may indeed have been the glider re-worked. It looked surprisingly modern with its overhung top wings, tractor propeller and neat tricycle undercarriage. The wings arched gracefully upward at the tips, and the pilot sat somewhat precariously between them on a raised seat immediately aft of the motor. From his seat a long fan shaped tailplane with rectangular elevators ran back,

The first de Pischoff design; it is shown taxiing, but not flying. (Courtesy of the Musée de l'Air et de l'Espace/Le Bourget-France)

joined at the trailing edges by a thin spar which ran through a cut-out in the fin. It was damaged in a test in November 1907, and did not actually fly.

(Span: 10 m; wing area: 25 sqm)

<u>Autoplan:</u> In 1909 de Pischoff returned to his native Austria; and working with 2 German engineers Werner and Pfederer, designed and built at Wiener-Neustadt the monoplane known as the Autoplan. Before the summer of 1910 de Pischoff had brought his new machine back to France: it still carried on its side fairings the initials PWP, which disappeared subsequently. The Société Autoplan was formed before the 1910 Salon to exploit de Pischoff's patents.

The Autoplan was designed roughly as a winged car with a real ash chassis. The 60 hp water-cooled ENV engine nestled inside an aluminum top cowl with an automobile-style radiator in front; seats were side-by-side behind the motor. The monoplane wing was supported well above the nacelle; it was built with rigid leading edges and flexible trailing edges, and the tips curled up and were joined by springs so that one would go down if the other went up in a gust: automatic stability was the goal of too many French designers of the period. The tail was set at the ends of 4 tailbooms arranged in a trapezoidal section, and comprised a Blériot-type tailplane with tip elevators, 2 small rudders above it, and a small secondary triangular tailplane above them; the whole assembly rested on 2 castering tailwheels, while the front end used 2 non-castering main wheels. In France the PWF initials on the sides were replaced by PAP, and de Pischoff's name appeared on the rudders.

(Span: 11 m; length: 9.7 m; wing area: c 27 sqm; empty weight: 365 kg; 60 hp ENV)

The general arrangement of the subsequent Autoplans did not vary much from that of the first one. It is likely the first propeller was geared down to 700 rpm, with a diameter of 3.14 m and a pitch of 2.75 m. In 1910 it was likely to be direct-driven at 1200 rpm with a diameter of 2.5 m. The engine cowl was extended around the 2 seats. At the 1910 Salon the Autoplan was offered with a 50 hp Daimler; and also with a 60 hp motor, as a Type Militaire. After de Pischoff's school moved from Issy to Juvisy, the 50 hp Daimler version was tested in January 1911, and was described as taking off after a long run and climbing slowly.

3 were said to be under construction at Boulogne-Billancourt, one of them meant for Russia; Shavrov confirms that 2 were bought for Russian flying clubs, first with 50 hp ENVs and later with 70 or 85 hp Labor-Aviations, and that all performances were poor. At the same time that the Autoplan was being described in France as having a gross weight of 520 kg, a 4-cylinder 70 hp Labor driving a geared propeller of 2.85-meter diameter and 1.8-meter pitch at 900 rpm was installed. The 2 seats

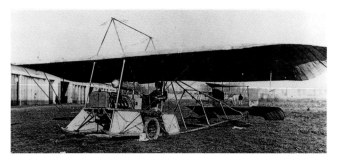

One of the de Pischoff Autoplans; the pilot seems to be driving an automobile. (Courtesy of the Musée de l'Air et de l'Espace/Le Bourget-France)

were replaced by a single one. In 1913 the span was increased to 13 m (gross weight 570 kg) with no better performance.

But by 1911 de Pischoff had sold his assets in the design to Cornet, at Juvisy, and for a while the Autoplan was known as the Cornet. In 1920 de Pischoff developed a tiny biplane powered with a small flat twin. The pilot sat on the tail-boom like a motorcycle; in 1922, testing an improved variant, de Pischoff spun in and was killed.

Pivot

Before joining Koechlin to develop the Pivot-Koechlin monoplane in 1911, Pivot had designed and built a small monoplane with the assistance of Doutre. The wings were trapezoidal with heavy dihedral, wire-braced, with struts from the undercarriage underneath; the fuselage was triangular in section and uncovered; a small angular rudder stood alone above the large tailplane and elevator. A tailwheel supported the rear, and a pair of wheels and a forest of struts supported the front. A 50 hp 5-cylinder Anzani was installed behind a triangular metal plate. The machine was reported tested at Issy in August 1910, flown by Vasseur.

(Span: c 6 m)

In 1924 Pivot was building automobiles in small quantities.

Plaisant

Completed in May 1910, Gustave Plaisant's tractor monoplane represented yet another method of control: the parasol wing was shaped

The relatively simple Pivot monoplane, with an extremely complex undercarriage arrangement. Someone at the time wrote Yvonne across the face of the lady pilot...? (Courtesy of the Musée de l'Air et de l'Espace/Le Bourget-France)

like a bird's, even with rectangular plates overlapping each other at the trailing edge like feathers. The whole wing rocked from side to side for control. A long uncovered framework on 3 wheels supported the rectangular tailplane, and there was no vertical surface anywhere. The Journals report that it "stalled" at Issy in September 1910, and flipped onto its back at Béthény in December.

(Span: 8.7 m; length: 8.18 m; wing area: 22 sqm; 40 hp inverted inline Gyp)

Photographs taken in his shop (20, Boulevard Malesherbes, Paris) show the same fuselage and undercarriage, and only the tilting center-section of the wing, but with a new Plaisant invention which he called Propulseur Cycloïdal. It was fitted to the airframe in 2 versions, each more remarkable then the other. One featured a rotating bar of 3-4 meters in length fitted to the propeller shaft, with chains driving 2 separate propellers of perhaps 2 meters in diameter, one at each end. The central bar turned, and each of the propellers turned as it turned. The other featured a complex 4-armed structure with a geared differential mounted in the middle, and 4 small propellers turning separately at the ends of the arms. The whole rig was wire-braced; gears everywhere. It is possible that Plaisant tried the Propulseur Cycloïdal before the feathered wing design.

Platel
J Platel was a toy manufacturer who had a flimsy-looking copy of the Demoiselle built in 1909; the fabric was laced to the spars. It sat on 3 wheels, and apparently could be driven on the ground with wings folded; it arrived in this way at Bagatelle. The first flights were 2000 m in length at a 2-meter altitude.

(Span: 6 m; length: 7 m; wing area: 12 sqm; weight: 149 kg; 24-28 hp Anzani)

Poignard et Tranchard
Octave Poignard had a biplane built by Tranchard at Brinon-sur-Sauldre; a photograph shows it being assembled in a rough shed. A large divided rectangular forward elevator was mounted on triangular outriggers, the biplane tail cell on another pair. The wings had curved tips and were single-bay, seemingly very short for this machine and this period.

Then he had the same firm build his monoplane in 1911. The airframe was entirely of ash, the tail boom being attached to the fuselage with 2 sleeves; a cruciform swallowtail rode at the end. Ailerons were mounted at the tips of the rectangular wings. The undercarriage was set like the Antoinette on a single post, and was apparently steerable. The 9-cylinder engine cowled in aluminum plates was "cooled by radiance" and drove a clutched 2-bladed propeller at 1100 rpm.

(Span: 11 m; length: 10 m; wing area: 24 sqm; empty weight: 330 kg; Antoinette)

The Plaisant rocking-wing monoplane, complete with feather-like wing covering. (Author's collection)

One of at least 2 versions of the Plaisant Propulseur Cyclöidal propeller arrangement. This one comprises a rotating bar with spinning propellers at each end, the whole thing chain-driven and mounted in what looks like the fuselage of his aeroplane. (Author's collection)

Another version of the Plaisant Propulseur Cyclöidal system, with a rotating cross with 4 small propellers set into the corners. Note the complex gearing: his 40 hp engine would not have sufficed for all this. (Author's collection)

Poire

Alphonse Poire became known for looping a Henri Farman. He was reported to have started his flying career at Issy on an aeroplane of his own design, but no trace of this machine seems to have survived. Poire (also spelled Poirée) may have contributed to the design, construction, or testing of someone else's aeroplane, and then pretended as some did that the aeroplane had been his own. He died in a crash at the end of 1922.

Poix et Deroig

Poix et Deroig showed their big monoplane at the 1911 Salon; they had built it in Reuil, west of Paris, clearly with the Hanriot in mind, but with some original structural innovations. From the wings aft the fuselage was wood and covered with veneer, but the forward part with the engine was built around a metal girder. The rectangular wings could warp. The undercarriage resembled that of the Hanriot, with 6 struts, 2 skids and 2 wheels.

(Span: 11 m; length: 10 m; wing area: 25 sqm; gross weight: 580 kg; 110 hp 4-cylinder inline Clément-Bayard)

Pompeien Piraud

A scene-painter turned dentist, Jean-Claude Pompeien Piraud began patenting ornithopters in 1870; he tried models, unsuccessfully. During this period he passed on to Gabriel Voisin what little was known at the time of aviation science. Gabriel Voisin reported in his autobiography:

> M Pompeien Piraud had contrived an ornithopter-like flying machine; and overcoming incredible difficulties, he was building himself, near the Parc de la Tête d'Or, a cock-and-bull apparatus powered by a steam-engine... The previous models he had built could not fly... He then had the idea of tying his machine to pulleys under a cable and to stretch that between 2 poplars...

The model had bat-like wings actuated through balancing poles by the motor, which was mounted inside a roughly streamlined hull.

(Span: 6.25 m; hull length: 2 m; hull width: .6 m)

In 1898 he began a full-sized machine which was frequently publicized in 1907, shortly before he died.

Ponche et Primard

Charles Ponche and Maurice Primard were metallurgists in Long, Somme, in northern France. In 1911 they designed a monoplane similar to the de Pischoff Autoplan, though built entirely of metal. Known as Tubavion, it was built around a long tubular boom, on which was mounted the rectangular wing and the pusher engine; the pusher propeller turned on bearings with the boom as axis, and the tailplane and elevators were attached to the end, to which the semicircular rudder was hinged. The pilot sat below with the passenger beside him, immediately aft of the cowled engine, which drove the propeller above through a rearward shaft, chains, and sprockets. Fitted between the 2

The lightweight Demoiselle copy by Platel, in 1909. (Author's collection)

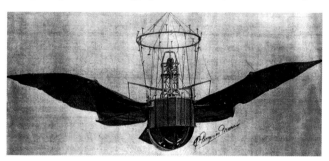

A signed photograph of a model of Pompeien Piraud's 1870 flying machine. (Author's collection)

pairs of wheels, the engine behind its curved rectangular radiator was cowled. The wing and tailplane were of thin sheet aluminum with aluminum ribs fixed on top; instead of welding they used the method of "hot nesting inside forged aluminum casings." The machine was shown at the 1911 Salon.

(Span: 9.7 m; length: 9.5 m; wing area: 18 sqm; empty weight: 320 kg; gross weight: 420 kg; 70 hp water-cooled Labor turning the propeller at 800 rpm)

After unsuccessful tests, the Ponche et Primard underwent many modifications. It was reported to have made its maiden flight in March 1912, and to have been taken to Reims in May. Photos taken at the end of 1912 show the engineers' efforts to lighten their aeroplane: cowling and seat fairings were removed; 2 of the 4 wheels were taken off, and 2 tandem seats replaced the double one. One version had a handsome streamlined nacelle in aluminum with the 2 seats in tandem. Fabric covering was applied to the top of the wing; new tail

An early version of the Ponche et Primard Tubavion, still with the low-set engine and side-by-side seating, and with only 2 wheels. (Courtesy of the Musée de l'Air et de l'Espace/Le Bourget-France)

surfaces covered in fabric only were substituted for the all-metal ones, and a new 70 hp Gnôme was on top the top of the wing aft of the propeller: it is likely that a 50 hp Gnôme was also tested. The new wing had to have the center of the trailing edge cut out to allow for the rotation of these new engines. The test pilots at Reims were Goffin and Mère.

Ponchel

Under this name a steam-powered design was shown in 1901 at the Salon de l'Auto.

Ponnier

Ponnier's early work appeared while he was working for Hanriot; his first designs were known as Hanriots. The F1, the first design to carry his name at all, also bore the name of Pagny – the Ponnier-Pagny was a single-seat armored pusher biplane with an 80 hp Gnôme. The covered nacelle was shovel-nosed; the outrigger tail structure was triangular in section with the single beam at the bottom.

(Span: 13 m, 8 m; length: 7.95 m; wing area: 30 sqm; weight empty: 240 kg; weight loaded: 550 kg; speed: 105 kmh.

A second version had an uncovered box nacelle with a distinctively sloping front.

The first of his machines to bear Ponnier's name alone – though it appeared in one of the Hanriot catalogs with the name Hanriot – was the D.I, the most famous of which flew at Reims in 1912 and 1913. It was a pretty little Nieuport single-seater monoplane look-alike, but with the familiar Hanriot 4-legged undercarriage and a small pyramidal pylon structure.

(Span: 8.9 m; length: 7.08 m; wing area: 18 sqm; loaded weight: 465 kg; speed: 110 kmh; 50-60 hp Gnôme)

A later version, with the trailing edge-mounted Gnôme, and the aluminum tandem-seated nacelle. Note the generous use of castings at all the joints. (Courtesy of the Musée de l'Air et de l'Espace/Le Bourget-France)

The Ponnier F1 with the covered nacelle. (Courtesy of the Musée de l'Air et de l'Espace/Le Bourget-France)

Below: The second version of the first Ponnier, the F1. (Author's collection)

Even more famous than the D.I, the D.III was flown in the Gordon-Bennett race at Reims, also in 1913, by Védrines; his machine was marked F5.

(Span: 7 m; length; 5.5 m; wing area: 8 sqm; loaded weight: 500 kg; speed: 200 kmh; 160 hp Gnôme)

In the same year a variant was designated Type Cavalrie, with divided elevators as opposed to the one-piece set of the D.III.

(Span: 9.2 m; length: 5.26 m; wing area: 13 sqm; weight empty: 215 kg; weight loaded: 375 kg; speed: from 60 to 135 kmh)

Ponnier also built a small 2-seater trainer, Type Ecole, in 1914. It had a 3-cylinder engine and an uncovered fuselage supported by a 4-legged undercarriage. In July 1914 the firm offered the L1, also a Type Cavalrie, a small single-seater biplane with a 50 hp Gnôme.

(Span: 8 m, 7.2 m; length: 5.5 m; wing area: 20 sqm; weight empty: 260 kg)

Pons

Between 1910 and 1912 Pierre Pons probably formed the SAFA (Société Anonyme Français d'Aviation). This firm may have built or rebuilt and sold Caudrons and the curious machine described below.

The all-metal pusher canard biplane built by Pons in 1911 for Captain Morel was already being referred to by the end of the year and early into 1912 as the Morel; it made its few short flights at Issy in April 1912. Pons and Morel may have been partners, or Morel the sponsor and Pons the designer; more likely, Pons was the constructor and Morel the designer.

The rudder and elevators were mounted on top of the long pointed nose, and the pilot sat high on the fuselage amidships. The most distinctive feature of the Pons was the arrangement of its wings, very close together; the top one was fixed on the upper longerons at the rear end of the fuselage, and the lower one pivoted on its main spar, each side differentially, for aileron control. It was braced to the fixed upper wing with 2 V-shaped panels on each side, pivoted on the main spar of the lower wing; the outer V on each side was covered to serve as a fin. The top wing was of airfoil section, the lower was flat.

The structure was of steel tubing covered by sheet aluminum, and sat on a tricycle undercarriage, 2 close-set wheels forming the forward point of the triangle. Only 9 bolts were needed to disassemble the entire machine.

(Span: 9 m; length: 6.5 m; wing area (top): 11 sqm; total: 22 sqm (Pons claimed the wing area when the lower wing was pivoted fully was only 15.2 sqm); weight: 400 kg; 60 hp Anzani)

Poulain-Orange

Gabriel Poulain was a famous bicycle-racer who held at least one speed record on the track. In 1910 his first aeroplane appeared, a handsome design similar to the Hanriot, with a long rectangular-section covered fuselage, Blériot-style pylon, triangular fin and tailplane, and

Jules Védrines in the Ponnier D.III at Reims. (Courtesy of the Musée de l'Air et de l'Espace/Le Bourget-France)

The Ponnier Type Ecole. (Courtesy of the Musée de l'Air et de l'Espace/Le Bourget-France)

A close-up of the Pons canard. Note abrupt change in cross-section of the forward fuselage. (Author's collection)

trapezoidal rudder and elevators; the motor was probably a Labor-Aviation. The machine was damaged in a crash in 1911; and to escape the draft, Poulain fled to Germany and opened a flying school at Johannisthal.

In 1911 he showed another monoplane, this one with tail surfaces like the Antoinette's, a Blériot undercarriage, and Poulain in big letters on the big fin.

In 1912 his third design appeared, this time with a long triangular-section fuselage, sometimes fully covered, sometimes covered only in front. The wings were rectangular with nearly square tips; the undercarriage repeated the Blériot style, but the pylon was now a 4-strut pyramid. The Antoinette triangular rudders were replaced by 2 curved

The Poulain-Orange No 1 of 1911. (Courtesy of the Musée de l'Air et de l'Espace/Le Bourget-France)

sections. The engine was an Argus, and a streamlined fuel tank was fitted under the fuselage between the undercarriage legs. An Anzani was later substituted, with a rectangular fuel tank in front of the pilot to serve as a windscreen.

He also exhibited a "giant monoplane" of 18-meter span, built by Mallet, powered by a 24 hp Labor-Picker.

Le Prieur

Towards the end of 1909, Yves le Prieur, a young Navy officer and attaché to the French embassy in Tokyo, designed and tested a large biplane glider resembling the Henry Farman III. The equal-span wings had no dihedral and the cell was mounted on 6 tiny wheels; the biplane tail cell with side-curtains and central rudder was attached to the ends of 4 outriggers, and a large square surface served as forward elevator. Ailerons were fitted to the lower wings only. On the side-curtains of the tail cell was painted Le Prieur No 3; nothing is known about No 1 or a possible No 2. The glider flew in Japan, towed by a car; it may have been the first heavier-than-air machine to fly in Ja-

A later Poulain-Orange, but in the same year. (Author's collection)

pan. In 1916 Le Prieur invented the air-to-air rockets to be used by French fighters against German observation balloons.

Proudhon

This aeroplane appeared in 1911, a tractor monoplane with a long uncovered triangular-section fuselage, a tall rectangular rudder, 2-wheel undercarriage, and skids.

De Puiseux

In 1909 the Comte Gustave de Puiseux struggled to fly his Cycloplane,

The Argus version of the Poulain Orange No 3. (Courtesy of the Musée de l'Air et de l'Espace/Le Bourget-France)

The Anzani version of the same machine. (Courtesy of the Musée de l'Air et de l'Espace/Le Bourget-France)

built by Vinet, at Ouistreham, on the Channel coast. It resembled a 2-cell box-kite with short wing extensions, all mounted high above a bicycle, whose rear wheel served as a giant pulley for a belt (or bicycle chain) driving a tiny tractor propeller out ahead of the front cell. It may have been tried later with a 1.5 hp motor, and may also have been the mock-up for a bigger machine called La Mouche (fly), with 2 counter-rotating propellers. The wing panels, broad and short, were to fold down on each side so La Mouche could be driven on the highway; it seems also to have been designed to be converted from a glider to a powered aeroplane. It had a box-girder fuselage, slightly tapering aft, which rested high above a 4-wheeled rectangular frame on which sat the motor, forward radiator, and the pilot. It was tested, unsuccessfully, in 1910.

(Span: 7 m; length: 6.4 m; wing area: 10.9 sqm; weight (probably the kite cells only): 44 kg)

R

Ramel

Inspired by Santos-Dumont and Albert Moreau, G Ramel designed in 1911-1912 an automatically stable biplane, controlled by the pilot's movable seat. Fitted with both front and rear elevators, each with a central fin, and a rudder at the rear, the machine had a box-like nacelle with the motor forward and the seat aft. The seat, with the controls attached, was mounted on 2 perpendicular supports, each rolling on an arched rail, so the seat was horizontal at all times. Ailerons pivoted sideways between the outer wing struts. The machine sat on 2 wheels under the lower wing, with a stabilizing wheel at each end of the fuselage frame. It was built near Fismes, between Reims and Soisson, and tested by Trotton for the first time at Juvisy on 3 October 1911; it was never heard from again.

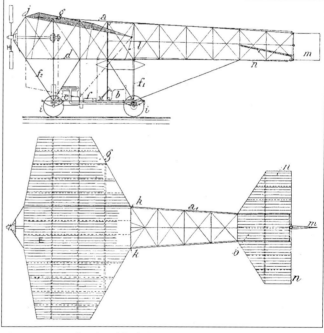

A contemporary drawing of the de Puiseux Cycloplane in its powered version. (Author's collection)

(Span: 9 m; 3-cylinder Anzani)

Ramet

Several gliders of this name were tested at Berck in 1908-1909; during 1909 at least one biplane and one quadruplane were tried. (The name might have been Ramel.)

Ranoli (Romoli?), Doye, et Légal

The names of this otherwise unknown aeroplane being built in 1911 may be incorrectly spelled, and the designer may have been yet a fourth man.

Ratmanoff

The designer and builder of the Normale propeller, Ratmanoff may have begun his aeronautical career with Avia at St Die, where he was reported testing a glider in May 1909. He built at least 2 of the de Beer monoplanes, and at least 2 2-seater monoplanes of his own design, one of which was exhibited beside one of the de Beers at the 1913 Paris Salon.

It was a neat side-by-side trainer, with rectangular wings of fixed incidence, unlike the de Beer. It had a covered fuselage tapering to a horizontal knife-edge at the tail, long triangular fixed tail surfaces, a 4-strut pylon and a half-cowled 10-cylinder radial Anzani. The wings warped through a sprocket and chain, operated by foot-pedals: the pilot could choose between large and small sprockets to adjust the sensitivity of the warp control. The arrangement for tightening the bracing wires in the fuselage was unusual: instead of turnbuckles, a small rod was passed through the base of each cross member parallel to the longeron, and the wires at each side were attached to the ends of the rod. 2 bolts ran through the longeron parallel to the cross-member; tightening them at the same time drew the rod closer to the longeron, tightening the wires. Meant to make rigging easier, this device only weakened the structure at every joint.

The other 2-seater sat the pilots in tandem.

Ravaud

Sometimes the distinction between aeroplane, hydroplane, and motorboat become blurred: the term "aéroscaphe" describes some sort of combination. Roger Ravaud built 2 different aéroscaphes, the first of which was built in 1908 and entered in both the aeroplane and motorboat races at Monaco in 1909. It had twin floats, with vertical frames to support 3 pairs of equal-span biplane wing cells; the pilot sat amidships at a tilted steering wheel. The rotary motor mounted on its back drove 2 contra-rotating pusher propellers through a vertical shaft and a gearbox. It was tested with and without the middle pair of wings, and on a 4-wheeled land-chassis. It was wrecked at the Monaco meeting.

(Span: 3.25 m; length: 8.5 m; 50 hp Gnôme)

Ravaud had a second aéroscaphe built by Saunders in England in 1913; it was clearly a hydroplane only, with inadequate wing area to do more than skim the surface. It too was intended for Monaco, but proved too slow, and never left England. It featured broad-chord delta wings with a smaller surface at a high angle of attack under the nose; 2 wide floats in tandem had their thin edges forward. A small rectangular rudder was pivoted above the nose; the pilot sat amidships in a long ply-covered fuselage, with the 50 hp Gnôme again mounted on its back to drive a pusher propeller through shafting and a gearbox. Ravaud had intended to substitute a 100 hp Gnôme and try for 96 kmh.

The automatically stable aeroplane of G Ramel in 1911-1912. (Author's collection)

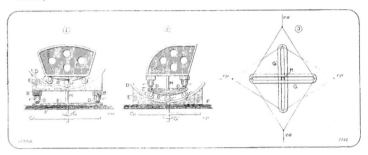

The rolling seat of the Ramel, which controlled 2 axes of movement. How the pilot steadied himself while swiveling his seat around is not clear. (Author's collection)

The tandem 2-seat Ratmanoff. (Courtesy of the Musée de l'Air et de l'Espace/Le Bourget-France)

Ravaud's first Aéroscaphe, at Monaco in 1909. (Courtesy of the Musée de l'Air et de l'Espace/Le Bourget-France)

Du Reau

The unsuccessful tandem monoplane built by du Reau at Malinge's garage at Angers was tested in the summer of 1910. The rectangular box fuselage was covered on the bottom only and rode high on 4 wheels, the front pair of which was Blériot-style. The rear wings consisted of fabric hung between the 2 spars filling with air as the machine gained speed; the front wings were rigid and probably flat in section, semicircular in plan and hinged on vertical pivots to move the center of pressure fore and aft or left and right. A 30 hp 3-cylinder Anzani drove a pusher propeller.

Régy

The Régy brothers were carpenters who subcontracted for other designers and builders, in particular for Borel; they also produced propellers. At the end of 1909 they were said to be building 2 monoplanes "copied from the Demoiselle, designed and drawn by them," and having a "stress girder with the seat below." These might be otherwise unknown machines built for Rossel and Peugeot, or for the Belgian Bothy.

Reiser

A monoplane of this name was reported at Juvisy in 1911. Perhaps it was the metal-framed German Reissner monoplane.

Reisler-Picard

This was a double (tandem) biplane, with the 2 pairs of wings each adjustable in angle of attack from 5° for level flight and the take-off run, to 15° for the take-off jump itself, to 30° for landing. A biplane cell elevator was set out ahead, and a vertical rudder at the rear. The engine was mounted amidships driving a pusher propeller; the mechanic sat behind the propeller and the pilot in front of the engine between the front pair of wings. The whole machine rested on 4 castering wheels. Probably built by the Voisin firm, the machine is said to have managed a brief hop or 2.

Reisler-Picard also designed an adjustable-pitch propeller, perhaps to be used on this aeroplane. The pilot could turn a handle attached to a spring-loaded collar on the propeller shaft, through which the adjustment could be made. A pressure gauge was fixed to register changes in the position of the collar, and the pilot made his adjustments from reading the gauge.

Renard

Lieutenant Charles Renard never succeeded in building a full-scale flying machine, but his experiments were noteworthy. In 1872 he showed a 10-winged model glider with a streamlined fuselage, aileron stubs on each side of the fuselage, and a cruciform tail. Renard tested his model from the tower at St Eloi in 1873, but the pendulum effect from hanging the fuselage from the tower of wings was opposite to his expectation, and the model first glided and then spiraled in.

In 1903 he was a colonel, and published the results of his studies on what he called sustaining screws – that is, propellers designed to lift weight directly. He also proposed an arrangement whereby a machine could lift itself off as a helicopter, and then proceed to fly as an aeroplane; unfortunately it was never built. In 1904, however, he did

The second Ravaud Aéroscaphe; the front end was at the left. (Courtesy of the Musée de l'Air et de l'Espace/Le Bourget-France)

The Renard Decaplan model. (Author's collection)

build at least one nearly full-sized model of his helicopter, with 2 rotors of 2.5-meter diameter, driven by twisted belts running bicycle rims, in turn driven by a vertical shaft from a small motor set into the apex of the inverted V that formed the frame.

REP

In 1904 Robert Esnault-Pelterie built a poor copy of the 1902 Wright glider from drawings and data published by Octave Chanute in an earlier issue of *L'Aérophile;* Chanute's figures and plan were in error, and Esnault-Pelterie compounded the errors. The pilot was slung underneath the rectangular wings on straps; a forward elevator and rear rudder were fitted; the wings may have warped on this first version. Control was to have been by weight-shifting in the sling.

The glider failed in May: the designer said the wing curvature was too great. In his lecture to the Aéro-Club in Paris on 5 January 1905, later reprinted in *L'Aérophile* of June 1905, he stated that the glider had been an exact copy of the Wrights', and that therefore theirs had also failed and their reports were untrue. Esnault-Pelterie rebuilt the glider in October 1904; the span was reduced to 9.6 m, the wing curvature to 1:50, and the forward elevator removed; it is likely that this version incorporated wing-warping; but he quickly gave it up.

(Span: 10.2 m; wing curvature: 1:20 (Chanute gave this figure for the Wright glider, where it should have been 1:20 to 1:30)

He modified the glider again and flew it, still in October; this time 2 forward surfaces were set out ahead of the wings. They could move together as elevators and separately as ailerons. He outlined further tests, since attempts to fly this last version behind an automobile proved unsuccessful, but there were no further tests.

REP 1: In 1907 Esnault-Pelterie designed a new 30 hp 7-cylinder radial engine and his first powered aeroplane. Trapezoidal wings were set at an anhedral angle; the short fuselage had a triangular section and rounded top, with a long keel surface underneath; a triangular tailplane was mounted immediately aft of the trailing edges; a single wheel was fitted under the fuselage with large supporting wheels set on each side of the main wheel, and a small tailwheel; there was no vertical surface. The wings warped. It made several flights in November and December of 1907, the longest 600 m. A modification removed the 2 supporting wheels from under the fuselage and put them onto the wingtips.

(Span 9.6 m ; wing area: 18 sqm; 30 hp REP)

REP 2. In 1908 a long angular fin was added on top of the rear fuselage, and a long trailing rudder underneath; the tailplane was enlarged; hydraulic brakes were added, the first in history on an aeroplane. It was tested several times at Buc; on 8 June it managed a 1200-meter flight at a claimed speed of some 88 kmh, and a claimed altitude of some 30 m.

(Span 8.6 m; wing area: 17 sqm; weight: 350 kg; 30 hp REP)

REP 2bis: This 1909 design was similar to the REP 2, with reduced wing area (15.75 sqm). The tail fin was enlarged, the tailplane was removed, and the elevator placed further aft still. One was modified for the 1909 Reims race, with long trailing fin surface marked with the number 1. This in turn was altered again, with what became the typical REP triangular fin and rectangular rudder; a tiny semicircular rudder surface remained underneath.

The first REP, No 1, with the 2 supporting wheels moved out to the wingtips. (Courtesy of the Musée de l'Air et de l'Espace/Le Bourget-France)

The REP No 2 of 1908, with changes as noted in the text. (Courtesy of the Musée de l'Air et de l'Espace/Le Bourget-France)

One of the stages in the development of the REP No 2, the 2bis, in a luckless moment. (Courtesy of the Musée de l'Air et de l'Espace/Le Bourget-France)

Type B: This new single-seater flew in 1910, the last REP to have the elaborate 3-part vertical surfaces of the 2bis. There was a long swallowtailed tailplane and semicircular elevators, tailskid, and a straightforward 2-wheel undercarriage with forward skid. The fuselage was triangular in section.

(Span: 12.8 m; length: 9.5 m; wing area: 25 sqm; empty weight: 480 kg; loaded weight: 600 kg; 50/60 hp REP)

A slightly larger version had 2 seats.

Type D: This 2-seater with a 60 hp REP engine was similar to the Type B 2, but with a diamond-shaped cross-section. One of them, slightly modified, survives uncovered in the Grande Galerie at the Musée de l'Air et de l'Espace.

Monoplan de Cours (Type Circuit Européen): This stubby machine was flown by several race pilots in 1911; some versions had a standard triangular fin and vertical rudder, while others had the earlier comma-shaped rudder only. All had the earlier triangular-sectioned fuselage. Most or all had the 60 hp REP engine. It was similar to the Type F of 1911.

Biplane 1911: This pretty 2-bay biplane was otherwise similar to the monoplane described above, also with the diamond cross-section.

    (Span: 11.3 m; length: 10.5 m; wing area: 40 sqm; empty weight: 500 kg; loaded weight: 900 kg; 60 hp REP)

Type F 1911: A 2-seater with the diamond section.

    (Span: 11.7 m; length: 7.75 m; 60 hp REP)

Type (?) 3 seater 1911: Another diamond section; perhaps a modified Type D.

    (Span: 13.5 m; length: 9m; gross weight: 500 kg; 85 hp REP)

Type F 1912: This was a 3-seater, about the same size as the D of 1911, but with an 85 hp REP, and a triangular fuselage section.

Series E-80: An 80 hp Gnôme powered this 1912 single-seater. It had a comma-shaped rudder, triangular-sectioned fuselage, and no skid.

Series K: This 2-seater was shown first at the Paris show in 1913, along with the I-80. Some were later fitted with a 90 hp REP,

The REP Type B single-seater. (Courtesy of the Musée de l'Air et de l'Espace /Le Bourget-France)

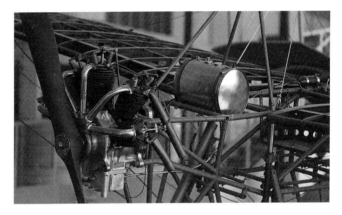

The uncovered REP Type D at the Musée de l'Air et de l'Espace. (Courtesy of the Musée de l'Air et de l'Espace /Le Bourget-France)

others with a 60 hp REP; some had a tall comma-shaped rudder; others had a triangular fin and rudder. The military version appeared in 1914. One K survives at the Musée de l'Air.

Hydro: A 2-seater Series K monoplane mounted on a large rectangular single float and small tail float. One of these, REP 1, flew at St Malô; another, REP 2, flew at Tamise.

The 1911 REP Type de Course. (Peter M Bowers collection)

Series I-80, K-80: The first of these 1913 designs was a stubby single-seater monoplane with 60 hp Le Rhône and 2 rudder styles, one of them the comma; the second was similar, with an 80 hp Gnôme, and a triangular fin fitted to the comma rudder. The K-80 appeared in photos of military trials of 1913.

Vision Totale: A parasol monoplane was entered in the 1914 Concours de Sécurité, similar to the K-80 but with a high parasol wing with considerable dihedral, and a taller comma rudder; the 80 hp Le Rhône was half-cowled.

The British Vickers-Maxim firm decided to go into aircraft construction. Their No 1 was basically a 1911-12 Type D monoplane, perhaps using part of an original REP fuselage, with double skids forward and 2 pairs of wheels. Subsequent Vickers designs, Nos 2-7, were based on it. Dr Mawson bought it almost immediately for his projected South Pole expedition. It was wrecked at Adelie, and some of the remains were until recently still visible at Cape Denison. It is thought the fuselage is still inside the shack there, but the building is now full of ice.

Réquillard

Réquillard's monoplane made its official appearance at Juvisy in June 1910, flown by Marc Pourpe, who went on to fame as a pilot. The machine was very slender and streamlined, with the pilot sitting on top in front of the control wheel, as in the Hanriot; the wings were large and ply-covered on the lower surfaces with curved tips like the Hanriot's. The fixed tail surfaces were long and triangular, the rudder in 2 parts connected at the trailing edges to allow the elevator to move up and down between them. A metal ring around the front of the fuselage, much smaller than the 50 hp Gnôme, carried the supporting steel tubes of the undercarriage, a very neat arrangement with trailing wheels and a short skid. The tailwheel was mounted on long legs so the machine stood horizontal on the ground.

It was reported to have flipped onto its back on its first tests.

(Span: 10 m; length: 7 m; wing area: 20 sqm; gross weight: c 400 kg)

Marc Pourpe was reported flying another small monoplane in 1911-1912; it had a covered fuselage and a tailplane with a swept-back leading edge. It may have been designed in association with Réquillard; it was reported to have crashed, and Pourpe to have given up designing and home-building.

Restan

A tractor monoplane of this name was photographed in 1911 at Point-à-Pitre, French Antilles. A single photograph shows heavily-cambered wings which were "flexible at the tips but not warping," and a heavy Blériot-style pylon structure.

(Span: 9 m; length: 7 m; 25 hp 4-cylinder Pascal Mercedes)

The 1912 REP hydro (a Series K monoplane on floats). (Courtesy of the Musée de l'Air et de l'Espace/Le Bourget-France)

The 1914 Concours de Sécurité REP Vision Totale. (Courtesy of the Musée de l'Air et de l'Espace/Le Bourget-France)

The 1910 Réquillard; perhaps the forward skid should have been longer. (Peter M Bowers collection)

Reuch et Cazaudran

A 1911 ornithopter?

Rheims et Auscher

The famous automobile-body builders also worked as aeronautical subcontractors before 1910.

RHM

At the end of 1909, with 2 partners unknown except for their initials (R, M), a young man named Heurtaux built a small biplane at Gouvieux, near Chantilly. It had "several rudders," inter-wing ailerons, front and rear elevators, wheels and skids; by early 1910 it still had no engine, and the designer was said to be planning a monoplane. He wanted to take his biplane to Creil, to escape his father who disapproved of his son's expensive and fruitless experiments.

Rimailho

The big awkward-looking Rimailho biplane appeared in 1912; the firm had designed and built the Rimailho 155 mm field gun, which had been in use since 1904, so their biplane may have been designed as a 2 – or 3-seater for the artillery. The long square-sectioned covered fuselage tapered sharply down to the tail starting just aft of the cockpits, giving the machine a broken-back appearance. The wings were of equal span, rectangular in shape, with a wide gap between the rectangular upper 2 wing panels. The rectangular tail surfaces were pivoted aft of their leading edges so they were balanced, but there were no fixed surfaces; small castering tailwheels were fixed at the ends of the elevator spars. The landing gear was similar to that of the Antoinette, but without a skid. The engine was fully cowled in a severe rectangular box, and the radiators were flat along each side of the nose.

Rivière

A machine of this name was mentioned at Juvisy in 1911.

Robart

Many of the early aviation pioneers are known only through one or more photographs of the same aeroplane; but when even partial information about their work chances to survive, it sometimes then becomes clear that they in fact had studied carefully for years, step by step; and although they may have stopped short of success, they achieved as much as many others better known. This is the case with Henri Robart, whose name was even at the time often misspelled as Robert.

Born in 1876 the son of a mechanic in Amiens, in northern France, he was soon cycle-racing with some success. He was about 20 when he began his research on flying machines; though he flew balloons regularly, his prime interest was in heavier-than-air. In 1899 he studied helicopters, building propellers of varying sizes up to 10 meters in diameter, some of them contra-rotating, which he than tested with electric motors. In February 1901 he obtained lift measured at 8 kg with 2 propellers each 2.5 m in diameter and driven by a 100 kg electric motor. At this same time he began work on gliders, which he tested at Berck. There he met such pioneers as Ernest Archdeacon, Robert Esnault-Pelterie, Gabriel Voisin, and Ferdinand Ferber. In April 1904, on Archdeacon's request, he tested Voisin's biplane glider. By this time he had himself built a monoplane glider. The 12 hp motor Robart was building may have been meant for this glider: the motor weighed 30 kg.

This may be the only surviving photograph of the 1911 Restan monoplane. (Author's collection)

The big Rimailho biplane. Note the twin tailwheels mounted at the ends of the one-piece elevator spar. (Peter M Bowers collection)

(Span: 8 m; wing area: 12 sqm (reported foldable); weight: 12 kg)

In 1908 Robart began testing a large monoplane which underwent substantial alterations before hopping on 21 December. The rectangular wings, covered only on the bottom, curved gracefully upwards at the tips. The rectangular fuselage was covered on the sides only; the triangular tailplane, also curved up at the tips, was covered only on the bottom. There was a forward elevator with a triangular fin set like an arrowhead in the middle; a triangular rudder was fitted on top of the tailplane. The machine stood on 2 close-set wheels with a single tailskid aft and a semicircular skid fitted with shock-absorbers out in front. The overall construction seemed rough, the fabric loose. Modifications leading to flight included removing the forward fin, replacing the long rudder with a tall rectangular one, and adding a straight rectangular wing panel, also covered on the bottom only, above the middle of the monoplane wing. It retained the 4-cylinder water-

The first Robart monoplane of 1908. (Courtesy of the Musée de l'Air et de l'Espace/Le Bourget-France)

cooled 40 hp Antoinette with the 2 tractor propellers on outriggers from the nose.

(Span (with upper wing): c 12 m; length: c 12 m)

On the airfield of La Croix Rompue (broken cross) near Amiens, the tests of the monoplane were most likely unsuccessful in spite of its hops; and Robart built a second aeroplane, this time a biplane, Le Papillon (butterfly). It was patterned on the Wright, with 2 pusher propellers driven through chains, one crossed, the Antoinette motor on the lower wing. Forward outriggers carried a single forward elevator with 2 triangular fins, again like arrowheads. A single pair of rear outriggers carried a single tailplane and long rudder underneath it. 2 main wheels with a third under the trailing edge carried the aeroplane; but in May 1909, when it was finished, it did not fly.

(Span: 12.75 m; length: c 12 m; wing area: 50 sqm; weight: 400 kg; 50 hp Antoinette, with the same propellers as on No 1)

Lacking more money, Robart had to abandon his work, but remained a locally famous balloonist for years, even many years after WWII, making a flight on every national holiday at Amiens, where he became eventually a popular driver's license examiner.

Roberthie
He designed a monoplane in 1912, naming it Rob.

Roche et Laborde
E Roche and F Laborde designed and built what may be the only true tandem delta monoplane in the history of aviation; it was tested unsuccessfully on the parade ground at Cercottes, near Orléans, c 1910. A large open box-like frame sat on 4 wheels, 2 at each end; in the middle of the box near the front was a Gnôme driving 2 counter-rotating tractor propellers on outriggers on each side through chains. Fore and aft of the box were the 2 V-shaped horizontal surfaces, each with a triangular fin underneath. The front surfaces were set at c 10° incidence, possibly hinged at the trailing edge to allow variations down to 0°.

Roger
A "variable surface" monoplane associated with the name Georges Roger was mentioned briefly in 1911: aluminum flaps could double the wing area to 20 sqm; the wings warped for control. The engine was the strangest feature, a 60 hp Breton. Designed in 1909, it was a 12-cylinder rotary with 3 crankshafts arranged like 3 flat-4 motors together. The propeller shaft turned at 1600 rpm, but the whole engine turned at only 400 rpm. Power could be varied from 20 to 60 hp through the control of the exhaust valves.

(Span: c 5 m; chord 2 m; length: 8.5 m; 60 hp Breton)

The modified Robart, no more successful than in its first version. (Courtesy of the Musée de l'Air et de l'Espace/Le Bourget-France)

Robart's second and no more successful machine. (Courtesy of the Musée de l'Air et de l'Espace/Le Bourget-France)

A close-up of Robart's big biplane. Its ragged construction shows clearly here. (Author's collection)

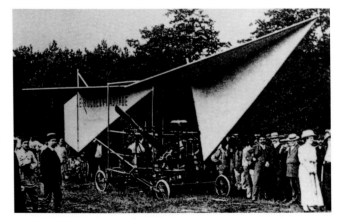

A crowd of admirers surround the awkward-looking Roche et Laborde tandem delta in 1910. (Courtesy of the Musée de l'Air et de l'Espace/Le Bourget-France)

Roissard et Belley

An otherwise unknown design of this name was registered for the Concours Militaire, but it was probably not finished.

Roshar

A multiplane of 1908?

Roshon

Possibly the same as the Reusch et Seux, of 1908...?

Rossel-Peugeot

The former co-worker of Clément Ader, FC Rossel, obtained the necessary financial backing from the 3 Peugeot brothers, whose automobile company, founded in 1900, was proving extremely successful. With their help he patented in 1908 a gearing system to drive 2 contra-rotating propellers with a single motor; and a little later, a spring device to tilt wings during take-off to increase lift through a steeper angle of attack. Rossel built a biplane, sometimes referred to as a Peugeot, in 1909, based on this patent.

Inspired by both the Wright and the Voisin, it featured round-tipped wings, 2 shaft-and-gear driven pusher propellers. Tail-booms carried the biplane tail cell with an hexagonal rudder set between the surfaces. The 2-wheel undercarriage was fitted to a long axle supported by 3 triangular covered frames, and the rear was carried on a pair of small tailwheels. The motor may have been one of Peugeot's.

The second Rossel-Peugeot appeared in 1910, at the same time as the Régy brothers were reported building 2 monoplanes for Boillot and Goux, famous drivers for the Peugeot racing team; only one machine appears in the photographs. Designed by Rossel and developed by Taris, the aircraft was patterned on the Antoinette, with a long narrow triangular fuselage, an Antoinette-like undercarriage with extra struts and a wheel set forward under the skid, an Antoinette-like tail and large tailwheel, and trapezoidal wings not so wide nor so deep as the Antoinette's. A 7-cylinder rotary Rossel-Peugeot provided the power.

(Span: 10.2 m; length: 9.3 m; wing area: c 20 sqm; gross weight: c 350 kg)

In 1910 Rossel and the Peugeot brothers formed the Société Anonyme des Constructeurs Aériennes Rossel-Peugeot in Valentigney, in eastern France; the firm seems to have given up the construction of aircraft to focus on a series of small rotary engines. About 100 examples of the 30 hp Type A Rossel-Peugeot and the 50 hp Type B were built. Subsequently the firm built under license the 50 hp 4-cylinder inline Aviatik motor designed in then-occupied Alsace.

De Rougé

The firm designed and built 2 helicopters and 2 biplanes. The first helicopter may not have been finished. It had a small ragged-looking 4-blade rotor and a 3-outrigger tail. The second, marked II on the tail, had a single rotor of some 8 sqm in area and 5 m in diameter, whose torque was to be balanced by a single huge square fin at the tail: it was to be powered with an Anzani and was supposed to carry 60 kg over its weight of only 130 kg. Perhaps it flew.

A close-up of the Roche et Laborde on the same occasion. Note the centrally-mounted Gnôme. Accommodation for the pilot do not seem clear in this photograph. (Courtesy of the Musée de l'Air et de l'Espace/Le Bourget-France)

The first Rossel-Peugeot aeroplane, a biplane, of 1909. (Peter M Bowers collection)

The graceful Rossel-Peugeot monoplane. (Peter M Bowers collection)

A less happy photograph of the Rossel-Peugeot; we do not know where in its history this accident occurred. (Courtesy of the Musée de l'Air et de l'Espace/Le Bourget-France)

One of the tractor biplanes had an airfoil of flat section, a stabilizer and no rudder, 2 wheels and a single skid, and an Anzani motor – perhaps the same one as in the helicopters. The other had wide fixed flat spars in each wing, with wide trailing sections like sails attached for the full length of the wings. The tractor propeller was mounted far forward with the engine amidships; the fuselage was a long box uncovered except for the top surface. A curved rudder and broad tailplane brought up the rear; the whole machine ran on 2 wheels and a double tailwheel.

Rousseil

A Rousseil is reported to have designed at least 3 aeroplanes in Scée, the last completed when he was 18 years old. They were likely to have been gliders with wing areas of c 20 sqm.

Roux, Charles

When he left the disbanded Avia firm, Charles Roux founded his own firm ACR (Aéroplanes Charles Roux), at first advertising for his own designs. The office was located first at rue de Provence in Paris, and then on the Ile de la Grande Jatte – made famous by the painter Seurat – west of Paris. His metal monoplane, probably his 7th design (cf Avia and his first 6), was designed early in 1911 and completed on 1 March: everybody, including Roux, was amazed at its first easy 700-meter flight across the field at Issy-les-Moulineaux. Wooden wings were mounted on top of the triangular metal fuselage; the tailplane was a long triangle, and the rudder was shaped like a kidney. The engine was a 45 hp Anzani.

Victor Garaix was the former mechanic of Charles Roux while Roux was with the Avia firm, and later became his chief pilot at ACR at Issy. When Roux gave up, ACR became Aérotourisme Victor Garaix, and the so-called Garaix monoplanes were actually ACRs. Garaix achieved his brevet in October 1912 on one of these machines. Garaix was advertising 40 or 50 hp Anzani-powered monoplanes at 6000 and 8000F, and 60 or 80 hp 2-seaters at 10 and 12000F; it is likely that most were not built. These prices were low for the period, and suggest that Garaix was not selling them well.

(Span (2-seater): 9.4 m; length: 8.5 m; wing area: 18 sqm; empty weight: 260 kg; fitted initially with a 50/60 hp Dutheil et Chalmers when the machine was known as an ACR)

Eventually Garaix returned to Chartres, and then he gave up the business. While at Chartres he seems to have sold a single monoplane to Alexandre; the machine was then described as an Alexandre. He became chief pilot for Paul Schmitt, and did the few record flights upon which his reputation now rests.

After leaving ACR, Charles Roux worked for a while for other firms: he was chief designer for CINA (Compagnie Internationale de Navigation Aérienne, also known as SNA, or Société de Navigation Aérienne), where he worked on the Shigeno and the Demazel. He also worked in a firm titled Aérogarage. It is possible that he was hired away from ACR by CINA, leaving Garaix to handle the business.

The first de Rougé helicopter. (Courtesy of the Musée de l'Air et de l'Espace/Le Bourget-France)

The second de Rougé helicopter. The rotor still seems small for the size of the machine. (Courtesy of the Musée de l'Air et de l'Espace/Le Bourget-France)

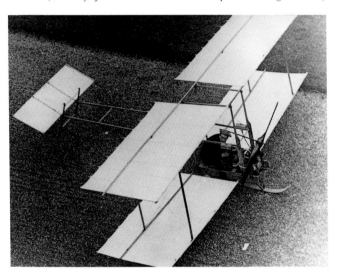

The first of the de Rougé biplanes. (Courtesy of the Musée de l'Air et de l'Espace/Le Bourget-France)

The metal Roux monoplane of 1911. (Courtesy of the Musée de l'Air et de l'Espace/Le Bourget-France)

A later single-seat Roux-Garaix-ACR-Aérotourisme Victor Garaix monoplane. (Courtesy of the Musée de l'Air et de l'Espace/Le Bourget-France)

Roux (F or G or Charles?)

An F or G (or perhaps Charles) Roux is mentioned in 1903 and 1904 as a designer who had built an ornithopter.

Roux, MP

In 1896 (1904?) an MP Roux built a large steam-powered model ornithopter with birdlike wings and a streamlined fuselage with a tractor propeller; it was tested down a long inclined ramp, evidently without success.

Roy

Very little information remains of Le Moustique beyond several brief mentions and a single postcard. The young Roger Roy built his rough Demoiselle copy in 1910 in Thouars, near Les Essarts, where de Rougé had begun his own experiments. The high wing was heavily framed and flat in section; the pilot sat below it, and a single heavy spar held up the Antoinette-shaped cruciform tail, braced with many wires from a single high kingpost. The V2 motor, probably a Buchet, was set on the leading edge and drove a short all-metal propeller.

Rozé, Perret, et Chaffal

This large overhung biplane designed by François Denhaut was made partly of steel tubing. It had a single trapezoidal tailplane aft only, and no apparent vertical surfaces. The arrangement of the 2 pusher propellers was similar to that on the Wright. It was damaged in 1909 at Poitiers.

Roziers

Gaston Roziers was a builder and/or owner at Chalôns in 1908.

Ruchonnet

A Swiss citizen, Ruchonnet was one of the earliest pilots when he purchased the Antoinette VIII; he went on to work with Voisin and then Hanriot, before starting his own firm in 1910. At La Vidamée he founded a flying school and did his design work: he built at least 2 monoplanes and perhaps 4.

The Rozé, Perret et Chaffal biplane with twin Wright-style pusher propellers. (Courtesy of the Musée de l'Air et de l'Espace/Le Bourget-France)

His Cigare is mentioned for the first time in July 1911, a slender monoplane with long narrow tapered cylindrical fuselage made of thin strips of citron wood rolled over a mold. In September it was described as modified: "lighter and more gracious," with the 60 hp Verdet rotary mounted in front outside the fuselage. The wings were rectangular, almost flat in section with slightly cambered leading edges, braced through a tall 4-legged pylon. A large cylindrical fuel tank was strapped in front of the pilot as a windshield. The undercarriage was made of wood and steel struts, high and narrow, attached to a short horizontal bar under the fuselage, and fitted with 2 short skids. The strut arrangement varied in different photographs. On 12 January 1912 Ruchonnet was killed in a dramatic crash in his new monoplane, leaving behind a pregnant wife.

On 30 April 1913 the Swiss pilot C Schemmel took off from Paris in an attempt to fly to Russia and win the Coupe Pomméry; unfortunately he was forced to land near Cologne in Germany. His monoplane was reported as a Ruchonnet-Schemmel, similar to the Ruchonnet but with narrower undercarriage and a lozenge-sectioned fuselage cowled in front over the motor. The rudder had been replaced with a Blériot-like unit.

In 1914 Schemmel registered in the Monaco competition, again with a Ruchonnet-Schemmel, probably the same machine but now fitted with a 100 hp Gnôme. A rare photograph of poor quality shows the Cigare in front of another monoplane, similar to a Blériot with

Ruchonnet's Cigare of 1911. (Courtesy of the Musée de l'Air et de l'Espace/Le Bourget-France)

shorter wings, and a 3-cylinder Anzani. The undercarriage resembles that of the Cigare; the machine may have been a Blériot modified by Ruchonnet. Sometimes these machines were described as Schemmels; one had a diamond-section fuselage.

Rumeau

A very small "rigid" monoplane which could easily be disassembled was reported under construction in 1909 near Toulouse by the "two brothers Rumeau."

The Ruchonnet-Schemmel, with different fuselage and undercarriage. (Courtesy of the Musée de l'Air et de l'Espace/Le Bourget-France)

S

Saconney

An unmanned full-sized machine of this name was described in 1913 – perhaps a kite. There is a possibility that Saconney built manned kites starting in 1906.

Sala

This was small monoplane similar to the Blériot XI, with the fuselage entirely uncovered, rectangular wings and a single strut for the upper pylon, and a 2-piece rudder which moved up and down with the elevator. It had an ENV, and appeared at Issy.

Sallard

Henri Sallard demonstrated his first aeroplane at the 1914 Concours de Sécurité; *L'Aérophile* described it as automatically stable in pitch and roll, thanks to its shape and CG position, with a great excess of power which allowed throttle maneuvering – that is, taking off, climbing, or descending by using only the throttle without touching the controls:

The big Sallard for the 1914 Concours de Sécurité. (Courtesy of the Musée de l'Air et de l'Espace/Le Bourget-France)

The aeroplane being nose up will not slide on its tail if throttles are cut, but pitch down by itself and recover its gliding attitude by itself... If in a bent turn (inclined), pressure on the rudder is released, the apparatus will recover its horizontal position, sliding slightly on (low) wings to follow the new direction straight forward.

It was a big handsome biplane of metal construction, with a long fuselage tapering to a horizontal tail-post, and cut off square in front behind the engine; the pilot sat immediately behind the engine, ahead of the wings, and the passenger was behind and slightly above him. The upper wing was much longer than the lower, both with gracefully rounded tips, with ailerons on the top wing only. The tail was long and tapered, small in comparison with the rest of the machine. It rested on 2 pairs of wheels with short skids in between.

(Span: (upper) 15 m; (lower) 11 m; length: 9 m; wing area: 37 sqm: gross weight: 600 kg; top speed: c 100 kmh; 100 hp 10-cylinder Anzani)

The first Sanchez-Besa, a Farman copy, of 1910. (Author's collection)

Salles

In 1912 a 45 hp Anzani-powered biplane was introduced as having been built by the A Salles Company; it was in fact a 1911 Caudron single-seater.

Sanchez-Besa

The Chilean aviator Sanchez-Besa was well known in French aeronautical circles for his Spanish accent and his flights in balloons; he went on to design 7 or 8 different heavier-than-air machines from 1909 to 1913, all more or less copies, all more or less unsuccessful. He had been following the careers of Santos-Dumont, Henry Farman, and Léon Delagrange, when at the end of 1908 he went to Mourmelon to fly Voisins.

His first aeroplane was little reported on: 2 or 3 may have been built. A Farman copy, it was introduced in May 1910 at Mourmelon, and later 3 were registered for the 1910 meet at Reims, though they may not actually have been built. One, possibly the first one, possibly the only one, was sold to South Africa in September.

(Span: 11 m; length: 12.5 m; wing area: c 50 sqm; gross weight: 500 kg; 60 hp ENV V8)

Below: The Sanchez-Besa seaplane at Monaco in 1912. Note complex tail-boom box structure. (Courtesy of the Musée de l'Air et de l'Espace/Le Bourget-France)

One of the 1912 Sanchez-Besas patterned on the contemporary Voisins. This photograph has been variously labeled both Voisin and Sanchez-Besa. (Peter M Bowers collection)

Another 1912 Sanchez-Besa, this one with a Canton-Unné. (Courtesy of the Musée de l'Air et de l'Espace/Le Bourget-France)

Subsequent Sanchez-Besa machines were patterned on the Voisins of the period; Voisin had worked for Sanchez-Besa until at least 1913. His influence even on the Sanchez-Besa Type E monoplane, actually the Sommer Type F, was reported after the 1913 Salon.

Three Sanchez-Besas were shown in 1912, all biplanes. The first is likely to have been built in 1911 as a military type, very similar to 2 earlier Voisin-designed military biplanes: unequal-span wings had hanging ailerons on the top only, the 2 pilots sat in tandem in a streamlined covered nacelle made partly of steel tubing; the single rudder was set under a monoplane tailplane. The machine rested on 4 wheels. The machine was better known as a seaplane, mounted on 2 floats, the nacelle now uncovered: it flew at many contests, notably Monaco and St Malô. 2 were reported delivered to Chile in March, but it was also reported that 2 biplanes delivered to Chile were Voisins.

(Span: 15 m; length: 9 m; useful load: 110 kg; 80 hp water-cooled Canton-Unné)

The third Sanchez-Besa design was also a Voisin-type pusher seaplane, similar to but larger than the previous one; the tail-booms came together at the tail in plan view, instead of being parallel like the Monaco machine. Benoit flew it at the Tamise meet in Belgium at the end of the summer of 1912. It carried 3.

(Span: 16.4 m; length: 10.11 m; wing area: 60 sqm; empty weight: 900 kg; 100 hp Renault)

The fourth design was unlike all the others; it was built in 1912, likely by Voisin, and shown at the Salon of that year. The wing and tail were those of the previous seaplane – or very like them; the engine was buried between the lower wings in the low-set fuselage behind the 2-man crew and was connected through a chain to the pusher propeller. 2 main wheels supported it amidships, with 2 more in the front as in many of the Voisins; a skid held up the tail.

It is quite possible that Sanchez-Besa's early Voisin-like designs were in fact actual Voisins, more or less. At this time Gabriel Voisin, he of the terrible temper, had few customers, and Sanchez-Besa may have been a kind of sponsor to his work, as Henri Deutsch de la Meurthe was to be a few months later.

At the end of 1912 Roger Sommer gave up his business, and Sanchez-Besa bought back his shops and those of Train, at Mourmelon. Some time earlier Sommer had left to Léon Bathiat, his chief test-pilot, the rights to Sommer's monoplane, to which Bathiat made some useful improvements. Bathiat then joined Sanchez-Besa to form a new firm, Bathiat-Sanchez.

The first machine from the new combination was introduced at the end of the spring of 1913 and was developed directly from the third Sanchez-Besa, but with equal-span wings, a rudder extension above the elevators, and tail-booms joined at the tail. The floats were large and flat and turned up at the nose. A rotary engine was mounted at the rear of the nacelle and through a chain drove a pusher propeller. Rugère tested it on the Seine, apparently with little success, since a few months later the firm produced a new seaplane for the Paris-Deauville race and the meet at Deauville at the end of August 1913.

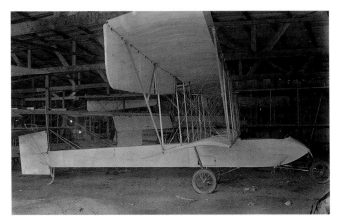

The odd Sanchez-Besa landplane, with a buried engine. (Courtesy of the Musée de l'Air et de l'Espace/Le Bourget-France)

The 1913 Bathiat-Sanchez with its single float being tested on the Seine; similar to the machine at Deauville. (Courtesy of the Musée de l'Air et de l'Espace/ Le Bourget-France)

But this machine was nothing more than the 1912 Voisin military biplane pusher fitted with a large flat pontoon float and wing-tip floats: it was known as the "13.5 meters" and became the Type L.

The last Bathiat-Sanchezes were shown together at the 1913 Salon. The first was known as Type E, originally a Sommer Type F with slight differences: the wings had no dihedral and resembled a Morane. Some articles on the Type E were illustrated by the earlier Sommer – but Sommer Type E, not Type F!

(Span: 8.9 m; length: 7.1 m; wing area: 16 sqm; empty weight: 290 kg; top speed: 115 kmh; 50 hp Gnôme)

The second Bathiat-Sanchez; note outrigger construction and tail bracing. (Courtesy of the Musée de l'Air et de l'Espace/Le Bourget-France)

The second Bathiat-Sanchez at the 1913 Salon was another big pusher biplane, looking very much like some of the Voisins of the period, also built partly of metal. The single elevator had no tailplane, and the twin rudders showed above and below it; the tail-booms came together at the elevator leading edge, changing direction along the way and further braced to the tops and bottoms of the 2 rudder posts. The 4-wheel undercarriage was typically Voisin, with a pair of close-set nose-wheels. There were a great many rigging-wires, even for 1913: the machine was dubbed Sanchez-bizarre.

(Span: 13.5 m; length: 10.1 m; wing area: 46 sqm; gross weight: 825 kg; empty weight: 550 kg; speed: c 90 kmh; the 70 hp Renault was soon replaced by an 80 hp Gnôme)

And in 1921 appeared the Toussaint, also by Sanchez: it featured no fewer than 21 wings!

Sanchis

Léon Delagrange tested this Wright copy at Issy in June 1909, crashed it due to wind on 11 August, and flew it on 17 August; it was wrecked in November in Germany.

The engine was set in the leading edge of the lower wing with the pilot sitting behind it above the drive-shaft. The forward elevator cell was upheld by 2 pairs of curved crossed outriggers; the rear tailplane cell had a fixed fin and (first) rounded and then rectangular rudder between the surfaces. 2 castering wheels set in what looked like bicycle forks supported the front, and 2 small tailwheels the rear.

(Span: 12 m; length: 11.5 m; wing area: 49 sqm; gross weight: 450 kg; 3-cylinder 45 hp Anzani)

Santo

The monocoque form of construction posed a real challenge to the home-builder, and few took it up. The Santo monoplane of 1912, built in Marseille, was one of the few exceptions; besides its advanced construction it sported several other innovations, including provision for a pilot's canopy of mica and aluminum, and a tail unit unlike any other machine. The single tailplane was rigged to move up and down as an elevator control; but it could also pivot around the fuselage to stand vertically and move sideways, for rudder control. The wheels were attached to a skid forward of the undercarriage leg; each skid pivoted on the ends of its leg, and an extension of the skid ran back up to the fuselage where it was attached to a heavy spring which functioned as a shock-absorber. The engine was set in the nose within a streamlined conical cover. An 80 hp Anzani was planned, which would have brought the overall weight to 310 kg; but it is likely that only an 18 hp Dutheil et Chalmers was fitted.

The all-purpose swiveling tail surface seems not to have been used. Instead, a conventional unit appeared, with semicircular elevators and a fishtail.

Santos-Dumont

The extremely rich grandson of a French immigrant and son of a Brazilian coffee-plantation owner, Alberto Santos-Dumont set himself

The Sanchis under construction in the Despujols workshop in 1909. (Peter M Bowers collection)

The 50 hp Anzani installed in the Sanchis, apparently immediately following the previous photograph. (Bill Lewis collection)

Variations on a theme: the completed Sanchis, quite different from its initial stages. (Author's collection)

up in France in 1891. There he became fascinated with automobiles and motors, and later with flying machines. He hired teachers to help him learn what he thought he needed, and thus met Emmanuel Aimé, a math teacher, a founder of the French Aero Club, and its first general secretary; Aimé helped Santos-Dumont till 1906 with his most difficult calculations. Later Aimé went on to work with Salmson on another heavier-than-air machine.

Santos-Dumont's first flying machine was a little round balloon named Brazil: at the time, in 1898, it was the smallest man-carrying balloon in the world. His last dirigible was his No 14, built and flown in 1905; it was famous as the lifter of his first heavier-than-air design, No 14bis, which made its first hop the following year. But he had been making model aeroplanes and model gliders for some time. A photograph shows him and his mechanic Chapin at Neuilly in the winter of 1905, holding a large model. It features a semicircular wing with a long flexible boom at the tip of which is fixed a triangular tailplane. A string is stretched from the nose: apparently it is being tested as a kite. The design was developed into a glider with a wing area of 22 sqm which was apparently built and tested behind a motor-boat. A 1906 drawing shows the same design but larger, with a push-pull propeller combination in which the rear one turned on the boom itself. To have been known as No 11, this one was not built.

No 12: In 1905 appeared his drawings of a helicopter with 2 large rotors turning in opposite directions, and a single tractor propeller, all driven through a shaft, spoked wheels and belts. The propellers were designed with the help of Victor Tatin and were formed of steel tubes, ribs, and fabric, weighing less than 9 kg each. The engine was tried with the 3 propellers and found inadequate and the helicopter was not completed.

(Rotor diameter: 6 m; length: 12.5m; 24 hp Antoinette V8)

No 14bis: His dirigible No 14, built and flown in 1905, was a long drooping cigar with a small car suspended far below. Planning to use it the following year to carry a heavier-than-air machine, he rebuilt it with more volume, and worked at the same time to design and build the aeroplane, to be known after the dirigible as No 14bis. It was an awkward canard biplane pusher with a 3-bay wing cell and 6 side-curtains. The pilot stood up in his cockpit, the narrow car from an earlier balloon, and controlled the aircraft through hand-wheels. At the front of the long cov-

Santos-Dumont and his mechanic and their model, 1905. (Author's collection)

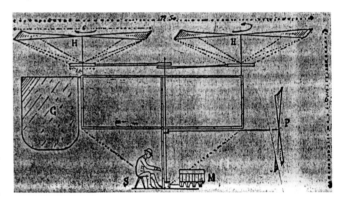

A 1906 drawing of Santos-Dumont's helicopter project. (Author's collection)

Moving the Santos-Dumont 14bis very carefully through a gate, Alberto Santos-Dumont himself leading the way. (Courtesy of the Musée de l'Air et de l'Espace/ Le Bourget-France)

Above left: A close-up of the aft end of No 14bis, the pilot to stand upright at the control wheel at the left. (Courtesy of the Musée de l'Air et de l'Espace/Le Bourget-France)

Left: A real photograph of the No 14bis in flight. (Courtesy of the Musée de l'Air et de l'Espace/Le Bourget-France)

ered fuselage hung a biplane cell, pivoted to work as both elevator and rudder. The whole machine rested precariously on 2
wheels. A 24 hp Antoinette was mounted between the wings,
driving the large Tatin propeller taken from the dirigible No 14.

It was tested under the belly of No 14 on 22 July 1906 at
Bagatelle; soon afterwards he slung it from 2 pulleys on a cable
at Neuilly St James, as Ferber had done for his own aircraft at
Meudon. The Tatin was replaced by an aluminum paddle-bladed
propeller built by Levavasseur, and further tests were run to check
the working of the controls, the aeroplane being towed back to
the starting point each time by a donkey named Quino. Santos-
Dumont had a 20-meter ramp built for eventual take-off trials,
but did not use it. On the first test the propeller was broken, and
the 24 hp Antoinette was replaced on 21 August with a 50 hp
version.

On 4 September he tried again on the parade ground at Bagatelle in the Bois de Boulogne, and damaged the forward elevator, which had been reworked to control pitch only; 2 polygonal
flaps had been installed between the outer wing-curtains to act
as air-brakes and to control yaw. These were operated with wires
attached to the pilot's back. On 7 September it taxied for 17 seconds, pitching up but not flying; on 12 September the propeller
was changed for a larger one. On 13 September it hopped for a
distance of at least 7 m, and France went wild; but it was damaged in the effort. On 23 October it flew 60 m at a height of some
3 m; on the 26th it flew even further, and Santos-Dumont was
awarded the Archdeacon cup for the 25-meter prize.

Further efforts damaged the machine; then on 12 November at Bagatelle, at near-zero temperatures, Santos-Dumont made
3 unsuccessful tries; the fourth was against the wind, and he flew
82 m; a fifth managed 220 m, slightly higher than 7 m, and turning to port. The machine was damaged upon landing. No 14bis
flew only once more, on 4 April 1907, at St Cyr, when it covered
another 50 m.

Though a modest achievement, even for the time, this performance can be considered a decisive impulse towards heavier-
than-air flight in France and Europe.

Santos-Dumont's further efforts to fly his No 14bis resulted
only in the destruction of the entire fuselage. Today, models have
been wind-tunnel-tested; a full-scale reproduction was recently
tested at Le Bourget. The results were very clear indeed: the
aeroplane should not have flown!

(Span: 11.5 m wing area: 52 sqm; weight: 300 kg; 24 hp
(50 hp) Antoinette)

No 15: On 22 March 1907 he brought out a curious tractor biplane with wings made of okoume wood ply sheeting, a large
dihedral angle, 5 side-curtains; 2 long bamboo outriggers, one
above the other, carried the biplane tail cell and its 2 rudders.
The engine was mounted on the top wing with the pilot sitting
below it; a single forward wheel and complex tailskid, aided by
wing skids, supported the machine on the ground. Forward elevators were to have been fitted, and ailerons later were added,

*Santos-Dumont (L) working on his No 15 with plywood sheet surfaces and a
precariously-positioned 50 hp Antoinette. (Courtesy of the Musée de l'Air et
de l'Espace/Le Bourget-France)*

*Another view of No 15. Note the 2 thin outriggers supporting the tail. (Cour-
tesy of the Musée de l'Air et de l'Espace/Le Bourget-France)*

set outboard and forward of the wings. On 27 March, at St Cyr, it
was wrecked while taxiing.

(Span: 11 m; length: 5.5 m; wing area: 13.9 sqm; empty
weight: 295 kg; 50 hp Antoinette from No 14bis)

No 16: In the meantime he built a dirigible, which does not strictly
belong in this account, except that a 100 hp Antoinette was
mounted with a small wing behind it; this motor was later replaced with 2 small 6 hp motors on outriggers, and photos of this
arrangement – the car with the twin engines – are sometimes
confused with one of his heavier-than-air designs.

The twin 6 hp engines on the Santos-Dumont No 16. (Author's collection)

No 17: His next heavier-than-air machine was a development of No 15, and powered with the same 100 hp Antoinette ordered for the earlier machine. Again, the plywood wings and high dihedral; but the tail of this one was mounted on a long rectangular-section frame. The engine was set onto the leading edge of the lower wing, and the machine rested on 2 main wheels and 2 V-struts with a cross-axle. Sometimes reported not to have been built, No 17 was indeed begun but not completed.

No 18: This was a wingless 3-float hydroplane with the same 100 hp Antoinette and the big 3-bladed propeller from No 17 mounted high and forward, and the driver at the wheel at the very stern. Photographs of this machine are sometimes confused with those of a flying machine experiment.

No 19: By the end of 1907 Santos-Dumont had completed his first real monoplane, a tiny tractor monoplane which he named Libellule (dragonfly); later he renamed it Demoiselle (another more common name for dragonfly, as well as for a young girl). It was built of bamboo and silk, weighing less than 60 kg: the rear fuselage was a single bamboo spar, with the small cruciform tail set on a universal joint at the end. The wings were nearly square in plan, with 2 spars and only 7 ribs on each side. The motor was perched at the center of the leading edge, and the pilot sat on a strap below, aft of the wings, between the wheels; a third wheel right behind him kept up the rear. Wing-warping was controlled by wires attached to the pilot's back. On each side of the machine, immediately outboard of the wheels, was a hexagonal surface coordinated with the swiveling tail; a small hexagonal forward elevator was set just ahead of the pilot's feet. After one crash, Santos-Dumont replaced the single propeller with 2 small ones, one on each side of the motor, driven on big sprockets by belts, one crossed; a 3-bladed fan cooled the motor. Santos-Dumont weighed only 49 kg ("without shoes and with gloves"), and could easily take off in the little plane at Issy.

(Span: 5 m; length: 8 m; wing area; 9 sqm; gross weight: 110 kg including pilot and gasoline; 17-20 hp flat twin air-cooled Dutheil et Chalmers driving a single Antoinette-style aluminum paddle-bladed propeller, or 2 Tatin built-up propellers)

No 19bis: But No 19 proved unsatisfactory, and was modified with the substitution of a 24 hp Antoinette mounted this time between the pilot's legs and driving a larger-diameter Tatin propeller through a wide belt and 2 pulley wheels, one large and the other enormous. The wings were enlarged to 13 ribs on each side, and the 3 hexagonal surfaces were removed; these changes did not improve the little machine.

No 20: Early in 1909 he introduced his next and most famous aeroplane, also called Demoiselle, and sometimes known also as Bébé or Joujou. The single tail-boom of No 19 proved too flexible and was replaced with a triangular frame made of bamboo

There are not many photos of Santos-Dumont's No 17 – it may not even have been finished. Here Santos-Dumont stands against the tail outriggers and the 100 hp Antoinette; the sheet plywood wings go up and off to the right, with one rectangular strut frame showing at the right. (Author's collection)

Santos-Dumont aboard his hydroplane, No 18. (Author's collection)

The Libellule (later Demoiselle), No 19, with the single bamboo tailboom and forward elevator. (Courtesy of the Musée de l'Air et de l'Espace/Le Bourget-France)

poles fitted together through metal casings and braced with short metal struts. A third wheel at mid-length supported the tail. For this new machine Santos-Dumont designed and had Darracq build a 30 hp water-cooled flat twin; it was mounted above the pilot on the top wing, and the radiator tubes were wrapped around the upper boom. The Chauvière propeller was of constant chord.

Above: The first modification of No 19. Note that only the propeller at the right was belt-driven; the other turned by a connecting-rod, but may have been designed for its own belt. (Courtesy of the Musée de l'Air et de l'Espace/ Le Bourget-France)

Right: A close-up of the drive used in No 19bis; the 24 hp Antoinette replaced the 17-20 hp Dutheil et Chalmers. (From Lougheed's Vehicles of the Air)

In March 1909 No 20 was damaged at Issy; it was repaired and taken to St Cyr – still today a small airfield west of Paris. It reappeared with a new Chauvière and new radiators, this time the tubing laid chordwise under each wing. The tailwheel was gone, replaced by a tall skid under the rear fuselage. A large cone-shaped tank appeared immediately behind the pilot. This version was sometimes referred to as Demoiselle II; in it Santos-Dumont flew the 8 km from St Cyr to Buc in 5 minutes to win a bet with Guffroy.

The Demoiselle was sometimes described as "flying like a butterfly;" it was sometimes also called the Infuriated Grasshopper. Very unstable and quick for its time, it allowed only the lightest pilots to fly it, and few did it well. Several were built at Santos-Dumont's factory, and he generously allowed the public access to his patents, so many more were built in garages and back yards. Some larger firms wanted to take advantage of his offer; he delivered an uncompleted No 20 to Dutheil et Chalmers as a model to build from. This may be the machine, seen in some photographs, fitted with a Dutheil et Chalmers flat twin early in 1910.

Though advertised at only 5,000 Francs, the Dutheil et Chalmers machine was never produced, and the machine delivered by Santos-Dumont was abandoned until it was recovered by Charles Dollfus and taken to the Musée de l'Air et de l'Espace, where it was restored and is now displayed. It features a horizontally-mounted steering wheel.

(Musée de l'Air et de l'Espace aircraft – span: 6.4 m; length: 6.75 m; wing area: 10 sqm; take-off weight: 118 kg; top speed: 90 kmh; 25 hp Dutheil et Chalmers)

Earlier in 1909 the firm of Clément-Bayard became interested in the Demoiselle project, and the modified original Demoiselle was thus fitted with the 4-cylinder inline Clément-Bayard from the former Maurice Clément biplane, and tested unsuccessfully in September 1909. Since the engine was too heavy, Clément-Bayard made plans for mass production of the Demoiselle at 7500F each, 2,500 more than the projected Dutheil et Chalmers, though nearly 20,000F less than any other production aeroplane. The Clément-Bayard machines had all-metal tail girders and wooden wings, and were powered with 30 hp flat twins: still the aeroplanes were tricky and could only be flown by the lightest-weight pilots. It was unstable on all axes, with inadequate power and lifting surface. Sometimes the Clément-Bayard version was referred to as Santos-Dumont No 21.

Roland Garros, who became known as a Demoiselle pilot, and his friend Edmond Audemars, undertook unsuccessfully to build a Demoiselle copy. And Morane-Saulnier did the same in 1913, a 2-seater with a low-set Gnôme and Morane wings.

A Demoiselle ground trainer, in which the rear fuselage of a Demoiselle, complete with pilot's seat and overhead engine and propeller, was mounted inside a large semicircular track in which the whole device could rotate 90° in each direction, at the same time moving forward on a large 3-wheeled chassis.

But by this time the ingenious little Brazilian was beginning to suffer from the disease, probably sclerosis, that caused his early retirement and withdrawal from aviation. In 1914, already bitterly depressed and horrified by the War, through a misunderstanding he was accused of being a German spy. Enraged, he destroyed all his papers and returned to Brazil. In and out of sanitariums, he returned to Rio in 1928: a surprise welcome demonstration turned to disaster in front of him when the committee's big seaplane crashed in the harbor; in 1930 the British airship R101 was destroyed; his own country burst into

A revised No 20; note the conical tank behind the pilot. The third wheel is gone. (Author's collection)

The No 20 in flight: it looks as if deserves its name, "Infuriated Grasshopper"! (Courtesy of the Musée de l'Air et de l'Espace/Le Bourget-France)

Alberto himself at the controls of one of his No 20s. (Author's collection)

Garros and Audemars attempted their versions of the Demoiselle, too; this one had a 50 hp Gnôme on the leading edge of the wing. (Courtesy of the Musée de l'Air et de l'Espace/Le Bourget-France)

The Demoiselle ground-trainer. (Author's collection)

revolution. Sick, and feeling guilty about his part in the development of aviation, on 23 July 1932 he hanged himself.

Sarri

A monoplane of this name was reported at Juvisy in 1911.

Sarrus

Sarrus was the pilot and perhaps the builder as well of a monoplane seen in Marmande, in southern France, about 1911. A crude Blériot copy, it had rectangular warping wings, a pylon composed of 4 struts coming together at the top, like the Sommer. The fuselage was covered in front, and deep enough for the pilot to sit in up to his shoulders. Sarrus' machine was called Elan II (thrust, energy): there seems no record of Elan I.

Saulnier

After graduating in 1905 from the Ecole Centrale, an engineering school, Raymond Saulnier was drafted into the artillery, and then vainly searched for a job in Brazil, finally joining the Blériot company in 1908 as a "pair engineer." Here he did the calculations for various types including the famous XI; he was not the designer of this most famous of the Blériot machines, as has often been reported. After Blériot's Channel crossing, Saulnier was not given a permanent appointment; he wrote a book and contributed to the *Encylopédia de l'Aviation*; and in October 1909 he founded his own firm, named Société des Aéroplanes Saulnier, at Courbevoie, north of Paris.

Here he designed a monoplane, of which several were reported built: 2 are known, unless the second was in fact the first modified. It was rolled out in March 1910 and taken to Mourmelon where Saulnier had rented a hangar. Its rectangular fuselage tapered to a horizontal tailpost; a triangular tailplane and dorsal fin were also unlike the Blériot; the pilot sat on a strap hanging inside the uncovered frame. The wing-bracing pylon comprised an inverted V and 2 kingposts. Wings and undercarriage and castering tailwheel bespoke their origins. The aeroplane was damaged in March 1910.

(Span: 8 m; length: 7.2 m; empty weight: 280 kg; 30 hp air-cooled Darracq)

The second machine (or modification of the first) showed little difference: the pylon was formed of 2 inverted Vs and a horizontal bar, the fuselage was covered on the top rear, and the elevator was now in halves to clear the larger rudder. The engine was a 50 hp Anzani; the machine was reported to have flown on 27 May 1910, reportedly sometimes by Anzani himself. In June 1910 a Saulnier monoplane was described at Juvisy with a Labor-Picker engine. Saulnier also built a biplane for de Lesseps.

The Saulnier company was bankrupt in September, and on 3 October 1910 the assets – no aeroplanes included – were sold at auction. He met Morane at a Borel event – Borel was selling the Blériot XI – and in 1911 Saulnier became involved with the formation of a new and more successful firm, the Société Anonyme des Aéroplanes Morane-Borel-Saulnier. Saulnier went with Morane when Morane left the new firm.

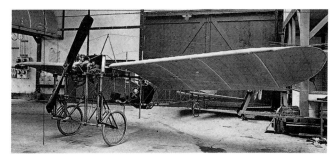

The first Saulnier design. Note the pilot suspended in his seat-strap. (Peter M Bowers collection)

The second Saulnier monoplane. (Courtesy of the Musée de l'Air et de l'Espace/ Le Bourget-France)

The second Saulnier in full flight. (Bill lewis collection)

Saulquin

A Sergeant Saulquin of the 13lst Infantry Regiment tested a biplane of unknown design in the spring of 1911. The pilot sat above and to the rear of the lower wing.

(Span: (upper) 9 m; (lower) 4 m; length: 8.75 m; wing area: 26 sqm; 50 hp Gnôme)

Sautereau

A machine of this name was described at Auxerre in 1907.

Savary

Robert Savary was born 13 June 1888, and quickly became interested in heavier-than-air flight. He built 2 gliders, RS1 and RS2, apparently unsuccessful. In March 1909 he had the firm of Léon Bollée at Mans build him a tractor biplane, and flew it successfully several times at Chartres in May. It had an aileron fitted at the middle of each forward outer wing-strut between the wingtips, a 40 hp Dutheil et Chalmers, trailing wheels with long forward skids, and a biplane tail. 2 vertical surfaces were set immediately aft of the ailerons.

The first Savary, a tractor biplane. (Author's collection)

When the Société des Aéroplanes Robert Savary was incorporated in June 1910 at Neuilly, a western suburb of Paris, the assets included his patents from 1909, various subcontracts, and "a biplane." It was a Wright Flyer copy, built and tested at Leon Bollée's facility where Wilbur Wright had made his first European demonstrations. Savary's machine featured a biplane rear elevator, 2 pusher contra-rotating pusher propellers driven through one chain by a 40 hp water-cooled engine; there were 2 ailerons, and 2 flaps mounted vertically between the wingtips to control yaw. The pilot sat on the lower wing behind a large horizontally-mounted steering wheel. The motor was mounted to the pilot's right, behind a distinctive circular radiator.

The new Savary of 1910. Note the forward-mounted vertical radiator. (Peter M Bowers collection)

(Span: 10 m; length: c 8 m; wing area: 44 sqm)

In 1910 a new Savary was shown at the Reims meeting, a much larger biplane. It retained Wright-style wings and there were now 4 vertical shutters hinged to each of the 2 rear outer wing struts. The biplane elevator cell was retained from his first aeroplane, but this time the engine, mounted on the lower wing behind a tall rectangular radiator, chain-drove 2 tractor contra-rotating propellers; the 2 pilots sat in tandem immediately behind the engine. The 2 castering main wheels were fitted under the trailing edge at the rear of a long uncovered structure of triangular section which served as forward fuselage and skid at one end and supporting skid at the other. The machine was rather heavy, a problem with all of the Savary designs.

An intermediate Savary design: it had 4 ailerons, but the hinged elevators and covered nacelle had not yet appeared. (Courtesy of the Musée de l'Air et de l'Espace/Le Bourget-France)

(Span: 8.5 m; length: 9 m; wing area: 30 sqm; 60 hp ENV V8 driving the 2 Savary propellers at 500 rpm)

In 1911 his big 1910 design was modified: the large forward structure was replaced by a lighter unit to carry the central skid and rubber shock-absorbers attached by cables to the castering wheels. Ailerons were now built into all 4 wing panels. The control surfaces were hinged to the triangular tailplanes; the rudimentary fuselage nacelle was now covered and fitted behind the engine and the 2 chain-driven tractor propellers. 3 variants were built in 1911: a racer of 10-meter span, and a 2 – and a 3-seater; the latter 2 were entered in the 1911 Concours Militaire, each with overhung top wing panels and doubled wheels to meet the Concours requirements.

(2-seater: span: (upper): 14.5 m; (lower): 10 m; length: 11 m; wing area: c 52 sqm; empty weight: 600 kg; payload: 220 kg; speed: c 90 kmh; 70 hp water-cooled 4-cylinder inline Labor)

(3-seater: span: (upper): 19.5 m: (lower): 14 m; length: 12 m; wing area: c 69 sqm; empty weight: c 700 kg; payload: 420 kg; speed: c 90 kmh; 70 hp Labor)

Though the pilot Level was killed in the crash of the 3-seater, Joseph Frantz, who was later to be credited with the first air combat victory in 1914, managed so well with the 2-seater that the Army ordered 9 of them. One was delivered in 1911, the next in 1912, and the remaining 7 in 1913.

In 1912 Savary was offering for sale his 2 – and 3-seat military machines, a 2-seater with double controls for training, and a "type de course, long voyage, extra-léger" (a lightened long-range cross-country racer) all powered with the 70 hp Labor. The same year he tested one of his aeroplanes with propellers running without reduction-gearing, the engine set well ahead of the propellers; results were not satisfactory. All the 1912 designs were fitted with the rectangular nacelle of his 1911 models.

A seaplane with twin 3.7-meter Tellier floats and with retractable wheels was finished at the end of 1912. The vertical shutters were shorter with rounded corners, and a small semicircular rudder was fitted between the tail outriggers ahead of the biplane tail cell. The machine was wheel-tested at Juvisy on 2 January 1913, powered with a 75 hp air-cooled Renault, though it was later re-engined with Savary's favorite 70 hp Labor.

The basic Savary designs used various motors at different times. On 13 March 1913 Frantz flew 9 passengers on one of the twin tractor Savarys using a 110 hp Salmson Canton-Unné engine.

Two more Savary designs were shown at the end of 1912. The first was a big military tractor biplane with overhung wings similar to his previous designs but with a 50 hp Gnôme set in a circular cowl at the front of a rectangular-section nacelle whose rear end was a handsomely streamlined cone; the pilots sat side by side.

(Span: (upper) c 12 m; (lower) c 8 m)

The last design of 1912 was very different; it was shown on the last day of the Paris Exposition. It was a very modern-looking sesquiplane with a thick-sectioned mid-wing set into a completely covered cylindrical fuselage. The 80 hp Gnôme cowled inside the nose drove through chains the 2 tractor propellers which were set into the leading edge. The high undercarriage had a shorter wing of c 4-meter span between the wheels, all made of steel tubing and wire-braced. The wheels were unusual: the rim and tire rotated around the wheel disc which itself was set on the end of the axle off-center so the whole wheel could pivot backwards on landing, to cushion the shock. An internal spring attached at one end to the lower wing limited travel of this unlikely – and evidently unsuccessful – arrangement.

Right: The last Savary of 1912 shown on the last day of the 1912 Exposition. Then it seems to have disappeared. (Author's collection)

One of the 1911 Savarys with overhung wings and undercarriage sprung from the center skid structure. (Peter M Bowers collection)

One of the 1911 military Savarys. Note the double wheels. Clearly the nacelle was not designed for 7 passengers. (Courtesy of the Musée de l'Air et de l'Espace/Le Bourget-France)

The Savary seaplane. Note the covered nacelle and the hinged elevators. Ailerons were fitted to the top wings only. (Courtesy of the Musée de l'Air et de l'Espace/Le Bourget-France)

The 1912 Savary with a streamlined tail cone. The grain in the wood of the lower longeron shows clearly in the original photograph; it is wildly erratic. (Peter M Bowers collection)

Savary stopped building aeroplanes in 1913, as did many other constructors, for want of business, since the military was cutting back its aircraft orders,

Schmidt et Bauer

Unknown design or designs in 1908 – possibly the same builder as Schmitt?

Schmitt

Paul Schmitt tried for years to develop a device to make aeroplanes automatically stable: he was finally one of the winners of the 1914 Concours de Sécurité with his 7th design, Type 7. Records are incomplete concerning the previous 6; some of the earlier kites and gliders built between 1904 and 1909 may have been included in the numbering system.

The first known Schmitt aeroplane was built by Lucien Chauvière and brought to Chartres for assembly in March 1910; it was tested in April. It was a biplane resembling a headless and tailless Wright. A heavy chassis rested on 4 wheels and 2 skids, with the pilot at the front and a large 4 – or 6-cylinder inline engine on the center of the lower wing, driving a single pusher propeller at the rear through shafts and chains. Diamond-shaped rudder surfaces were attached to the rear outermost wing struts. The second Schmitt – or perhaps it was the first modified – had enlarged rudder surfaces, and a pair of long outriggers on each side carried small horizontal surfaces far out in front and to the rear. The forward undercarriage skids curved up much higher – perhaps to ensure safety in landing.

The second major Schmitt design formed the basis for most of his later aeroplanes: a trapezoid-section box frame to carry wings and engine, with some sort of tapered fuselage covered only at the rear to carry the pilot and a single elevator at the tail. This was the first Schmitt to employ his distinctive stabilizing method: by pivoting the wing-cell on a pin mounted high in the cabane structure he could vary the incidence to keep the center of lift in the same plane as the center of gravity, allowing the fuselage to remain horizontal during climb and descent. The pilot turned a crank with an attached worm gear to achieve this result: it worked.

This machine was developed up to Type 7. The first development was probably another similar machine with unequal-span wings, a 3-place design with a 70 hp engine built in 1911. There was no rudder: small vertical rudder surfaces were still fitted to the rear outboard wing struts. The single large rear elevator pivoted on the very tip of the long rear fuselage. This may have flown, but was reportedly less successful than its predecessor.

Another version of the Schmitts. Still no rudder, except for the upright wingtip vanes. (Courtesy of the Musée de l'Air et de l'Espace/Le Bourget-France)

The first version of the first Paul Schmitt. Note the trailing triangular rudder flaps attached to the aft wingtip struts. (Courtesy of the Musée de l'Air et de l'Espace/Le Bourget-France)

The first Paul Schmitt, modified. The angle of attack of the whole machine seems to have been increased. (Courtesy of the Musée de l'Air et de l'Espace/Le Bourget-France)

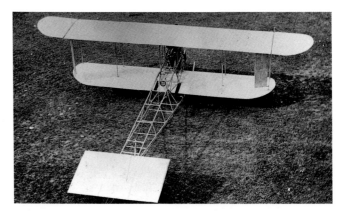

One of the first stages of the development on the way to the Schmitt Type 7, this one with a water-cooled engine. (Courtesy of the Musée de l'Air et de l'Espace/Le Bourget-France)

The next Schmitt variant appeared in 1912, a big 3-bay biplane still with the distinctive trapezoid-section fuselage, but with a rudder; the wing-tip rudders were gone. The unequal-span wings had long inset ailerons; there seems to have been no elevator.

Schmitt's classic Type 7 appeared in 1913, was shown at the 1913 Salon, and was advertised to fly between 30 and 120 kmh. In February, April, June, and July 1914, Victor Garaix, Schmitt's appointed test pilot, broke 43 world records: altitude with 4 to 9 passengers, speed with 4 to 6, distance with 6 and endurance with 3 and 6 passengers. It had an all-metal frame without brace-wires. The fuselage section began as a flattened rectangle forward, became nearly square amidships, then triangular, and finally tapered to a horizontal tailpost. The wings still pivoted at the cabane pivot; the undercarriage was heavy, with skids and 2 pairs of wheels. Type 7 was sometimes fitted with an extra pair of wheels at the skid-ends, 6 wheels in all.

(Span: (upper) 17.5 m; (lower) 13.5 m; wing area: 49 sqm; empty weight: 650 kg; gross weight: 1500 kg; incidence variation: between 0° and 12°; speed variation from 40 to 116 kmh)

After he achieved second place at the 1914 Concours de Sécurité, he sold Type 7 to the Army, and Schmitt was encouraged to develop a

Still another early Schmitt, different from the previous 2 photographs. (Courtesy of the Musée de l'Air et de l'Espace/Le Bourget-France)

The Schmitt Type 7 of 1913. (Courtesy of the Musée de l'Air et de l'Espace/Le Bourget-France)

A 1914 development of the Schmitt Type 7; in one of these Garaix flew 5 passengers for 2,250 m, and 6 passengers for 1,700 m. (Author's collection)

smaller 2-seat Type 8 which was not finished before the outbreak of the war. Type 9, a still further development, was eventually ordered in quantity in 1916. These later Schmitts were fitted with 2 or 4 wheels.

Schmutz

On 15 June 1906, an Albert Schmutz brought his odd flapping-wing glider to a foot-bridge above the Seine at St Cloud. Painted red, white, and blue, the apparatus was made of steel tubing with a 5-meter long inverted half-cylinder covered with silk set above it like a roof. The wings of steel tube, rattan, and silk, each 2.5 meters long, were arranged through V-shaped levers and rubber cords to flap. The test lasted the few seconds of a vertical drop into the Seine.

Above: The first Schreck Diapason. (Courtesy of the Musée de l'Air et de l'Espace/Le Bourget-France)

Schreck

Louis Schreck had been a Wright pilot. Before he became famous as a builder of flyingboats, some of which were still in service at the start of World War II, Louis Schreck began his own design work in 1911 with a strange machine which actually flew.

> Diapason I: It resembled a baby carriage, the curved handles of which supported the front elevator; the covered frame was set on 4 wheels, and the wings swept back in wide curves, resembling a tuning-fork – hence the name Diapason. Small round-topped rudders were set above the trailing wingtips, with elevators hinged to the ends. The engine was in the nose and through a long shaft drove a pusher propeller at the rear of the fuselage.

> (Span: 12 m; length: 14 m; wing area: 32 sqm; weight: 400 kg; 50 hp Gnôme)

It was also photographed with a 50 hp water-cooled Chenu, the fuselage left uncovered: this version may have been an earlier one.

The second Diapason. Note the differences from the first. (Courtesy of the Musée de l'Air et de l'Espace/Le Bourget-France)

> Diapason II: In this version, also Gnôme-powered, small trapezoidal rudders were set above and below the wingtips, with small control surfaces hinged to the tips themselves. One of the Diapasons was to have been fitted with a "retractable amphibian undercarriage," apparently in 1911-12.

In 1912 Schreck turned to more conventional designs. He bought Tellier's patents from the Chantiers Alphonse Tellier when Tellier left his firm to work on his own. Schreck formed the Anciens Ateliers Tellier with Gaudard as chief designer. In the meantime Denhaut had also been designing flyingboats, and he merged with Donnet, Levêque, and Conneau to form Donnet-Levêque; he subsequently left Donnet-Levêque and worked first with Borel and then Goupy. Levêque then left Donnet-Levêque to build his own flyingboats; and the remains of the Donnet-Levêque firm merged with Schreck's Chantiers d'Artois to form FBA (Franco-British Aviation) with Schreck as director. Some wartime FBA flyingboats are described as Schrecks.

Sclaves

This tractor biplane powered by an acetylene motor was tested at Ambérieu in 1910 by a man from Lyon named Sclaves. At least one photo shows a 50 hp Prini-Berthaud engine. The rectangular wings were braced entirely by one pair of outboard struts on each side and wires from double kingposts on top. The heavy forward box structure seemed made of pipes; the rear fuselage was uncovered. The 2 wheels were castering.

Seguin (Augustin)

Marc-François Seguin had married into the famous ballooning family de Montgolfier; his son Marc became an engineer, with inventions in many areas including steam boilers and iron cable suspension bridges. Marc's son, also named Marc, married a distant cousin from the same Montgolfier family, and one of their sons was Augustin, named after his mother and his grandmother. Augustin married 3 times, once to another Montgolfier cousin (not Augustine this time!). With his first wife he had had several sons, one of whom was Louis; with his third wife he had several more, one of whom was Laurent. Louis and Laurent were the inventors and builders of the Gnôme rotary engines. Still another cousin, Germaine-Marie de Montgolfier, married Henri Fabre. But Augustin was the only Seguin who built any aeroplanes.

At Annonay he built at least one flimsy biplane glider with heavily-staggered wings featuring straight ribs and fabric laced to them. Then in 1909 he commissioned his cousin, Henri Fabre, to build him a lifting surface of 10 sqm for another glider, this time a canard, the pilot sitting in a covered fuselage girder of triangular section. The front spars were of typical Fabre design and construction: a pair of thin spanwise flat wooden strips with zigzag cross-members making them a girder, the fabric laced on behind. This one too had a wing area of 10 sqm, "too little to carry a man, and therefore unsuccessful in the several short flights we made."

On a later occasion, Augustin brought Fabre a small toy canard monoplane, and suggested that such a design would be the best in which to use the Gnôme! Thus Henri Fabre built a small monoplane, again of 10 sqm wing area, again too small: but eventually came the famous Fabre flyingboats.

Seguin (Gabriel)
A machine of this name, otherwise undescribed, was entered on the Monaco list for 1909.

Serraillet
Serraillet, the Marseille representative of the Fiat company, built a Voisin copy in 1909 or 1910. A fixed biplane tailplane cell was set at the end of the 4 outriggers of the aft structure with a rectangular rudder set between them; the nacelle was uncovered, with the typical Voisin front elevator perched on the nose. The wings were short and rectangular and non-warping; odd movable surfaces were hinged to the ends of all 4 wing panels. The forward elevator was operated from a steering wheel; other controls worked through a wheel on the starboard side of the nacelle.

Servais
In July 1912 the local papers at Chartres were starting a subscription to buy a man named René Servais an engine for his monoplane.

Seux
The details of the career of Edmond Seux are not clear, and it is difficult to sort out his designs. Born in Annonay, the home city of the Montgolfier brothers, he is said to have begun early with models. In June 1904 he had the Surcouf firm build him a triplane "parachute à réaction," fitted with "lateral planes." It was tested unsuccessfully in February 1905.

In 1907 he had the firm of Ronnet at Lyon build him a monoplane; it had a "waving wing" with flexible tips "for stability" mounted on a complex uncovered frame set on 4 wheels, 2 large ones in front, 2 smaller behind. 2 pusher propellers were mounted on shafts driven by twin belts and large pulleys. A forward elevator was on triangular outriggers and a cruciform tail was mounted on a pair of horizontal booms. The wing leading edge was thick, and the wing plan was that of a large bird. The aeroplane was tested on 15 May at Grandchamps, a nearby parade ground; it is reported that the front wheels lifted off

The big Sclaves all wire-braced biplane. (Courtesy of the Musée de l'Air et de l'Espace/Le Bourget-France)

The Serraillet Voisin copy. Note the 2 control wheels, and the wingtip surfaces. (Courtesy of the Musée de l'Air et de l'Espace/Le Bourget-France)

The "waving wing" Seux monoplane. In this photo, the tail looks wavy, too. (Author's collection)

and the tiny rear wheels collapsed. Seux planned to refit tandem wheels, but did not get to do this.

(Span: 10 m; wing area: 24 sqm; weight: 450 kg; 35 hp Anzani or Buchet V2)

In 1908 he had the workshops of Pierre and Louis Reusch build him a biplane, known as the Reusch et Seux. In the same year the 3 men also patented a pusher biplane patterned on the Wright, possibly not built, his first biplane not having been completed either. The Reusch et Seux had a forward elevator and a transverse engine driving 2 pusher propellers.

(Span: 10 m; length: 9 m; wing area reported as 50 sqm; 50 hp engine)

On 6 Nov 1909, Edmond Seux's body was found in the Rhône river: it was said he had killed himself because he could not repay his loans. He was 42 years old.

Above and right: Two views of the Roux-designed Shigeno, featuring its circular rudder. (Courtesy of the Musée de l'Air et de l'Espace/Le Bourget-France)

Shigeno

In 1912 the Japanese Baron Shigeno had a biplane built, probably by CINA, designed by Charles Roux and constructed by Thomann; it was tested by Demazel. The Baron showed up again during WWI in a French uniform.

The machine was all-metal with a fabric cover. The top wings overhung the lower, supported by diagonal struts, and were fitted with large ailerons. The fuselage was triangular in section, the rear uncovered. The circular rudder carried the Rising Sun (Homoru) in the center; the elevators were long and trailed to the rear on each side. Each wheel had its own skid, and the pair were set far apart on the axle. A pretty machine.

(Span: (upper) 8.8 m; (lower) 5.8 m; length: 3.1 m; wing area: 24.35 sqm; empty weight: 371 kg; gross weight: 501.4 kg; endurance: 3 hr; 6-cylinder Anzani)

Sigren

This name appeared in 1909 – but perhaps it was not French at all.

Sloan

From 1910 to 1912 the American John Sloan built his series of "bicurve" biplanes in a small workshop in the Paris suburb of Charenton. As with so many of the early designers and builders, it is difficult to determine how many of the machines appearing under his name were new ones, or merely earlier ones modified and developed.

His first was shown in 1910, typical of his bicurve designs with the shorter top wing arching down at the tips almost meeting inboard of the tips of the lower wing, with the extended leading and trailing edges of the upper wing joined to those of the lower. The lower wing

had some dihedral, and then its tips drooped also, with large ailerons on the trailing edges near the ends. The long uncovered rectangular fuselage sat 2 in tandem behind the engine; a tall rectangular rudder stood up at the rear above a long tailplane set at a high angle on the fuselage. The elevators were connected to a forward elevator mounted on outriggers. The aeroplane rested in front on 2 pairs of wheels with a skid between each pair, and a tailwheel; the latter was replaced with a skid before the end of the year. The lower wings were called lifting surfaces and the upper ones stabilizing surfaces: the theory was that the downward curve of the lower wings would "slow the chute if the engine cut."

(Span: (upper) 8 m; (lower) 10.95 m; chord: (upper) 2 m; (lower) from 2 to 2.9 m at the tip; length: 11.3 m; wing area: 49 sqm; speed: c 75 kmh; 50 hp Gnôme with a 2.5 m diameter Sloan propeller)

A similar machine, or the same one altered, was often photographed in flight. The forward elevator was gone, and a 35 hp Labor

The 1910 Sloan bicurve at the Paris Salon. (Courtesy of the Musée de l'Air et de l'Espace/Le Bourget-France)

A closeup of the first Sloan bicurve. Note the ailerons. (Courtesy of the Musée de l'Air et de l'Espace/Le Bourget-France)

provided power through chains to the 2 tractor propellers. The pilot sat in a sort of bucket. Another version – or modification – flew next, with the Gnôme and a single tractor propeller, front elevator, but with a less-drooping top wing. It crashed in 1911.

Reports appeared in 1911 of a new Sloan design, different from the 1910 type: it was shown at the Concours Militaire in August, a handsome conventional-looking 3-seater in green fabric "the color of a frog." The fuselage was covered only in front; the old high rudder was retained, and the top wing, now longer than the lower, drooped only slightly, where the lower wing waved substantially. Big ailerons hung from the top wing only. A leggy curved twin skid held up the tail.

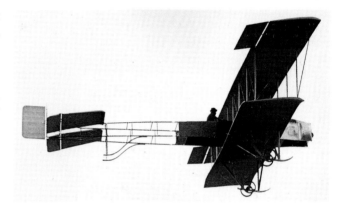

The 1911 Sloan entered in the Concours Militaire. The designer has retained the upturned aft fuselage and wavy wings from the beginning. (Courtesy of the Musée de l'Air et de l'Espace/Le Bourget-France)

Below: The twin tractor propeller Sloan. It is hard to see what if any components of the earlier aeroplane are used in this one. (Courtesy of the Musée de l'Air et de l'Espace/Le Bourget-France)

(Span: (upper) 13 m; length: 9.5 m; wing area: 49 sqm; empty weight: 500 kg; 100 hp Gnôme)

Sloan's penultimate reported flying machine was flying in 1912 at Issy, seemingly a throwback to the 1910 designs, with the twin skid of the Concours Militaire entry; a final design was similar to the 1912 military aeroplane but with a small inline 4-cylinder motor.

In the years 1911-1912 he was working on plans for a 18.5-meter span Calais-Dover passenger biplane, with a single big float and a boat-shaped fuselage and a 100 hp Clerget; it was not built.

Société d'Aviation Méridionale

One of many small companies founded as constructors, often subcontractors or representatives of larger firms, this one was the local representative for Nieuport in southern France.

Société de Construction d'Appareils Aériens

This firm, referred to also as SACAA as well as the Avionnerie de Levallois (an industrial suburb northwest of Paris), was founded in 1909 by George de Manthe, Clément Ader's son-in-law, with Espinosa, Ader's former mechanic. Until 1911-1912 they built a great number of flying machines designed by their inventors. In 1910, for instance, they were building 3 biplanes, one monoplane, one helicopter, and one helicoplane. Only one of their output, however, was advertised as a genuine SCAA: the Frégate, built for Robert de Lesseps. It is not clear now what parts Espinosa and de Lesseps played in the design, though Espinosa sometimes claimed it all as his own.

Alex Dumas in *L'Aéro* reported at the end of 1909 that 3 Frégates were being built for de Lesseps; the first one appeared throughout 1910 with many modifications. The most striking feature of the series was their M-shaped gull wings, like those of the frigate-bird, which showed up especially well after crashes and nose-overs. The spars were hollow and wrapped with fabric tape, a patented method copied from Ader's Avions. The long trapezoidal rear elevator was hinged at the leading edge on the top of the fuselage well forward of the stern. The first version had no rudder, depending on wing-warping for directional control, and the outer wing sections were crescent-shaped. A rudder was added to the second version, and the wingtips were shorter and more sharply swept back. The undercarriage consisted of castering main-wheels and a tailwheel.

(Span: 10 m; length: 6.5 m; wing area: 20 sqm; empty weight: 230 kg; speed: c 65 kmh; 25 hp Anzani)

At the 1910 Salon another – perhaps the third – Frégate was exhibited, this one with an uncovered fuselage and a 25 hp Anzani, though it never flew in this form. The wingtips were rounder, and the elevator was hinged at the stern. It was shown under the name SCAA, and was flown by Guillaume, the SCAA pilot.

Société d'Etude pour la Locomotion Aérienne

In 1909 the pilot Gaudard founded the Société d'Etude pour la Locomotion Aérienne (SELA), for which he was unable to collect the adequate operating capital of 300,000F. G Badini, their designer, built 2

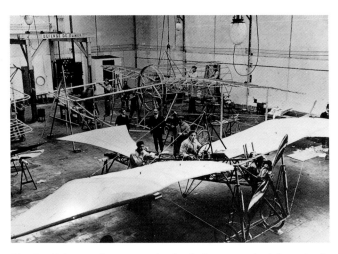

The first Frégate under construction for de Lesseps at the Avionnerie, the shops of the SCAA (Société de Construction d'Appareils Aériens). In the background, the remarkable Bertrand monoplane is taking shape at the same time. (Courtesy of the Musée de l'Air et de l'Espace/Le Bourget-France)

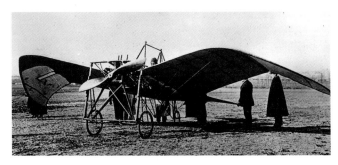

Probably the second version of the SCAA Frégate. (Author's collection)

The third Frégate, now with fin and rudder and nearly straightened wings. (Author's collection)

The pilot signed this photograph with his name, and "Pilote de la Frégate (no 3)." Note the addition at this time of what seems to be a small horizontal rectangular surface forward of the tailplane. (Courtesy of the Musée de l'Air et de l'Espace/Le Bourget-France)

Above: The second SELA (Société d'Etude pour la Locomotion Aérienne) monoplane, with the Aviatik engine. (Courtesy of the Musée de l'Air et de l'Espace/ Le Bourget-France)

similar aircraft, one which appeared in 1910 at St Cyr, powered by a 55 hp Aviatik engine; the other, a variant, in 1911. They were monoplanes with rectangular wings without dihedral and Blériot-built undercarriages. The first had a triangular tailplane (later removed) with a large rectangular elevator hinged to it with the rudder posts above and below fixed to the moving surface; the fuselage was uncovered.

The second had its fuselage fully covered, the corners of the wingtips clipped; the tailplane was now triangular and the rudder mounted firmly on the fuselage. Power was a 55 hp Aviatik. This machine was sponsored by *La Dentelle au Foyer,* a lace-workers' magazine which later bought a Farman for the Army, christened La Dentelle de Puy: the city of Puy was famous for its lace industry.

Société des Véhicules Aériennes
In 1910 Dajoigny and Beaussart had built a monoplane at Mourmelon under their own name, based on the Demoiselle and called the Simplex. A slender fuselage structure, first uncovered then later covered over, changing from rectangular to triangular section towards the tail, supported a warping tailplane and small elevator, vertical surfaces above and below; a trailing rear wing surface brought up the very rear. As in the Demoiselle the pilot sat in a sling seat under the wing. A water-cooled engine was fitted at least once. In January 1911 they founded a new firm, the Société des Véhicules Aériennes, at Issy, and ran a flying school there with a variety of monoplanes.

In June 1911 they were building the Minima, built mostly of bamboo and doped yellow; it was to feature "ailerons under the wingtips," and used a 25 hp René Gillet 4-cylinder X engine. The Minima may have been a development of an earlier glider of 1910.

(Span: 6 m; weight: 60 kg without the engine installed; 25 hp René Gillet)

Right: The third SVA, with a 6-legged undercarriage. (Courtesy of the Musée de l'Air et de l'Espace/Le Bourget-France)

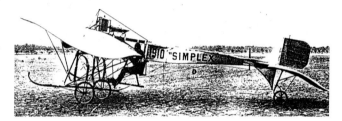

The Dajoigny et Beaussart monoplane Simplex, featuring a very low-set pilot. (Author's collection)

Dajoigny's and Beaussart's second design, put out under their firm name SVA (Société des Véhicules Aériennes). Note 4-legged undercarriage. (Courtesy of the Musée de l'Air et de l'Espace/Le Bourget-France)

At the same time the builders announced a 2-seater to be powered by a 3-cylinder bi-rotary Ligez, which turned opposite to its own crankshaft and propeller.

By 1912 the SVA was operating 2 different monoplanes, one smaller than the other, both patterned on the Blériot XI. The smaller differed from the Blériot in its 4-legged undercarriage and triangular fin and tailplane. The larger had its wingtips rounded at the trailing edge only; the fuselage longerons were parallel for most of their length; the undercarriage had 6 legs, the extra set of supporting struts from the engine mount.

(Smaller monoplane: span: 7.2 m; length: 6.8 m; wing area: 10 sqm; gross weight: 320 kg; 30 hp 3-cylinder Anzani)

A monocoque machine was announced for the end of 1912, but no further information is available. A photograph dated March 1913 shows the SVA monoplanes beside a third even larger one, probable an old 2-seater Sommer with a Gnôme: current publications reported without further details that the school was using 50 and 70 hp Gnôme-powered aircraft.

Soiron
An all-aluminum machine weighing 349 kg with a 70 hp engine was reported built in 1909 by a man of this name.

Solirène
Solirène was an early pioneer in southern France; among his designs was a glider begun in 1903 but not completed, a bat-shaped hang-glider with a fan-shaped tail and a long forward outrigger, in which he threw himself from a tower at Palavas-les-Flots in 1904 and fell heavily into the sea – luckily without hurting himself. His son went on with the work in 1906, also at Palavas, flying manned gliders. It is likely that the 2 of them built still other gliders and perhaps kites.

Sommer
Born on 4 August 1877, the son of a felt manufacturer at Mouzon, Roger Sommer became interested in machinery, won fame at age 18 as a bicycle-racer, and built a one-cylinder 4-wheeled car. By the end of 1908 he had built his first aeroplane, a large biplane which foreshadowed Henry Farman's Type III of 1909. It had a monoplane forward elevator, the pilot seated on the leading edge of the lower wing. Sommer's design included a pair of small wings at the middle of the 4 tail-booms, with the rectangular rudder placed just forward of the biplane tail surfaces. The engine, reportedly an Anzani, was mounted below the lower wing, driving a pusher propeller mounted in the middle of the airframe; but photographs show a 50 hp water-cooled Vivinus, which Sommer knew well, since he owned a 60 hp Vivinus automobile. The machine rolled on 3 wheels.

As the third aviator at Chalôns, Sommer had his hangar between Farman's and Voisin's, and his machine was tested there in the spring of 1909, achieving only occasional hops. There in May Sommer met Farman and bought one of his Type IIIs, which was delivered at the end of June; Sommer installed the 50 hp Vivinus.

Roger Sommer's first design, in 1909. (Courtesy of the Musée de l'Air et de l'Espace/Le Bourget-France)

The 1910 Sommer in one of its several versions. (Author's collection)

On 7 August 1909 he became famous by bringing back to France the endurance record previously held by Wilbur Wright: Sommer had flown for 2 hr 27 min 15 sec. In December he sold the Farman to Daniel Kinet, since he had finished his own completely successful design: this 1910 Sommer was to undergo many alterations, and several were built in different forms; by the spring of 1910 he had 58 aeroplanes on order and 60 men working for him.

The 1910 Biplane: Powered with a 50 hp Gnôme, the aircraft featured rounded ailerons extending well behind the trailing edge – the shape was modified at least once – and a monoplane forward elevator with 2 long flat curved skids at the tips, attached to the landing gear. But the most remarkable feature was the variable incidence tailplane. The control wheel for this device was set horizontally at the pilot's left, and was characteristic of all Sommer designs till 1911; the arrangement was used to control stability and the speed of the aircraft. For instance: the center of gravity on these aircraft changed when the wings were wet. A large rudder appeared initially ahead of this tailplane, but was soon replaced with 2 pairs of small closely-spaced surfaces both above and below. The pilot sat on the leading edge of the lower wing with the stick at his right, controlling only the front elevator; aileron control cables were first attached to the pilot's jacket, then to the top of the stick, when it was located between the pilot's legs. The fuselage and elevator could be unhooked to fold back against the wings.

Many Sommers of this type were exported, particularly to Great Britain (represented in 1910 by Charles Rolls), Belgium, and the Netherlands. One was sold to Russia and copied; another to Germany, in 1910; the Albatros firm applied for license to build these machines. Many variants appeared, with slight improvements to structure and airfoil.

(Span: 10.36 m; length: 12.5 m; total area: 36 sqm; empty weight: 330 kg; wing incidence: 9°; 50 hp Gnôme, Vivinus, Aster, ENV, among others)

As soon as he could, Sommer began to fly with from one to 3 passengers on what were then fairly long flights. The machine was slow, and heavy on the controls. In May he flattened the airfoil and reduced the number of vertical surfaces from 4 to 2; the stick was placed between the pilot's legs.

In June 1910 he produced a new variant, a 2-seater with Farman-type front elevator mounting, different rear skids, 2 rudders, and simplified undercarriage. The airfoils were changed again, the results being known as "a flat wing." 2 or 3 were sold to the Army, but they were all heavy on the controls and too fragile; one of them was never correctly rigged. The Army preferred the Farmans, to which they had grown accustomed through the Farman school.

In July or August, Sommer sent to the Reims meeting a new racer, similar to the original biplane but with a reduced lower span; and a larger machine with 2 more ailerons on the top wing, which increased the span to about 12 m. From this design came the later Aérobus.

At about the same time Sommer tested a twin-engined machine which flew at least once, on 27 September 1910. No record exists, not even in the Sommer family archives, of this machine, save that it existed. It probably had 2 engines hooked together to one propeller.

Grand Biplan (Aérobus): This was the first major replacement of the 1910 design; it appeared early in 1911, and retained the tail and airfoil of the earlier machines, but had a lengthened upper wing with high aspect-ratio ailerons mounted in pairs. Powered with a 70 hp Gnôme, it had seats in 2 banks: on 24 March 1911 it carried 7 children and then 9 adults, 2 of them standing up outside on the front skids. Later that day it carried 12. On 9 January Molla carried 5 passengers for 66 m – a world record; but had to land because of the cold and snow. 2 Aérobuses flew at the Concours Militaire, one with a skid, the other without.

(Span: 12 m; length: 12.5 m)

Type de Course: This was a 1911 tractor biplane, built with the nose of one of his monoplanes (cf below), and shortened biplane wings with 2 ailerons; it was designed for racing.

From mid-1911 Sommer started designating his designs with letters according to a system for which the key seems lost.

Type K: This was an all-wood biplane with a faired-in nose for the pilot, and a forward elevator mounted on 2 outriggers. The wings were narrower than those of previous machines. It was not successful, being designed for the Army who was not interested in it, since at the time the Army wanted heavier, more powerful aircraft.

Above and below: two views of the 1911 Sommer Grand Biplan (Aérobus). It doesn't look as if any of the crew or passengers wore seat-belts. (Courtesy of the Musée de l'Air et de l'Espace/Le Bourget-France)

The 1911 Sommer Type de Course (racing type). (Peter M Bowers collection)

Right: The 1912 Sommer Type K. (Courtesy of the Musée de l'Air et de l'Espace/ Le Bourget-France)

(Span: 12 m; length: 12 m; total area: 20 sqm; empty weight: 230 kg; 50 hp Gnôme)

Type Léger: The pilot sat out in front of the narrow-chord wing cell; the tail consisted of a horizontal tailplane with 2 rudders below it, the whole supported on 2 booms.

Type L (Type Rapide): This design, also unsuccessful, had an all-steel frame. The wings were of unequal span with gap smaller than previous types, and the upper wing was made in 3 panels, the outer 2 of which pivoted on the single steel tube spar to act as ailerons; a single row of steel struts was set between the wings. There was a small forward elevator whose stated purpose was to provide an orientation point for the pilot against the horizon, and an elevator fitted to the rear of the Sommer tailplane. Covered in green, it was shown at the 1911 Paris Salon, and immediately was called La Grenouille (the frog); and also Le Populaire, because of its low price, 8500F. Sommer fitted a new carburetor of his own invention, designed to prevent popping back.

(Span: (upper) 12 m; (lower) 7.8 m; length: 9 m; wing area: 26 sqm; empty weight: 290 kg; gross weight: 515 kg; speed: 90 kmh (no faster than the other Sommer biplanes); 50 hp Gnôme)

Type de Campagne: This was developed for the Army from the Type L, but it proved to be too light. It lacked any forward elevator, and showed a double row of interplane struts.

Type R (Type de Place – fortress type): The last of the Sommer biplanes, and the most successful, developed in several variations throughout 1912. By mid-1912 these were called Rl, R2, and R3; but by the end of the year only R and R3 were still mentioned. By the time Sommer was building the R-types, he had re-staffed his factory, with the new workers coming from the armament industries and being familiar with precision assembly-work. This big biplane was more modern than it appeared: built of wood, the struts by the engine were steel tube, and the steel-tube landing gear struts were wood-filled. The wooden wing struts were hollow. Controls were mounted in ball-bearings, and piano wire was replaced with cable running through guides of copper tubing. Two rudders were set below the tailplane with its rear elevator, and a forward elevator might be also fitted at will, again to orient the pilot. R2 was a 2-seater, R3 a 3-seater. The crews sat in a cockpit in front of a Renault engine; the fairing on the R2 was open in front, and covered on top on the R3. Different sets of wings were used. One photograph shows 4 ailerons, 2 large and 2 small on the upper wings (R2?); others show 6, with 2 more on the lower wings (R3?). All hung down at rest. 2 of the ailerons were linked to the rudders, supposedly helping in turbulent weather. Type R was fitted with a variety of engines: a 50 or 70 hp Gnôme, or a 50 or 70 hp Renault. One Type R was tested in December 1912 with an 80 hp de Dion Bouton V8. The fam-

The Sommer Type de Campagne. (Courtesy of the Musée de l'Air et de l'Espace/ Le Bourget-France)

The 1912 Sommer Type R3, the 3-seater. (Courtesy of the Musée de l'Air et de l'Espace/Le Bourget-France)

ily archives show a Type R with a water-cooled Canton-Unné of probably 110 hp, and a front elevator.

(R3 – spans: 15.5 m, 12 m; length: 11 m; length including front elevator: 11.7 m; total area: 54 sqm; top speed: 93 kmh; take-off run: 60m; landing run: 30 m; empty weight: c 50 kg; gross weight (fuel and oil for 4 hr): c 900 kg; various engines)

Type Reliable: This light wooden machine appeared in the press in April 1912; designed for tactical reconnaissance, it was quickly foldable. A pusher, it had no forward elevator, and the pilot sat well forward of the lower wing leading edge. The engine was mounted aft of the propeller. The tailplane had an elevator fitted to it, and the same vertical rudder as on the Types K and L pivoted around a vertical axis at about 1/3 chord, with a tailskid mounted on its leading edge.

(Spans: 12.5 or 12.8 m, 9 m; length: c 9.5 m; empty weight: 275 kg; 50 hp Gnôme)

During the summer of 1912, Sommer flew a seaplane on Lake Geneva; it was fitted with an 80 hp Salmson Canton-Unné engine, and was similar to the Type R without the faired fuselage. Tellier provided the 3 floats. Sommer and Burri operated a scheduled service between Evian in France and Lausanne in Switzerland. In August it was entered in the Lausanne competition: there seems to have been only the one. A simpler 50 hp Gnôme seaplane had been flown previously.

Sommer also built monoplanes of many kinds, although they are designated only as Type E (and probably Type F); they appeared in 3 major series sometimes described as Blériot types, Deperdussin types, and Morane types.

<u>Type Blériot</u>: The first was a rough copy of the XI, with a Hanriot-type undercarriage and a Blériot-style center-section support overhead. It appeared both as a single-seater and a 2-seater, unstable and very fragile with bolted spars. Léon Bathiat, the Sommer chief pilot, moved the wing a foot further to the rear, making the machine much more stable. The engine was covered with a flat ring to prevent showers of castor oil, the front of the fuselage was covered with steel plates, and the underside with fabric.

(2-seater – span: 11.5 m; length: 9 m; empty weight: c 270 kg; gross weight: c 410 kg; wing area: 17 sqm; 70 hp Gnôme)

(Single-seater – span: 10.5 m; 50 or 70 hp Gnôme)

Several weeks later Sommer showed a monoplane with fuselage completely covered, and a smaller, lighter undercarriage with 2 skids. It was followed by another, with the main section aft of the engine covered with a single steel plate; the skids had been taken off the undercarriage, and the masts were in the form of a small pyramid in front of the pilot. All these early monoplanes had typical 4-longeron wooden fuselages, with the long-

The 1912 Sommer twin-float seaplane. (Courtesy of the Musée de l'Air et de l'Espace/Le Bourget-France)

The first Sommer monoplane, like the Blériot XI with altered undercarriage and covered underside. (Peter M Bowers collection)

erons tapering regularly in section; all the fuselages were covered along the bottom.

<u>Type Deperdussin</u>: These designs were variants of the Type E, all single-seaters and the most successful and the most famous

A variant of the Sommer Type E, labeled Centre Sommer (Sommer school). (Courtesy of the Musée de l'Air et de l'Espace/Le Bourget-France)

of Sommer's aircraft. The first had a bird-shaped fuselage profile, with the wheels and the upper pylon brought forward. The tanks in front of the pilot canted upward to form a windbreak, and the inboard leading edges sloped forward to the engine cowling, resembling the Deperdussin racers of the period. A second version had a much higher rudder.

On the earlier monoplanes the tail unit was fitted with the same device as on the still earlier biplanes, but on the Type E it was replaced with a Type de Sécurité (safe elevator): a slow push or pull on the stick controlled in the normal way. But a sudden sharp movement on the stick produced a much larger movement of the elevator: the idea was to help the pilot recover suddenly. Needless to say, it was not successful. The Type E completely covered in fabric was ordered by the Army; 20 monoplanes with serial numbers over 100 were bought and formed the Centre Sommer (Sommer School), which was not an operational unit. The Type E was fitted with a 50 or 70 hp Gnômes which gave speeds of 105 or 135 kmh, or with a 35 hp Anzani. All the military Type Es had the starboard trailing edge cut out for better visibility.

In January 1912 Bathiat achieved a top speed of 150 kmh (average speed 144 kmh) on a 70 hp Gnôme-powered Type E; a little later Jules Védrines achieved 169 kmh on a 140 hp Deperdussin.

For the Circuit d'Anjou in the summer of 1912 Sommer got ready a new 2-seater with an 80 hp engine for his friend and pilot Kimmerling. It crashed at Chalôns during its first tests, killing both Kimmerling and Tonnet, Sommer's chief engineer. As a result, the warping cables were redesigned on all the Sommer monoplanes.

(Span: 8.7 m; length: 6.7 m; empty weight: 270 kg; gross weight: 440 kg; wing area: 16 sqm; 50 or 80 hp Gnôme)

Type Morane: During the 1912 Salon, a new monoplane was shown on the Sommer stand. It had a cowling similar to those on the Moranes, and the top of the fuselage was slightly rounded. This may have been the Type F described by Alex Dumas, unless it was in fact another variant of the Type E. At the end of 1912 Roger Sommer suddenly announced his resignation; he noted that he had built a total of 182 aircraft. He explained that the Army had not confirmed its orders for the Type R and the automatic stabilizer monoplanes. In fact, the Army still preferred the Maurice Farmans, from which the Type R was not significantly an improvement – and the monoplanes were still inadequate in their performance. He sold his interests in 1912 to Léon Bathiat, who went into partnership with Sanchez-Besa and sold the monoplanes under the name Bathiat-Sanchez. During World War I Sommer went on to found, in association with Bathiat, one of the most important aircraft factories of the War, turning out great numbers of Spads and Caudrons. He later devoted his time to the family felt business, which became one of the main European carpet producers, the Sommer Allibert Group.

Sotinel, Guérin, Corneloup, et Karganiantz

A monoplane built by Sotinel, Guérin and Corneloup-Karganianz appeared in 1909. It may not have been finished – or perhaps it was in fact the subsequent monoplane built with Janoir. Sotinel also worked with Bastier and de Brageas, but he seems soon to have left these associations. The Guérin-Corneloup machine was under construction in a hangar guarded by a goat said to be fond of castor oil. One account described the machine as a "differential balance... to be auto-

The Sotinel, Guérin, Corneloup et Karganiantz automatically stable pendulum monoplane. (Author's collection)

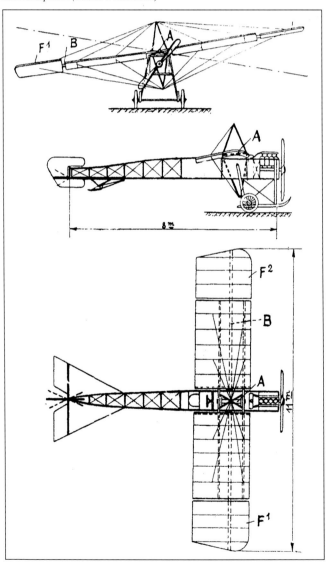

Contemporary drawing of the SGCK monoplane showing the range of wing/fuselage movement. (Author's collection)

The 2 Souchet monoplanes in front of the Brulé et Souchet flying school hangar. Both show minor variations on the Blériot XI theme. (Courtesy of the Musée de l'Air et de l'Espace/Le Bourget-France)

matically stable in bank and climb." The fuselage worked as a pendulum and was connected to the wingtips. When one wing was raised by a gust, the tips automatically moved with the fuselage to level the aircraft. Change in speed or altitude could be made by varying the angle of attack of the wings. The description ended by saying that "the bird has not yet finally borne out all that is claimed for it, although the design is certainly very ingenious."

(Span: 11 m; length: 9 m; wing area: 21 sqm; gross weight: 400 kg)

Souchet

The Brulé et Souchet flying school at Issy-les-Moulineaux operated at least 2 little-documented Souchet monoplanes resembling the Blériot XI, powered by 3-cylinder 30 hp Anzani engines. One of them had an undercarriage like that on the early Sommers – 2 skids and 2 wheels – and the other a Morane-like gear. They were likely both modified Blériots, or built from Blériot spares. Variants, like the Grazzioli, might have been made by at the school. This Brulé may have been the same Brulé who worked with Girardot in 1911.

Stanley, Schaerf, et Savage-Landor

These names together belonged to a group of owners or builders in 1908.

Stoeckel

A strange little tailless monoplane appeared at Issy in 1908-09. A tiny engine drove 2 little tractor propellers through belts. The frame resembled a wheelchair, with a skid (sometimes a wheel instead) immediately behind the seat. Above the pilot was the single wing wildly curved in every direction, with a third panel, also curved, above the

A close-up of one of the Souchet aeroplanes. (Courtesy of the Musée de l'Air et de l'Espace/Le Bourget-France)

center-section. Stoeckel designed the wing to resemble a bird's half-folded wing; his aeroplane might have fared better with the wings unfolded. Stoeckel was also a Blériot XI pilot.

(Span: 6 m; length: 5 m; wing area: 28 sqm; gross weight: 300 kg; 4-cylinder 12 or 25 hp Revel)

Strofe

A machine referred to as the Tri-Aéro was reported at Nancy, associated with this name.

Da Sylva

Gomez da Sylva was a Portuguese who in late 1909 built a curious pusher biplane whose most distinctive feature was the curved down-turned center-sections of both wings, coming to horizontal knife-edges. The fuselage was an uncovered rectangular box, with a pair of eleva-

Two above: two views of the odd little Stoeckel. It is difficult to make out from only one picture how the machine is arranged. (Courtesy of the Musée de l'Air et de l'Espace/Le Bourget-France)

Right: The sculptured da Sylva pusher biplane. The 2 forward surfaces move independently. (Author's collection)

tors forward which moved up and down independently; controls were 2 sticks on each side – there were no rudder pedals. Outriggers supported a pair of rudders and a rear tailplane. The whole thing sat on 4 wheels, the pilot far forward.

(Length: 6.5 m; wing area: 25 sqm; weight: 250 g; 60 hp Anzani)

T

Taris

A graduate of the Polytechnique, Taris contributed to the design of at least 3 aeroplanes in 1909 and 1910, and also taught aeronautics at the Ligue Nationale Aérienne. The first machine on which he is known to have worked was the Taris-Bucheron biplane, tested by an infantry officer between September 1909 and August 1910 at Juvisy and Moulins. Descriptions of the machine are not clear, and extant photographs very poor. Even at the time it seems to have been difficult to describe, for a writer for *La Vie au Grand Air* wrote: "It partakes of all existing styles of aeroplanes."

It stood high above 2 skids and 2 pairs of wheels, its long narrow rectangular wings joined by a forest of 22 struts. The pilot sat in a frame hung out ahead of the lower wing. The 50 hp Gnôme was set on the trailing edge of the lower wing and drove a geared 4-bladed Taris propeller. The tiny cruciform tail was supported by booms, with 2 large rudders between the wings near the tips. The working of the control system is not clear; it may have been reworked several times. One photograph shows the pilot holding a horizontal lever with his left hand and a vertical one with his right. The machine was built at Espinosa's SCAA where Taris may have met Robert de Lesseps.

Later in 1910 Taris worked on the design of a monoplane known sometimes as the de Lesseps, sometimes as the Taris. De Lesseps had ordered it as "an aeroplane for speed." The triangular-section fuselage was covered aft of the straight wing; the uncovered nose protruded far ahead of the leading edge. The pilot's seat was let into a

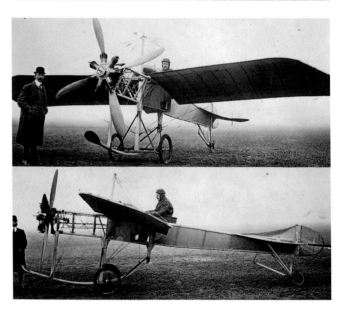

Two views of the second Taris, built for de Lesseps. (Peter M Bowers collection)

triangular swelling in the fuselage, leaving a curious triangular floor outside the aeroplane. The 2-wheel one-skid undercarriage resembled that of the Antoinette; a tailwheel on a complicated structure brought up the rear. The propeller was another Taris, this time 4-bladed and (some said) ground-adjustable. The aeroplane was expected to be fast, but it was not; it crashed early in 1911.

(Span: 8.5 m; length: 7.5 m; wing area: 14 sqm; gross weight: 350 kg)

Tatin

Victor Tatin's name was associated with a variety of advanced aeronautical designs and design projects. Born in 1843, by the time he was 31 he had made his first flying model, a little ornithopter made of feathers and weighing 5 grams. Although this flew, he turned quickly to fixed wing designs, to which he had been introduced by Alphonse Pénaud. In 1879 he designed and built a compressed-air powered model, now at the Musée de l'Air, which flew tethered to the center of a circle. The cylindrical tank with conical ends was the fuselage; the engine drove a long connecting rod on each side out along the monoplane wings, driving through cranks 2 tractor propellers. The tail was fan-shaped, like a pigeon's. The design showed Tatin's concern for reducing drag, and influenced the designer's later aeroplanes. Tatin would not be followed in these efforts till Edouard Nieuport in 1909.

In 1881 Tatin designed the propeller of the first electric dirigible, shown at the Paris Electrical Exhibition of that year. The airship was built by Gaston and Albert Tissandier; the motor was a 1-1/2 hp Siemens, and inadequate to the task. The spar-mounted spoon-bladed propeller, however, was to appear often in the next few years on more successful French heavier-than-air machines. And in 1890 Tatin invented an aneroid recording barometer that was to be used as one of the first altimeters in 1891.

The same year, with Professor Charles Richet, later of Breguet-Richet helicopter fame, Tatin designed and tested a large model which resembled Stringfellow's. An angular boat-shaped fuselage carried the steam engine with a propeller at each end of the hull, the rear one turning in an opening in the long flat horizontal surface that became the tail. Trapezoidal wings with a nearly flat airfoil section showed considerable dihedral. Damaged in the same year and then tested over the sea in 1897, it achieved a distance of 140 m before stalling and falling into the water.

(Span: 6.6 m; wing area: 8 sqm; weight: 33 kg; 1-hp steam engine)

In 1904, financed by Henri Deutsch de la Meurthe, he tested a model of a twin-rotor helicopter, at the same time contributing to Santos-Dumont's dirigibles.

In 1906 he designed what was to have been his first full-sized aeroplane, a monoplane sponsored by Jesus Fernando Duro, a member of the Aéro Club de France and founder of the equivalent in Spain. Construction began at Maurice Mallet's shops. Unfortunately Duro died from typhoid in August 1906, and the monoplane was left unfinished. It seems likely – but there is nothing left to show what this machine looked like – that some of its elements or basic design appeared again on his next monoplane, this one designed for Count Henri de la Vaulx, and built by Clément-Bayard.

Described as a "soaring plane," it was meant originally to have elliptical dihedral in both the elliptical wing and tailplane; it turned out to have slight dihedral only in the outer wing panels, and neither surface was elliptical in plan, but trapezoidal. The square-sectioned fuselage sat low to the ground, a 50 hp Antoinette set transversely behind the pilot driving 2 Tatin pusher propellers between the tail-

Above and below: two views of the big Tatin twin-prop model of 1890, before and after covering.. Note the steam boiler. (Courtesy of the Musée de l'Air et de l'Espace/Le Bourget-France)

De la Vaulx tested and crashed this second big Tatin machine in 1907. (Author's collection)

booms. The pilot sat well within the fuselage which was tapered at each end.

In his special crash-suit de la Vaulx tested his aeroplane at St Cyr in November 1907. On the 18th he is reported to have taken off after a 50-meter run downwind and stayed aloft for 70 m. In flight, the starboard wing failed: Tatin was known as a skilled clocksmith, not a carpenter: his structure was too weak, although evidently aerodynamically sound.

(Span: 15 m; fuselage length: 6.75 m; overall length: 13.25 m; wing area: 60.4 sqm; gross weight: c 400 kg; 50 hp Antoinette)

In the 1908 Salon Tatin showed his next monoplane, this one sponsored by Louis Paulhan. It was a handsome development of his previous machine, and named Aéro-Torpille No 1. The fuselage was now spindle-shaped ("spindle" in French is "fuseau," hence the word "fuselage"); the wings were again trapezoidal, very thin, set on the top of the fuselage, with Tatin elliptical dihedral. A device to adjust the angle of attack was patented at the end of 1911; it may have been fitted to Aéro-Torpille No 1. The engine was inside the fuselage amidships, and a long drive-shaft turning on 5 bearings ran back to the tail-

Above and below: two complementary views of the handsome Tatin Aérotorpille No 1. (Courtesy of the Musée de l'Air et de l'Espace/Le Bourget-France)

mounted propeller, kept off the ground by a long skid. The undercarriage had 2 wheels each attached at the bottom of inverted wooden arches, the axle running between them. It was reported to fly at about 145 kmh, but was difficult to control. (Bill Hannan, the famous Peanut-scale model-builder, reports that in a recent model meet the little Tatin model flew quicker and with more stability than any of the other models entered.) The fate of the aeroplane is not known, but features of it were copied afterwards – cf Riffard and Ruby, for instance, and Paulhan's Aéro-Torpille of 1911.

(Span: 8.6 m; length: 8.6 m; wing area: 12.5 sqm; empty weight: 360 kg; 50 hp Gnôme)

Tellier

Alphonse Tellier was the son of the founder of the Chantiers Tellier, which built fast motorboats on the Quai de la Rapée on the Seine in Paris, and he eventually took over his father's firm. At the Quai de la Rapée he met both Victor Tatin and Léon Levavasseur before 1900. In 1905 he drove one of his own speedboats, La Rapière, to tow Voisin's glider on the Seine; in the same year Hubert Latham drove another of Tellier's boats, Antoinette, named for Léon Levavasseur's daughter. (The name Antoinette referred first to Levavasseur's daughter, then

The first Tellier, of 1909. (Peter M Bowers collection)

to his motor-boats, then to his V8 engines, and last to his aeroplanes.) Growing more interested in flying machines, Tellier began designing propellers and testing them on a hydroplane; by 1908 he had built a catapult to test lifting surfaces.

In 1909 following the Reims meeting, he was asked by Emil Dubonnet to design and build him an aeroplane. Construction began

Above: One of the second versions of the Tellier, still with wings shaped like those of the Blériot XI. (Courtesy of the Musée de l'Air et de l'Espace/Le Bourget-France)

at la Rapée and was completed in Tellier's new facilities at Juvisy, also on the Seine. Painted brilliant yellow, the aeroplane resembled a much-elongated Blériot XI, with tapered wings braced from a single tall inverted V tower extending above and below the 2-seat fuselage; the wings were constructed with riveting and brackets. He later patented brackets of celluloid to facilitate wing-warping-perhaps these were used on his first machine. A triangular fin carried a small semicircular rudder set high above the one-piece tailplane and elevator, the whole carried by an early-style tailwheel. The radiator was set into the fuselage below and behind the engine. Testing took some time: at first, Dubonnet, who did not know how to fly, learned to taxi with a 20 hp motor, the planned 35 hp Panhard-Levassor not being ready. Finally, with the larger engine, Dubonnet first flew it on 8 March 1910 and was breveted on it on 17 April. While still unlicensed, on 3 April, he was awarded a prize from the magazine *La Nature* for a 100 km flight taking nearly 2 hours from Draveil to La Ferté sous Jouare, during which flight he landed near Orléans to ask his way. 20 days later he took off from his private field at Draveil and landed at Bagatelle, having achieved the first flight over Paris (at an altitude of 30 to 100 m). On 28 May a landing accident destroyed the aircraft.

(Span: c 11.7 m; length: c 11.9 m; wing area: 24 sqm; empty weight: c 310 kg; gross weight: c 475 kg; 35 hp Panhard-Levassor)

It is said that 5 of these fuselages were built in 1910 at the Tellier School at Etampes; a second variant was built before the end of the year. One of these was equipped with the 60 hp Panhard-Levassor and sold to Russia in October, and which fitted with the 60 hp REP sold late in 1910 to the Comte de Nissole. The second variant was better streamlined then Tellier's first design: the engine was faired

A late 1911 Tellier, probably built under the name ACT, or perhaps under the later firm name d'Artois. (Courtesy of the Musée de l'Air et de l'Espace/Le Bourget-France)

underneath like the LVG of 1915. The undercarriage was simplified, smaller, and lighter; the tailwheel was replaced by a skid, the pylon tower by a single post, the tapered wings by Blériot look-alikes. This may have been the Type de Course sometimes referred to in the contemporary press.

In 1910 Tellier's whole business went bankrupt, some of the workers went to work for Levavasseur to build Antoinettes; and in January 1911 Armand Deperdussin bought up his works and then sold the aviation division to Louis Schreck. Deperdussin then helped Alphonse Tellier start a new company on the island of La Grande Jatte, on the Seine – today more famous for Seurat's great painting than for anything done there by Tellier. The new firm continued to build boats, floats, and hulls for flyingboats; there in 1912 he built the hull for the big Breguet flyingboat, La Marseillaise; and during the War he built seaplanes. The Tellier construction method was successful and later much imitated: 2 layers of slatted mahogany, covered with fabric and varnished, riveted perpendicular to each other, were screwed on frames or strakes.

In unpublished short memoirs, Tellier wrote that he had no money to patent this technique, but that Blériot, Béchereau, and some of the managers at Nieuport recognized later, in 1916, that the construction of most monocoque fuselages depended on Tellier's system.

In the meantime Louis Schreck had reorganized the aviation section into a company called ACT (Anciens Chantiers Tellier) in the former Tellier works, and was continuing to sell Tellier monoplanes. In April 1912 he moved all the facilities including the school to Longuenesse, near St Omer, in northern France.

By the end of 1911, ACT was offering 3 variants on the Tellier theme: a single-seater, a 2-seater, and a racer. The latter was tested by Marc Pourpe in mid-1911, and it was sometimes referred to as the Pourpe monoplane: it was probably unrelated to the earlier Tellier Type de Course racer. It had straight rectangular wings and a short all-covered fuselage; the undercarriage was further simplified from the second design, and standard V-legs supported a long cross-axle that extended far beyond the apices of the Vs. The machine was sometimes referred to as Type 1912, and was shown in advertisements by ACT.

(Span: 9 m; length: 7.8 m; empty weight: 350 kg; 45 hp Panhard-Levassor)

Early in 1912 a Tellier monoplane was reported with a 50 hp Chenu engine, and up to 7 were reported built by May 1912. The question remains as to how many were built after Schreck took over the firm, and who exactly was responsible for the later machines. It is possible that the Chenu-powered machines may have been earlier Telliers retrofitted. Anciens Chantiers Tellier was not successful, and was soon disbanded to reappear as Chantiers Artois or simply d'Artois, with Gaudard as Chief Designer. A year later this new firm merged with the Société des Hydroaéroplanes Levêque to form Franco-British Aviation (FBA), also under Schreck.

In 1913 Tellier was building floats for seaplanes in his new firm Alphonse Tellier et Compagnie; in August 1914 Tellier worked briefly with Voisin and then reopened his factory on La Grande Jatte, building floats and motor-boats. In 1916 he worked on a big new flyingboat using the 200 hp Hispano-Suiza, and went on to build great numbers of flyingboats during and after the War.

Théodoresco, Lecoq, Rossi

One of several young Rumanians who went to France to study engineering early in the century, Teodorescu's name (Théodoresco in French) appears first early in 1911 when it was reported that he was having a monoplane built at Raymond's, the builder of the nacelle of the dirigible Pax. In April it was being assembled by Lecoq and Rossi's shops at Issy les Moulineaux. First trials were expected in mid-June, but the aeroplane was not tested before 20 July. Théodoresco's first attempt was into the wind; he pulled back on the stick, "took off, flew backwards, and fell down." Alexandre Anzani may also have flown the monoplane – or perhaps he was there only to install the engine. In September the wings were modified and it flew short distances.

The rectangular monoplane wing had rectangular wings and inset ailerons. The fuselage frame resembled a pair of wide-open shears with an elevator at each end, interconnected: the actual surfaces may have been Blériot spares without the Blériot movable tips. A long small rudder was mounted under each elevator. The engine and tanks were set above the wing, with a pusher propeller. The whole device

The oddly graceful Théodoresco monoplane of 1911. And it flew. (Courtesy of the Musée de l'Air et de l'Espace/Le Bourget-France)

The Thomann of 1910 – the second, or perhaps the first modified. Note the change in fuselage cross-section under the trailing edge. (Peter M Bowers collection)

rested on 4 castering wheels, each with its own highly curved small skid. Altogether a remarkably pretty aeroplane.

(Span: 11.8 m; length: 11.5 n; wing area: 26.8 sqm; 60 hp Anzani)

Thézenas et Reynaud

A man named Thézenas or Tézenas had formed a company called Société Forésienne d'Aviation (SFA) at St Etienne, near Lyons, and had built at least one monoplane and one biplane; little is known of either. Early in 1909 he was reported fitting an engine to a monoplane of his own design. Later, Thézenas and Reynaud were said to be building a biplane of 9.5-meter span, with a biplane elevator and rudder, 2 pusher propellers behind the wings and 2 more "lifting" propellers. The pilot sat on a saddle.

In 1912 a TRAL monoplane was mentioned in one aeronautical review, spanning 7 m, with a length of 6 m and a wing area of 12 sqm; it is possible that the first 2 letters stood for Thézenas and Reynaud.

Thomann

Thomann built bicycles: he was familiar with welded steel tubing and had worked with Delagrange, and when he began building aeroplanes by his own he used this construction. His first monoplane was built in Suresnes, a western Paris suburb. Delagrange had been killed in January 1910, and it is possible he had helped with the design. Similar to the Blériot XI, it differed in its fuselage: it was of rectangular section forward, triangular aft, fully covered; the frame was built in 3 sections joined with bolted collars as in bicycle construction. It also differed in the tail, which consisted of one long triangular tailplane on each side of the fuselage with a single elevator, a long triangular fin, and a small rudder at the end of it with another below the fuselage.

A second monoplane flew at the end of the summer of 1910; it may well have been the first one rebuilt. The fuselage was uncovered aft, and the typical Blériot high angle of attack was reduced; a rectangular tailplane was added below the aft fuselage.

(Span: 8.8 m; length: 7.5 m; empty weight: 175 kg; gross weight: more than c 200 kg; speed: 70 kmh; 25 hp Anzani – when fitted with a 45 hp Anzani, speed was said to be c 90 kmh)

At the time of this new machine, Thomann was reported building aeroplanes designed by others; Thomann's own designs were held by the CINA at Issy, where Thomann built and flew his machines. Early in 1911 the hangar at Issy was described as a "ruche" (beehive) with "half a dozen monoplanes" parked in it. The later Thomanns had fuselages of all-rectangular section and were very sturdy; one photograph shows 8 men sitting on one of them laid across 2 packing cases, and another shows 4 men climbing into a fuselage held vertically. The tail surfaces were more rounded, with the tailplane now set between the upper and lower fuselage longerons. One photograph shows 3 machines, one with the earlier tail, another with a large 5 painted on the fin.

After the war Thomann built motorcycles.

(Span: 8.5 m; length: 7 m; wing area: 17 sqm)

Thorand

Thorand is a forgotten pioneer of southern France. In 1910 he was completing a "curviplan" of 12.5-meter span; an unclear contemporary description talks of what might be a biplane with wings "joined at the middle," featuring 2 triangular cells. In August 1911 he was flying a monoplane at La Brague, Antibes; it might have been his own design.

Thuau

Victor Thuau was a former bicycle racer who turned to aeroplane design with little talent and little luck. He had built models before his only full-scale machine, a Demoiselle-based monoplane he called the Héroclite Phenomenon. The short rectangular wings were basically loose sails, each with 8 ribs and a leading edge; the tip of the leading edge was braced with a long spar running diagonally back to the aft fuselage, and the outer triangles of the sails worked as ailerons. The tailplane was deeply arched, apparently to increase lift at the tail. The fuselage frame was wide and squat, with the 10 hp V2 Anzani level with the top longerons; power was increased with the substitution of a 28 hp 3-cylinder Anzani. A different propeller of Thuau's own design was fitted to each engine, one of them with adjustable pitch. The whole ugly little machine weighed 120 kg; it was tested unsuccessfully at Issy in July 1910.

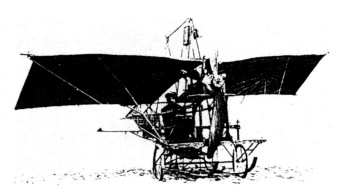

The Héroclite Phenomenon, Victor Thuau's semi-Demoiselle. (Author's collection)

Torchon

Paul Torchon brought a glider to Le Touquet in 1909.

Toussaint

An Albert Toussaint was mentioned as associated with aviation in 1909.

Train

Emile Train was the son of a manufacturer at St Etienne, near Lyon, and today is more famous for his motors and motorcycles built after World War I than for his early aeroplanes. These were of excellent design, but Train lacked the funds to compete with better-established builders, and his steel tube construction required skills that were not always available. Expert in mechanics and oxyacetylene welding, Train built his fortune by designing and building automatic vending machines. By the end of 1909 he had set up a hangar southwest of the camp-site at Mourmelon and began work on his first monoplane. After 3 months he was able to fly it, and he was breveted on 9 April 1910.

His monoplane was an all-metal copy of the Demoiselle, using wood only for the ribs. There were no turnbuckles, for ease of disassembly, and many parts were interchangeable, using bolted collars. The fuselage was deeper than the Demoiselle's, and the elevator was fitted under the rudder. The rectangular wings were double-cambered, thickening slightly behind the leading edge, and the tail surfaces consisted of a standard set, unlike the Demoiselle and its universal joint. The Anzani was mounted on the leading edge above the pilot.

In December 1910 Train had modified his monoplane and was building a 2-seater which flew early in January; it was developed from the single-seater by simply bolting on outer wing panels and fitting side-by-side seating in the front fuselage which had fabric-covered streamlined panels on either side, giving the appearance of a tear-drop-shaped nacelle. The undercarriage was strengthened, and the engine was now set slightly ahead of the wing. Some machines had a streamlined fairing behind the engine; some had a gutter to keep oil from the crew. The 1911 catalogue emphasized the Train's stability and ease of handling in gusts or strong winds, which Train himself often demonstrated.

The first Train aeroplane, a sort of all-metal Demoiselle. (Courtesy of the Musée de l'Air et de l'Espace/Le Bourget-France)

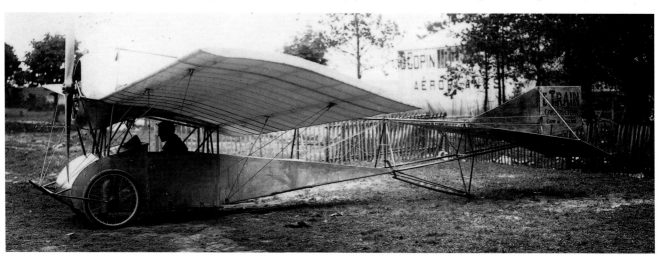

Basically the same Train with fabric-covered sides. Note the neatly-cowled Gnôme on the leading edge. (Courtesy of the Musée de l'Air et de l'Espace/Le Bourget-France)

The later 1912 Train monoplane with 3-4 seats. (Courtesy of the Musée de l'Air et de l'Espace/Le Bourget-France)

(Single-seater: span: 9.3 m; length: 8 m; wing area: 16 sqm (20 sqm): empty weight: 260 kg; 30 or 60 hp Anzani or 50 hp Gnôme)

(2 seater: span: 10.6 m; length: 8 m; wing area: 20 sqm; empty weight: 280 kg; 30 or 60 hp Anzani or 50 hp Gnôme – 70 hp Gnôme recommended for 2-seater)

The Train monoplanes remained generally unnoticed until Train's accident at the Paris-Madrid race in May 1911, when his engine cut out just after take-off; he tried to get back to the field at Issy to avoid horsemen ahead of him. He pulled back on the stick just before flare-out, stalled, and crashed onto a group of VIPs wandering out on the field, killing the Minister of War. The crash put Train and his aeroplane on the front page. It was clear, and quickly admitted, that the pilot was not to blame; Train was allowed to begin the race again the next day in another machine (some reported it was the same one, repaired), and the aviation press printed frequent laudatory articles about the designer and his aeroplane. The Train proved very reliable in this and future competitions.

The biggest operating advantage of the Trains was that the steel-tube structure did not deform in wet weather; primarily for this reason 5 (some reports say 7) single-seaters were bought by the Army for tests in the Colonies in Algeria, and they were sent to the school at Biskra, in the Sahara. These particular aircraft had 3-cylinder Anzanis instead of Gnômes to save weight. In 1911 Train offered a seaplane, either similar to the 1910 Anzani-powered model or the same machine, with 2 short floats replacing the wheels and a third fitted to the tailskid.

Although his aeroplanes were good ones, Train could not manage without financial assistance, and this was provided in 1911 by Henri Deutsch de la Meurthe. Train sold his hangar facilities to Sanchez-Besa, and his designs became part of Astra, as Astra-Train. In 1912 a new Train seaplane appeared, this time with a large rectangular pontoon with extensions on each side forward, apparently to protect the pilot. This huge float, 3 m long and 2 m wide, proved unsatisfactory and was abandoned.

(Span: 12.94 m; length (with float): 8.44 m; wing area: 21 sqm; 50 hp Gnôme, fully cowled)

In 1912 Train was building metal monoplanes similar to Nieuports and Borels. They had all-covered fuselages and simple rectangular rudder and elevators; the 2-wheel undercarriage had 6 legs like the Hanriot.

(Single-seater: span: 8.5 m; length: 8 m; wing area: 16 sqm; weight: 240 kg; speed: 78 kmh; 20 hp Darracq, 40 hp Anzani, or 50 hp Gnôme)

(2-seater: span: 9.9 m; length: 8 m; wing area: 20 sqm; weight: 270 kg; 40 hp Anzani or 50 hp Gnôme)

A drawing appeared of a different monoplane, with gracefully curved underbelly, split vertical surfaces above and below the rear fuselage, trapezoidal wings with wing-tip ailerons, an undercarriage similar to the Blériot XI but with 2 long curved skids beginning under the fuselage.

By the end of 1912 the heavier-than-air designs of Astra were merged with those of Nieuport, and an entirely new Train design appeared, a 3-4-seater monoplane with an all-covered fuselage, apparently inspired by the Nieuport. E Train, Constructeur was painted on the fuselage. The engine was fully cowled; the undercarriage resembled that of the Hanriot, a rectangular box-frame with trailing skids fore and aft. The upper pylon was an odd 3-legged tower from which the guy-wires braced the long wings – probably the same wings used on the Astra-Train. The triangular fin was later removed in favor of a balanced rudder; the large rectangular elevator had a box cut-out for the rudder.

(Span: c 13 m; length: c 8 m; wing area: 24 sqm; 70 hp Gnôme)

In 1913 Train was reported flying Nieuports at Mourmelon.

Trebeudin
A biplane, c 1913.

Trochu
A constructor or builder of this name was reported in 1908.

Turlin
This name was associated with some sort of flying machine with the name La Cigogne (swan).

U

Union des Aviateurs de la Côte d'Azur
A biplane glider of this name was flown in 1909, with front elevator, rear rudder, and a 10-meter span with a wing area of 41 sqm.

Union Française Aérienne
In 1909 this association was flying both a triplane and a monoplane; the former spanned 8 m with a 10 hp engine. Further details unknown.

V

Vaniman
Melvin Vaniman worked as music teacher, actor, opera singer, and airplane mechanic; he settled finally in Gennevilliers, a northern suburb of Paris, where he was hired by the American balloonist Walter Wellman to redesign his airship's car and put in a 75 hp automobile engine. To his balloon the America Vaniman and Wellman added an equilibrator, a 120' long leather tube filled with food for the trip that was to serve as a drag-rope for Wellman's Atlantic try. The first attempt started on 2 September 1907, failed, and in 1909 they tried

again – and failed again. On 15 October 1910 Wellman, Vaniman , 4 crewmen, and a cat named Kiddo started once more, again with the equilibrator, now a long bag full of gasoline for a second engine. The apparatus failed again, Wellman and his crew were saved, and Wellman abandoned the attempt. But Vaniman continued: he had a new airship, the Akron, built by Frank Seiberling of the Goodyear Tire and Rubber Company, and started again on 2 July 1912. Shortly after take-off, the airship exploded, and Vaniman and his 4-man crew died in the attempt.

But in the meantime, in Paris in 1907 he had designed an aeroplane first described as a monoplane, but which was in fact a monstrous canard triplane of which 2 variants are known. A large steel-tube structure carried 3 wings of 11-meter span each. The pilot sat on the lowest wing beside the 70 hp Antoinette engine which drove a single pusher propeller. The forward elevator was first mounted ahead of the tall rectangular rudder; then it was re-set lower on another pair of Wright-style outriggers; there was no rear tail surface at all. The whole rig rested on a 4-wheel chassis.

The triplane was modified in 1908 and reported as No 1bis. Ailerons were added at the tips of the middle wing, controlled through the pilot's elbows. Fixed horizontal and vertical surfaces were added at the rear, supported by 3 high-set parallel spars, the pusher propeller churning away below the booms. The forward surfaces were now carried by a complex set of spars, and the machine rested on 3 wheels instead of 4; tip wheels were fixed under the tips of the lower wing. Although on wheels, the second version of the Vaniman ran on special rails: one photograph shows it flying, but the photo may be dubbed.

(1st version: span: 11 m; length: 6 m; wing area: 72.6 sqm; empty weight: c 300 kg: 70 hp Antoinette)

In May/June 1908 Vaniman showed another awkward triplane; its relation to the first one is unclear. It had wings of a much shorter span, each 12 rib-bays in length, and what resembled the awkward forward rectangular rudder of Vaniman 1bis. A deeply arched rear tail surface and a low-slung flat forward elevator were to provide longitudinal stability.

Vasserot-Delassor

A monoplane of this name was reported to have flown 100 m on the beach at Cesson, near St Brieuc, in northern Brittany, on 13 November 1909. A postcard dated October 1909 shows a large Vasserot tractor monoplane named La Mouette Géante (giant sea-gull) on the beach at Cesson. The short rectangular-sectioned fully-covered fuselage rested on an Hanriot-style undercarriage; the trapezoidal wing was set at large angles of incidence and dihedral. The drooping triangular wing-tip surfaces gave the sense of a gull wing. The pylon was a trapeze, with one of its supports 2-legged, the other 3-legged. The long triangular tailplane drooped on each side, with a large vertical surface underneath; the trailing edges may have warped for control.

Vedovelli

The 1910 Vedovelli Fantôme resembled a huge alligator tangled in a forest of bent struts. Start with an alligator-shaped hull of square sec-

The sense of the 2 machines in this and the following photograph is basically the same: a triplane, with twin-boom outriggers, a high rectangular vertical surface, a single pusher propeller. But the 2 Vaniman triplanes are otherwise quite different. This one is the 1907 machine. (Author's collection)

And this is the 1908 Vaniman. (Courtesy of the Musée de l'Air et de l'Espace/ Le Bourget-France)

A somewhat simplified – retouched – rendering of the big Vedoveli in one of its several forms. (Author's collection)

tion, the jaw parts lined with transparent windows, and the pilot's bridge, also glazed, where the animal's eyes would be. A large rectangular rudder with rear-facing balances was hinged to the vertical bow. A wing with attractive elliptical dihedral was mounted on bent struts above the hull; a similar one, higher still, behind it, on more bent struts; another, similar, set well forward and low ahead of the nose; and yet another, set well aft and low. A tall rectangular fin rose up at the rear. These latter 2 were mounted on a pair of arches half-covered, as if to provide some rear fin area; gracefully bent skids were fixed at each end of each arch. Another much smaller rectangular wing, like an afterthought, lay on top of the hull amidships. 2 wide-set wheels forward and a nose-wheel allowed movement on the ground; 2 propellers were set into the middle of the side arches. The front rudder was painted SDA 4 SDA, but the meaning is unknown. Watching the Fantôme taxiing 200 or 300 m at 3 kmh was described as "dumb-founding": trails of dust were scraped from the field at Issy by the rear skids.

It crashed once, and was rebuilt with a simple 2-wheel undercarriage, wire bracing instead of steel tubing for the wings, and a reduced forward rudder. It was rebuilt again, now with the sides fully covered and a single propeller between the side-curtains; the rear rudder was gone.

The same year, taking time off from his electric-equipment factory, Vedovelli patented a motor and propellers, and a paddle-powered hovering machine.

Vendôme

<u>No 1</u>: Raoul Vendôme's first aeroplane appeared in 1908, a flimsy-looking monoplane with broad arched wings with the ribs on the top surface. A broad flat basketwork paddle ran back to support 2 large rectangular horizontal tail surfaces, one on each side. A single high pylon post braced the wings from above; wheels are visible in the single extant photo, splayed out, one on each side and far apart. It may not have been finished.

<u>No 2</u>: The new design was shown at the 1908 Paris Salon, quite different from its predecessor. The fuselage was long and covered, curving up at the tail, and supporting a single huge arched horizontal tail surface. The monoplane wings were also deeply arched, supported by a 4-strut pylon above; small movable surfaces above the leading edge of the wingtips were to provide control. 2 undercarriage wheels were set forward, and a third halfway back.

<u>No 3</u>: This pretty little monoplane of December 1909 set the pattern for several to follow. The fuselage consisted of a single boom with the familiar arched horizontal surface set above the

The Vendôme No 1 in the shop. The tail surfaces do not seem to be movable. (Courtesy of the Musée de l'Air et de l'Espace/Le Bourget-France)

Above and below: two views of the Vendôme No 2 photographed in 2 separate locations. (Courtesy of the Musée de l'Air et de l'Espace/Le Bourget-France)

Above and left: The Vendôme No 3. Note the first appearance of the later Vendôme trademark landing gear. (Peter M Bowers collection)

tail end; a small trapezoidal fin was below it, and a small square rudder behind that. The wings were rectangular, with odd movable eyebrow surfaces on top at the tips; an inverted V pylon supported the wings. The undercarriage was formed of a heavy arch and 2 trailing wheels.

(Span: 11.5 m; length; 9.5 m; weight: 210 kg; 30 hp Anzani)

A smaller version of No 3 had a slender covered fuselage, a Blériot-style trapezoidal pylon, rectangular wings, an arched undercarriage frame, and a rectangular rudder mounted aft and underneath an arched stabilizer surface. The eyebrow ailerons had disappeared; the names Odier-Vendôme appeared on the fuselage sides.

La Moustique (mosquito), was photographed on 13 November 1909, a tiny monoplane with a scalloped wire trailing edge, and typical Vendôme structure otherwise. An additional small horizontal triangular surface was sometimes fitted on the top of the fuselage between the wing and the stabilizer. A 12 hp engine was mounted below the nose, driving the propeller through a wide belt.

Odier-Vendôme biplane: Henri Rougier was born in Marseille, the location of the automobile firm Turcat-Méry; he became a race driver, using Turcat-Méry cars. He learned to fly in 1909, and in 1911 a new firm, Turcat-Méry-Rougier, was established north of Paris at Levallois-Perret to build engines and aeroplanes. He commissioned the firm of Vendôme to design him a new machine, a biplane which also carried the name of Odier, Vendôme's engineer. It appeared in 1910, with wings on each side arched like spoons from a straight center-section; the odd Vendôme eyebrow surfaces appeared at the lower wingtips, though it was also built with ailerons. Tiny wheels were set into arched undercarriage legs. Twin boom structures supported the biplane tail with its semicircular central rudder. It was underpowered with its 18 hp Turcat-Méry engine. A second version (No 2?) appeared the same year, this one with less severely arched wings, the 2 booms of the first biplane combined with the single arched tailplane of the Vendômes. 2 small rectangular rudders fitted under the tailplane; the trailing wheels had high curved horns in front to carry the shock cords.

A later version of the No 3 Vendôme. (Courtesy of the Musée de l'Air et de l'Espace/Le Bourget-France)

The tiny Vendôme Moustique. (Peter M Bowers collection)

Another view of the little Vendôme: a truly light aeroplane. (Bill Lewis collection)

Below: The Odier-Vendôme biplane of 1910. (Courtesy of the Musée de l'Air et de l'Espace/Le Bourget-France)

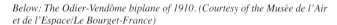

(No 2: span: 8 m; length: 8 m; 18 hp Turcat-Méry)

Demoiselle copy: In 1910 Vendôme also built a Demoiselle look-alike, with a single boom, high arched tailplane set ahead of the Demoiselle-style rudder, and a tailwheel fitted to a leggy strut.

The Odier-Vendôme biplane in flight. (Peter M Bowers collection)

In September 1910 appeared at Issy a tiny Vendôme monoplane with arched wings and flexible deckled trailing edge extensions (or ailerons?); long triangular horizontal and vertical fixed surfaces comprised a large rudder and separate elevators joined with a single rod to provide control. The familiar Vendôme arched undercarriage was used here, too.

In February 1911 another Vendôme monoplane flew at Issy. It showed off gulled wings at shoulder height, the familiar arched undercarriage beam with trailing wheels, and a covered fuselage of diamond-shaped section. The large tailplane had the separated elevators joined with a strut at their trailing edges. 2 different rudders were fitted, one tall and rounded, the other tall and angular; the latter version had a Viale engine.

Also in 1911: a pretty design with elliptical wings, the Vendôme arched landing gear, rounded tailplane and elevators, and a new rounded comma-shaped rudder. The cockpit was set up in a raised cowling behind the 5-cylinder Anzani.

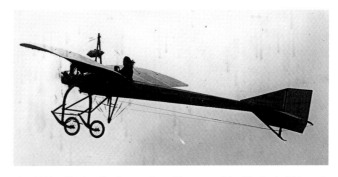

The 1911 gull-wing Vendôme at Issy. (Courtesy of the Musée de l'Air et de l'Espace/Le Bourget-France)

Type Militaire: In 1912, a clean little shoulder-wing monoplane with trapezoidal wings and inset elevators, a rectangular tailplane in at least 2 forms, each with long trailing elevators. The new comma rudder was retained. The machine could be disassembled in 5 minutes. The wheels were huge, 1.8 m in diameter.

(Span: 8 m; length: 6.8 m; wing area: 16.9 m; Anzani engine)

In 1914, a new monoplane featured a V-leg undercarriage, and curved trailing edges to the wings with cut-outs on each side next to the fuselage. A small rectangular rudder stood up by itself, over the large rectangular horizontal tail.

Also in 1913 Gibert flew his new machine at Issy and soon crashed it on the roofs of Paris, a stubby little monoplane similar to the one of the previous year, but with a triangular fin and D-shaped rudder.

Another 1911 Vendôme monoplane. (Courtesy of the Musée de l'Air et de l'Espace/Le Bourget-France)

Monoplace Repliable: This design of 1914 featured a slender covered fuselage, and the arched undercarriage of the earlier Vendômes, but it gave way to the next 2-seat design, lighter, with the same engine.

(Span: 9.15 m; length: 7 m; 50 hp Gnôme)

Two views of the 1912 Vendôme Type Militaire. (Courtesy of the Musée de l'Air et de l'Espace/Le Bourget-France)

<u>Type Militaire</u>: In 1914 Bossano flew this Le Rhône-powered 2-seater at Issy, a handsome machine with triangular undercarriage legs, a raised cowling in front of the pilot, and an uncovered aft fuselage. It may have flown with a 4-bladed propeller. It could be disassembled in 70 seconds.

(Span: 8.2 m; length: 5.8 m; wing area: 14 sqm; empty weight: 197 kg; speed: 130 kmh; 50 hp Gnôme)

Villard

Henri Villard was a French national who moved to Belgium from 1898 to 1914 to work out a series of helicopters, 6 in all, among his other studies of aviation subjects.

<u>1</u>. In 1901 he built a propeller – or perhaps a rotor. No further aircraft for it has been discovered.

<u>2</u>. A machine was being completed at Tarbes in 1909. It or another was later being completed at La Seyne-sur-Mer, near Toulon. In August 1909 he was sent a 50 hp Gnôme and completed his rig, which he thought would lift 3 people.

<u>Aviator</u>: an early, perhaps the first, Villard effort at vertical flight, consisted of a large umbrella-like rotor of 9.1-meter diameter on a shaft, off which the pilot sat with a horizontal propeller in front of him and a steerable circular rudder behind him. The rotor was a disc of silk stretched over a wheel of double wire spokes, and was to serve as a gyroscope for stability as it turned, and as a parachute in case of trouble. A photograph shows a similar helicopter with 2 overhead rotating discs – either a modification of the first Aviator, or a new machine. The first one was finished in 1902.

<u>Ornis-1</u> was a heavy wooden-framed helicopter machine built in 1906 which never flew. The pilot sat forward in a half-covered nacelle with an up-curved skid in front

<u>Ornis-2</u> was Villard's second version in 1913 at Schaerbeek, and it was shown in 1914 at the third and last Salon de l'Automobile, du Cycle, et de l'Aéronautique in the great hall which is now occupied by the Belgian Air and Space Museum. A small 4-bladed rotor turned immediately above a long drooping wing of deeply arched airfoil section built on 2 spars. The small openwork fuselage, similar to that of Ornis-1, was covered in front, and sat on 2 wheels. A contemporary account of the flight trials follows:

> The Burgermaster of Schaerbeek, M Kennis, allowed M Villard to install his machine in the courtyard of the town hall, where he made a hellish noise, without succeeding in rising due to the weight of his motor. Learning of this, Albert I summoned M Villard and offered him an 80 hp Anzani and the use of a shed at the Parc du Cinquantenaire so that he could pursue his experiments.

The 1914 Vendôme with wing cut-outs. (Courtesy of the Musée de l'Air et de l'Espace/Le Bourget-France)

The 1902 Villard Aviator – there seem to have been several of them. (Courtesy of the Musée de l'Air et de l'Espace/Le Bourget-France)

The 1906 Villard Ornis I helicopter. (Courtesy of the Musée de l'Air et de l'Espace/Le Bourget-France)

They proceeded successfully, since the helicopter, piloted by Tony Orta and Henry Gérard, began by lifting itself a meter off the ground. On 28 June 1914 the machine was taken to Berchem-Ste-Agathe, and Albert I went himself went to watch the trials each time more convincing; but not attentive to the presence of his sovereign, M Villard, quite distracted, greeted him with "Good day, Mr Lord!" Baptized l'Ornis, the helicopter was taken and destroyed when the Germans took Berchem-Ste-Agathe, several months later.

Albert had paid for a 120 hp Anzani; but for some reason an 80 hp engine had been delivered, and Albert asked Villard to build a third machine.

Ornis-3 was the third Villard design to be royally funded, and consisted only of bare steel tube struts mounted on 4 tubular floats; it used a larger engine, possibly the 120 hp Anzani meant for Ornis-2. It was tested by Henri Gérard at Ostend shortly before the War broke out. What may have been its immediate predecessor or perhaps a subsequent modification was similar, but was set on 3 big square-cornered floats.

(Rotor span: 2.7 m; rotor speed: 1100 rpm; weight: 410 kg; 120 hp Anzani (?))

Vinet

Another well-known automobile – and automobile-body builder, G Vinet became interested in aeronautics in 1904, when he built Archdeacon's first glider. In 1907, much more ambitious, he was planning an aeroplane in the shape of a bird, with 2 propellers, a 10-meter span, and a 12-15 hp engine; it was probably not completed. In 1909 his firm, Vinet Boulogne, had settled in Courbevoie, a northwestern suburb of Paris, and was building spares for aircraft. By 1910 it was selling Blériot wings and fuselages, and built aircraft by other designers such as Farnier, Milord, and de Puiseux.

From 1910 to 1913 the firm built a series of monoplanes of its own design; these took basically one of 3 forms. Letters were assigned to various types; B, D and F were mentioned the most frequently, but the variations were much more numerous than this suggests.

The first Vinet was a Demoiselle derivative in 1910, test-flown at Issy. The uncovered fuselage was of triangular section, the upper 2 longerons being light girders. The wings were trapezoidal, with odd upturned tips; the tail surfaces were of conventional form, unlike the Demoiselle's.

(Span: 10.5 m; length: 7.4 m; 40 hp water-cooled inline Labor, and other similar engines)

Type B: In 1911 Vinet advertised his Type B, claiming that his former aeroplanes (Type A?) had been "test machines without direct commercial consequences." Similar to the Blériot XI, the uncovered fuselage was slender; the undercarriage was a lighter version of the Hanriot's, where a 4-legged frame supported 2 long skids, across which was bound the axle. A long triangular tailplane supported tiny triangular elevators; the triangular rudder had no fin.

(Span: 9 m; length: 7.8 m; wing area: 16 sqm; empty weight: 210 kg; speed: c 90 kmh; 40 hp Gyp)

Vinet produced a racing variant for the Circuit Européen in June 1911, but it is not clear whether in fact it was entered. It had slightly less wingspan and weighed fractionally less than the Type B. Another similar machine was photographed in March 1912 at Issy – perhaps the same one modified, with Blériot-style pylon instead of a 3-legged tower.

The third Villard helicopter, Ornis-3. (Courtesy of the Musée de l'Air et de l'Espace/Le Bourget-France)

The first Vinet, similar to the Demoiselle. (Courtesy of the Musée de l'Air et de l'Espace/Le Bourget-France)

The Vinet Type B. (Courtesy of the Musée de l'Air et de l'Espace/Le Bourget-France)

Type D: The Vinet Type D was completed before the end of June 1911; it was the first of a series of similar machines designed by P James, all with a low-set covered fuselage below a parasol wing with the engine mounted above the leading edge. It was tested in August 1911 at Chateaufort but was found unsatisfactory.

(Span: 8.64 m; length: 6.58 m; wing area: 15.32 sqm; empty weight: 250 kg: 50 hp Anzani)

Type F: At the 1911 Paris Exposition, Vinet showed his Type F, similar to the D but better finished, with larger wing, smaller tailplane, and narrow tread, with a 35 hp Dansette-Gillet. Reports of the period describe it with a 50 hp Gnôme as either a single – or 2-seater.

(Span: 8.7 m; length: 6.5 m; empty weight: 180 kg; 35 hp water-cooled Dansette-Gillet)

On 28 February 1912 a Vinet crashed, this one with much wider tread and a large rectangular rudder; at the 1912 Salon a further development was shown with a huge tank set into the center-section of the wing, and a rotary engine. At least 2 versions appeared, with differences, before Vinet stopped building them.

Viriot
An all-metal monoplane was shown under this name at Issy, powered by a 35 hp Anzani.

Voisin
Any account of the work of the brothers Voisin must cope with the problem, greater with this firm than with any other, of the number of aeroplanes designed and built in part or in whole by the Voisins for other people whose names then became associated with the aircraft. The Voisins decided early on to accept work from others; these basically Voisin designs will appear in this section, though since some have become better known under their owners' names, they will be described more fully elsewhere.

Born on 5 February 1880, Gabriel Voisin became early interested in things mechanical, and he and his brother Charles built some pieces at the machine shop in his father's gas-works. They built kites; and discovering Hargrave's work in Australia, developed several large box-kites, and by 1898 they became interested in flying machines, and tested gliders at Neuville au Saône. In 1899 they added a pair of bars under one of their big Hargrave-type kites and tried it several times, unsuccessfully, stopping the tests before attempting to launch Charles from a 60' cliff in a quarry. At the 1900 Paris Salon he met Ader and saw his Avion; inspired, he went on to study the work of Octave Chanute, and based on the American's trussed box structure, the brothers built another glider.

Glider 1903: a biplane built of bamboo with cruciform tail copied from Chanute: this form was flown as a man-carrying kite, and the tail removed and replaced with the rear cell of their Hargrave kite. It was modified, or at least 2 and possibly 3 others were built in addition by 1908.

(Span: 6.4 m; wing area: 18 sqm; empty weight: 24 kg)

At Chalais-Meudon Voisin met Ernest Archdeacon and saw his Wright-based glider; Archdeacon asked Voisin to pilot it in 1904 at Berck-sur-Mer on the Channel coast, and subsequently to be the engineer in a new aeroplane-building firm, Le Syndicat d'Aviation. The gliders built by this firm are described under Archdeacon. One of the observers at the tow-testing from the Seine of the later Voisin-built Archdeacon glider was Louis Blériot, who asked Voisin on the spot to

The Vinet Type D, with the Anzani. (Peter M Bowers collection)

The Vinet Type F 2-seater. (Courtesy of the Musée de l'Air et de l'Espace/Le Bourget-France)

build him a similar machine and become a partner in aeroplane-building; their first three products, Blériots II, III, and IV, all unsuccessful, are described under Blériot. After these failures the partnership was given up.

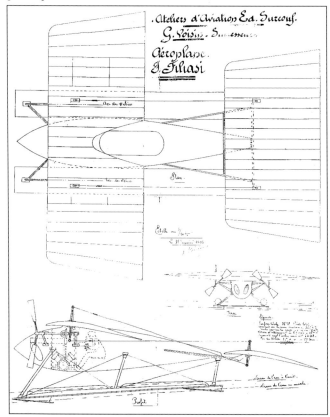
An original drawing by Gabriel Voisin himself of the 1906 hydroplane (aeroplane?) designed for Filiasi. (Author's collection)

In late 1906 the Voisin brothers hired a draftsman, Maurice Colliex, and formed a new firm, Les Frères Voisin, thus becoming the first manufacturers of aeroplanes – the first real aircraft factory. They had 2 plans: first to build the often bizarre and complicated and generally unsuccessful projects of rich amateurs who wished to make something original, and thus to collect enough capital to carry out their second plan: to develop their own early designs tested on the Seine into a successful flying machine. To attract customers to both plans, Voisin decided to name the machine after the purchaser rather than himself; the firm's name appeared in small print under the buyer's. In January 1906 they designed a remarkable streamlined twin-propeller hydroplane (but Voisin's own drawing is titled Aeroplane...) for a M Filiasi.

Their first customer, Florencie, had an ornithopter designed and built; then he ordered the nacelles for first one and then another unsuccessful machine – these are all described under his name. Their second customer for whom they designed an aeroplane was Henri Kapferer, whose little Buchet-powered biplane appears under his name.

Then came the sculptor Léon Delagrange, who is better known today for having been one of the first customers of Charles and Gabriel Voisin than for his fine flying and contemporary fame as a pilot. Though he never took part in the design of any of the aeroplanes he bought – Voisins and later a Blériot XI – he usually eventually modified them.

The Voisin-built Delagrange No 1 in flight, 30 March 1907. (Author's collection)

The Delagrange No 1 on floats. (Author's collection)

Delagrange (No 1): Henri Kapferer recommended the firm to his friend Delagrange who in December 1906 ordered his own machine designed and built by the Voisins; 3/4 of the purchase price would be paid only upon proof of a successful flight. Voisin attempted the first flight on 20 February 1907; it lifted briefly, but the fuselage failed. He tried again on 16 March at Bagatelle, but the torque of the motor drove it into the ground on its left wing. Adjusted, as Pénaud had done to his design of 1872, with 2 kg of dead weight added to the right wing, the machine flew successfully for 60 m on 30 March.

With the announcement of the Archdeacon Deutsch de la Meurthe prize, the Voisins wanted to buy the aeroplane back, but Delagrange wanted to enter it himself; and Voisin recommended testing it with floats. Taking off the wheels, Voisin assisted with the tests of and alterations to the seaplane glider in 1907 on Lake Enghien, near Paris, and then again with wheels, finally wrecking it irreparably in a crash. The aircraft showed what was to become typical Voisin design: big biplane cells for the wings and tail, big side-curtains as vertical tail surfaces and later between the wing struts, forward elevator, big rectangular open-box structure for the tail outriggers supported at the end by 2 tailwheels, and a castering 2-wheel undercarriage.

(Span: 11 m; length: 11 m; wing area: 60 sqm; dry weight: 450 kg; 50 hp Antoinette)

The following year he replaced the Antoinette motor in one of his Voisins with a 50 hp Chenu. In the same year he bought a Channel-type Blériot XI with a 3-cylinder Anzani and substi-

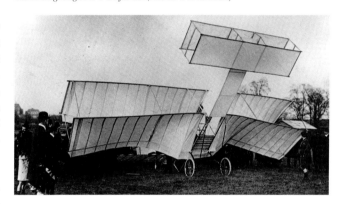

The Delagrange No 1 crashed at Vincennes. (Courtesy of the Musée de l'Air et de l'Espace/Le Bourget-France)

tuted a 50 hp Gnôme, renaming his machine Monoplan Eclair (lightning). With a strengthened undercarriage it was the first 50 hp XI, and also the fastest: on 30 December 1909 he achieved an average speed of 78.3 kmh with a top speed recorded of 86 kmh. A few days later, on 4 January 1910, he died when his Blériot crashed in a turn.

In March 1907 the firm also built the nacelle, propeller, and control surfaces for the dirigible Ville de Paris. They continued to build and test Chanute-type gliders mostly for the Aéro Club de France in May. Then they built in 5 weeks a little 50 hp Antoinette-powered biplane with a movable nacelle for the German Hans Reissner, who went on to work with Hugo Junkers on all-metal aircraft structures. The firm also built an unsuccessful large 100 hp helicopter for the Russian, Prince Chelmiky.

Henry Farman (HF 1): Ordered on 1 June as being "the same as Delagrange's one," on the basis of payment after a one-kilometer flight, and finished at the Voisin works in August 1907, the first Henry Farman was a big boxkite arrangement covered in silk with a big biplane tail cell with a central flap for a rudder; there were no side-curtains in the wing cell. The long pointed fuselage nacelle was uncovered, with a small biplane forward elevator pivoted at the front. The wheels castered, as on the Blériot. It hopped on 30 September 1907, but managed a 30-meter flight on 7 October.

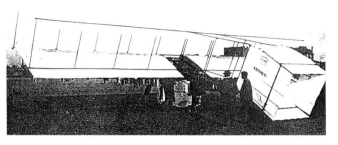

The biplane built for Hans Reissner. (Author's collection)

(Span: 10.8 m; length: 13.45 m; wing area: 42 sqm: empty weight: 320 kg; loaded weight: 550 kg; speed: 60 kmh; 50 hp Antoinette)

It was modified over time: a monoplane forward elevator replaced the biplane cell; the nacelle was covered; the rudder was moved aft inside the tail cell. Then the tail side-curtains were reduced and the rudder brought forward again. Then the tail cell was shortened; a gas tank was set on the top wing and a water tank above the engine. On 13 January 1908 it made a world record flight, one kilometer, closed-circuit. It then returned to the factory and reappeared as the Ibis.

The slightly modified Henry Farman No 1. Note the tank on the top wing. (Courtesy of the Musée de l'Air et de l'Espace/Le Bourget-France)

HF Ibis: The machine was restored and now covered with Continental cloth, and re-engined with a 50 hp Renault until May 1908, when the Antoinette was restored. In Belgium it received side-curtains on either side of the nacelle; in this form it flew from Châlons to Reims on 30 October, 27 km in 20 minutes. Farman's first design contribution was to modify the Ibis to triplane configuration (described under Farman).

Below: The Delagrange No 3, a modified version of No 2, itself a copy of the Henry Farman No 1. (Bill Lewis collection)

Right: The de Caters No 1 triplane. Note typical contemporary French use of castings. (Peter M Bowers collection)

HF II (Voisin): Henry Farman ordered this machine with a 2-meter gap instead of 1.5, but did not accept it. It may have been used as an "appareil d'essais," for testing engines.

Delagrange No 2: Seeing the success of the Farman machine, Delagrange ordered an exact copy of it from the Voisins in the fall of 1907 and flew it successfully in January 1908.

(Span: 10.2 m; length: 10.5 m; 50 hp Antoinette)

The Flying Fish: In February 1908 Henry Farman ordered a monoplane originally designated Henry Farman No 2; it is described under Farman, but was patented by Voisin.

Auffm-Ordt: Voisin built this little monoplane in April 1908, described under Auffm-Ordt.

Goupy No 1 triplane: In May 1908, the first of the 2 1908 Voisin triplanes, described under Goupy. It was powered with a 50 hp Antoinette.

Vaniman triplane: Built in August 1908 – described under Vaniman.

Delagrange No 3: Delagrange added side-curtains to his No 2 in September 1908, one on each side close to the fuselage, and renamed it No 3, with an Antoinette engine.

De Caters No 1 triplane: In October 1908, this was the second Voisin triplane, based on Goupy's but improved.

(Span: 7.5 m; length: 9.8 m; wing area: 44 sqm; empty weight: 475 kg; speed: 54 kmh; 50 hp Anzani, or perhaps a 60 hp Vivinus.)

Moore-Brabazon No III: Built for the Englishman in November 1908 with a 60 hp Vivinus engine. (See below, under Standard Voisin)

De Bolotoff: This big triplane is described under de Bolotoff.

Zipfel: Armand Zipfel had earlier built a glider to Voisin's instructions; he later ordered an aeroplane from the Voisin firm, patterned almost exactly on the Delagrange No III. It was built at the Ateliers d'Aviation du Sud-Est de Villeurbane, near Lyons, and Zipfel flew it first in November 1908. Later he took it to Germany, making the first significant powered flights in that country. He went on to build Voisins under license. (See also Zipfel.)

Standard Voisin: The firm put their best model into production, the first one being completed in December 1908. The ribs in both wings and tail were identical; 19 types of aluminum castings were used, and a variety of sheet-steel engine mounts al-

The Standard Voisin of Bunau-Varilla. (Peter M Bowers collection)

Henry Fournier's No 1 Standard Voisin; the engine has not yet been installed. Note the chalk lines on the rudder to guide the painter. (Peter M Bowers collection)

Paulhan's Standard Voisin. (Courtesy of the Musée de l'Air et de l'Espace/Le Bourget-France)

lowed variation in selection of powerplants. The first aircraft was sold to JTC Moore-Brabazon, who called it Voisin No III, since he had attempted to fly in 2 earlier aeroplanes, one of which may have been Goupy's abandoned triplane. Initially fitted with a 50 hp Vivinus automobile engine, it was later re-fitted with a 50 hp Antoinette with the nacelle covered. Moore-Brabazon then ordered a second Voisin, this one called No IV, fitted with an ENV and wider gap. 60 or so were built, exhibited, sold, and raced, in the course of 1908 and early 1909.

(Span: 10 m; length: 10.5 m; wing area: 49.75 sqm; empty weight: 445 kg; 50 hp Antoinette)

Among the purchasers were the Aeroclub of Odessa; de Baeder; Bregi (this machine was offered by *L'Aviation*); Bunau-Varilla; de Caters; Dufour; Ferber; Fournier (No 1); Gaudart (Daumont I); Gobron; Hansen; Jacquelin, Kluytmans, Koch; Legagneux; Lesire; Ligue Nationale Aérienne (2 a/c called Alsace and Ile de France); Metrot; Morveaux; Paulhan (who won it in a contest – see Paulhan); Poillot; Richer; Rigal; de la Roche; Rougier (No 1); de Salvert; Sanchez-Besa; des Vallières; Vivinus. Similar Voisins were license-built in Italy for Anzani, Cagno, and Florio.

<u>Voisin tractor,</u> 1909: The replacement for the popular but now outdated 1908 model featured a 4-cylinder Voisin-built engine; it was now a tractor biplane with an uncovered arched fuselage similar to that used in the Flying Fish. There were 2 sets of side-curtains and no forward surfaces, and the tail cell could move in 2 directions. It showed no improvement over the earlier models. In 1910 Edmond Jacquelin bought it and modified it further.

(Span: 10 m; length: 9 m; wing area: 49.75 sqm; 40 hp Voisin)

<u>Voisin Type de Course,</u> 1910: This entirely new design – and the smallest so far – was another effort to replace the standard model still in use throughout the world. It featured steel tube wing and outrigger beams. The design was gradually improved, appearing in races and airshows; one was flown by Bielovucic in his flight from Paris to Bordeaux. The new ones replaced the biplane tail cell with a single upper surface and a single rudder below it, which survived throughout WWI; and the drooping ailerons set

The author could not easily find a photograph of the Standard Voisin owned and flown by the Baronne Raymonda de la Roche, so he settled for this fine photograph of the lady herself. The baroness set many records and was world-famous, finally dying in one of her own aircraft. (Courtesy of the Musée de l'Air et de l'Espace/Le Bourget-France)

The 1910 Type de Course (racing) – this one was flown by Bielovucic. The design appeared in many variations, as shown by the following photographs. (Peter M Bowers collection)

The 1909 Voisin tractor. It was later sold to Jacquelin – see under Jacquelin for further information. (Author's collection)

De Rougier's Voisin Type de Course. (Courtesy of the Musée de l'Air et de l'Espace/Le Bourget-France)

into the trailing edges of the upper wings only, or of both. The Voisins sold both wood – and metal-framed versions of the standard model, along with the new improved ones at the same time; at least 6 of these were built.

<u>Type Bordeaux:</u> This was a 2-seater; one was equipped with a 38 mm Hotchkiss rapid-firing cannon and shown at the 1910 Paris Salon. Voisin also tested a rotary-engine-powered model with chain drive and sprockets of different sizes to test optimum pro-

Above: Another Type de Course, this one flown by Métrot at Reims. (Peter M Bowers collection)

peller speeds. Unlike the one-off Racing Biplane, the Type Bordeaux was in production.

(Span: 11 m; length: 10.5 m; wing area: 46 sqm; empty weight: 480 kg; 55 hp ENV)

Type Tourisme: Developed from the Type Bordeaux, this version was a little smaller than its parent and lacked the nosewheel. It featured a full dual control system.

(Span: 11 m; length: 9.5 m; wing area: 32 sqm; empty weight: 400 kg; 50 hp Gnôme)

Type Militaire, 1910: Also developed from the Type Bordeaux, this one had folding outer wing panels and kept the nosewheel; it also had dual controls.

(Span: 11 to 16 m (unfolded); length; 9.5 m; wing area: 42 sqm; speed: 87 kmh; 50 hp Gnôme)

Astra Triplane: Sponsored by Henri Deutsch de la Meurthe, Voisin was called to help the Astra firm design and build a huge armor-plated triplane made of steel tubing; even the wing bracing was steel tubing and not wire. 4 huge main wheels were centered on the lower wing leading edge, 2 on each side, 2 small wheels, one on each side, held up the rear end of the fuselage. One 75 hp Renault V8 was considered power enough to fly the huge machine; it did in fact fly, carrying its crew of 2. Big hanging ailerons were fitted to the 2 top wings; the long covered fuselage and neat single tail unit were remarkably modern-looking for 1911.

A 2-seater Type de Course. Note the extension shaft on the Gnôme. (Peter M Bowers collection)

Accident. A luckless Voisin Type de Course. (Courtesy of the Musée de l'Air et de l'Espace/Le Bourget-France)

(Span: 13 m; length: 7 m; 75 hp Renault)

Type Militaire, 1912: Resembling the Type Militaire of 1910, it featured doubled wheels.

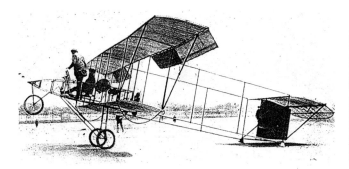

The Voisin Type Militaire of 1911. (Author's collection)

The big Astra triplane flew – with 6 wheels – on only 75 hp. (Courtesy of the Musée de l'Air et de l'Espace/Le Bourget-France)

A close-up of the Astra triplane. The struts all seem very light. (Courtesy of the Musée de l'Air et de l'Espace/Le Bourget-France)

The Voisin Type Militaire of 1912. Note the doubled wheels. (Author's collection)

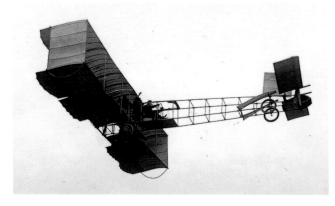

The 1911 canard prototype in full flight. Not quite in its first form, this version has the new forward eyebrow winglets. (Courtesy of the Musée de l'Air et de l'Espace/Le Bourget-France)

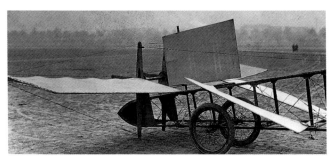

Details of the front end of the new Voisin canard. (Peter M Bowers collection)

Probably the Voisin canard prototype in a later form, in full flight. (Courtesy of the Musée de l'Air et de l'Espace/Le Bourget-France)

Left: Probably the second canard, it is being tested by Colliex on the Seine, on 6 August 1911. (Courtesy of the Musée de l'Air et de l'Espace/Le Bourget-France)

Canard prototype, 1911: This new design used one of the old rib-shaped triplane fuselages, probably from the third of the earlier triplanes, or perhaps from the abandoned Flying Fish. The fuselage frame was hung between the wings of the biplane cells – taken from a standard Voisin – with wires, to avoid the stresses of struts on a fuselage not designed for it. Ailerons were fitted to both upper and lower wings. In the course of testing, winglets were added behind the forward elevators, the fuselage was covered, and the front fin was enlarged. It carried up to 3 people, and was later mounted on floats.

(Span: 10 m; speed: 76 kmh; 50 hp Gnôme)

The second canard design, larger than the first, was meant as an amphibian, with 4 floats and attached wheels. Voisin demonstrated this 17-meter span machine by taking off the wings and driving it through the streets of Paris.

Production canards, 1911: Larger than the prototype, 3 of them were sold to Russia. They each spanned some 11 m. One 3-float amphibian, different from the others, was built in 1912 specially for the French Navy.

Seventeen-Meter: With increased wingspan the Type Militaire became known as the Seventeen-Meter. Some 47 were built.

(Span: 17 m; length: 11.5 m; empty weight: 970 kg; 70 hp Renault)

A revised version with shorter fuselage with a mica window in the nacelle floor, and a 4-wheel undercarriage, was tested in 1911, and in development it introduced the L-Series which served through World War I in various forms.

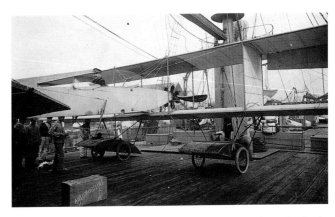

One of the 1911 production canards of 1911, specially built for testing by the French navy. Here it is on board La Foudre. (Bill Lewis collection)

One of the 3-seat canards of 1912. Note the variation among these later canard designs. (Peter M Bowers collection)

Another view of the aircraft in the preceding photograph. (Courtesy of the Musée de l'Air et de l'Espace/Le Bourget-France)

Below: Voisin built this all-metal monoplane for the chairman of the Bristol Aeroplane Company in 1911. (Courtesy of the Musée de l'Air et de l'Espace/Le Bourget-France)

Above and right: two more – and different – Voisin canards of 1912. Note the variations in the front ends, and the attachment of the forward elevators. Sometimes photographs can be matched through the patterns of oil and grease spots. (Courtesy of the Musée de l'Air et de l'Espace/Le Bourget-France)

<u>Canard 1912</u>: Further 3-seater canard developments of the 1911 design were built, experimenting with various combinations of rudder and front elevator controls.

(Span: c 17 m)

<u>Bristol-Voisin:</u> In 1911 the British Bristol firm commissioned an all-steel monoplane built by Voisin intended for the chairman of Bristols. Powered by a Gnôme, it had a triangular-sectioned fuselage, a complex forward structure, 2-wheel undercarriage and tailskid. The rectangular wings had ailerons and corrugated upper surfaces, reminiscent of the later work which Professor Reissner, himself a Voisin purchaser, did with Hugo Junkers.

<u>Type Monaco (canard)</u>: The final Voisin canard was similar to the 3 previous, but smaller, with 4 floats, built specially for the meet at Monaco. Voisin built 2 for the Monaco meet.

<u>Sanchez-Besa</u>: Built in 1912, this was the last of the Voisins built to the designs of others; it is described under Sanchez-Besa.

<u>Icare</u>: Henri Deutsch de la Meurthe ordered an aero-yacht from the firm. Colliex and Voisin used a standard Voisin structure combined with a Ricochet motorboat. Behind the pilot on opposite padded benches in an open bathtub-like cockpit sat 6 passengers; there was also provision for 2 small cannon and ammunition – the reason for the latter is unclear. The big Clerget was set into the flat-bottomed square-sterned hull and drove through chains a pusher propeller mounted high between the wings. The 4-bladed propeller was made by bolting together a pair of 2-bladed propellers. A single big rudder was fitted between the twin tailplanes, the whole mounted on outriggers. The aeroplane was tested at Issy with an added 6-wheel undercarriage.

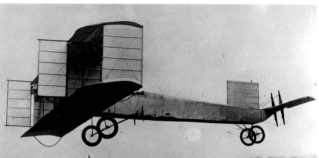

One of the 2 Types Monaco built by Voisin for this meet in 1912. (Courtesy of the Musée de l'Air et de l'Espace/Le Bourget-France)

(Span: 22.5 m; length; 12.5 m; wing area: 62.5 sqm; loaded weight: 2050 kg; speed: 110 kmh; 200 hp Clerget)

The L Series of 1913 was developed from the variant of the Seventeen-Meter, described above, and the series in its various forms was the Voisin design built in the largest numbers. By the end of 1918 more than 6,000 had been built, by Voisin, by other French firms, and by other countries. From these came the even bigger, frequently cannon-carrying, Voisin pushers, which served valiantly during the War. One survives today as the center-piece of the WWI Gallery at the National Air and Space Museum in Washington.

Vuia

Trajan Vuia, a Doctor of Law from Budapest living in Paris, designed and built his first monoplane between 1903 and 1905; it was tailless, with folding wings, 4 large motor-bicycle wheels, and a Serpollet motor

Two views of the one-off Voisin Icare Aero-Yacht. (Courtesy of the Musée de l'Air et de l'Espace/Le Bourget-France)

In February 1913, the prototype of what would become the Voisin 13.5-Meter, the forerunner of most of the wartime Voisin pushers. (Author's collection)

The 13.5-Meter Voisin of 1913. Note the extension shaft. (Author's collection)

A 13.5-Meter Voisin on floats for the French Navy. (Author's collection)

The Voisin 1L. Its lineage is pretty clear. (Courtesy of the Musée de l'Air et de l'Espace/Le Bourget-France)

The Voisin Petit Blindé (little armored one) of November 1913. Note the all-new tailboom and tail structures. (Author's collection)

A later Voisin, with tail structure like le Petit Blindé, but with more wheels. (Courtesy of the Musée de l'Air et de l'Espace/Le Bourget-France)

modified to use carbonic gas, giving some 25 hp. The front wheels turned with the rudder, and the wings could be warped and their angle of incidence changed in flight. Vuia tried it at Montesson, taking off briefly on 3 March and 12 and 19 August 1906, managing at most a hop of 12 m at a few centimeters in height, but it was underpowered and not controllable.

(Span: 8.7 m; wing area: 20 sqm; weight: 241 kg; 25 hp Serpollet)

He modified his machine as No Ibis, without the variable incidence mechanism, and with a rear elevator; it, too, was not successful. It is now visible, but tailless, at the Musée de l'Air et de l'Espace.

(Wing area: 23 sqm; weight: 275 kg; same engine and propeller)

Then he rebuilt the machine entirely: the No II was equipped with a 24 hp Antoinette and an Antoinette propeller with aluminum paddle blades. The fuselage box was now square in section instead of pyramidal as in the first 2, the rudder was larger, and the tires were much heavier; but it made little difference. 2 trials, in June and July 1907 at Bagatelle, were failures; and Vuia abandoned his machine and his efforts. One photograph shows what looks like either a further-modified No II with a horizontal tail surface, or perhaps a No III.

He built at least one helicopter as well, Hélicoptère Vuia No 1. The machine stands on 3 wheels with a vertical rudder upright between 2 outriggers. There seem to be 2 rotors, a big one on top and a smaller one perhaps turning among the various flat-surfaced wings or control surfaces. The prospect of its flight, at least in retrospect, seem doubtful.

Vuitton-Hubert

This firm in Paris built at least 3 aircraft, 2 of which were helicopters; there is no record that any of them ever flew.

I: This one was shown without a motor at the Paris Exposition of 1909. 2 counter-rotating rotors each with 4 elliptical blades were driven directly from the engine mounted on its back low on a 4-wheel chassis; the rotors were built up like long thin wings, with spars and ribs. A smaller propeller was fitted at the rear for horizontal thrust, driven by a gear from the main shaft. Steering was done by the pilot's leaning, combined with a rudder hung at the tail. A fixed triangular vertical surface was set forward.

(Rotor diameter: 4 m; length: 4.25 m; 50 hp Farcot)

II: The second machine, an odd monoplane, was shown at the 1910 Paris Salon. A long uncovered triangular frame of square section had a small cruciform tail at the very end; the front end of the fuselage was a cubical box, all uncovered, with a motor driving a huge 3-bladed paddle tractor propeller; above was set a large angular low aspect-ratio wing with upturned tips.

III: This was displayed at the same Salon, marked Vuitton III. It was similar to No I, an uncovered 4-sided pyramidal frame on 4

Trajan Vuia's No I, without a tailplane. (Author's collection)

The Vuia No Ibis, with a tailplane. (Author's collection)

The second Vuia aeroplane, with a squared box frame. (Author's collection)

This remarkable photograph shows one of the Vuia aeroplanes in a precarious position: it may be No II, with enlarged tailplane. No further information is available on this incident, at least by time of writing. (Courtesy of the Musée de l'Air et de l'Espace/Le Bourget-France)

wheels, with a central vertical drive-shaft and 2 counter-rotating rotors, the top one with 3 short blades, the lower with 2 long thin ones. The rear-mounted pusher propeller was still there, but the 2 vertical surfaces did not appear.

W

Wehrle
A machine of this name was reported in 1909 as being built on skates and/or floats.

Wilkes
British-built, an awkward-looking Wright copy appeared, perhaps with a Gladiator motor, at Le Havre in 1909 or 1910. The wings seemed floppy; a biplane forward elevator was balanced by the familiar Wright double rudders behind. The machine ran on 4 wheels. The twin propellers featured huge paddle blades.

Witzig-Lioré-Dutilleul

<u>WLD 1</u>: The first WLD was shown in 1908, a fragile-looking biplane with overhung top wings, long uncovered nacelle ahead of the wings carrying a single forward elevator; a large floppy rectangular tailplane with 2 rectangular rudders fitted below it with 2 tailwheels attached. Between the tailplane and the top wing were set, at graded height and interval, 2 short horizontal panels the span of the tailplane; the aeroplane was supported on a tall undercarriage structure with 2 trailing wheels. By the time the wings were attached, the single forward elevator had been replaced by a biplane cell, and the landing gear legs and pivoting girders for the wheel supports had been changed, with the wheels forward instead of castering aft. But with this arrangement the whole structure sagged visibly.

(Span: 8 m; length: 12 m; wing area: 50 sqm; weight: 550 kg; expected top speed: 15 km/second (this seems not to have been a misprint!); 50 hp Renault)

It was subsequently modified further, with a heavier supporting box structure for the aft fuselage, and various combinations of the supplementary rear panels; the wheels once again were reversed, to trail aft.

<u>WLD 2</u>: This appeared in 1909, a much simplified version of No 1. It had a straightforward 4-boom outrigger, a single forward elevator, ailerons set partly into the lower wings, and 2 small rectangular rudders set between a pair of large back-staggered tailplanes. The wings were of equal span.

Right: One of the first revisions of the Witzig-Lioré-Dutilleul No 1, with the wheels set too far forward, resulting in the distortion of the whole airframe. (Author's collection)

The Vuia helicopter No 1. (Courtesy of the Musée de l'Air et de l'Espace/Le Bourget-France)

The Vuitton-Hubert No 1 helicopter. (Courtesy of the Musée de l'Air et de l'Espace/Le Bourget-France)

The 1910 Wilkes, which appeared, but perhaps did not fly, at Le Havre. (Bill Lewis collection)

Ferdinand Lioré's first monoplane was exhibited in the WLD display at the 1909 Salon; it is described under Lioré.

Wright

Wright aeroplanes were built under license with Barriquand et Marre motors by la Société des Chantières de France, organized by Lazare Weiller. One such machine was used by Etévé to work out his automatic stabilizer. The Société Ariel, whose Director was Michel Clémenceau, had the monopoly on the sales of Wright aeroplanes.

Z

Zenith

This 1910 monoplane was built by Georges and Gendre at Villemobile (or by L Tatte Ch de Langhe and Corville) from plans by M Tabarly. It had arched undercarriage, a Blériot-style wing and trestle pylon, and tail à la Vendôme – the tailplane set above the rear end of the fuselage, with small semicircular rudders above and below, and triangular fins. Pictures also show it without the upper fin.

(Span: 8.5 m; length: 8.5 m; wing area: 16.2 sqm; speed; 70 kmh; 3-cylinder Anzani)

Zens

Paul and Ernest Zens produced at least 3 designs:

1. In 1908, a ragged-looking pusher biplane with a 50 hp Antoinette, with wings set at a large dihedral angle; a single forward elevator set into the nose of a long streamlined covered nacelle. 2 triangular outriggers supported a single rectangular tailplane and 2 tailwheels, with no vertical surfaces. It managed to make a few short hops.

2. In 1911: this was a high-wing monoplane with a long uncovered rectangular fuselage structure, single tailplane and elevator; a single rudder (in some pictures, a pair) set aft of the elevators. The ailerons were inset into the wing. The pilot sat on the floor below the trailing edge, the engine being set into the leading edge. The machine was supported on 2 pairs of wheels, a pair of long curved skids connected at the tips.

3. In 1912: this was a conventional-looking monoplane with level rectangular wings, a slender covered fuselage with a small rect-

Above and below: two views of the final version of the WLD 1, with the wheels safely back supporting the engine. (Courtesy of the Musée de l'Air et de l'Espace/Le Bourget-France)

The Witzig-Lioré-Dutilleul No 2, more like other designs of the period. (Courtesy of the Musée de l'Air et de l'Espace/Le Bourget-France)

A Wright built by la Société des Chantières de France, with many wheels. (Author's collection)

Left: The 1910 Zenith monoplane. Note the arched undercarriage beam. (Courtesy of the Musée de l'Air et de l'Espace/Le Bourget-France)

Above and right: The first Zens. Note absence of vertical surfaces; even the fuselage sides are curved. (Courtesy of the Musée de l'Air et de l'Espace/Le Bourget-France)

angular rudder above and below the tailplane. A single N-shaped girder on the fuselage centerline carried a skid across the lower ends of the N, and the axle lay across the skid. The whole structure was wire-braced to the wings.

Zipfel

In 1908 Armand Zipfel built a glider from instructions from the Voisins, put a motorcycle motor and propeller in front, and made short runs off the ground. A later aeroplane designed by Zipfel was built by the Voisins, and is described under their name.

Right: The Zens brothers are moving towards a more standard form with this their second aeroplane. (Courtesy of the Musée de l'Air et de l'Espace/Le Bourget-France) Below: The attractive third Zens design, this slender monoplane is eager to fly in this photograph. (Courtesy of the Musée de l'Air et de l'Espace/Le Bourget-France)

Zodiac

The Société Zodiac developed in 1911 from the firm begun by the painter Maurice Mallet to build dirigibles; the Comte de la Vaulx was named technical director. This firm built some 63 dirigibles with no fatal accidents, and later, at least 3 different aircraft:

1. In 1910: a Blériot-like monoplane built for the Prince de Nissole, named L'Albatros, with a double pair of wheels and skids on an elaborate undercarriage structure. The horizontal tail was set below the rear of the fuselage, with a trapezoidal rudder at the far tip.

2. Another monoplane for the Prince de Nissole, with Antoinette wings and ailerons, a long uncovered rectangular fuselage, rectangular elevators, and Antoinette-style fins and rudders. A small aileron (?) surface was visible on each side of the fuselage under the wing. A tailwheel was fitted.

3. In 1911: a Farman-style pusher biplane with equal-span wings and an uncovered wedge-shaped nacelle. A forward elevator rode on outriggers; the biplane tail cell had a single rectangular rudder between the surfaces. Labouchère flew it at Issy. It also ap-

The Zens in flight. (Bill Lewis collection)

The first Zodiac monoplane, built for the Prince de Nissole. (Courtesy of the Musée de l'Air et de l'Espace/Le Bourget-France)

The second Zodiac monoplane for the Prince de Nissole, L'Albatross. (Courtesy of the Musée de l'Air et de l'Espace/Le Bourget-France)

Above: The third Zodiac, this 1911 biplane. It appeared shortly after appearing here, modified as seen in the next photograph. (Courtesy of the Musée de l'Air et de l'Espace/Le Bourget-France)

Right: The third Zodiac in its later form, with covered nacelle and overhung top wings. (Courtesy of the Musée de l'Air et de l'Espace/Le Bourget-France)

peared with the nacelle covered, and top-wing extensions braced with pairs of diagonal struts.

4. In 1911: a handsome big 2-seat 3-bay 1911 tractor biplane with overhung top wings and inset ailerons, it had an Antoinette-style undercarriage with a pair of small wheels at the tip of the skid, and Antoinette-style tail surfaces. Power was a neatly-cowled Gnôme. In 1912 it appeared again, now with 2 hexagonal rudders instead of the single rectangle, and a skid instead of the single tailwheel.

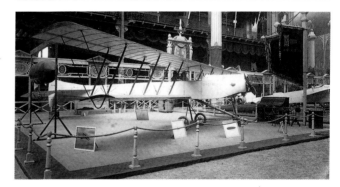

The big 2-seat Zodiac of 1911. (Courtesy of the Musée de l'Air et de l'Espace/ Le Bourget-France)

Appendices

Appendix I: More Aeroplanes, Perhaps

So far the author has not been able to find anything more about these names, except perhaps for a single reference in a book or magazine. Some of them may be misspellings of more familiar names which appear elsewhere in this book. They may be builders, designers, financiers, pilots- or perhaps mere errors.

Alaires 1908
Archambaud

Baleira, de
Belin
Bellocq
Bernardin
Bloudinat
Bonafous
Bonnemaison
Bonneville, Louis
Brancolard
Briais
Brun et Martin
Bucciali
Budig et Rigaud
Budin
Buguet
Buisson
Bussoli

Caminade
Camus
Chapuis
Chaubourg

Dauvergue
David
Decobre le Duée de Varenne (1908)
Deletang
Delizy Dubuet (1908)

Desmots
Dolfuss (1908)
Dufer
Duncant
Dupuit (Système Dupuit)

Felber et Fils
Ferrus
Fifils
Fornet
Foulac
Fournier (not Voisin)
Frachet
Franchomme
Friboulet

Gaillard
Gourrier
Guérin

Joux, de

Lageais
Landé
Lantereau
Lechevalier
Leflot
Lefrève
Lestage
Lorin
Lormain
Losse

Malvina
Mangeot
Marra
Massip
Masson
Mauve
Mayene
Mercier
Milin
Millet
Minard
Miscarol
Moncher, Guy
Montpensier, de
Moreau-Berthaud
Mousset
Moulin
Mourain

Nunait

Olivert et Brunet
Opperman (German?)

Partiot
Penkala et Penkala
Percival
Philippi (Philippon?)
Picot
Poan, FJ
Poignard, Octave
Poitrot

Pommier
Porporato
Proton
Poupelard

Rabelle
Rabiola (Robiola?)
Raze
Richard
Robyns
Rolle
Rylski
Richel
Ringard

Saint Germain
Sarard
Sautereau
Serrailler
Simms (Voisin)

Tenier
Terce
Timaskian (Timaksion?)
Touéry
TournierTruffault

Verdaguer
Verlet

Zanii

Appendix II: More Aeroplanes, But Which?

These photographs, some of good quality, some not, are of aircraft of the period whose names and histories have become separated from their pictures. Some seem similar to others elsewhere in this book – they might be developments or variants– but others just seem different. Perhaps some day their names and their pictures will come together. In the meantime we can wonder about them. (Unless some of the readers of this book can recognize some of them.) The numbering is only for reference. (All the photographs are from the author's collection.)

1

2

3

4

5

6

7

8

9

10

11

12

13

14

15

16

17

18

19

20

21

22

Appendix III: The Names

The names listed with no parenthetical explanations appear in alphabetical order in the section titled *The Aeroplanes*. Others can be found in the places designated.

A

AAE (cf Ateliers Aéronautiques de l'Est)
Abeille (cf de Marçay-Moonen)
ABL (cf Bonnet-Labranche)
Abric-Calas
Acier
ACR (cf C Roux)
ACT (cf Tellier)
Ader
Aéral (cf Fernandez)
Aérobus (cf Bourgoin et Kessels)
Aérogarage (cf C Roux)
Aéromobile (cf Constantini)
Aéronautique Club de France (cf Archdeacon)
Aéroplane Gyroscopique (cf Lataste)
Aérostable (cf Moreau)
Aérotourisme Victor Garaix (cf C Roux)
AGA (cf Association Générale Aéronautique)
Aiglon (cf Chazal)
Aillaud (cf Lecoq-Monteiro-Aillaud;
   Goyard-Aillaud))
Aimé (cf Aimé-Salmson, Santos-Dumont)
Aimé-Salmson
Akron (cf Vaniman)
Albatross (cf Zodiac)
Albert
Albessard
Alexandre
Alkan
Alvarez et de Condé
Aman (cf Etrich)
Amiot
Anciens Chantiers Tellier (cf Tellier)
André, d'
Antoinette
Anzani
Archdeacon
Ariel (cf Wright)
Armorique (cf Guillebaud)
Arnaud
Arnoux
Arondel
Artois, d'
Asquier-Régence
Association Générale Aéronautique
Astanières, d' (cf Constantin-d'Astanières)
Astra
Astra-Train (cf Train)
Astruc
Ateliers Aéronautiques de l'Est
Ateliers d'Aviation du Sud-Est (cf Voisin/Zipfel)
Ateliers et Chantiers de Dunkerque
Ateliers Vosgiens d'Industrie Aéronautique
   (cf Avia)
Aubry
Aubry (cf Météor)
Audemars et Garros (cf Santos-Dumont)
Audenis (cf Jacob et Audenis)
Audineau
Auffm-Ordt
Auto Aérienne (cf Pichou)
Auto-Aviateur (cf Bousson-Borgnis)
Auto-fiacre
Autoplan (cf de Pischoff)
Auzely
Aventino, Mingozi, et Paletta
Avia
Aviator

Avionnerie de Levallois (cf Société de
   Construction d'Appareils Aériens)

B

Babillard, Le (cf Henry Farman)
Bachelard
Bachelier-Dupont-Baudrin
Bacqueville, de (cf Pioneers)
Badaire
Badini (cf Société d'Etude pour la
   Locomotion Aérienne)
Baignoire, La (cf Lucas-Girardville)
Baillod
Bailly
Balassian de Manawas
Balaye
Baleine, La (cf Chassagny et Constantin)
Balsan
Baratoux (cf Compagnie Generale de
   Navigation Aérienne)
Barbichet, Le (cf Janicot)
Barillon
Barker
Barlatier et Blanc (cf Blanc)
Barlazzi
Baron
Bastier
Bathiat-Sanchez (cf Sanchez-Besa)
Baudrin (cf Bachelier-Dupont-Baudrin)
Baylac
Bazin
Beaufeist
Beaurin
Bébé (cf Santos-Dumont)
Bébin
Bécue (cf Garbero)
Bédélia
Beer, de
Bellamy
Bénégent
Berger-Gardey
Berliaux et Salètes
Berthaud
Bertin
Bertrand
Besnier (cf Pioneers)
Besseyre (cf Gilbert)
Besson
Bethenot (cf Perrin et Bethenot)
BGV (cf Guyot)
Bicurve (cf Sloan)
Billard
Billard et Lanzi (cf Lanzi et Billard)
Biot-Massia (cf Biot)
Biot-Massia (cf Pioneers)
Blanc, Henri
Blanc, Maurice
Blanchard (cf Pioneers)
Blanchard et Viriot
Blard
Blériot
Blinderman et Mayeroff (cf Kassa)
Bluebird (cf Moisant)
Bobba (cf Jourdan; also Ladougne)
Bobenreith
Boeswillbald (cf Guyot)
Boillot et Goux (cf Rossel-Peugeot)
Bonamy

Bonnet-Labranche
Bordier
Borel
Borel-Denhaut (cf Denhaut)
Borel-Morane (cf Morane-Saulnier)
Borel-Odier (cf Borel)
Borel-Ruby (cf Ruby)
Borgnis et Desbordes de Savignon
Borgnis-Bousson (cf Bousson-Borgnis)
Bosano, de (cf Dussot)
Bothy
Boucheron
Boullay
Bourbeau et Devaux (cf Bédelia)
Bourcart
Bourdariat
Bourgoin et Kessels
Bourhis
Bourniquet
Bousson-Borgnis
Boutard
Boutaric
Bouyer (cf Denhaut)
Boyenval et Jouhan
Brageas, de
Brazier
Breguet
Breguet-Richet (cf Breguet)
Breton
Breuil, du
Bridoulot
Briel
Brissard
Brissaud
Bronislawski
Bronislawski (cf Farman)
BRT
Brulé (cf Brulé-Girardot)
Brulé et Souchet
Brulé et Souchet (cf Souchet)
Brulé-Girardot
Bruneau (cf Parent)
Brunet
Bruyère et Sarazin
Buchet
Buéno et Demaurex
Bulot
Bunzli
Burdin (cf Kapferer)
Bussac, de-Chepaux (cf Chepaux)

C

Caille
Calvignac
CAM (cf Clerget)
Canton et Unné
Capon
Carlier
Carton-Lachambre
Castagne et Cambageon
Casteljou
Caters, de (cf Voisin)
Caudron
Caux et Camboulive
Caye
Cayol
Cayre
Cazalot et Prevot

Cazaudran (cf Reuch et Cazaudran)
Caze, de
Ceita
Celle, de la
Cellier (cf Guyot)
Certonciny et James
César
CGM (cf Comte, Gournay et Michaux)
CGNA (cf Compagnie Générale de
   Navigation Aérienne)
Chabeau et Biffu
Chaffal (cf Roze, perret, et Chaffal)
Champel
Chantiers d'Artois (cf Schreck)
Chantiers de France (cf CGNA)
Chapiro
Charmiaux
Charpentier
Chassagny et Constantin
Chaussée
Chauvière
Chazal
Chazal (cf Pacchiotti)
Chèdeville
Chelmiky (cf Voisin)
Chepaux
Chéramy (cf Gibert)
Chesnay
Chevallier et de Clèves
Chevallier, Yves
Christollet (cf Delabrosse et Christollet)
Cigare (cf Ruchonnet)
Cigogne (cf Turlin)
CINA (cf Compagnie Internationale de
   Navigation Aérienne)
Clémendière, La (cf Meugniot et La Clémendière)
Clément (Louis)
Clément (Maurice)
Clément-Bayard
Clerget
Clerget-Archdeacon-Marquézy (cf Clerget)
Clèves, de (cf Chevallier et de Clèves)
Cluzan
Coanda
Colibri (cf Goyard-Allard)
Collardeau (cf Lecoq-Monteiro-Aillaud)
Collieux (cf Voisin)
Colliex-Jeanson (cf Jeanson-Colliex)
Collin de Laminières
Collomb
Colombe (cf Ladougne)
Combes
Comète (cf Labanhie et Puttet)
Compagnie Générale de Navigation Aérienne
Compagnie Internationale de Navigation Aérienne
Comte, Gournay, Michaux
Constantin
Constantin (cf Chassagny et Constantin)
Constantin (cf Chassany et Constantin;
   Constantin-d'Astanières)
Constantin-d'Astanières
Contal
Contenet
Copin
Coquard (cf Nord Aviation)
Corbadec
Corbeau (cf Moisant)
Corignan
Corneloup (cf Sotinel, Guérin-Corneloup-
   Karganiantz)
Cornet (cf de Pischoff; Landron; Lassagne)
Cornu
Corville (cf De Langhe)
Couade
Courrejoux
Coursier

Courtet
CPC
Crépin (cf Goulois-Crépin)
Curviplan (cf Thorand)
Cussac
Cycloplane (cf de Puiseux)
Cyrnos (cf Filippi)

D
Dajoigny (cf Société des Véhicules Aériennes)
Danard et Nayot
Danton (cf Denhaut)
Dardelet
Daucourt et Pourrain
Dauheret
De Bolotoff
De Coster
Debort
Debougnies
Décazes
Deflers
Defries
Delabrosse et Christollet
Delagrange (cf Blériot; Voisin)
Delaisis
Delalandre
Delamare (cf Gassier)
Delamotte
Delasalle
Delaunay-Belleville
Delbrel (cf Janicot)
Demazel
Demoiselle (cf Santos-Dumont)
Demouveaux
Denhaut
Denissel et Godville
Deperdussin
Dergint
Dernaut
Deroig (cf Poix et Deroig)
Desbrouères (cf Gabardini)
Deschamps et Blondeau
Desfons
Desfontaines
Desforges (cf Pioneers)
Desmonceaux, de Givray, et Gallisti
Desprat (cf Aubry)
Desusclade
Detable et Tabary
Devaux
Dewailly et Vertadier
Dhumbert
Diapason (cf Schreck)
Dinoird
Dion-Bouton, de
DNP (cf Danard et Narjot)
Domingo
Donnet (cf Denhaut)
Donnet et Denhaut (cf Denhaut)
Donnet-Levêque (cf Denhaut)
Dorade (cf Mainguet)
Dorand
Dottori
Doutre
Drouhet
Drzewiecki
Dubois-Rioux
Dubreuil
Dufour
Duhany-Suthy
Dumas
Dumont
Dumontet et Talon
Dumoulin
Duparquet
Dupont (cf Bachelier-Dupont-Baudrin)

Duray-Mathis
Dussot
Dutel
Dutheil et Chalmers
Duvernois

E
Ecrevisse, L' (cf Moisant)
Elan II (cf Sarrus)
Enfin, Le (cf Alkan)
Enigma (cf Lucas-Girardville)
Eparvier
Epervier, L' (cf Blériot)
Equevilly-Monjustin, d'
Ernoult (cf Melin)
Ery (cf Kassa)
Esnault-Pelterie (cf REP)
Espinosa (cf Société de Construction d'Appareils
   Anciens; and Denhaut)
Essor, L' (cf Fabre)
Essort Aérien
Etevé
Etienne et Cie
Etrich
Euler (cf Voisin)

F
Fabre
Fabrègue, de
Farcot
Farman, H
Farman, M
Farman, H & M
Farnier
Fauber
Fauré
Fauvel
FBA (cf Franco-British Aviation Company, Ltd)
Ferber
Fernandez
Feure, de (cf Deperdussin)
Filippi
Fillon
Flèche, La (cf Lange et Billard)
Florencie
Flugi (cf de Coster)
Fouin
Fouquet
Fournier (cf Voisin)
Franchault
Franco-British Aviation Company, Ltd
Frégate, La (cf Société de Construction d'Appareils
   Aériens)
Fritsche (cf Voisin)
Fumat

G
Gabardini
Gabelle, Hauguet, Riard et Martin
Galeotti (cf Givray et Galeotti)
Galvin
Gambier
Gangler
Garaix (cf C Roux)
Garaix, L
Garbéro
Garnier
Garros et Audemars
Gary
Gasnier
Gassier
Gastambide-Mengin (cf Antoinette)
Gaudard
Gaudard (cf also Legrand, d'Artois)
Gaulard (cf Société d'Etude pour la
   Locomotion Aérienne)

Gauthier
Gavault
Gavault
Gayot
GBS (cf Guyot, Boeswillwald et Stahl)
GBV (cf Guyot, Boeswillwald et Stahl)
GC (cf Guyot-Cellier)
GCJ (cf Guyot-Cellier-Jaugey)
GCK (cf Sotinel, Guérin, Corneloup,
    et Karganiantz)
Genuel, Chaboussant, et Giraud
Gérard
Gérard (cf Pioneers)
Géraud
Germe
Gibert
Gibert (cf Kassa)
Gilbert, E
Gilbert, O
Gildorf
Gillebaud (cf Guillebaud)
Gilly
Girardot (cf Brule-Girardot)
Girardville (cf Lucas-Girardville)
Giraud-Pastorino
Givaudan
Givray et Galeotti
GJC (cf Guyot-Cellier-Jaugey)
Gobbi
Goeland (cf Fabre)
Golant
Goldschmidt
Goliesco
Gonnel
Gonthier (cf Leclerc)
Gouin
Gouin (cf Blériot)
Goulois-Crépin
Goupil (cf Pioneers)
Goupy
Gourgas (cf Chazal)
Gourvène
Goyard-Aillaud
Gramaticesco
Grapperon
Grazzioli (cf Huet, Grazzioli, et Lombardini)
Grégoire-Gyp
Gregory
Gremaud
Groffaud et Jolly
Gron
Groos
Guedon
Guée
Guercin
Guérin (cf Sotinel, Guérin , Corneloup
    et Karganiantz)
Guigardet
Guillaume
Guillebaud
Guillemin
Guinard
Guy et Bollon
Guyard
Guyot
Guyot et Verdier
Guyot, Boeswillwald et Stahl (cf Guyot)
Guyot, Boewswillwald et Villem (cf Guyot)
Guyot-Cellier-Jaugey (cf Guyot)
Gyp (cf Grégoire)
Gyroscopic Spinning Top (cf Lucas-Girardville)

H

Hamelis, Delamare, Mathieu et Gassier (cf
    Gassier)
Hanriot

Hans
Hansen (cf Voisin)
Hartmann (cf HF-BV)
Hayot
HDMG (Hamelis, Delamare, Mathieu,et Gassier)
    (cf Gassier)
Hein (cf Voisin)
Hekking
Helicoplane (cf Philippon)
Helliot
Henry
Hérard (cf Pioneers)
Herbster
Herbster (cf Gramaticescu)
Hervé
Hervieux
Heurtaux (cf RHM)
HF-BV (cf Hartman et de Virel)
Hirondelle (cf Lemaitre, Maucourt, et Legrand
Homoplane (cf Marcal)
Hornstein (cf Chapiro)
Hornust
Huet (cf Huet, Grazzioli, et Lombardini)
Huet, Grazzioli, et Lombardini
Hugues (cf Leray)

I-J

IAL (Imbert et Latour)
Illinschulz
Imbert (cf IAL)
Jabiru (cf Loisel, Farman)
Jacob et Audenis
Jacquelin
JAL (cf de Lailhacar)
Janicot
Janicot et Delbrel (cf Janicot)
Janicot et Mouricot (cf Janicot)
Janin (Jeannin?)
Janoir
JAP
Jaugey (cf Guyot)
Jaugey (cf Guyot)
Javigny (cf Juvigny)
Jeanson-Colliex
Jerme (cf Germe)
Joliot (Julliot?)
Jolly (cf Groffard et Jolly)
Jorwitz
Jospe (cf Vinet)
Joujou (cf Santos-Dumont)
Jourdan
Juge et Rolland
Juvigny

K

Kapferer
Karganiantz (cf Guérin-Corneloup-Karganiantz)
Kaspar
Kassa
Kaufmann
Kaulbars (cf Voisin)
Kellner (cf Voisin)
Kerchone-Aman (cf Etrich)
Kessels (cf Bourgoin et Kessels)
Kluytmans
Koch (cf Voisin)
Koechlin
Korvin, de
Korwin, de (cf de Corvin)

L

Labaudie et Puthet
Laborde (cf Roche et Laborde)
Laborde et Roche (cf Roche et Labord)
Lacaille et Lemaire
Lachassagne

Ladougne
Lagasse
Lailhacar, de
Lalouette et Maillaud
Laminne
Lamotte
Lamoureaux
Lanbanhie et Puttet (cf Labaudie et Puthet)
Landeroin et Robert
Landron et Cornet
Lane
Langhe, de
Langhe, de, et Corville (cf de Langhe)
Lanzi et Billard
Lartigue
Lassagne
Lasternas
Lasternas et Lepers (cf Lasternas)
Lataste
Latopp
Latour (cf IAL)
Lautard
Lavesvre et Veillon
Lavezzari
Lazard et Lemoine
Le Bris (cf Pioneers)
Le Papillon (cf Robart)
Le Prieur
Leau (cf Norrep-Leau)
Lebeau
Leblic
Leclerc
Leclère (cf Leclerc)
Lecoeur
Lecomte
Lecoq (cf Théodoresco)
Lecoq, Monsevro et Aillaud
Leduc
Lefebure
Lefebvre
Leforestier
Legagneux et Martinet (cf Martinet, Legagneux,
    et Riffard)
Léger
Legrand
Legras
Legraton
Lejeune
Lelièvre
Lemaire
Lemaitre
Lemaitre et Legrand (cf Lemaitre, Maucourt,
    et Legrand)
Lemaitre, Maucourt, et Legrand
Lemoine (cf Lazare et Lemoine)
Lepers
Lepers (cf Lasternas)
Lepin
Leray
Leroy et Marzollier
Lescars
Lesna
Lesquins
Lesseps, Paul de (cf Taris)
Lesseps, Robert de (cf Société de
    Construction d'Appareils Aériens)
Letellier-Bruneau (cf Parent)
Letord et Niepce
Letur (cf Pioneers)
Leuilleux et Babry
Leuilleux et Fardel (cf Leuilleux et Babry)
Levasseur
Levasseur (cf Fernandez)
Levavasseur
Levêque
Levêque (cf Denhaut)

Levy-Gaillat
Leyat
LG
Libellule (cf Blériot, Farcot, Santos-Dumont))
Light (cf Léger)
Linzeler
Lioré et Olivier
Lis (cf Perron)
Liurette
LL (cf Lasternas et Lepers?)
LM (cf Lecoq-Monteiro-Aillaud)
LMA (cf Lecoq-Monteiro-Aillaud)
LML (cf Lemaitre, Maucourt, et Legrand)
Loctin (cf Franchault)
Lods
Loisel
Loitron et Delage
Lombardini (cf Huet, Grazzioli et Lombardini)
Lonnet
Loubery
Lucas-Girardville
Ludwig
Lumière
Lunel (cf Letord et Niepce)
Luxior (cf Berthaud)

M
Mabelly
Maglione
Magnard
Maigrot
Maillot
Mainguet
Malecot
Malicet et Blin (cf Filippi)
Malloire
Mamet
Marcal
Marçay-Moonen, de
Marigny, de
Marin la Meslée
Marque
Marquézy (cf Clerget)
Marzollier (cf Leroy et Marzollier)
Martin
Martinaisse
Martinet (cf Martinet-Legagneux-Riffard)
Martinet et Legagneux-Riffard
Mas, de (cf Anzani)
Massia-Biot (cf Biot)
Mathieu (cf Gassier)
Maucourt (cf Lemaitre et Legrand)
Mauriac, de
Mauriac, de (cf Guillaume)
Maurice
Maurin et Willaume
Maxima (cf Société des Véhicules Aériennes)
Mayeroff (cf Kassa)
Mazoyer
Mélin
Melvin Vaniman (cf Vaniman)
Méry et Rougier (cf Voisin)
Metalloplan (cf Mazoyer)
Météor (cf Aubry)
Meugniot et La Clemendière
Michaud
Mieusset et Monin
Milord
Minima (cf Société des Véhicules Aériennes)
MLR (cf Martinet-Legagneux-Riffard)
Moineau, Le (cf Noël)
Moisant
Molon
Monaco, Le (cf Gabardini)
Monge, de
Monin (cf Mieusset-Monin)

Monnier-Harper
Monoplane W (cf Berthaud)
Monsevro (cf Lecoq-Monteiro-Aillaud)
Monteiro (cf Lecoq-Monteiro-Aillaud)
Montel
Montéry
Montgolfier
Monthier et Calamard
Morane (cf Morane-Saulnier)
Morane-Borel (cf Morane-Saulnier, Borel-Morane)
Morane-Saulnier
Moreau
Moreau et Berthaud (cf Passerat et Radiguet)
Morel (cf Pons)
Moteiro-Aillaud (cf Lecoq-Monteiro-Aillaud)
Mouche, La (cf de Puiseux; also Vinet)
Mouette Géante, La (cf Vasserot-Delassor)
Mouette, La (cf Lefebvre; also Perrot-Duval
    and Bulot)
Mouillard (cf Pioneers)
Mounier
Mouramet (cf Moutatet)
Moustique, Le (cf Roy, and Vendôme)
Moutatet
Mullot
Mulot (cf Mullot)

N
Nantes Aviation (cf Leroy et Marzollier)
Nau
Nault
Nautilos (cf Astra)
Nayot (cf Danard et Nayot)
Neubauer (cf Voisin)
Nezières (cf Dumontet et Talon)
Niçois (cf Maurin et Willaume)
Nicolas
Nieuport
Nissole, de
Nissole, Prince de (cf Zodiac)
Noel
Nord Aviation
Norrep-Leau
Noue, de (cf Obre)
Nourry (cf Illinschulz)

O
Obre
Octavie III (cf Paulhan)
Odier (cf Vendôme; also Borel)
Odier-Vendôme (cf Vendôme)
Olga (cf Garnier)
Olivier
Orange (cf Poulain-Orange)
Ouarnicr
Outrey
Ouvrière

P
Pacchiotti
Pagny (cf Ponnier)
Pajo (cf Besson)
Papin et Rouilly
Parent
Parent, Letellier et Brunot (cf Parent)
Pasquier
Passerat et Radiguet
Pastorino (cf Giraud-Pastorino)
Patte (cf De Langhe)
Paulat
Paulhan
Paulhan-Curtiss (cf Paulhan)
Paulhan-Fabre (cf Paulhan)
Paulhan-Kapferer (cf Kapferer)
Paulhan-Tatin (cf Tatin)
Paulhan/Peyret/Tatin (cf Tatin)

Paumier
Péan
Pégase
Pelletier et Sergeant
Pelliat
Pénaud (cf Pioneers)
Pentéado, de (cf Chauvière)
Perret (cf Rozé, Perret et Chaffal)
Perrin et Bethenot
Perron
Perrot et Duval
Petit-Conchis
Peugeot-Rossel (cf Rossel-Peugeot)
Peyret
Peyret
Peyret (cf Kapferer)
Philippon
Piau
Picat du Breuil (cf du Breuil)
Pichou
Picot et Christophe
Pierlot
Piffard
Piquerez
Piraud (cf Pompeien Piraud)
Pischoff, de
Pischoff, de, et Koechlin (cf Koechlin)
Pivot
Plaisant
Platel
Poignard et Tranchant
Poire
Poix et Deroig
Pompeien Piraud
Ponche et Primard
Ponchel
Ponnier
Pons
Popp (cf Copin)
Popp et Copin (cf Copin)
Poulain (cf Poulain-Orange)
Poulain-Orange
Pourpe (cf Requillard)
Prestwick (cf JAP)
Prévot (cf Cazalot et Prévot)
Prini-Berthaud (cf Berthaud)
Protin-Contal (cf Contal)
Proudhon
Puiseux, de
Puthet (cf Labaudie et Puthet)
PWP (cf de Pischoff)

R
Radiguet (cf Passerat et Radiguet)
Ramel
Ramet
Ranoli (Romoli?), Doye, et Legal
Ratmanoff
Ravaud
RDL (cf Ranoli, Doye et Legal)
Reau, du
Rebikoff (cf de Korvin, Morane-Saulnier)
Régy
Reiser
Reissner (cf Voisin)
Reister-Picard
Renard
Renaux (cf Pioneers)
REP
Réquillard
Resnier (cf Pioneers)
Restan
Reuch et Cazaudran
Reusch et Seux (cf Seux)
Révillard (cf Copin)
Rheims et Auscher

RHM
Riffard (cf Martinet, Legagneux et Riffard)
Rimailho
Rioux (cf Dubois-Rioux)
Rivière
Rob (cf Roberthie)
Robart
Roberthie
Robur (cf Balaye)
Roche et Laborde
Roche, de la (cf Voisin)
Roger
Roissard et Belley
Rolland (cf Juge et Rolland)
Roshar
Roshon
Rossel-Peugeot
Rossi (cf Théodoresco)
Rougé, de
Rougier (cf Turcat-Méry-Rougier)
Rougier (cf Voisin)
Roux, Charles
Roux, MP
Roy
Rozé, Perret, et Chaffal
Roziers
Ruby (cf Borel-Ruby)
Ruby-Borel (cf Borel-Ruby)
Ruchonnet
Ruchonnet-Schemmel (cf Ruchonnet)
Rue, de (nom de plume for Captain Ferber; cf Noël)
Rumeau

S
SAAD (cf Doutre)
SACAA (cf Société de Construction d'Appareils
    Aériens)
SACAA (cf Société de Construction d'Appareils
    Aériens)
Sacconey
SAFA (cf Caudron, Pons)
Salamanca, de (cf Nicolas)
Sallard
Salles
Salmson et Aime (cf Aime-Salmson)
Salvez, de (cf Berthaud)
Sanchez-Besa
Sanchis
Santo
Santos-Dumont
Sarazin (cf Bruyère et Sarazin)
Sarri
Sarrus
Saturnian (cf Dumoulin)
Saulnier
Saulquin
Saunier (cf Chauvière)
Sautereau
Savary
SCAA (cf Société de Construction d'Appareils
    Aériens)
Schemmel (cf Ruchonnet)
Schmidt et Bauer

Schmitt
Schmutz
Schreck
Sclaves
Scott (cf Avia)
Scrive (Scrive-Van Damme) (cf Nord Aviation)
SEA (cf Bonnet-Labranche)
Seguin (Augustin)
Seguin (Gabriel)
SELA (cf Société d'Etude pour la Locomotion
    Aérienne)
Servais
Seux
SFA (cf Thézenas et Reynaud)
Shigeno
Sigren
Simms (cf Voisin
Simplex (Société des Véhicules Aériennes)
Sirius (cf Bénégent)
Sloan
SNA (cf Charles Roux)
Société Anonyme de Fabrication de l'Aéroplane
    (cf Caudron)
Société d'Etude pour la Locomotion Aérienne
Société de Construction d'Appareils Aériens
Société de Construction de l'Aéroplane la Muette
    (cf Lefebvre)
Société de Navigation Aérienne (cf Charles Roux)
Société des Appareils Aériennes Doutre (cf Doutre)
Société des Chantières de France (cf Wright)
Société des Véhicules Aériennes
Société Forésienne d'Aviation (cf Thézenas
    et Reynaud)
Société Générale de la Fabrication de l'Aéroplane
    (cf Dumas)
Soiron
Solirène
Sommer
Sotinel, Guérin, Corneloup et Karganiantz
Sporta (cf Monthier et Calamard)
Stanley, Schaerf et Savage-Landor
Stoeckel
Strofe
Surcouf (cf Astra)
SVA (cf Société des Véhicules Aériennes)
Sylphe (cf Gassier)
Sylphide (cf Moreau-Berthaud)
Sylva, da
Syndicat de l'Aéronautique (cf Archdeacon)

T
Tabary (cf Detable et Tabary)
Tambarly (cf de Langhe)
Taris
Taris-Bucheron (cf Taris)
Tatin
Tatin-de la Vaulx (cf Tatin)
Tatin-Paulhan (cf Tatin)
Tellier
Temple, du (cf Pioneers)
Théodoresco, Lecoq, Rossi
Thézénas et Reynaud
Thibault de St André (cf Pioneers)

Thomann
Thorand
Thuau
TLR (possibly the same as Thézenas et Reynaud?)
Torchon
Toussaint
Train
TRAL (cf Thézenas et Reynaud)
Trébeudin
Tri-Aéro (cf Strofe)
Trochu
Tubavion (cf Ponche et Primard)
Tunmer (cf Dutel)
Turcat-Méry-Rougier (cf Vendôme)
Turgan (cf Archdeacon)
Turlin

U
UACA (cf Union des Aviateurs de la Côte d'Azur)
UFA (cf Union Française Aérienne)
Unic-Bertrand (cf Bertrand)
Union des Aviateurs de la Côte d'Azur
Union Française Aérienne
Uniplan (cf Gonnel)

V
Van Damme (cf Nord Aviation)
Vaniman
Vasserot-Delassor
Vaulx, de la (cf Tatin)
Vautour (cf Etrich)
Védovelli
Vendôme
Verdier (cf Guyot)
Vermorel (cf Givaudan)
Villard
Villem (cf Guyot)
Villotrans (cf Levavasseur)
Vinet
Virel, de (cf Hartmann)
Viriot
Vivinus (cf Voisin)
Voisin
Vosgien (cf Avia)
Vuia
Vuitton-Hubert

W
Wakadori (cf Shigeno)
Wehrle
Wilkes
Witzig-Lioré-Dutilleul
WLD (cf Witzig-Lioré-Dutilleul)
Wright
Wroblewski (cf Berthaud)

Z
Zenith
Zens
Zipfel
Zodiac
Zyx (cf Lartigue)

Bibliography

The following list represents most – I'd like to say all – of the various books and magazines and pamphlets used over more than 15 years in the preparation of this book. They were – and are – published in several countries over a very long period; some came in partial sets studied in aviation museums in Washington, Ottawa, Paris, New York, and Berlin; others came in the form of xerox copies or partial xerox copies from friends and enthusiasts worldwide. Special mention should be made of the Musée de l'Air et de l'Espace in Paris, whose reference library, photograph files, and photographic services were made specially available to me for this project: I was allowed to stay unsupervised in the records room while everyone else went out to lunch. And in France, lunch takes a good 2 hours!

My own collection of miscellaneous photographs, postcards, and clippings dates from the early 40s to the present; where these images came from originally is now impossible to determine. I hope that the fellow enthusiasts who recognize their gifts to me of many years ago will accept this collective and grateful aknowledgement of their generosity and support.

Magazines, Journals
Aéro, L'
Aero & Hydro
Aero, The
Aeronautics (London)
Aeronautics (NY)
Aeronautics Magazine
Aéronautique, L'
Aérophile, L'
Aeroplane Monthly
Automobilia and Flight
Avia
Aviation Illustrée, L'
Bericht
Brussels Air 98 Museum Magazine
Conquête de l'Air
Deutsche Luftfahrer Zeitung
Deutsche Zeitschrift für Luftschiffahrt
Deutscher Luftfahrer Zeitschrift
Encyclopedia of Automotive Engineering
Enthusiaste, L'
Exposition Aérienne 1907
Exposition Aérienne 1910
Exposition Aérienne 1912
Flight
Flug und Motor Technik
Flugsport
Flugwerfen und Motor Technik
Flying and Aero Club of America Bulletin
Icare
ILA
Illustrierte Aeronautische Mitteilungen
Illustrierte Zeitschrift für Automobilism und Aviatik
Luchtvaart
Luftverkehr
Mitteilungen des Osterreichische Aero Clubs
Mois Aéronautique et Automobile
Motor
Motorluftschiff
Motorwagen
Navigazione Aerea
Osterreichische Aero Club
Osterreichische Flug Technische Verein
Osterreichische Flug Zeitschrift
Pégase
Pilot
Revue de l'Aviation, La, 1910
Rivista Aeronautica
Rivista Technica di Aeronautica
Scientific American
Suisse Sportive
Taschenbuch der Luftflotte
Technique Aéronautique
Trait d'Union, Le
Verein für Luftschiffahrt
Vie au Grand Air, La
Vie Automobile, La
Viertrijahrsberichte
Wiener Aeroklub
Wiener Luftschiffe Zeitung
Zeitschrift für Flugtechnik und Motorluftschiffahrt
Zeitschrift für Motorfahrzeuge

Books
Abbal, Odon. Il Etait une Fois St Hippolyte-du-Fort et les Aéroplanes. St Hippolyte-du-Fort: Librairie Coularou, 1993.
Andrews, Allen. The Flying Machine: Its Evolution Through the Ages. 1977.
Au Temps de Clément Ader. Staff of l'ANAE (l'Académie Nationale de l'Air et de l'Espace). Toulouse: TEKNEA, 1994.
Bedei, Francis, and Max Joy. L'Histoire Port-Aviation 1909-1919. Le Mée-sur-Seine: Editions Amatteis, 1993.
Bénichou, Michel. Roger Sommer, Constructeur 1977-1965. Anciaux.
Berger, Alphonse. Conquest of the Air. NY: Putnam and Co, Ltd, 1909.
Blériot, Louis. Blériot. Paris: Arte Adrien Maeght, 1994.
Bonte, Louis. L'Histoire des Essais en Vol. Paris: Docavia, 1974.
Bordeaux, J. Etude Raisonnée de l'Aéroplane. Paris: Gauthier-Villars, 1912.
Brewer, Robert WA. Art of Aviation. London: Crosby Lockwood, 1911.
Bruce, JM. Nieuport Aircraft of World War One. London: Arms and Armour Press, 1988.

—. *Warplanes of the First World War, Vols Four and Five*. London: Macdonald and Son, 1972.

Chambre, René. *Histoire de l'Aviation des Origines à nos Jours*. Paris: Flammarion, 1958.

Chanute,Octave. *Progress in Flying Machines* (reprint of 1894 edition). Long Beach: Lorenz and Herweg, 1976.

Christienne, Charles, and Pierre Lissarague. *Histoire de l'Aviation Militaire Française*. Paris: Charles Lavauzelle, 1980.

Constant de Destournelles et al. *Pour l'Aviation*. Paris: Librairie Aéronautique, nd.

Crouch, Tom. *Blériot XI*. Washington,: Smithsonian Institute Press, 1982.

Cuiche, Myrone N. *De l'Aéronautique Militaire 1912 à l'Armée de l'Air 1976*. Turcoing: 1978.

Davilla, James and Arthur M Soltan. *French Aircraft of the First World War*. Flying Machines Press, 1978.

Dollfuss, Charles, and Henri Bouché. *Histoire de l'Aéronautique*. Paris: Les Editions de L'Illustration, 1942

Dollfuss, Charles, et al. *L'Homme, l'Air et l'Espace*. Paris: Les Editions de L'Illustration, 1965.

Dollfuss, Charles. *Avions*. Paris: Robert Delpire, 1962.

Drôles de Machines. Paris, Musée de l'Air et de l'Espace, 1995.

Early Military Aircraft of the First World War, Vol 1, Landplanes, and vol 3, Seaplanes & Motors. Dallas: Flying Enterprises, 1963, 1971.

Eiffel, Gustave. *Nouvelles Recherches sur la Résistance de l'Air et l'Aviation*. Paris: Librairie Dunod et Pinat, 1914.

Fabb, John. *Flying and Ballooning*. London: BT Batsford, Ltd, 1980.

Fabre, Henri. *J'Ai Vu Naître l'Aviation*. Grenoble: Guirimand, 1980.

—. *Les 3 Avions d'Henri Fabre*. Grenoble, Guirimand, 1979.

Ferber, Ferdinand. *L'Aviation*. Paris: Berger-Levrault, 1910.

Flying Book, The: The Aviation World Who's Who, nd.

Foxworth, Thomas. *The Speed Seekers*. NY: Doubleday, 1974.

Gaston, R de. Les *Aéroplanes de 1910*. Paris; Librairie Aéronautique, nd.

—. *Les Aéroplanes de 1911*. Paris; Librairie Aéronautique, nd.

Gaston, R de, et Alex Dumas. *Les Aéroplanes de 1912*. Paris: Librairie Aéronautique, nd.

Gayraud, Didier. *Maïcon: les Compagnons des Gabians*. Nice: Serre, 1994.

Gibbs-Smith, Charles H. *Early Flying Machines 1799-1909*. London: Eyre Methuen, 1975.

—. *Invention of the Aeroplane 1799-1909*. London: Faber and Faber, 1966.

—. *Rebirth of European Aviation*. London: His Majesty's Stationery Office, 1971.

Grahame-White, Claude, and Harry Harper. *Aeroplanes Past, Present and Future*. Philadelphia: Lippincott, 1911.

—. *Heroes of the Air*. London: Henry Froude, 1912.

Harper, Harry. *Evolution of the Flying Machine: Balloon, Airship, and Aeroplane*. Philadelphia: David McKay, 1930.

Hayward, Charles B, et al. *Cyclopedia of Automobile Engineering, Vol I*. Chicago: American Technical Society, 1912.

Jane's All the World's Aircraft 1913, ed Fred T Jane.

Jane's All the World's Aircraft 1914, ed Fred T Jane.

Jane's All the World's Airships 1909, ed Fred T Jane.

Jane's Historical Aircraft from 1902 to 1916, ed CG Grey. Garden City: Doubleday, 1973.

Kaempfert, Waldemar. *The New Art of Flying*. NY: Dodd, Mead, 1911.

Kurc, Alain. *Les Pionniers de l'Aviation en Beauce*. Châteaudun: Société Dunoise, nd.

Lartigue, Jacques-Henri. *Jacques-Henri Lartigue*. NY: Aperture, 1976.

Lessard, E, and E Brodin. *Le Triomphe de l'Aviation*. Paris: Albert Méricant, 1911.

Lieberg, Owen S. *TheFirst Air Race*. Garden City: Doubleday and Co, 1974.

Liron, Jean. *Les Avions Farman*. Paris: Docavia.

Livre d'Or de la Conquête de l'Air, Le

Loening, Grover. *Military Aeroplanes*. Boston: WS Best, 1918.

—. *Monoplanes and Biplanes*. London: Mann and Co, 1911.

Lougheed, Victor. *Vehicles of the Air*. Chicago: Reilly and Britton Co, 1910.

Marchis, L. *L'Epopée Aérienne*. Paris: Dunot et Pinat, 1910.

Mayoussier, Roger A. *A Tire des Ailes*. Lyon: Créations de Pélican, 1996.

Milestones of the Air: Jane's 100 Significant Aircraft. NY: McGraw-Hill, 1969.

Motor, Staff of. *The Aero Manual*. London: Temple Press, Ltd, 1909 and 1910.

Nicolaou, Stéphane. *Les Hydravions*. Paris: ETAI, 1996.

—. *Deauville 1913: Capital de l'Hydraviation*. Paris: Musée de l'Air, 1993.

Peterson, Houston. *See Them Flying*. NY: Richard W Baron Publishing Co, 1969.

Petit, Edmond. *La Vie Quotidienne dans l'Aviation en France*. Paris: Hachette, 1977.

—. *Nouvelle Histoire Mondiale de l'Aviation*. Paris: Librairie Hachette, 1973.

Prendergast, Curtis, et al. *The First Aviators*. Alexandria: Time-Life Books, 1980.

Rapport Officiel sur la Première Exposition Internationale de Locomotion Aérienne (1909). Paris: Librairie Aéronautique, 1910.

Rapport Officiel sur la Quatrième Exposition de Locomotion Aérienne. Paris: Blondel la Rougery, 1913.

Rapport Officiel sur la Quatrième Exposition Internationale de Locomotion Aérienne (1912). Paris: Blondel la Rougery, 1913.

Rivière, Pierre. *Les Hydro-Aéroplanes*. Paris: Librairie Aéronautique, 1912.

Sahel, Jacques. *Henry Farman et l'Aviation*. Paris: Bernard Grasset, 1936.

Schatzer, Hans. *Propeller Nostalgie*. Graz: S Weishaupt Verlag, 1981.

Simon, E, and R Lemaire. *L'Aéronautique Avant 1914*. 1985.

Smith, Laurence. *The Romance of Aircraft*. NY: Stokes, 1919.

Straub, Jerry M, ed, *Fly 1908-1909*. Seattle: Superior Publishing Co, 1971.

Voisin, Gabriel. *Men, Women, and 1000 Kites*. London: Putnam and Co, Ltd, 1963.

Weber, E. *L'Aviation*. Paris: Editions Nilsson, nd.

Wragg, David. *Flight With Power*. NY: St Martin's Press, 1978.

Wykeham, Peter. *Santos-Dumont: a Study in Obsession*. London: Putnam and Co, Ltd, 1962.